True South

True South

Henry Hampton and *Eyes on the Prize,*
the Landmark Television Series
That Reframed
the Civil Rights Movement

Jon Else

VIKING

VIKING
An imprint of Penguin Random House LLC
375 Hudson Street
New York, New York 10014
penguin.com

ISBN 9781101980934 (hardcover)
ISBN 9781101980958 (eBook)

Printed in the United States of America
1   3   5   7   9   10   8   6   4   2

Set in Minion Pro
Designed by Francesca Belanger

For Porgie and Bob

Contents

Author's Note

We have by now many fine chronicles of the civil rights movement; I have not tried to write another. *True South* assumes that the reader comes with a basic understanding of that history and may be interested in how one group of filmmakers struggled to tell it.

Much of this book will make better sense if you have seen at least some of the fourteen-part documentary series *Eyes on the Prize I* and *II,* readily available from many sources.

I have generally followed terminology described by Henry Hampton in guidelines for *Eyes on the Prize* narration: "We had heated debates, but finally chose to call the southerners who opposed the civil rights movement 'resisters' rather than 'racists.' We did so because we wanted to keep this valuable history accessible and not lose viewers before we had engaged them in the story." Here I have used both those terms as well as "segregationist" and "white supremacist," depending on the context. I have occasionally employed the traditional term "Negro" when the history warrants it, but more often "black," "Afro-American," or "African American."

Henry Hampton's lawyer Ike Williams said, "Once in a while you get those little glimpses of race having affected Henry, but otherwise it was the most dispassionate kind of thing . . . deeply interested in how the civil rights movement came about, but not approaching it from any position of color, only from a position of justice; how do we achieve justice." My own connections to the civil rights movement and to Henry Hampton run deep, so I cannot claim dispassion, but have tried to be accurate and honest.

The statements and opinions expressed in this book are solely those of the author and do not in any way represent the official history or views of Blackside, Inc.

True South

Introduction

Throughout the winter of 1964–65, Selma, Alabama, simmered in a state of siege, broken by sudden explosions of violence and finally, on March 7, "Bloody Sunday."

Two days later, twenty-four-year-old African American Henry Hampton set out along Broad Street toward the Pettus Bridge, together with his friend Rev. James Reeb and a thousand other marchers, led by Martin Luther King Jr. and Ralph Abernathy. Their goal was to deliver a voting rights petition to Governor George Wallace at the state capitol in Montgomery. A quarter mile ahead, on the other side of the Alabama River, waited hundreds of heavily armed Alabama state troopers, flanked by Sheriff Jim Clark's famously brutal mounted posse.

Hampton was on church business, sent by his Unitarian employers in Boston. Strikingly handsome and athletic, but slowed by the heavy steel leg brace he had worn since a childhood bout with polio, Henry found himself "marching between a black Alabama sharecropper and the wife of Senator Paul Douglas. . . ." He had a hard time keeping up with the crowd, and began to worry what would happen if he fell behind and became easy prey for white thugs prowling to thin the herd. But then Henry realized that half a dozen black citizens of Selma had, as if by magic, formed a protective circle around him, moving toward the troopers on the other side of the bridge at his pace, "my own personal honor guard."

Only forty-eight hours before, those same lawmen, determined that black men like Henry Hampton would not have a voice in Alabama, had savagely beaten, bullwhipped, and gassed hundreds of peaceful men, women, and children. Local whites cheered from the sidelines. Outraged clergy across the nation answered a call from Dr. King and leapt into action. Henry, the lay national director of information for the Unitarian Universalist church, joined hundreds of northern ministers converging on Selma.

Now the new march was on, in violation of a federal judge's order, headed for another confrontation. Cresting the bridge, they saw the helmeted troops arrayed across the highway, daring the marchers—under federal injunction not to cross the county line—to come forward. Still on the bridge, near the spot where lawmen beat John Lewis unconscious two days before, Dr. King unexpectedly stopped and knelt down while Ralph Abernathy led the demonstrators in tense prayer. Newsreel footage from that day shows the eerie image of a half dozen ministers standing around the kneeling King so that he would not present a clear target to a sniper.

What Henry Hampton and those thousand marchers did not know as they awaited their destiny was that King had brokered a secret deal with the White House only hours before: they would stop at the county line and go on to fight another day. Because they desperately needed the federal courts and President Johnson on their side, the Southern Christian Leadership Conference leaders were loath to violate federal judge Frank Johnson's injunction against marching on to Montgomery.

With a sinking feeling, Henry now saw King and Abernathy turn around and lead the bewildered marchers—who had come to lay their lives on the line and see this thing through all the way to the state capitol—back into Selma. What had begun as a mass expression of courage and moral witness ended in a meek retreat before the same forces who had smashed the Bloody Sunday march, all to avoid angering the president. Henry didn't know what to think, but suspected that the moral muck of national politics had caught up with the principled clarity of the civil rights movement.

Unfolding before the news cameras in the "Turnaround March" that afternoon was a harsh lesson in pragmatic *realpolitik,* resonating under the crisp moral shadow of its already famous big brother, Bloody Sunday. They would, in fact, live to fight another day, and very shortly brought American apartheid to its knees. As he trudged back to Selma instead of on to Montgomery, in that very jumbled strategic, tactical, and political moment, Henry—a church representative, not yet a filmmaker—thought to himself, "Someday someone is going to make a great story out of this. This is going to make great television."

As sweet as their victory would eventually be, it was the process itself, the messy workings of history, that fascinated Henry. Over the next quarter century, in his battles with commercial television, public television, his own staff, historians, and the estate of Martin Luther King, he would never retreat from the complexity of that great story.

On a February night in 1986, two decades after the Battle of Selma, Henry Hampton met me curbside at Boston's Logan Airport. In his youthful days as a cabdriver, how many late-night fares had he picked up at Logan?

We were then in our seventh month of production on *Eyes on the Prize: America's Civil Rights Years,* and I had logged ninety-nine flights in economy class on "the Hampton Air Force," mostly puddle jumpers over the piney woods of Alabama and Georgia, to film the aging foot soldiers of the movement, many of whom had marched on the Pettus Bridge. Tonight he looked haggard but wanted to talk, so for the next couple of hours we drove around Boston in a miserable freezing rain, with Archie Shepp playing on his aging Jaguar's stereo. He had always been soft spoken, with the voice of a long-ago heavy smoker, but this night I could barely hear him.

We parsed the lurching progress of *Eyes* editing, had a late bite to eat at Chef Chandler's, and stopped at an all-night drugstore for Henry to pick up the largest bottle of antacids I'd ever seen. Unpaid film lab bills mounted, the roof at the office still leaked, half his staff were in angry revolt over late paychecks, and no funder would step up with money to complete his civil rights television series. Prowling the wet South End streets, I could see that the "great story" that someone would someday tell was grinding him down.

Henry was wrung out from throwing himself at the mercy of cynically polite corporate executives who never intended to give him a dime to tell the messy story of the civil rights movement. All his energy went to the fund-raising he hated, and little to the filmmaking he loved. He had just turned forty-five, and in the last few months post-polio syndrome had begun to weaken his good leg.

In happier times that fall, heady from filming in Mississippi and Alabama, our late-night drives had been a lark: planning a civil rights themed restaurant, "Eyes on the Pies," and talking about our fathers, about his epiphany in Selma in 1965, about my own days in Selma that same winter, the sublime power of freedom songs, my other life shooting television commercials in California, the small but mounting victories for the freedom struggle in South Africa. We pondered whether Martin Luther King could have been elected president, and asked *where* exactly did King get that zinger, "The arc of the moral universe is long, but it bends toward justice!" And Henry was already planning a second civil rights TV series, *Eyes II,* picking up in 1965 with the rougher, *really* messy history of the Black Panthers, affirmative action, Malcolm X, and urban rebellions. But tonight he was melancholy.

Around midnight, I followed as he slowly hauled himself up the stairs to his Blackside office at 486 Shawmut Avenue—books and folders stacked high, a picture of Dr. King on one wall, the philosopher/poet W. H. Auden on the other, Gandhi in the corner, and his "grand rambling mess" of a desk at the convergence of their force fields. He spread out dozens of rejection letters from corporations and foundations, sank into his chair, and said, "Why don't they just give us the goddamn money." At that moment, with footage for his epic six-part civil rights story nearly all in the can, with producers, researchers, and editors hard at work, archive material pouring in, and a full head of steam, we had run out of money. We couldn't meet the next month's payroll. It was the end of the line.

It should have been easy. Six years before, back in 1979, his naive first attempt to produce the "great story" of the civil rights movement for commercial television had ended in humiliating failure. And now he knew his second try, for PBS, was going down in flames and taking him with it. He knew—and I knew—that if we laid off the staff on Monday morning, notified the creditors, turned off the heat, and closed the door, his life's dream would expire for good. Our exhausted producers would scatter back to their exasperated families, the aging civil rights warriors we still needed to film would die in obscurity, and telling the grand saga of the southern freedom struggle would fall to someone else—maybe Ken Burns or Oprah Winfrey—sometime in the future.

We stacked up the rejection letters and called it a night.

The next day Henry arrived at the office around noon and told me he had gotten up, gone to his bank, and—risking personal financial ruin for the sake of a story—mortgaged his house. He got enough cash to meet payroll, calm the creditors, and keep us working for those critical two weeks until PBS and the Ford Foundation came in with the tipping point grant.

Henry Hampton was seldom at a loss.

CHAPTER ONE

Cave Painting

1940–68

This man who would spend his adult life telling stories of the poor and dispossessed was born into the most privileged life a young Negro boy could reasonably expect in segregated St. Louis, Missouri, in the mid-twentieth century. His was a bright world.

Henry's father, Dr. Henry Hampton Sr., was a star, first chief surgeon and medical director at the renowned Homer G. Phillips Hospital for Colored. Dr. Hampton was by all accounts a genial and self-assured man of means—every cent of which he'd earned—with a thriving practice in a modern office. He enjoyed profitable investments, new cars every year or two (a big black Buick for himself, a Buick station wagon for Mrs. Hampton and the kids). His wife and three children enjoyed security and material comfort that would have been the envy of any midwestern family, black or white. Dr. Hampton's name and photo appeared in the *St. Louis Post-Dispatch* for community leadership, his work with charities, his medical research, and his testimony before the city council, and once when a burglar broke into his home and stole fifty suits and a television set.

The senior Hampton was a politically savvy Democrat, and extremely well connected in both the black and white communities, despite the exclusionary protocols of Missouri segregation. Back in 1949 he had been named to the Board of Freeholders, tasked with writing a "home rule" charter for the city of St. Louis, the only identified Negro among thirteen white judges, labor leaders, a state senator, and the president of the County Farm Bureau, and he chaired the board's Health and Public Welfare committee.

His daughter Judi remembered, "He knew everybody, and we always used to say that he would have made a great mayor or governor. Pop got into every structure, the kind of guy who could reach out to everybody: the church hierarchy, the guy who ran the car dealership, every social circle." His son, Henry Eugene Hampton Jr., born August 19, 1940, would grow up to acquire the same sort of far-reaching network of influential social connections in his adopted home, Boston, and by the 1980s more than a few of us asked Henry Jr. when he was going to run for public office.

In 1928, Dr. Hampton graduated with honors from the traditionally black Meharry Medical College in Nashville, a first-rate school that in the 1930s trained many of the best and brightest Negro medical professionals who would have gone to the University of Missouri, Harvard, or Yale had they been white. It was there he met his future wife, Julia Gullatte, a practical nurse.

Judi Hampton said, "Mother was warm, a good mom, endearing and gracious, easygoing, and sweet." Henry was the middle child, his big sister, Veva, four years older, and little sister, Judi, two years younger. His best friend, Dan Raybon, remembers Mrs. Hampton always asking what she could do for Judi, Henry, and Veva. "It wore her out. She always wanted to do something special for Henry's birthday. She adored Henry Jr. and gave him slack, waited on him *hand* and *foot*."

He was the young prince. Judi remembered, "Our dad ruled the roost. When Mom gave birth to Henry she got a mink coat. When she gave birth to my sister and me she got a 'Thanks for the good job.' Our mom was conservative, not a feminist." Nor was her husband; the kids' childhood friend Ellen Sweets described Dr. Hampton as a good fellow, but with attitudes of the time "just short of misogyny."

"Doc" ran a small pharmacy out of the home, and the kids earned spending money filling pill bottles. Their house, amid modest 1920s bungalows, was the biggest and best-looking home in the area, clad in red brick, custom designed for Dr. Hampton in 1941 by St. Louis's premier modernist architect, Harris Armstrong. It was large and striking, in the International Style of Frank Lloyd Wright, standing at 1751 Laclede Station Road, just on the white side of the dividing line between white and colored neighborhoods a few miles south of then 100-percent-white Ferguson, Missouri. The Hampton family also enjoyed a little getaway farm with horses and chickens in the country a couple of hours west of St. Louis. All the years I knew him, Henry kept the framed deed for the farm on the wall of his office.

The Hamptons were apparently among the few blacks able to skirt the strict de facto racial restrictions on St. Louis housing and reside just within the white section of Richmond Heights. Their black neighbors, the

Raybon family, lived up the street at 2019 Laclede, just across the line in the working-class colored section of Maplewood. Young Dick Gregory and Chuck Berry lived nearby.

Their grand home with its big backyard, rock garden, and pond was a magnet for the kids' friends, who spent long summer afternoons bouncing from the Hamptons' to the Raybons' and back. The big paved lot in between served as a roller rink, basketball court, and tennis court. (Blacks were barred from most public courts in St. Louis except for a half day a week after 5 P.M.) "The lot was a sanctuary for us, it was protection, fenced all the way around; that kept the white folks from bothering us," said Dan.

Blacks were only allowed to sit in the balcony of St. Louis mainline movie theaters, which the Hamptons refused to do, so their early film education was at black theaters, the Comet or the Douglass (named for Frederick Douglass and "entirely built by Colored Labor"), drinking Cokes, watching musicals, gangster films, Westerns, and the news of the week from the Negro newsreel services.

The Hamptons purchased one of the neighborhood's first televisions, Judi recalled, "a box as big as the room, with a tiny little picture." In the fifties the new medium was timid, not yet feeling its muscle, and virtually all white on screen, except the demeaning *Amos 'n' Andy* and *The Little Rascals,* featuring Buckwheat, the crudest sort of nappy-haired Negro stereotype. Henry recalled that as kids their mainstream media image of blackness was bounded by only "knowing our history through Tarzan and cannibals . . . hair and cosmetics ads . . . sensing ourselves as a different kind of American." Once in a blue moon came a welcome Sammy Davis Jr. or Nat King Cole guest appearance. Few had yet really grappled with blacks' representation on television, an issue that would consume Henry later in life.

He and the girls watched *Leave It to Beaver, Howdy Doody,* and *The Lone Ranger,* and saw Elvis Presley sing on *The Ed Sullivan Show* in 1956, as well as tens of thousands of commercials for laundry soap, breakfast cereal, beer, and cigarettes. And like so many of us kids in those early fire-in-the-cave days of television, they sometimes just zoned out on the couch watching the test pattern when broadcasts stopped at 10 P.M., transfixed by the mesmerizing novelty of it all.

Henry was a round-faced, cheery kid, not fat, not skinny, just strong and beefy, the way he would be for the rest of his life. Henry, Dan, and Judi collected eggs at the farm and sold them house to house, with Judi riding on the wagon. They had a little grass-cutting service, competed in soapbox derbies, and went up and down the street in the colored neighborhood looking for lawns to cut. "We did everything," said Dan. "Henry and I rode our bikes everywhere; one time we rode twenty miles, all the way to the Mississippi River. Henry always had the attitude 'Let's do it!'"

The Hampton household was evidently quiet and conservative. They seldom dined out because restaurants in white St. Louis would not serve them, and they didn't find the restaurants in black St. Louis much good. The parents neither drank nor smoked, and Mrs. Hampton's cooking was in the tradition of her native Texarkana, Texas. "Food was a centerpiece, especially on holidays and weekends; baked ham and spare ribs with lots of butter, and gravy on everything," said Judi. "Gravy on your Cheerios."

They subscribed to *Ebony* and *Jet,* and were fully engaged in the energetic black community of St. Louis. Dr. Hampton, an Alpha Kappa Alpha man from Fisk University, belonged to the Royal Vagabonds, a local men's club of black professionals: lawyers, doctors, academics, social workers, and Nathaniel Sweets, the publisher of the *St. Louis American,* one of the city's four black newspapers. Judi remembered, "Our family valued education, community involvement, excellent manners, a life of purpose." Ellen Sweets recalled "a very strong middle-class black community of tremendous integrity. We kids were well versed in classical music, literature, well traveled, with very solidly middle-class values. The Hamptons were *upper* middle class . . . debutante coming-out parties with white dresses."

Decades later, when the triumph of the civil rights movement had swept many successful and well-to-do African Americans out of their tight-knit, self-supporting communities to join the mainstream white elites in schools, colleges, businesses, and social clubs, Henry said, "There was the irony of our victory when, in achieving our goal to integrate, we lost a large part of the dearly earned integrity of our communities."

Resolutely positioned in the black bourgeoisie, they shared hopes and aspirations as desegregation made its halting way across the South in the wake of the Supreme Court's 1954 *Brown v. Board of Education* decision. Inch by inch, changes in law and custom were now rolling back the brutal Jim Crow system that had prevailed since 1896.

Missouri had been the northernmost slave state only seventy-five years before Henry Hampton's birth, and slavery was in his grandparents' living memory. In 1917, on rumors that black men had been fraternizing with white women, a thousand armed white men had rampaged through

East St. Louis, burning whole sections of the town, killing one hundred blacks and leaving six thousand homeless.

Henry came of age in the forties and fifties, a time he would evoke in *Eyes on the Prize,* when blacks and whites, tempered by the Great Depression and World War II, lived side by side with separate but unequal lunch counters, bus station waiting rooms, theaters, drinking fountains, neighborhoods, swimming pools, churches, hospitals, public schools, private schools, taxis, housing, men's clubs, women's clubs, baseball teams, cemeteries, barbershops, and histories. The sole desegregated lunch counter in town was at City Hall. Dan Raybon remembered, "I would be walking down the street when I was a kid and some crazy guy would yell 'nigger,' and it took me a while to figure out he was talking about me. We played with the white kids across the alley when we were little, lower-income white people. And one day they said, 'We can't play with you anymore.'"

In what Bill Cosby's biographer Mark Whitaker aptly called "a segregated world of strivers," Dr. Hampton's family of the 1950s must have resembled an earlier version of Cosby's fictional Dr. Huxtable's family of the 1980s.

But while Henry and the girls were growing up, the Hamptons' life was closely and uniquely braided together with whites while at the same time segregated in a maddening dual existence. Dr. Hampton once saved the life of a white man pinned under a car. The Hamptons had white neighbors, and Henry's father treated both black and white patients in his private practice downtown (also designed for him by architect Harris Armstrong).

Because he was particularly skilled at treating multiple sclerosis, white doctors sought him out for advice on difficult cases, then began referring patients, and eventually white patients began seeking him out themselves. He even did house calls to white patients, extremely unusual for a black doctor in the 1950s, sometimes allowing one of the kids to tag along. Henry Jr. clearly inherited his father's ability to navigate comfortably in both white and black worlds, and in the race-agnostic spaces in between. Dan Raybon remembered that even as a kid, "Henry had no issues at all interacting with white people."

But blacks were shortchanged in nearly all of life's measures, and there were stark reminders of racism in St. Louis, as when Henry saw his father humiliated by an ill-mannered young white waiter who refused to serve the patrician doctor and his three children on a Sunday outing. Dan said,

"There was the constant specter out there. . . . It limited the way *I* thought, but I never felt that Henry was bounded by *anything*. I thought, 'What's the world *he's* living in?'"

As an adult, Henry talked often and eloquently about race in public and in private, so it is ironic that his parents didn't discuss slavery, segregation, or race within the family. Young Henry at one point growing up got interested in slavery, but couldn't inspire much of a conversation in the home. The Congress of Racial Equality (CORE) had staged one of the nation's first sit-ins in St. Louis in 1949, but it was long forgotten, and the 1917 East St. Louis white rampage was apparently never brought up in the Hampton family. "Our parents didn't dwell on the past, because racism was so much in our face: at school, or seeing the Black Sambo pickaninnies in front of peoples' houses. Little things, like I didn't get invited to the dance at the white school. Henry got around it by immersing himself in sports," said Judi.

Over it all hung the very real Cold War specter of nuclear attack, with "duck and cover" drills in every school the Hampton kids attended. "Henry and I were about as far left as you could get. I was big on ban the bomb; Henry was too," remembered Ellen Sweets, who refused to get under her desk during the drills. Nuclear weapons are race blind, and their shadow fell equally over Americans of all colors and classes in the mid-twentieth century. The Hampton family watched the same telecast I did at the height of the Cuban Missile Crisis on October 22, 1962, when JFK grimly announced on prime-time TV that a massive Soviet nuclear attack on the United States and a "full retaliatory strike on the Soviet Union" were tangible possibilities that very night.

Dr. Hampton was determined that his children should receive the finest possible education, and in those days Catholic schools were the best in St. Louis. The local archbishop, Joseph Ritter, unilaterally integrated nearly all parochial schools by decree in 1947 as a matter of simple justice, seven years before the U.S. Supreme Court did so nationwide. Dr. Hampton was so impressed that he and Mrs. Hampton converted the whole family to Catholicism.

The Hampton children were not entirely sure what they had converted *from*. There was little tradition of religion in the elder Hampton's family and the kids had never known any other religion until Judi, Henry, Veva, and their parents "became Catholic" and took to attending Mass every Sunday, the only black family in a white parish in Richmond Heights. As Judi recalled, Henry went to Mass "reluctantly, and not as often as the rest of us. He was definitely not devout."

The Catholic school a few minutes walk from their home was one of the few archdiocesan schools still segregated in the early 1950s, so Henry and Judi's father drove them half an hour downtown every day to St. Nicholas elementary school. Henry's sixth-grade report card shows excellent grades, except that Sister Noella notes his weak performance in Christian Courtesy, Reliability, and Penmanship. Nuns smacked him on the back of the hand with a ruler for being a smart-ass, but he excelled in Religion, Reading, and Social Studies. By the time I met him thirty years later, he certainly had become a master of Christian courtesy and was working on reliability, but his tiny cramped handwriting would remain forever illegible to anyone but the man himself. His fifth-grade schoolmate at St. Nicholas, William Clay, would grow up to serve in Congress and one day deliver a ringing tribute to Henry Hampton on the floor of the U.S. House of Representatives.

For Henry's 1954 school year, after the *Brown v. Board* school desegregation decision, Dr. Hampton enrolled him and Judi in the newly desegregated Little Flower school, where they were the first and only two black kids. They were not happy about changing schools, but their father, a farsighted, practical realist, said, "This is what's happening; suck it up and deal with it." Judi said that Dr. Hampton taught them that "'The world is not black,' and therefore had us go to a white suburban school," with the goal of studying hard, working hard, and eventually making enough money to guarantee freedom and independence.

After Little Flower, Henry moved up to the barely integrated St. Louis University High, a large A-list Jesuit prep school run by the socially conscious "gentleman scholars of Christian Education." Here he was one of only two African Americans in a class of 183. He is remembered as a *very* bright and very competitive teenager. In high school he was clearly a well-liked, strong-willed, and supremely confident young power player, a fine student, a member of the basketball and football teams, and a good tennis player. He and Dan swam with friends at the downtown YMCA during nighttime "Negro hours." "Henry played every sport and was good at them all. . . . He was an incredible athlete," said Dan. "He would have been a college football player. He just had that winning attitude. 'I'm going to win!' He did not like to lose."

He had inherited his fair-skinned mother's broad face and warm smile, and both his parents' solid good looks. There was something boyish in his fifteen-year-old countenance, and decades later I thought at times I could see the exuberant teenager in the grown man's face, now framed with flecks of gray. He was—and always would be—a sharp dresser like his dad, "though not that splendid." Ellen Sweets said, "He was *so* good-looking and a *really* sweet guy. When I saw that Henry Hampton played tennis, *I* wanted to play tennis. . . . I was crazy about him."

With great resolve, his mother and father had raised their children to know that the sky was the limit, and did everything to free their kids from what Judi called "the mental baggage of segregation. . . . Our parents never wanted us to succumb to victimhood." If it all turned out the way everyone hoped, Henry, Judi, and Veva's generation would leapfrog into a coming new America where at last race was not a deciding factor.

Theirs was a picture-book American childhood, coming of age with a tight-knit circle of friends, loving parents, good health, prosperity, fine schools, long idyllic summers, and the prospect of boundless possibility in the heartland. Surely in those years lay the roots of his optimistic patriotism. As we made *Eyes on the Prize* in the 1980s, Henry, generous to a fault toward the nation that treated his people so wretchedly for three hundred years, would again and again ask that we find and use images of "a black child holding an American flag."

Except that he was black in a racist city, Henry had it all. Then, in 1955, he was visited by two events that would jolt his fifteen-year-old universe to its core, set the course of his life, and eventually lead to *Eyes on the Prize*.

First was the murder in August of fourteen-year-old Emmett Till, killed by two white men in the hamlet of Money, Mississippi, for having talked fresh to a white woman, his savagely beaten body dumped in the Tallahatchie River. Till's reported sin was having said, "Bye, baby," after buying some bubblegum from a white store owner's wife.

Like hundreds of young black males before him, Till might simply have vanished into Mississippi's vast pool of lost souls, except that the boy's mother insisted on an open-casket funeral in Chicago, his hometown, "so that the world can see what they did to my son." Till's sharecropper uncle, Moses Wright, stood up alone in a Mississippi courtroom, defying death in a sea of white men, and pointed his finger at the men who had murdered his nephew. The all-white jury acquitted the killers anyway, but a hundred reporters and photographers were there, and the story was national news.

Living in a border state, Henry, Dan, and their friends had been insulated from the worst casual savagery of the Jim Crow Deep South. But when *Jet* published the unretouched photo of Emmett Till's mangled head, pistol-whipped to a pulp and pierced by a bullet hole, it sent shock waves through black America that summer. Henry told his sister that he "could not, just could not, get the image of the face out of his mind." The picture shook to their roots an entire generation of Negro teens just coming into adulthood in the 1950s, a ferocious warning of what could await young black men in the South when they stepped out of line.

Dan remembered, "Till's murder was talked about in our household. It rippled all up and down the African American community, in homes, in the barbershop, in the pulpit, everywhere. Everyone was saying, 'This could have been my kid.' Henry was moved by Till, he was beyond upset." Every single civil rights activist we interviewed in 1985 for *Eyes on the Prize* had been shaken by Till's murder thirty years before. Rosa Parks talked about it, and the aging Ralph Abernathy said, "We looked ahead to the day that it would happen to me." Young Cassius Clay was moved, and Rev. Fred Shuttlesworth told us, "Really, only God, only the books in heaven can know how many Negroes have come up missing and killed." It rattled Negro teenagers the way the deaths of Oscar Grant, Trayvon Martin, Jordan Davis, Michael Brown, Tamir Rice, and Freddie Gray would shake black America in the next century.

The Till case set a spark of resolve: Henry's generation was not going to take it anymore; they would rise up to end segregation. These were the young people who would lead the sit-ins, CORE, SCLC, and the Student Nonviolent Coordinating Committee. Henry was now part of the nationwide "Emmett Till Generation," most of whom would before long identify themselves as "black," no longer "Negro." This generation existed only within black America; as a white teenager growing up in a progressive family in California, I never heard of Emmett Till until I went to Mississippi in 1963. By the 1980s his case was all but unknown to Americans outside the movement.

Till, who had traveled from his home in Chicago to visit relatives in the Mississippi Delta for summer vacation, ran afoul of deadly racial codes he did not understand and was murdered for no real reason other than his color. Henry now realized that despite the perks and privileges of his class, education, athletic prowess, smarts, charm, and good looks, his young black life could be worthless in many parts of the country. The sky was not the limit.

He later said, "On the one hand, there is no reason that a black person needs to live a portion of his or her life being concerned about the color of people around him. On the other hand, if you don't, you're crazy." When we were working on the Till episode of *Eyes on the Prize,* he said it was inescapable: "If you're black in America, race is a factor in your life. Start with that assumption." With converse effect, the same is true of white Americans, though it seldom occurs to us. We can, if we choose, with a little effort, forget about race.

In the early 1950s a great polio epidemic swept across America, leaving young Till with a stammer in his speech. The virus often spread in public swimming pools, striking all races without favor or prejudice, with special cruelty to youth. By 1955 the Salk polio vaccine was still in the testing stages, and would not be fully licensed until later that year. Dr. Henry Hampton Sr. was holding vaccine samples at his office, reluctant to use it on his own family.

Young Henry woke up one morning and couldn't move his legs. He tried again, but couldn't make it happen. Judi remembered, "My dad got really worried and said, 'We've got to get him to the hospital.' He knew what it was. . . . Polio in those days could be a death sentence unless they caught it early, and those were the days of the iron lung. We had a vigil at home; it was awful."

Dan said, "Henry and I were both doing a lot of swimming, and he was the one who got the disease."

On July 26, 1955, the *St. Louis Post-Dispatch* headlined "Two New Cases of Polio," one of whom was Henry Hampton Jr. But then, Ellen Sweets said, "When Henry got polio there was suddenly a great mysterious silence. They didn't talk about it. We didn't go there for a long time. We were afraid to swim in any pool. It was like AIDS." Ellen kept up on Henry's case only by eavesdropping on adults whispering, or by picking up the extension when she heard her mother talking in low tones on the phone.

With legs completely paralyzed and both arms partially paralyzed, a quadriplegic for all practical purposes, Henry could do little but stare at the hospital ceiling. "It's terrible, but how do I get through this? Meanwhile you have a dike of anxiety and fear that's pushing at you and if you let it come over you it will wash you under. So you learn to control that even in the room with that sense of fear."

He got through the worst of it and came home in a wheelchair. Judi said, "I remember in the living room watching him fall to the floor, because it was the only way he could get out of the chair." He lay at home sick for weeks, then months. A white physical therapist, Vanamie, came to the house and worked with the crippled young man for months as they toiled together to reclaim the use of his hands and arms. Henry began building the powerful upper body strength that would serve him well for the rest of his life. Their goal then was for him to walk at graduation with his high school class.

He mustered astonishing resolve against what must have brought many a teenage polio victim to suicidal despair. Dan remembered, "Polio didn't slow him down. . . . Henry was so involved in just *living*. He was *never* idle, always moving. 'Let's go do it!' We played wheelchair basketball on the lot, had some extra wheelchairs around, and I'd hop in one, and his attitude was 'I'm going to play wheelchair basketball and I'm going to be the best there is' . . . as soon as he could after he got out of the hospital. Henry was *never* a down talker. 'Life is going on, and I'm going to be part of it.' He had a feeling about the polio that 'This is temporary . . . Let's go, let's go, let's do it!'" Back in school, his Catholic friends carried him up and down the stairs in his wheelchair to physics class, Henry terrified they would drop him.

He said, "We—all of us kids who had polio—were all taught that 'You're going to beat this.' OK, you can't use that leg, but we'll put a brace on it and off you go. I was fifteen. It is powerful and frightening. You can only do so much. . . . Small successes are very important." And later in life, when severe health problems arose one after another, he never surrendered, and stubbornly refused to allow himself to be defined by illness.

But Judi said, "Not until he got polio did he really understand being rejected."

After six months of intensive physical therapy, strength slowly returned and he regained the use of first his right arm, then his left, and nearly all of his right leg, but the left was a goner. Supported with the three-foot-long hinged steel brace that would be his lifelong companion, Henry was at last able to walk upright. "Sometimes he got frustrated when he didn't get his brace snapped right before he got up, he was in such a hurry to 'go do it.' That brace tore up some pants, but it didn't stop him," said Dan. His dad built him a little bachelor pad in the basement where he and Dan listened to Motown and Dave Brubeck, and built powerful gas-powered model airplanes.

His father, haunted that he had not vaccinated the kids, bought the young man a brand-new fire engine red 1956 Thunderbird on his sixteenth birthday, "as a way to deal with the crisis." Dan remembered, "There was no car like it in town. . . . We drove that fire engine red baby everywhere we could, driving out in the country doing doughnuts. It was fun and it was liberating! It's a good thing the cops didn't get us. 'What are these black guys *doing*?!'"

Dan added, "I think the '56 T-Bird was also an act of defiance. Papa Doc Hampton knew about the racism and hatred, and I think he thought that this was just another way to throw craziness back at the haters. And, of course, it was a great rehab gift for Henry."

Henry recalled the reactions of other blacks, and especially white people, "and I began to see the kind of responses it got; there was a bit of real hatred that I had this thing that they didn't. It taught me some real lessons about how you exist in a society that is predictably racist and how you can come at it from different places to change it. And ultimately I got rid of my Thunderbird. . . . I astounded my father and my friends by saying, 'This is too flashy; it reflects on me . . . in a bad way.' In some ways the way you treat yourself is the way you treat others, and if you're sitting there reveling in the wealth of a successful family it does not really pay homage to the kind of contribution you're going to make to bring others with you."

Henry bought himself a dumpy little Renault Dauphine, "more than humbling," said Dan. But that didn't stop the two teenagers from driving to San Francisco. They "held it together with rubber bands and chewing gum . . . got to San Francisco Bay, saw it, turned around, and drove back to St. Louis." Back home, Dan would sometimes ride along for the fun of it when Henry went to the church to do "a really quick confession—confess sneaking into the drive-in, come out, and off we'd go, sneaking into the drive-in again. I'd think, 'What is *this* all about?' . . . We never talked directly about God or spirituality. We talked about cars a lot."

The Montgomery bus boycott and other stirrings of the infant civil rights movement were making their way onto televisions in American living rooms, including those of the Hampton and Raybon families. Now older, the kids took notice. "We did talk some about politics. But we mostly were just teenagers, talking about teen stuff, not about politics," said Judi.

In all, Henry spent two years in physical therapy, studying hard in his Catholic high school, busy growing up, busy becoming Henry Hampton. As his friend Bob Hohler put it, "Henry was the product of a Jesuit high school education, trained in rhetoric and reasoning, and the rigorous experience sharpened an already tough analytical intelligence."

On the day of his graduation from St. Louis University High School in June 1957, he walked haltingly from the back of the auditorium all the way to the front, supported by a crutch and the brace on his leg, with black and white students, teachers, and parents clapping all the way, cheering when he finally reached the podium. Judi broke down in tears.

He later told me, "The only upside to polio was that it probably saved me from being a too-small halfback on a lousy college football team."

Henry excelled with a vengeance in high school, and was able to apply to college with excellent grades. Because of ongoing de facto segregation in Missouri, many children of black professionals went off to out-of-state colleges. Henry's friend Ellen Sweets set out for Antioch and remembers that on her block alone black kids headed to Harvard, Oberlin, and Vassar. Dan went to the prestigious Washington University in St. Louis, and Henry's sister Veva, already a junior at Wellesley, was on her way toward medical school.

Henry applied to a half dozen colleges and was accepted at "a couple of Ivy Leagues and Williams," but "I went to Catholic schools, so a Catholic college was logical. The Jesuits convinced me I'd like it at Holy Cross. My father disapproved; he wanted all of us to go to Ivy League schools." Hampton surely would have made the grade as one of the only black undergraduates at Williams or Yale.

He arrived at the nearly all-white Jesuit college in Worcester, Massachusetts, in September 1957, just in time to watch on television as armed federal troops escorted black students into all-white Central High School in Little Rock, Arkansas. Isolated and hamstrung by the tight discipline, he tried to endure Holy Cross, but it was an "absolute disaster. I mean, it's painful getting up at seven o'clock every day for chapel. In bed with lights out by ten?" And that year at Holy Cross capped Henry's growing frustration with the Church.

His weariness with Holy Cross may also have had to do with a peculiar tendency among liberal churched whites at the time to smother Negroes with pandering attention. He later told his friend Ike Williams that Holy Cross "'kinded' me to death. I mean, I never felt I could take off my shirt or let down for a minute because everybody was, 'How you doin'? Come over for a pizza' . . . and so there was nothing but support. Hats off to them, but I never could relax. . . . I was so lonely. . . . Who could I ever tell that I'm lonely? I'm the most token of token people in the world. So I left."

Deciding now to follow his father and sister into medicine, he returned home to St. Louis that year to study premed and English at Washington University, not far from his parents' home. He found himself supremely comfortable at Wash U, did well in physiology, organic chemistry, and English, got broad exposure to the liberal arts, and solidified his lifelong love of poetry and literature. He discovered and devoured the great science fiction works of Ray Bradbury and Robert Heinlein and the philosophical poetry of W. H. Auden. It was during those college years that he developed his unshakable belief—sometimes against all evidence—in the power of the word, in particular the influence of spare and elegant speech.

At Wash U he reunited with his best friend, Dan Raybon. Henry took flying lessons in his junior year, inspired by the complex and powerful model planes he and Don had built in the basement, and by his uncle Reginald Woolridge, one of the first black pilots in World War II. He coaxed the terrified Raybon into taking off from an airstrip outside town. Dan gritted his teeth and figured, "Well, OK, let's do this." And Henry somehow found time to lead the 1960 St. Louis Rolling Rams wheelchair basketball team, which defeated Brooklyn in the national tournament. Henry was named to the tourney's all-star team and won the sportsmanship trophy.

In the student lounge he found time to watch a little television. Occasional strikes like Edward R. Murrow's *Harvest of Shame* lit up the mostly desolate media landscape. In that groundbreaking documentary Murrow introduced to broadcast journalism a halting forerunner of the decent, smart, and respectful discussion of race and class that Hampton would perfect years later. Television was not exactly the overt voice of the oppressor in those days, but it certainly enabled its own veiled strains of oppression simply by the near-complete exclusion of blacks. It is quaint now to look back at Murrow's all-thumbs white producers trying to figure out how to talk with poor black people on camera, and the poor black people trying to figure out how to answer, everyone trying to do the right thing but not knowing how. And in 1960, TV took fleeting notice when South African police killed 69 protesting black men, women, and children, most of them shot in the back, and wounded 180 more in what would be remembered as the Sharpeville Massacre.

Henry wrote, "Whatever television was, it was not a revolutionary force in our society." The chairman of the Federal Communications Commission in 1961 called it "a vast wasteland."

Looking back, standing in the Wash U quad decades later, he said, "In 1961, America was a landscape with a calm surface but with a flawed moral center. It was a time when shows like *Father Knows Best, Leave It to Beaver,* and *I Love Lucy* generated more discussion than the barbaric system of institutionalized and de facto racism that dominated this country. Racism was as far off as the Freedom Rides and Little Rock, and as close as the segregated restaurants that would not serve us, just a few hundred feet from this spot."

Toward the end of his time at Washington, inspired by the kids in Little Rock, Henry became head of the campus NAACP. Later he had his first taste of activism, with sit-ins at a local bank and Santoro's segregated restaurant, marching with brace and crutch. Dan says, "We were very involved in the NAACP and CORE, both of us. We'd march and picket in front of a bank until the cops came and made us move." Helping to organize the actions was Dr. Hampton's colleague in the surgery department at Homer G. Phillips Hospital for Colored, Dr. Leslie Bond, cousin of Julian Bond. Dr. Bond made sure that teachers, lawyers, and other black professionals marched in unity. Dr. Hampton was supportive but did not participate.

Henry said, "We did the good cop/bad cop thing. I would put on my Brooks Brothers suit and very narrow tie and go in and they would say, 'No, we can't serve you.' I'd reply, 'Why can't I sit here?' and then try to engage them in a reasoned argument. It never worked. Then the bad cops [other blacks] would come in with, 'We want it *now*,' much more aggressive, no reasoned arguments." They succeeded in desegregating Santoro's and other establishments. Ellen Sweets said that in the end, "St. Louis had it pretty good sailing through desegregation, largely because the Catholic archdiocese, B'nai B'rith, the National Conference of Christians and Jews, and black church leaders worked hard together to ease the transition." It was the first time Henry had witnessed the power of a coalition across racial and religious lines, and he never forgot it.

Henry Eugene Hampton Jr. graduated from Washington University on June 5, 1961, with a degree in English literature and all of his premed requirements complete, just as the first Freedom Rides left Washington, D.C., headed for trouble in Alabama.

"We watched and saw a movement. It began in the Deep South, fired largely by unlettered, simple people who said, 'No more.' The civil rights movement was the first big television event in this country over a sustained period. TV was just beginning to learn the lessons of graphic violence, thriving on confrontation. Suddenly television discovered that Mosaic conciliatory gesture of those individuals who with strength stood up and appealed to the country and its conscience. . . . That was great television. . . . The industry learned that this was not only something that would, in fact, draw ratings, but that people would immediately understand and react to."

But for Henry Hampton the movement would have to wait; he was on the high-achievement track, with a well-stocked brain, a powerful imagination, and boundless energy. He could have been a fine writer, lawyer, business leader, probably anything, even a pastor.

He packed off to McGill University Faculty of Medicine in Montreal, Quebec. It is not hard to imagine Henry Hampton Jr. as a fine doctor like his father: patient, kind, soft-spoken, a keen listener and diagnostician, exercising reserved authority but with the steel nerve to cut open your chest if he had to. But Henry could not endure the life of a medical student, with its strict routines. "My parents expected that I would become a doctor but that was not to be." After one miserable term at McGill he knew he would never be a physician and withdrew, again to his parents' everlasting disappointment. Years later, as the frail senior Dr. Hampton lay on his deathbed, still not entirely sure what his son Henry Jr. the film-maker did for a living, he leaned over and whispered, "You can still go to medical school." But Henry went on to become a healer of a different sort, and seldom looked back. When his longtime companion Suzanne Weil asked in 1990 if he ever regretted leaving medical school, Henry replied, "Every time I see a Maserati."

Now a dropout twice over, he rambled around as a short-order cook; drove a Mister Softee ice cream truck; moved to Boston in 1961, where his older sister, Veva, was in medical school at Tufts; wrote poetry; and did a little graduate work at Boston University. "I drove a cab, practiced classical guitar three hours a day, fooled around at BU with girls, had a wonderful time. I didn't know what I was doing, but I was happy to have given up the notion of medical school." Dan recalled, "Henry wanted to do something for the social good," but wasn't quite sure what it was.

How many of our generation did the same? Equally unsure, I had dropped out of Yale around that same time, and remember those dreamy unsettled times in the early sixties, when so many of us who had worked so hard to get ourselves into elite colleges decided to just take a hike, to our parents' dismay. We had the freedom to try life on the road, to drive a cab, work at the post office, load trucks, play around with the casual chic vagrancy of Orwell, Kerouac, and Woody Guthrie. We were in no hurry for careers, and a year at a rough factory job might pay pretty good money and teach us more about real life than a year of grad school. And there were so many guitar licks to learn. We had never experienced hunger, and most of us never did anything really dangerous, except for a few guys unlucky enough to get drafted and sent to the mysterious little war ramping up in Vietnam. We changed colleges as often as we changed jobs. My young wife and I between us attended seven different universities before we were done, job-hopping as we school-hopped.

Henry adopted Boston, with its eighteenth-century neighborhoods, labyrinthine streets, nearby Atlantic Ocean, and vibrant university culture, as his new home, and he never left. "Midwesterners gravitate toward the coasts, and probably since I've taken a lot of my experience out of books and a sense of history, I came here. I love the quaint old buildings in New England country towns. Maybe in some ways I even thought I'd be free of race for a while. Like James Baldwin going off to Paris, it's part of the black experience to want to be free of it and think you're living in a place where it's not going to determine or dictate a portion of your life."

By chance, one of his taxi fares in Boston on a summer morning in 1963 was Royal Cloyd, firebrand of the Boston arts scene and administrator for the Unitarian Universalist Association. Bob Hohler remembered Cloyd coming into the UUA office and saying, "I think I've got someone

I'd like you to interview tomorrow, met him in a cab on the way here from the airport. . . . We did grab a cup of coffee and talked for a while, about poetry mostly. He shut off the meter."

"You interviewed the cabdriver?" Hohler asked.

"I think he said something about studying for his MA in English at BU. I thought he'd be a good editor . . . he thought he wanted to be a writer . . . he isn't sure what he wants to do—at twenty-three few do—young, energetic, still mightily undisciplined."

Henry picked up the story. The job turned out to be at the Unitarian headquarters on Beacon Street. "Royal Cloyd always found bright people, young people, and gave them a chance. So after seven or eight months of editing the *Directory*—which is exactly what it sounds like—suddenly I'm director of information at the age of twenty-four, publishing a couple of magazines, making films, with absolutely no experience."

Henry Hampton, lapsed Catholic, ex-athlete, polio survivor, medical school dropout, former cabdriver and ice cream man, became, according to Hohler, the youngest African American professional to hold a major post in a mainstream Protestant denomination. Hohler added, "Henry fit right in. This was, after all, a place centered on the search for truth and understanding, a continuing, never-ending quest." Hohler noted the old Unitarian joke: Those on the road to the Pearly Gates will come across two signs. One reads "This way to heaven." The other reads "This way to a discussion about heaven," and there was little doubt which road Henry would choose.

Henry's new Yankee mentors and colleagues were as different as they could possibly be from the southern parents and midwestern Catholics who nurtured him. Their theology rejected the Holy Trinity and posited Jesus as a great man, prophet, exemplar, and model for living one's life but certainly not the Son of God. Charles Darwin, Thomas Jefferson, and Ralph Waldo Emerson were Unitarians, as was Henry's fellow St. Louis native, poet T. S. Eliot (until he converted to the Church of England). Above all, Unitarians were humanists, placing their faith in rational thought; no received wisdom there. Young Martin Luther King, at his wife Coretta's urging, had considered becoming a Unitarian minister. Henry was ready for this.

I was raised in the Unitarian Church, and Henry himself created some of the printed materials that arrived at our provincial congregation in California's wind-swept Great Central Valley back in the early sixties. Except for my mom, whose family had been at it for generations, nearly everyone in our congregation came from somewhere else: former reformed Jews, lapsed Catholics, Buddhists, a few black ex-Baptists, and my Lutheran/Episcopalian/atheist father.

Those Unitarian Sunday services were thin on passion but loaded with dialectic, irony, pluralist politics, skeptical clear thinking, and tepid singing. As a boy I always half wished our family were Catholic so we could revel in a little mysterious ritual; or better yet why couldn't we join one of the "shouting religions," Baptist, maybe, with rock and roll in church, belting out a joyful noise unto the lord. The Unitarian sermons Henry and I heard were well-crafted lectures, explications on history, politics, the moral philosophy of civil rights and nuclear disarmament. He once called them "the droning monotony of the white pulpit," a far cry from the passionate preaching we would later come to know in the South.

They may have been short on pageantry, but oh, did the Unitarians know about forcing social change upon the United States of America. They practiced the Social Gospel as well as any of their Christian brethren, and their long history of bold activism in matters of race, starting with the abolitionist movement, was grist for Henry. Transcendentalist Rev. Theodore Parker welcomed escaped slaves into his Boston Unitarian congregation in 1851, in open defiance of Massachusetts's Fugitive Slave Law, and wrote his sermons with a loaded pistol on his desk. Parker was, in fact, the originator of King's "arc of the moral universe" phrase that Henry so loved.

Henry flourished in his new community with the left-liberal white intellectuals of Beacon Street. The lively culture of debate and rational engagement suited his Jesuit-trained mind. "They were on the edge of the civil rights movement, and then the antiwar movement was their meat. They went to the 1963 March on Washington. They marched from Selma to Montgomery in 1965 and I went as part of my job. What I saw in the South stayed with me: individuals taking responsibility as leaders and followers. It was a remarkable groundswell of people collecting themselves, cutting through the bullshit that keeps people apart, and tracking toward an objective. When do you get close to that? It's a potent lesson and one you don't get over. You keep believing it could happen again."

He had a bit of Whitman in him, some Emerson, Thoreau, and a lot of Frederick Douglass held just below the surface. Henry was at ease around the Unitarians, with whom he would occasionally socialize after work.

During a summer afternoon staff party at the suburban home of the UUA executive vice president, hearing a cry from the backyard swimming pool, Henry leapt in, leg brace and all, and rescued seven-year-old Tanya Jane Miller, daughter of his coworker, Rev. Orloff Miller.

All of this was unfolding in an America blessed with a vibrant liberal political culture, as rambunctious on the left as the Tea Party would later become on the right, though with less malice. It was the banner year of civil rights. Liberal LBJ had trounced conservative Barry Goldwater ("The Fascist Gun in the West"), and hundreds of thousands of Ban the Bomb marchers were turning the arms race around. The best and brightest practical progressives owned Congress in the mid-1960s and drove the socially liberal missions of a dozen Great Society agencies. I vividly remember the heady sense of hope that permeated society, the belief that we could at last make American democracy deliver on its founding promises.

Working for the Unitarians, Henry may have thought he could live a race-neutral life in Boston, may have thought, like Richard Wright in France, that he could be simply a man for a while, immune or unaware of fierce nativist and racial currents coursing just below the surface in Boston. "But surprise! There were little things all along. . . . I dropped my white secretary off once in the North End and the next day all four of her tires had been punctured."

Bob Hohler said of Henry's time working for the church, "He developed the ability to navigate though the force fields that raced across the nation and the world . . . these forces were converged and circling one another. As a communications officer and as an activist, as writer and editor, filmmaker and poet, interpreter and analyst, facilitator and conciliator. Henry was in the middle of it all. I think of this five-year period as the equivalent of Henry's doctoral program. Somewhere along the line he picked up the notion that it was actually, literally, possible to change history."

Henry's older sister, Veva, never became directly involved in the civil rights movement. But Judi had grown up to become an activist in her own right, and left college in the fall of 1964 to go south and work in Canton, Mississippi. "I worked on the CORE voter registration . . . lived in Freedom House with my white boyfriend, Phil Sharp." Judi's mother supported her but feared for her life. Her father said, "I'll have a heart attack." Both parents were sympathetic in the end, but would dearly have preferred that Judi had not gone.

Police in Canton were "incensed by interracial couples, and were constantly breaking in at night to see who was sleeping with whom. . . . The cops would stop us when we were out in the pickup truck." Judi and Phil worked though the winter of 1964–65 as part of the skeleton crew (at the same time Henry went to Selma) and considered staying in Mississippi to make a life there, but left in the spring of 1965. Judi went to work as a program director for the War on Poverty in New York at the Addie Mae Collins Head Start center on 127th Street, and did drug rehab work. She eventually completed her degree at Boston University, and went on to do graduate work in comparative literature at Columbia. Judi's path followed a common trajectory of the time: I left my Student Nonviolent Coordinating Committee job in Georgia that same spring to work for the War on Poverty in California before finally finishing my degree at Berkeley a few years later.

Judi said one way to think about the three Hampton kids and how they dealt with race was: "I was a civil rights worker, Henry made *Eyes on the Prize,* and Veva tried to move on from racism by becoming a physician."

By then Judi and Phil were planning to be married, and Henry, very protective of his little sister, advised against it, saying, "I don't think this will work." Nonetheless, he made arrangements for them to wed in the beautiful chapel at Arlington Street Unitarian Church, and gave them his blessing. Their mother, Julia Hampton, "hated Sammy Davis Jr. for marrying a white woman," and did not feel comfortable when Judi married Phil, but she accepted it. All three of the Hampton children eventually married or had very long-term relationships with white partners. Veva was on her way to becoming one of the nation's few black women psychiatrists. She and David Zimmerman, a white science writer, had been married in the International House at Columbia in 1963. Henry Sr. and Julia, in David's words, "were kind enough to come to our wedding, which was pretty nice. Neither of my parents came. . . . My mother disowned me for marrying a black woman."

Henry's Unitarian job in Boston was "a good gig for him," remembered David, the foundation of his real political awakening and lifelong commitment to mass media as a force for change. As director of information, he had his own minipulpit, and easy casual access to leaders in the liberal establishment.

After marching with King in Selma, he began testing the waters of filmmaking with a couple of church colleagues. "We drove to the South to look at why certain Unitarian and Universalist churches had come apart around the issue of integration. I remember sleeping in the backseat of a big Chrysler for a week or ten days. I'm not sure my two white colleagues were as frightened as I was, but I knew what that world was around us. We drove and we shot film in Atlanta and in New Orleans, and Florida and Louisiana. It gave me a chance to see what was going on there."

Then in January 1968, at the height of the Vietnam War, Henry made his first trip abroad, accompanying fourteen American religious leaders on a round-the-world mission, "exploring whether religion can find a working consensus around the issue of peace." He was spokesman for the group, which included SCLC's Ralph Abernathy, Unitarian leader Dana Greeley, Catholic and Methodist bishops, rabbis, and Protestant clergy.

They had meetings at the World Council of Churches in Geneva, at the Vatican, and in Istanbul, Jerusalem, and Delhi before going on to Saigon for a meeting with Ambassador Ellsworth Bunker and General William Westmoreland, "fresh from his helicopter."

Always alert to the messy side of history, Henry said, "The peace mission was a big reach. Religious people sometimes have an inflated sense of their ability, but they also have this courageous notion that the power of religion can change things. Meeting with General Westmoreland was prophetic in retrospect. Our people were talking about death and peace, ending the war, and he was talking about the need to complete this and not leave an open sore. I always believed, watching him, that he knew he couldn't win that war under the circumstances. . . . It would have taken enormous ethical and moral strength to stand up and say, 'We've got to stop this,' but he didn't."

Their "attempt for the first time to bring temple, church, mosque, and synagogue into meaningful support of the United Nations and other regional structures for peace," wrapped up with uncomfortably ambiguous results, did little to hasten the end of hostilities. The papal nuncio entertained them at a French villa outside Saigon and they then flew out on January 30, 1968, hours before the Viet Cong's massive Tet Offensive began. In his report he wrote, "The purpose of the trip was, of course, peace—'peace' couched in the melodious syllogisms of the pessimist, 'peace' in the guilty tones of men who had never felt the taste of war, 'peace' in the thudding repetition of concern that people somewhere were dying."

The carnage in Vietnam raged on for another seven years.

It was on the weary flight home that Henry first started thinking seriously about making his own documentary films. In those days no one really considered documentary film—"sermonizing by other means"—a career option.

The times and the Unitarians were changing. As the first golden age of civil rights began to fade after 1966, the civil rights movement had splintered and now had to share center stage with the antiwar movement. As Black Power, black arts, and black consciousness gained momentum across the country, African Americans formed their own caucuses inside white-dominated institutions, including many religious denominations. With growing militancy and activism in white-majority churches, black clergy and laity began questioning a "false kind of integration," in which all power remained in the hands of white men.

Within their 98-percent-white denomination, black Unitarians were one of the first and the best organized caucuses, with direct control over a million-dollar commitment from the parent organization. They commissioned radical public-service spots for network TV, supported alternative schools and Chicago's Blackstone Rangers community organization project. Henry became their spokesman, writing, "The trend to consider a separate black church is heightened by the current revolution in the humanities by black artists, musicians, dramatists, writers, and filmmakers."

The black caucus movement "says not to people in the South, not Washington, but to the *organizations* in which you are a participant, 'Hey, what about *here*? What's going *on here*?'" The Black Unitarian Universalist Caucus found itself at the center of bitter charges of racism—black and white—that engulfed the church for two years. Race exploded within the headquarters in Boston and in churches across the country, tearing apart congregations, families, and friendships, and nearly crippling the UUA.

Henry said, "We wanted to take resources and assets and play a full role within the Unitarian Church. And the way you do it is to go off by yourself, which flipped the Unitarians out, but provided me with a way to work with blacks in Boston. I became the director of press for the caucus, as well as the director of information for the UUA. It was clear there was a conflict of interest, so in 1968 I resigned from my church job."

It was time for Henry Hampton to move on.

CHAPTER TWO

"Racism Is Like a Loaded Gun"

1968–78

Henry and I and thousands of others had embraced the civil rights struggle in our teens and early twenties, in the righteous afterglow of World War II's industrial-scale slaughter, when our parents, aunts, and uncles had beat the Fascists fair and square. And then we had emerged from the civil rights movement in 1965 with our clear-thinking, compassionate, white southern president, Lyndon Baines Johnson, proclaiming "We Shall Overcome" on prime-time television. In that winter of 1965, the great levers of democracy apparently functioned well for more Americans than ever before. The good guys were on a roll, striding across a great historical divide.

But nothing in the 1960s turned out quite the way we hoped. The swing from hope to despair was swift and devastating; it began with the August 1965 Watts Riot, one of the largest insurrections in American history, only a few days after President Johnson signed the landmark Voting Rights Act. Watching Watts burn, I could feel the naive faith in the self-correcting power of American democracy rupturing, faith that I and Henry Hampton had soaked up in our high school civics classes, faith that had been our engine of resolve through the movement days.

Looking forward after Selma to our dazzling multicultural future, cheering the victory, how could we have missed the ominous signs? Wasn't LBJ actually just a conniving, war-mongering redneck who had smacked down the pleas of black supplicants from Mississippi the summer before? Hadn't we already seen plots against King's life, and been all too quick to dismiss John Kennedy's assassination in 1963 as a freak sociopathic glitch in the orderly working of our exceptional nation? Weren't the specters of de facto segregation, racist housing policy, poverty, and police brutality clearly on the march from New York to California?

Everything went wrong in 1968, not in slow motion but with a ferocious density of shock unequaled until we saw the Twin Towers fall in 2001. Malcolm X lay dead by the time Martin Luther King was shot down.

George Wallace, our racist Antichrist, was snarling his way toward a presidential nomination until he, too, took a bullet. Thousands of police in Washington, D.C., beat and gassed their way through the huge "Resurrection City" family encampment on the Mall—SCLC's desperate attempt to keep the country's eyes on economic inequality after King's murder, the movement's Little Bighorn. Massive violent rebellions blew up in a hundred black ghettos in the summer of 1968. That year seemed both fleeting and interminable; would it ever end? Time slowed, stopped, turned back on itself.

Hunter Thompson called the late sixties "that place where the wave finally broke and rolled back" into the ocean, where we found ourselves suddenly adrift in a dark whirlpool we could never have imagined only a few years before. Henry later said, "It was one thing to stand in Selma in '65 and feel a sense of possibility and expectation, and another thing, four years later, to be absolutely distraught because the leaders were dead, the War on Poverty was a shambles, and Resurrection City had failed." Henry quoted King: "We had integrated the master's house, only to discover that the master's house was on fire."

The plague of military draft hung over us, our friends dying in the apparently aimless calamity raging on and on in Vietnam, a war we were now losing. We had half a million American troops on the ground, and 17,000 of them died in 1968 alone—more than all the U.S. deaths in Iraq and Afghanistan combined over ten years. And that year, 250,000 Vietnamese died. My close high school buddy, USMC Pfc. Jim Peschel, on combat duty in Quang Tri Province, had become disgusted with the war and applied for conscientious objector status; his commanding officer reacted by sending him out on the most dangerous patrols, and Jim died in hand-to-hand fighting at a jungle fire base. When riot police charged the crowd during a night antiwar demonstration in San Francisco, I actually reached down and picked up a brick on the street, despite all those nonviolence workshops. The Democrats' 1968 convention exploded in mass bloody mayhem in the streets of Chicago, and the New Left itself soon fell to fratricide.

Henry said, "The awful war, Vietnam, pulled away the resources, it pulled away the cadre of leadership that had been formed that was ready to assault the real problems of economic and educational inequality. It drained our spirits. We regrouped and went on to fight and win a monumental battle to end a bad war, but our chance to transform this society into one based on true equity was lost for the moment and for us." We heard rumors that the United States planned to use atomic bombs in Vietnam if things really went south. And Henry, wonk that he was, certainly knew that that war was unfolding in the shadow of 38,000 nuclear weapons we and the Soviets had at the ready, enough to end all human life on the planet. Bummer. (At a rally in Berkeley I heard Stokely Carmichael describe the arms race as "two white guys standing next to a swimming pool full of gasoline arguing over who's got more matches.")

Except for the music—the Grateful Dead channeling Lightnin' Hopkins on acid, James Brown channeling James Brown—1968 was a terrible year to be American. You did not have to be all that paranoid to fear that the rampaging civil unrest in the streets just might flash over into civil war. I know that neither Henry nor I could entirely shake the possibility. No one was sure the center would hold, and on a bad day many of us felt it would not.

The incendiary mayhem went global, in France, Mexico, Indonesia, Algeria, Japan, and a dozen other countries. There was no escape, and there were, indeed, no bystanders in this revolution. Soviet tanks rolled into Prague. On June 5, 1968, in a crowded alley in Paris stinking of tear gas, I heard from behind me a stranger's voice, a Frenchman, snarling, "Hey, American! Your Bobby Kennedy, he's dead." Bobby had been our last hope.

Our parents' generation was hardened in the crucibles of the Great Depression, the Holocaust, and the war; ours was little prepared to be ambushed by tragedy. For Henry and me and those of us who had spent our entire young lives in the stability, good fortune, and expansion of democracy, it was like stumbling into hell. And then drugs hit, and it was hell on happy pills. When I had left Yale for Mississippi in 1964, only a few years before, there were whispered tales that one of our classmates smoked marijuana—only a single one out of nine hundred young men; people would point him out, the hipster creep, across the Old Campus. Now, in '68, grass and LSD had become widespread anesthetics of choice, racking up their own casualties. At an antiwar rally in Berkeley in 1967 I ran into a guy who had worked with me in Mississippi, who talked about how much marijuana he was smoking and how much he loved it; another Mississippi friend swiftly derailed his life with cocaine and heroin.

And then a perfect capstone on the devil's own year came when some crazy woman shot Andy Warhol in the stomach, South Carolina cops shot SNCC field secretary Cleve Sellers in the back, and the citizens of the United States elected Richard Nixon.

That was the year Henry Hampton decided to start a documentary company.

His was an act of loony optimism and naive faith in the American system. Hampton, plugging away with the Unitarians, had kept his cool while the rest of us slipped into anxious loathing. His Jesuit education stood by him and he confessed to being a shameless idealist: "I aim to appeal to the better side." But his documentary venture did not spring up in a vacuum. As the traditional black/white coalitions forged in simpler times began to fray, ventures like the Congressional Black Caucus and the Unitarian Black Caucus staked out Afrocentric space in civic institutions and in commercial ventures, alongside vehement vanguards like the Black Panthers and newly reimagined all-black SNCC. By this time I noticed that even white people talking in private to other white people had abandoned "Negro" for "black."

And he did glimpse a few smidgens of hope in '68: hundreds of newly elected black officials in the South, Julian Bond put forward as the first-ever African American vice presidential candidate. Mississippi Freedom Summer organizer Allard Lowenstein was running for Congress. Who can forget when we saw our first photograph of the whole earth from space that year, a splendid blue and green orb of life, "earthrise" over the barren surface of the moon, a home worth saving.

Henry had become increasingly concerned with the token role of African Americans on screen and offscreen in film and television, and tokenism's effects on what stories got told, how they got told, and who told them. Even the Kerner Commission investigating causes of the Watts rebellion concluded: "The world that television and newspapers offer to their black audience is almost totally white, in appearance and attitude."

Surveying the media landscape in 1968, who could miss the overwhelming white male dominance of ownership, management, and content creation? If television was a new driver of the national conversation, what sort of meaningful dialogue could be had without major participation by minorities? African Americans were making faint inroads behind the camera in Hollywood, working on a few Sidney Poitier and Harry Belafonte movies, but there were probably no more than a dozen working in nonfiction television across the nation, hardly enough to even form a caucus.

So why not create a black film company? While he was still on staff with the Unitarians, Henry had, in fact, quietly filed incorporation papers in June 1967 for Blackside, Inc. The business address was 88 Lambert Avenue, his home in Roxbury. What would Blackside be? What would Blackside do? How would black stories be told? There were many questions, and not nearly as many answers, but in his mind he had no choice; he couldn't not do it. He later wrote, "The responsible parties of our society are those who understand, as did Martin Buber, that responsibility takes two things: a sense of obligation and the ability to act. . . . And they then turn away from our time of small and shriveled dreams of things, and give us a vision of a world as we would have it, for it is only in shared dreaming that we become responsible for changing it." On that philosophy of obligation and agency he launched his raw little institution.

On June 28, 1968, Henry officially ditched his comfy career and cozy office at the Unitarian Universalist Association headquarters up on Beacon Hill and began his new independent life as president, CEO, executive producer, and sole employee of Blackside, Inc., across town in the ghetto. From that day forward, for the rest of his life he was master of his own destiny, and would never again work for anyone else. "Two things coincided: the Black Power movement and my own personal need for independence. There's a part of me that never wanted to work for anyone. That was bred into me by my father, because if you work for anyone ultimately your destiny belongs to someone else, so creating a company was the logical step. I was twenty-eight."

Henry said he chose "Blackside" as a variation on "Blackstone," the name of a nice little city park on Shawmut Avenue in Boston's South End. And, of course, the company would offer the "the black side" of American history and culture that was not represented in the media and seldom taught in schools. The very name itself planted the Afrocentric flag— nothing wishy-washy like "Rainbow Television"—and surprised some of Henry's friends, who saw him more as enthusiastically multicultural, suspicious of doctrinaire ethnic identity, and as much a courtly faculty club type as a race man. And throughout Blackside's thirty-year run, the name would conjure false folklore that it was a black-only company, which it never was.

He had two clear, concrete goals: to produce powerful films relevant to the African American experience, and to produce young filmmakers of color. These he would do until his dying day. His scrappy little company would eventually train hundreds of minority filmmakers, produce sixty major projects (including some flops), and become the largest minority-owned documentary film company in America. For a while it would be the largest independent documentary company in America owned by anyone of *any* color. Henry later said, "I am not numbered among the powerful, never found my way into the traditional television management structure, and because there was no place for me there twenty years ago, I built a business outside of it." He felt the obligation and ability to fill the mentoring gap and make good, useful films at the same time, "to create an instrument that would be available to black folks when they wanted to compete in the media landscape."

His long-term mission was lofty, expansive, and nothing short of visionary: Blackside would make stories about "the real functioning of democracy as a permanent, accessible, and even popular subject for broadcasting . . . serving democracy, diversity, culture, and civil society . . . by producing powerful, dramatic, engaging and accessible stories about American social progress." And with the savvy and intelligence that were his mark, he added, to "explore the responsibilities of the government to its citizens and vice versa." That calling would finally come to full flowering in *Eyes on the Prize* years later.

He was inspired by Murrow's *Harvest of Shame* and Frederick Wiseman's searing cinema verité documentary *Titicut Follies*. But for now, the work was far more modest. Baby steps at a time, he was getting his TV chops by doing 3-minute comedy sketches with his Unitarian friend Howard Dammond on *Say Brother*, an important weekly black-run WGBH show, "just trying to see who could be funnier." *Say Brother*, born in the wake of Dr. King's death, produced by African Americans for African Americans, was a deep dive into blackness with a strong commitment from WGBH, at a time when it was rare to have black people on television, and when the Boston Brahmin whiteness of WGBH bordered on parody. *Say Brother* was wall-to-wall black faces.

With its proud "stamp of blackness," *Say Brother* was smart, relaxed, and professional, presenting a rollicking mix of live funk, soul, and early hip-hop music, debate, and community arts, with occasional documentary shorts produced and narrated by Hampton. His think pieces included a short, acerbic documentary look at Richard Nixon's inaugural speech in light of the continuing exclusion of blacks from electoral campaigns aimed at middle-class whites.

Young Hampton, sharply dressed, urbane, well spoken, served from time to time as an excellent host for studio roundtable discussion on issues of the day. He and everyone else smoked on camera, sending clouds of cigarette smoke drifting through close-ups of participants. And he was also running a 1 A.M. community service outreach effort at Kaiser Broadcasting's WKBG. Steve Fayer, one of the managers, said, "Kaiser, like every other company in the country, was panicking about FCC license challenges and serving minority communities, so the word came out that we were going to create ties to the black community and Hispanic community. We offered him late-night use of the studio for his 'Operation Night Train,' a Hampton-directed effort to train minority young people in broadcasting."

But nurturing newly founded Blackside was his first priority. Henry's first hire was Howie Dammond, who had "grown up in the killing fields of Pittsburgh and the Bronx," gotten a degree from Brandeis, was just out of grad school at Yale, was mentored by Rev. Jack Mendelsohn at the Arlington Street Church, and "had an Afro 100 feet tall." Then Henry snatched *Say Brother* associate producer and Alabama native Carol Munday to be Blackside's director of operations. The only piece of film equipment they owned was a Nagra tape recorder. Henry quickly set out hustling around town in a "little rusted-out $400 Volkswagen," and oversaw the first Blackside film shoot only a few weeks after launching the company.

It was a 30-second spot in a series of public-service announcements that first made people sit up and take notice of Henry Hampton as a new player in Boston's media world. Steve Fayer, the go-to guy when anything questionable came up at WKBG, recalled, "This guy who was head of the film department, a Boston Irishman, comes down the hall and says, 'You got to see this, man, this came from that colored company.'"

The infamous half-minute "Gun Spot" has now vanished into history; apparently no copy exists. Written and directed by Henry and shot by Werner Bundschuh, the "Gun Spot" featured an angelic seven-year-old blond boy whom Howie Dammond had found, in close-up, doing something with his hands just offscreen, you're not quite sure what, until the camera pulls back to reveal that he's expertly fieldstripping a real .45 automatic pistol and then loading it with live rounds, with the tagline "Racism is like a loaded gun." That was all. It was strong stuff for 1969, when the only civilians with firearms on television were private detectives, criminals, and Black Panthers.

Henry struck up a friendship with Steve Fayer, and sensed correctly that he was not cut out to work as a commercial television bureaucrat. Fayer was, in fact, spending every spare minute writing fiction. He had been around the block: Jewish kid from the Bronx, navy veteran, first mate on a gaff-rigged schooner, *C'est La Vie*, topside man with an underwater salvage operation in the West Indies "until it went bust when the two principals were collared by police in St. Martin's for smuggling." He had done the Iowa Writers' Workshop and was now chafing at his job as director of audience promotion at Kaiser Broadcasting.

When Henry asked him to help out getting Blackside's accounting in order, Fayer pitched in for a couple of weeks before setting sail for the Galapagos with one of the former smugglers.

Steve didn't see Henry again until the summer of 1972 at a mutual friend's wedding in the Waspy yachting town of Marblehead, Massachusetts. "As the Hamp and I walked up the steps of the Corinthian Yacht Club he remarked that this was probably the first time someone of his complexion had entered through the front door. I responded that it might be the first time for someone of the Hebrew persuasion as well." Over drinks at the reception Henry not only persuaded Steve to come and join Blackside full time, but to move into a room on the second floor of his home/office up on Lambert Avenue in Roxbury. "Henry had confidence in me when I had no confidence in myself. . . . Within a few days, I wrote my first government public-service spots for Blackside." Steve was to become one of the finest documentary writers in America, and worked with Blackside for the next thirty years, where he served as chief writer on *Eyes on the Prize,* and patiently taught dozens of filmmakers, including me, the craft of documentary writing.

Over the coming decades many would mistake Blackside for a nonprofit, but it was from the beginning a for-profit corporation (though sometimes thoroughly unprofitable), and Henry took home what profit the outfit could generate. He started the company with a few thousand dollars of his own money, quickly began winning contract bids, and within a year was actually earning enough to support himself. He said, "Making a living then didn't seem much of an issue—$10,000 a year seemed like a lot of money. The staff was me and one or two other people. I've never worried about being able to make a living. That's part of the middle-class confidence that your parents give you." A used MGB sports car took the place of the rusted VW.

I was at that moment launching my own film career, parallel to Henry's, in film school in California. The hot tickets were Jean-Luc Godard's baffling, splintered post–New Wave diatribes; the seductive cinema verité of Maysles, Leacock, and Wiseman; and Eastern European bummers that were proudly avant-garde in the worst possible way. Emile de Antonio released his unforgettably nasty Vietnam film, *In the Year of the Pig,* that year, and Bill Greaves, one of the few black documentary makers in the country, was busy shooting *Symbiopsychotaxiplasm* in Central Park. These films would not easily give up their secrets; it seemed that one of their goals was to make us feel stupid. Opacity was a virtue, clarity a weakness.

It took a lot of nerve for Henry to set out making documentaries, by far the most expensive, cumbersome, and complex form of nonfiction. He could more easily have founded a little magazine or launched a radio show. It was puzzling. And at that cultural moment when all hell was breaking loose in cinema, he was conservative and far against the grain in setting out to make conventional *educational* documentaries. In our intoxicating film world, educational documentaries were the meat loaf of cinema cuisine: bland, square, predictable, utilitarian. This was Henry's chosen path?

Henry, the prolific idea man, was in Howie's words "an impassioned critter." He never claimed to be a hands-on filmmaker, surprising for such a mechanically adept fellow who grew up hot-rodding cars and fixed his own plumbing. As far as anyone could see, he was a fumble bunny with cameras, lights, sound, and editing equipment, and happy to admit it. So among the people he hired to run the practical filmmaking operation was the young technical savant Romas Slezas, Blackside's first professional filmmaker. Romas was an elfin, sharp-talking Lithuanian refugee whose family had fled the Russian invasion during World War II, spent his early childhood inside Nazi Germany, and lived in a displaced-persons camp before fleeing to the United States. Fayer claimed that Romas bore "shrapnel scars of mysterious origin." At the time Henry hired him he was producing *Garsos Bongos,* a Lithuanian-language radio show, and had just finished the graduate film program at Boston University. When government contracting officers asked Blackside to list ten company holidays, Fayer noted they were probably the only minority company in history to come up with Lithuanian Independence Day. In years to come Romas would play the practical take-care-of-business Steve Wozniak to Henry's entrepreneurial visionary Steve Jobs.

He gathered a growing cast of collaborators to the little company, giving eager young filmmakers their first break, in a generous and shrewd pattern he would follow for years. Black Roxbury natives Mark Harris and Henry Johnson had played on the same church basketball team, and enrolled together in the class with the largest number of black men ever to attend Harvard, where Mark studied with the renowned ethnographic filmmaker Timothy Asch. African American filmmakers Jackie Shearer and Billy Jackson and Romas's white Boston University classmate Werner Bundschuh soon joined up.

Over the next decade the Blackside cadre did their work in a bewildering succession of spacious lofts and crummy storefronts in Roxbury, the South End, and Back Bay—22 Greenwich, 145 Dartmouth, 238 Huntington, 501 Shawmut, 88 Lambert, 486 Shawmut, the old Back Bay train station, and a vacant bank building where they kept their magnificent new Arriflex BL 16mm camera—the $30,000 envy of every cinematographer in the country—in the cavernous vault. Blackside's offices had their share of neighborhood hassles. Steve said, "Eighty-eight Lambert was broken into every weekend that Henry and I and the West Indian tenant were away." A brother pulled up on a motorcycle and put a shot into the conference room at 486. Leslie Harris once had to expel "drug dealing pimps on the fourth floor" with a .357 Magnum.

Jean-Philippe Boucicaut signed on as their first professional editor. When J-P was thirteen years old, his father, General Jean-René Boucicaut, chief of staff of the Haitian armed forces, tried unsuccessfully to overthrow Papa Doc Duvalier, and fled with his wife and children to asylum in the Venezuelan embassy, where they hid for a year before escaping to the United States. J-P would work with Blackside for decades, eventually editing the last film Blackside ever produced.

Some of the crew were political, some were just young people embroiled in the business of being young, not necessarily following the twists and turns of Black Power, the arms race, or the war in Vietnam, just wanting to "do well and get laid." Like surprisingly many producers of industrial and educational films, the Big Idea man—Henry—was a

thoroughgoing intellectual, a cultural, historical, philosophical, and political triumph of Jesuit engineering. If the occasion called, he could speak
about almost any subject with warm, eloquent ease, without ever dominating the conversation, a true polymath.

But to the young guys he could sometimes seem the distant boss, an
elder at thirty-two, "the Sphinx." Jean-Philippe Boucicaut remembered,
"Henry was quiet, with a sense of mystery about him, just like Romas. I
never knew exactly what he did, sitting in the office; he would come for a
screening, give his thoughts, and leave."

They were an extraordinary, eclectic bunch, and many of them would
work with Henry for decades to come. In those days before diversity compliance forms, I doubt anyone took inventory, but Henry and that first
posse had all lived life in some way as outsiders in mainstream America,
as the Other, excluded in major and minor ways from full citizenship and
civic life. They were blacks, immigrant Jews, Eastern Europeans, disabled,
children of the segregated South, a few Asians, refugees, and, in later
years, gays. They had personally felt the sting of discrimination in ways
that Wasp males—what Judy Richardson called "ordinary white guys"—
never had. Even twenty years later, working on *Eyes on the Prize,* I was
one of only four ordinary white guys on a staff of thirty-three. The Blackside roster was nothing if not thoroughly American.

Like so many little independent documentary companies staffed by
young writers, auteurs, and baby Marxists, Blackside paid the bills by
churning out a blizzard of commissioned films, radio spots, slide shows,
pamphlets, and even vinyl LP records. Henry produced dozens of shorts
that served a blunt practical purpose: *Steel Foundry Safety, Passage to
Profits, Child Safety Restraints in Cars, Seven Basic Skills of Wrestling,* and
the like, films on how to refuel ships or how to treat wastewater runoff.
Passage to Profits for Massport's *New Voices* for the Youth Employment
Development Authority, *Bravo Zero* for the coast guard, *Movin' Out* for
the navy, *Unemployment Insurance Test* for the Department of Labor, *The
Cleaner the Water* for the Environmental Protection Agency, *Non-Ferrous
Foundry* for OSHA, *Food-Borne Illness* for the Department of Agricul-
ture, *In Our Lifetime* for the U.S. Administration on Aging, *Be Good to
Your Baby Before It Is Born* with Diahann Carroll, *Runaways* for the Small
Business Administration—all now long forgotten. They did all the film
promos for the 1974 national 55-mph-speed-limit rollout.

These educational and industrial films were mainstays of new little film companies. They had pretty good budgets, and their direct lessons on how to properly carry out useful tasks probably made the world a better place. Those of us starting out in the business on both coasts gave them our all, reminding ourselves that the documentary genius Les Blank's first film was an industrial about chicken packing, and America's finest cinematographer, Haskell Wexler, put his colossal talent into Marlboro commercials. We tried to force as much art as we could into the commerce as we sharpened our craft, the documentary equivalent of serious young musicians pouring their souls into weddings, bar mitzvahs, and advertising jingles.

Anyone who ever worked on an industrial will recognize numbing lines of narration like "This completes an electrical circuit, energizing a solenoid-operated pilot valve. The valve allows the automatic fuel/defuel valve to go to the 'fuel position.'" But industrials were a fertile training ground and great fun to make, despite the values disconnect between the idealistic young filmmakers and their corporate/bureaucratic clients. While the Young Turks at Blackside were making them in Boston, I was doing the same in California, getting well paid to clamber around oil refineries, soda-pop factories, operating rooms, and manufacturing lines in the infant Silicon Valley, while I raised money for my first big documentary. On one job I counted twenty-two years of graduate school education among the crew intently focused on creating perfect folds in paper towels for a product shot; on another shoot a half dozen young Socialists grooming a Dodge car with chamois clothes traded snarky insults about the ad executives in charge.

Henry was patient, his grand documentaries about social movements on hold, just over the far horizon. But at Blackside in the seventies everything had a stealthy social purpose. Hampton was resolute in making sure that every corporate promo or dreary government training module advanced the visibility of African Americans on screen and their production work offscreen, whether the client noticed it or not. Sometimes the message was obvious and mandated in the contract, as in minority recruiting films for the armed services. Often it was sly, as in *Nuclear Defense at Sea* or *Shipboard Fueling and Defueling of Aircraft,* which were made by mostly minority crews and featured minority sailors on camera (and once, when they ran out of black sailors, a few Blackside crew members in borrowed navy uniforms). Every project, no matter how pedestrian, made strong subtle affirmations of diversity, both in how it was made and what it said on the screen. In its own quiet way, it was social justice activism by other means. They made *How Jojo Beat the Hawk,* a charming phonetics film for elementary-school children, featuring kids with giant Afros in his friend Leslie Harris's fourth-grade class.

Henry was building a tight community of filmmakers. The navy training films were written by Steve Fayer, produced by Henry Hampton with associate producer Judy Richardson, and shot at sea off San Diego by a crew that included his young Blackside professionals Michael Chin, Orlando Bagwell, Jean-Philippe Boucicaut, and Rick Butler, all barely out of college, on their way to becoming important players in American documentary.

He may have consciously taken a page from the playbook of the great British documentary pioneer John Grierson, who viewed documentary as "a pulpit." In the early 1930s Grierson staffed his film unit at the staunchly imperialist/capitalist/Tory Empire Marketing Board with young anti-imperialist Socialists. They successfully embedded pro-Labour sentiments and sly celebrations of indigenous culture into films promoting corporate interests and the imperial glory of the far-flung British Empire. Henry Hampton was certainly no Socialist, but he was an avowed multiculturalist who built every possible ounce of diversity into even the most pedestrian films for government and corporate clients.

Like Grierson, Hampton was a hell of a hustler; his skill at reeling in government contracts with ever roomier budgets became legend in those days of proliferating new agencies and affirmative action contracting. He and Fayer pounded out pitches and budgets on an IBM Selectric and a Smith-Corona adding machine: *Music for Living,* about the practical aspects of music (Henry wrote on the margin "I can sell this"); *Day Care: You Can Make a Difference; Achievement Motivation Training;* and *Prevention of Foodborne Illness in the Home.* They went at it hammer and tongs, always at the ragged edge of profit and loss, always overextended, like all the little production companies I knew out West, struggling to meet payroll despite their ferocious volume of production.

He and his little team burrowed their way through hundreds of pages of corporate and government bidding instructions. The Blackside archives are filled with numbing contract guidelines, memoranda, proposals, and contracts from and for Exxon, the National Park Service, the Small Business Administration, the Department of Health, Education, and Welfare, the Small Business Development Corporation, the General Services Administration, Bendix, and the Department of Labor, along with the Massachusetts Bay Transportation Authority's affirmative action plan and the Federal Railroad Administration guidelines, which noted, "We are certain that prospective firms who expect to submit an acceptable proposal will be interested in teaming with or subcontracting to qualified minority-owned firms in order to enhance their relative standing."

Amid all the paralysis and dysfunction of the late sixties, President Lyndon Johnson had launched the War on Poverty, a latter-day extension of FDR's New Deal. (Henry would later produce major television programs about both the New Deal and the War on Poverty.) It actually enacted policies aimed at correcting many of the systemic economic issues Dr. King was chasing when he was shot down. During the civil rights movement, activists and religious progressives had achieved stunning success in shifting the country's moral compass but little in implementing antipoverty action. The Office of Economic Opportunity's "Poverty Program," the home of Head Start and the Job Corps, marked what was perhaps the last time the liberal left managed to mount a strong practical response to poverty in America.

Most important for Henry Hampton, OEO was awarding film contracts to minority producers under an executive order requiring federal contractors to take affirmative action in hiring. Tiny minority-owned Blackside was perfectly positioned.

Hampton expressed anger at himself for not personally doing enough to end the war in Vietnam, "not bringing the full force of our moral power, as the civil rights movement had done." Despite his profound opposition to militarism in general and that war in particular, Henry made training films for the Pentagon, spurred by concern that racial injustice continued inside the military. (Black sailors had rebelled on the aircraft carrier *Kitty Hawk* during combat operations off the coast of Vietnam.) Henry calculated that if *he* didn't make military training films with a strong black component, they would get made anyway by someone else, without the black presence.

"I took some static about that because the war was not a popular thing among my friends, but some black Marine Corps officers came to me and said the enlisted men were getting increasingly black while there were almost no black officers. In all these films there was an underlying political message and they were getting to an audience that was difficult to reach. One of the films was about the responsibility to the black community or to the community as a whole—and here's the Marine Corps making copies and shipping them out to their people."

By Fayer's account, production on a film at El Toro Marine Corps Air Station was nothing if not quixotic. Blackside's toughest cameraman, Joe Mangine, up in a marine fighter jet, while another crew was "dodging artillery on the ground when the assigned helicopter failed to pick them up. . . . They hastily buried their equipment in the sand, set out twelve hours across the desert, and hitched a ride into L.A. with a drunken marine gunnery sergeant." Henry and Steve ended up in the commandant's office at Camp Pendleton protesting the near death of the crew and had their film confiscated.

Then came *Code Blue,* for the National Institutes of Health, a sharp-edged look at African American doctors and nurses working in emergency rooms in Oakland, Nashville, and Harlem, a hard-hitting film that would attract minority students to the medical professions. Howie Dammond produced the show. "I devoted eighteen months of my life to it, at a hundred dollars a month. Henry was a newbie as an executive producer, and I was out there with this crummy little budget, but in the end it gave Blackside credibility."

In approaching *Code Blue,* Henry had originally wanted to go "the bling-bling route, to sell the attraction of going into health care with fancy cars, expensive lifestyles, and the attraction of glitter." In the end the film made its pitch with simple, strong storytelling centered on emergency room medicine and the birth of a black baby "for its metaphorical value." Howie remembered shooting on the road: "Romas Slezas looked like a hippie with his beard and long hair, but he was a total filmmaker. He could walk with a 12–120 zoom like it was an extension of who he was. I thought, 'Here I am in Nashville with Picasso.'"

The 27-minute *Code Blue* was something for Blackside to be proud of, and was used in schools, community centers, and training programs for twenty years to come. Executive produced by Henry, the medical school dropout, it no doubt inspired thousands of African Africans to go to medical school. It won Blackside the CINE Golden Eagle, which was in those days nearly as important as an Oscar for fledgling documentary makers. Henry called it their "first real film."

Blackside's *Kinfolks,* produced by Mark Harris and former SNCC field secretary Dwight Williams, was the story of four black families in New

Haven, Connecticut, structured around a family reunion. The huge production, with a huge crew brought in from New York, Boston, and the West Coast, followed different generations of black families coming together. Mark Harris said, "It was nice being on location with an all-black crew. . . . They got it done."

Kinfolks marked the first time cameraman Bobby Shepard worked for Blackside. Bobby had served a Vietnam combat tour in the marines and then six years working on New York commercials as a union camera assistant. Hampton gave him his first break as a director of photography. In New Haven, "Everything that could go wrong did go wrong." When the producer lost his wallet, Bobby ended up putting all the rental cars on his credit card, and spent months pleading with Henry for reimbursement and back pay. "Blackside was the only black production company doing anything, but the director was making film school mistakes." After months of trying to collect his wages, Shepard swore he would never work for Blackside again.

Many others agreed that no one really knew what they were doing in New Haven. And like many Blackside projects, *Kinfolks* got in trouble because of budget oversight problems, and Henry's difficulty in articulating to the New York cutting room how he wanted the film structured. As we shall see, he was brilliant in conceiving bold ways of filmmaking, but often tongue-tied about how to do it or even exactly what the "it" was. Clear, timely guidance from the executive was critical in those days of 16mm film editing, when the cumbersome business of picture locking, negative cutting, and answer printing demanded long lead planning to meet a deadline. They got it done, but only after Romas dove in as the fixer to pull the project over the finish line.

Henry had perfect pitch for new talent. Orlando Bagwell, an unknown twenty-two-year-old black camera assistant from WGBH, had apprenticed at *Say Brother,* and when he did some good second camerawork on *Kinfolks* riding with the cops at night, it caught Henry's eye. Over the years I often saw Hampton debate with himself and his staff for weeks whenever it came time to hire journeyman filmmakers, but he was swift and impetuous in snapping up new young talent. He'd snapped up Bagwell in 1976.

"Henry offered me a job as producer/director/editor in our first meeting, but he put me in the editing room first, with Jackie Shearer, on a hospital film. There was this one scene that was shot really well, but it wasn't really that dramatic, and I created the sense of an emergency . . . I made it life and death. I gave it drama. And Henry remarked . . . 'That's a *really* good scene.' Then he asked me to do three Department of Labor films. I thought, 'I've died and gone to heaven; what a great way to start a career.' . . . I think Henry liked my spirit, liked my fight."

For a lot of people in the film business, the new white/black discourse was a work in progress, but Henry had no trouble talking, socializing, and negotiating across the color line, and he sensed the same ease in Orlando. "Henry was comfortable with whites, because he had lived in that space. . . . I was this young, kind of talky guy. But he knew I was comfortable in those white spaces . . . and I was as much at ease there as I was with my own. He needed those kinds of people to be in front of his work, or to be down in D.C. negotiating contracts with government clients, presenting the films."

Like Henry, Mark Harris, Jackie Shearer, and Henry Johnson, Orlando was well versed in the bizarre and often brutal ways of race in Boston. At the historical moment when Henry hired Orlando in 1976, Boston was in the throes of its school busing crisis. On April 5, 1976, Boston's *Herald American* ran a blistering photograph so loaded with irony and metaphor that it won the Pulitzer Prize for news photography that year for photographer Stanley Forman. Henry's friend Ted Landsmark, a Yale-educated black lawyer, was on his way to a meeting at City Hall when he came around a corner and stumbled into a crowd of whites demonstrating against court-ordered busing. Seeing a black man, the crowd suddenly became a mob, beating Landsmark. Frozen in the picture is white teenager Joseph Rakes with his long hair flying as he lunges at Landsmark with a ten-foot bronze-eagle-tipped flagstaff, using it as a lance, a huge American flag, now weaponized, billowing behind, while the black lawyer writhes to escape white anti-busing activist Jim Kelly gripping him by the vest of his three-piece suit. (Like so much in Boston that year, the photo is not exactly what it seems; Kelly was actually moving to protect Landsmark from the mob.)

The crisis had exploded when a judge ordered the busing of black kids from Henry's Roxbury neighborhood into all-white South Boston, and vice versa, to remedy de facto school segregation. The day after the flag attack, black teenagers in Roxbury dragged a white man from his car and crushed his skull with paving stones. A crowd of one hundred chanted, "Let him die! Let him die!" when the police arrived. A white mob dragged a Haitian cabdriver from his taxi and beat him to death. After a black teenager stabbed a white teenager, a white mob surrounded South Boston High, trapping inside black students who had been bused in from Roxbury. A black high school football player was shot by a sniper during a game in Charleston, and black homes were firebombed in Dorchester. In the end, five hundred police officers guarded four hundred students at South Boston High. The raw racial horror show engulfing Boston went on for months; tens of thousands of whites marched. For progressive black and white Bostonians like Henry, fresh from the sight of massed troopers, murders, and firebombings in the South, it was a northern nightmare come home to roost.

During the crisis, Orlando had been working as a substitute teacher in Boston's schools and was also directing a small after-school program at the Harriet Tubman House in Roxbury, where many of the black kids were being bused down to South Boston, center of white resistance. "I asked to be assigned to South Boston High in the year of the crisis. . . . All my kids from the Tubman Center were being sent there . . . and I knew what the school was like. . . . When a position opened up, I took it, teaching political science and history to black and white students. I looked young enough to be in high school. Because South Boston was so much in the news, I started using the news of the day in teaching." Orlando thought that his presence would lead to dialogue between black and white and "an understanding that you are just like me."

Heady with the joy of teaching, but overwhelmed with the work of being a new teacher, he usually stayed at school late to prepare for the next day's classes. Early one evening, walking to the bus stop, lost in thought with an armful of books, he "let down his jungle posture," and said "Hi" to a passing elderly white lady, who gave him an odd look. "I first let it go, thinking she's just one of those Southies who doesn't like black people. But suddenly I realized she's not looking at me, she's looking *beyond* me at twenty white guys following me. I was alone; I kept walking. Someone threw a bottle. Someone pushed me from behind. I dropped the books, got bashed in the head."

The mob surrounded the young high school teacher, throwing young men in one after the other to fight him. "I had taken karate, but I was pushing them away, didn't want to get into throwing blows, didn't want to hurt anybody. I shoved a kid who doesn't really want to fight and he hits a wall hard. I know I'm in trouble; they get me from all directions. Attacking me, kicking me in the back, out into the street, men and boys who fully intended to kill me. I'm down. I thought people would stop to help me . . . white motorists. But nobody helped me." Passing white drivers stopped and got out of their cars to join in the beating. "Racist people will kill you for no reason. I thought I was going to die. I felt profoundly lonely."

Suddenly Orlando heard honking, looked up, and saw a city bus bearing down on him through the crowd; the white bus driver opened the door, screamed, "Grab on, grab on, get in!" Orlando managed to get in and grip the bars, the mob trying to pull him out by his legs until he kicked loose and the bus pulled away with the mob chasing after. "And now I'm on a bus, bloody, with all white people. Some of them are crying." An elderly white woman, weeping, apologized to him, and Orlando stammered that it wasn't her fault. "I made it home to Roxbury, and the FBI knocks on my door within five minutes."

Federal prosecutors filed civil rights charges against the attackers. "So I'm a marked person in school; the principal is not happy, puts me on door duty, late afternoon hall duty, dealing with all these white hockey players." The headmaster treated Orlando as though he had brought this on himself; students wrote "nigger, nigger, nigger" on assignments. He no longer felt safe in the school building and resigned his teaching job. "That was the same year as the picture of the guy with the flag at City Hall," said Orlando.

Like Henry, Orlando was raised Catholic, had been an altar boy, attended Catholic schools, done premed studies in college, and driven a Boston Yellow Cab. He had come of age in New Hampshire, one of only a couple of thousand blacks in a state that was 99.5 percent white, laced with virulent color prejudice. In middle school his teacher led the class in singing "Old Black Joe" and "Swanee River" and talked about "darkies" while twelve-year-old Bagwell simmered with rage. He earned his BA at Boston University, then bummed around, picked apples in California, became a good conga player, and took long solo road trips around New England on his Harley-Davidson, sleeping in fields, repairing the bike himself on the side of the road.

After South Boston High, he was back doing political organizing and running the community youth center in Roxbury when a camera crew from WCBS came by to do a story and interview him. Seeing the film crew work, Orlando told the black cameraman, Rick Butler, "I want to do what you do." (Coincidentally, Rick and I had been classmates in film school, supporting ourselves working in a film lab, processing educational films on the day shift and girlie movies on the night shift.) Over the next few weeks Rick showed him how to load film magazines, and before long Orlando was working as Butler's assistant. The work with Rick eventually led Orlando to graduate film school at Boston University on an AFI grant, and finally to Blackside and Henry Hampton. In a complicated dance, like younger brother and older brother, Orlando and Henry would work closely together for the next quarter century.

Henry's big sister, Veva, was by now practicing psychiatry, and little sister, Judi, had graduated from Columbia in 1976. As Henry had feared, Judi's marriage to Phil Sharp did not last. After working for Head Start in New York and studying dance at the Martha Graham studio, she had embarked on a career in consumer affairs for Mobil Oil. A Mobil press release shows the attractive, stylish, and athletic young black woman, "one of the first women to set foot on an offshore drilling platform, 215 miles off Halifax." Brother and sister were both pioneering in fields previously closed to blacks, but Henry's Blackside and Judi's Mobil stood on opposite shores of the American corporate landscape.

Hampton had joined Boston's first wheelchair basketball team, playing several nights a week on a team of mostly Vietnam veterans from the Brockton VA hospital, and he was quickly elected captain. "It gave me a sense of moving." He was incredibly strong, fit, and hypercompetitive, with a barrel chest and powerful arms, and enjoyed holding up both his nephews, one with each arm, when he visited Veva and David's family in New Hampshire.

Orlando remembered, "Henry was a bull. We would play Ping-Pong until late . . . everybody else would go home and we were still there playing Ping-Pong. We played *forever.*" Howie Dammond added, "Don't try to play Ping-Pong with him. If you beat him you were on the shit list for a month." They played on the conference table that would be Blackside's town square for the next twenty years. "The big brown conference table was the Ping-Pong table, but it was *short,*" and Henry used this to his advantage.

Henry Hampton had the cultural sensibilities and probably the money to live in collegiate Cambridge, where Judi would eventually move, or up in the eighteenth-century cobblestone streets of Beacon Hill near his dear

friend Ruth Batson. But he chose the heart of Roxbury, once a Jewish en-
clave, now Boston's sprawling African American neighborhood, where
Malcolm X, Louis Farrakhan, and Senator Edward Brooke had come of
age after the Great Migration. It seemed to me the perfect Henry Hampton conundrum: the button-down television producer leaving a meeting
with white executives at WGBH, driving across town in his Jaguar to the
heart of the ghetto, where all of them were afraid to go. He was equally at
home with nouvelle cuisine or soul food, and one of his black friends sur-
mised, "Henry was like a lot of guys from privilege who felt they had to
show they were ghetto."

Fort Hill is indeed a big hill in the center of Roxbury, wrapped in a
maze of twisting streets, and Henry's big two-story house at 88 Lambert
Avenue sat near the top. It was more than a house, practically a compound, surrounded by a seven-foot-high brick perimeter wall, with a big
yard, and covering nearly half a square block. Surrounded by dingy projects and burned-out buildings, Henry's nephews remember it as "hard-
core ghetto." Judi said, "It looked like the Norman Bates Motel," with a
curious array of twenty-four small garages, which he rented out. His
nephew Toby remembers that when Henry bought the place, one of the
garages was "filled with upright pianos, one had a Porsche, one a Triumph
TR6. Previous tenants had disappeared." There was a Lotus sports car,
and Henry told me he had to evict some guys who were running a chop
shop, disassembling stolen cars in one of his garages.

Steve Fayer remembered, "At that time, Fort Hill in Roxbury was a big
drug dealing and stolen car area, streets were like the Wild West. Everybody in the house was packing, Henry included. Luther was one of Henry's
garage tenants, he'd come over almost every night with a .45 automatic
and his black Belgian Shepherd, Baron. Lu was restoring an early twenties
wooden-bodied Chevy truck, I think it was, and would work under the
truck while Baron patrolled the area." A 15-minute walk up from the
nearest T stop, Henry's place was an island of hip civility in a genuinely
rough area. When Howie Dammond was living in one of the second-floor
apartments during the summer of 1971, he had a party, and a gunman
invaded the first-floor apartment while the party was in full swing upstairs, held a gun to the guy, and cleaned him out. Gentrification was decades in the future.

Henry bought it for a song after Roxbury had endured a riot in 1967 and
another in '68 following Martin Luther King's assassination. Fort Hill had

been home to a dozen or so communes and collectives in the mid-1960s, until arson became rampant around 1970. White hippie homesteaders had vacated 88 Lambert after "a couple of brothers came in with knives and guns one night." In early 1972, for three hundred dollars a month, Henry rented Steve Fayer the upstairs Rainbow Room, so called because the hippies had painted an enormous rainbow across one of the walls.

Built in 1834, the house itself was magnificent, a lovely, big, rambling ten-bedroom, two-story affair with a huge porch, overflowing with books and most of the furniture from his folks' house in St. Louis. Howie, Romas, and Billy Jackson went up there for poker games, and it was *the* party house for young Boston media people, especially the nexus from *Say Brother,* BU, and Blackside. Marita Rivero remembered the place would be packed with people in their twenties and thirties, "grad students, people beginning their careers, mostly black, some white people. People in school, a lot of foreign students he picked up along the way. '*Oh,* you've been to one of *Henry's* parties?' We were young, probably not a lot of babies yet in our lives, grown-ups-in-the-making, not crazy wild drunk . . . these were older, postgrads. The parties stopped earlier than when you were young; you had to go to work."

Eighty-eight Lambert was Henry's home but it also housed the Blackside, Inc., office in those early days. Around twilight back on the evening of December 20, 1972, Steve Fayer had just pulled into the driveway after taking one of the secretaries to the train station. Two young black men lunged out of the shadows, one going after Steve's wallet while "the other attacker tried to stab me in the heart, and I turned away and caught the blade on my left shoulder, could feel it scraping along the bone." Steve yelled, Howie Dammond and Henry came out of the house, and one of the attackers, seeing the two black men, yelled, "Everything's cool, brother," and they took off into the dusk.

Howie went to work to stop the bleeding. "The guy had a long knife that went down through Steve's shoulder and into his chest. Everybody was freaking out. Because I knew the cops wouldn't come to the neighborhood, I called 911 and said a white girl had been stabbed by some black guys." Howie did stop the bleeding, and a couple of white cops showed up in a hurry before the guys raced Fayer to Brigham and Women's Hospital.

A few days later two Boston Police detectives questioned Steve and told him, "Get a gun, big gun, a .45 for next time. If you don't kill him with the first shot, shoot him again." A little kid from the neighborhood returned Steve's wallet in the mail with a nice note. Fayer said, "I tried to persuade Henry to move out of there but he wanted to stay in the community." Henry hired a rent-a-cop to guard the place at night, but Steve decamped to a little apartment in the quieter Back Bay, where he lived for the rest of his life.

Because the injury happened at Blackside's offices, and Steve was at the time director of business affairs, the company filed a workers' compensation claim with Marsh & McLennan, their insurance company, the only one in Blackside's storied history claiming benefits for a stabbing on the job.

A new era at 88 Lambert began when Hampton's friend Leslie Harris needed a place to stay and Henry rented him a room for two hundred dollars a month, partly because Harris came with a rapidly growing black Great Dane puppy, a potential guard dog. Eighty-eight Lambert was never broken into again. Harris began helping to fix the place up, rewired it, managed the garages for Henry, and ended up living there for the next fifteen years with his wife, teaching elementary school, starting a community association, raising three children, and going to law school. He eventually became a juvenile court judge in Boston.

Though Henry soon did move the company office down to 501 Shawmut Avenue in the South End, he lived in that big old house at 88 Lambert Avenue for another twenty-seven years. I and many other Blacksiders crashed there, and sister Judi visited often to cook St. Louis ribs and clean up the kitchen. The place became legend, ever more jam-packed as Henry stuffed it with more and more antiques acquired in his rambles around New England.

Henry said, "Think of history as the ancients did. Think of it as knowledge rushing away from us at the same time the future rushes in. Logic dictates that you try to hold on to as much as possible to understand what is to come." But aside from the news coming out of South Africa, the 1970s future rushing wasn't all that interesting. Our bittersweet 1960s, the communitarian Age of Everything (communal war, riots, drugs, love, civil rights), had slowly morphed into the Age of Nothing, with little to notice except atomized individualism and accelerating inequity. As the decade wore down, most of the energy had simply drained out of the traditional civil rights movement and antiwar movement, exhausted by assassinations, Watergate in 1974, and the fall of Saigon in '75. The Panthers were almost all jailed, dead, or in exile in North Africa with little to show for their zeal. And who could not finally notice that blacks and women received half of what white males earned for the same job? We were appalled that the richest 5 percent of the population now controlled 20 percent of the wealth. How could such imbalance have subverted the American bargain (work hard: live well) in our short lifetimes?

Our generation, so accustomed to winning, learned to live with frustration. With so many battles stalled, the national conversation about race settled into a long, polite mumble about the television series *Roots*. President Gerald Ford, as bland as the times, was more or less piloting the ship of state. We were down to seeds and stems.

But as America ramped down, Blackside ramped up. Working with Henry years later I got hints of how much his company had churned out in those rowdy salad days, without really understanding the sheer magnitude of it all until I got into the archives. They made dozens and dozens of films demanding all manner of filmmaking—verité, essay, animated characters, historical, educational.

I wasn't there, but it must have been a hell of a ride in that hustling first decade, young and brash, on a roller coaster always at the edge of trouble. Orlando and Romas were married with toddlers at home, but all the rest were unencumbered by family responsibilities. Howie Dammond told me, "Blackside was driven by all-nighters in those days, and there was an endless supply of plane tickets, for going to conferences." Mark Harris added, "We shot in L.A., lots of different places . . . to actually get paid to get on a plane, stay in a hotel . . . cool if you were twenty-three. It was *really* fun. We *all* thought we had died and gone to heaven." Steve Fayer said, "They would edit stuff on the Steenbeck, they would go out and shoot stuff, and I would say to myself, 'These colored people are crazy! They can do anything.' They didn't know what they didn't know."

Orlando, Billy Jackson, and Henry Johnson did a film about the Nation of Islam, and Orlando directed a film with Mark Harris about teen sexuality (those were a staple for small film companies in the seventies; we all worked on them). Henry sent Romas, Steve, and Howie to make a film about the legendary black photographer Gordon Parks. Parks welcomed them to his rented home in Beverly Hills for a day of shooting, and then they all climbed aboard the Santa Fe Railway's *Super Chief,* "the Train of the Stars," for the two-thousand-mile "guerrilla filmmaking" trip from Los Angeles to Chicago, with "the train as a metaphor for Gordon's life; a very poetic film." It was a sublime trip, the sort of production adventure that reminds you why you got into the documentary in the first place.

But it would be Howie's last Blackside film. He followed Carol Munday's exit, leaving only Henry from the original 1968 Blackside trio. Throughout it all had been a nagging undercurrent of complaint from many Blacksiders about getting proper credit and about endless struggles to get paid. Working for Blackside "was like joining a convent," said Howie. "I'm thinking, 'I'm giving up my life for this for a hundred dollars a week?'"

By 1978 Henry had been in the business long enough to develop an informed concern about the actual structure of American broadcasting: who controlled it, which programs made it to air and which did not, who got to tell stories in the media and who didn't. He paid attention throughout the 1970s as community activists tenaciously challenged commercial and public television stations, and lobbied for the inclusion of more programming by and for black Americans.

His critiques were not idle chatter. Henry joined a lawsuit brought by twenty-three white Bostonians and seven blacks, including his friends professor of psychiatry Ruth Batson and Polaroid vice president Thomas Brown. They challenged the license of CBS affiliate station WNAC-TV on the grounds of racial bias in hiring and broadcasting, and failure to provide adequate services to the local community. They finally won when the U.S. Supreme Court refused the broadcaster's appeal ten years later. Then Henry and several others actually purchased the FCC license themselves, making WNAC the only one of 956 television stations in the United States controlled by blacks. When he eventually sold his share of the venture a few years later, Henry sent Leslie Harris "down to D.C. to pick up the biggest check I've ever seen, well over a million dollars," much of which he put into *Eyes on the Prize*.

Fifteen years after settling in Boston, Henry was as well connected there as his own father had been in St. Louis. Now known as a public intellectual on the Boston scene, he had become involved with people and institutions that carried meaning and value for him that corporate/industrial/government work could never muster. In 1977, Harvard invited him to its School of Design on a Loeb Fellowship to study constitutional limitations and the nature of media and government information programs. On the sly (to Fayer's dismay) he had been writing company checks to support Royal Cloyd's Boston Center for the Arts. More important, he had met

Sue Bailey Thurman, the forceful and enigmatic founder of Boston's Museum of African American History. Thurman had discovered that a long-closed Jewish synagogue on Beacon Hill, damaged by fire and leaking through a badly patched roof, had originally been built by freedmen and sympathetic whites in 1805 as the African Meeting House. It was the oldest black church structure still standing in America. She convinced Henry to join her in forming a nonprofit to restore the decaying hall to its original spare elegance.

Ever since his dad staked out the family domain with a fine modern residence, office, and farm in Missouri, Hampton understood the need for African Americans to have bricks-and-mortar places they could call their own, racial and religious sanctuaries. "Hard space is not something we've had a lot of. We've built an awful lot of America, but we haven't had a lot for ourselves. The Meeting House was important to me; the fact that it exists is more powerful than simply the idea."

Of equally lasting importance for him, it was through Sue Bailey Thurman that Henry met her husband, the influential black theologian Howard Thurman, former dean of the Marsh Chapel at Boston University. Thurman had been a classmate of Martin Luther King's at Morehouse College and later King's close advisor and important direct conduit for the nonviolent philosophy of Gandhi, whom Thurman had visited in India. Through the Thurmans, Henry became more and more taken with the philosophy of the Social Gospel, especially the notions of social justice laid out with such clarity in Howard's classic 1949 book *Jesus and the Disinherited*. That thin volume, published by the Unitarians' Beacon Press, had profoundly influenced the leaders of the civil rights movement, and in it lay much of the eventual philosophical underpinning of *Eyes on the Prize*.

The book set forth Jesus as a poor and dispossessed Jew, not a Roman citizen, not a citizen of his own nation, and explored "what the teachings and the life of Jesus have to say to those who stand at a moment in history with their backs against the wall," enduring "the terrible pressures of the dominating world without losing their humanity, without forfeiting their souls." In the context of the infant civil rights movement, it answered the question of how Christianity, the religion of the American oppressor, was, in fact, "religion that was born of a people acquainted with persecution and suffering . . . secured by a ruthless use of power applied to weak and defenseless peoples." These principles Henry stashed away in his reserve of big ideas to revisit when the time came.

• • • • • •

With so much work in house, Blackside took on all the trappings of a proper small business: liability insurance, film negative insurance, auto insurance, vendor accounts, their first bookkeeper and accountant. Henry flew to New York and Washington for contract negotiations, often at the controls of his Beechcraft Sundowner airplane. Throughout all of his professional life, by any reasonable standard, Henry Hampton was at best an idiosyncratic manager of money. He was the "let's just do it" guy, not a fiduciary detail guy, never a balanced budget guy, and certainly not a rational cash-flow guy.

Over the years, most of us working with him smarted at how the disconnect between Blackside's phenomenal creative output and its constant financial fever put the whole enterprise in jeopardy. Perhaps it was because Henry had grown up free from financial worry. Perhaps it was his resolve to move forward always at all costs, to get every important project launched whether or not the money was in hand. Some of it was simply because he seemed comfortable living with risk. And he may have felt that Blackside was not any old business, making mousetraps or soap operas; his was not just a company, it was an *institution,* a black institution, its own minimovement, with a social mission, so the rules of management practice could and should bend for it.

Fayer, who had come with business experience, remembered, "We had a relationship to a bank that had saved Blackside time and time again . . . the Bank of New England. I was aware that the bank was doing it as sort of a community service. I would go down there with Henry and we'd beg for more money, and they kept giving it to him, they would put money in our account. We'd go in with the contracts, and say, 'Listen, we got this $150,000 job with NIH and we need operating cash.' We were supposed to pay interest on it. I don't ever remember writing a check back to the bank in those five years."

He and Romas also created a system of compensating producers with a piece of the action if they came in under budget and penalizing them for going over budget. Bobby Shepard recalls Henry offering him a producing/directing job with the enticement that if he brought the film in under budget Shepard could keep the difference.

"We had roaring arguments and disagreements," said Fayer. Though it was not entirely kosher, Hampton often paid off one government project with money from the next, supplemented by lines of credit and bank loans, occasionally by small infusions from a handful of investors. His willingness to risk his own finances spilled over into risk and hardship for other people, and throughout Blackside's long life as a company, the budget shortfalls more than once came out of his partners', producers', and freelancers' hides. They worked extra hours, days, and sometimes weeks without charging, grudgingly paid off company credit card bills with their own money when cash was short, cut Henry slack they would never cut to an ordinary boss because they so believed in Blackside's mission. Fayer said, "There were long periods when we did not take salary, with the company hanging on by its fingernails, just trying to pay the rent and the vendors, not paying ourselves."

Decades later, after four tractor trailers deposited the Blackside archives at the newly established Henry Hampton Collection in the Film & Media Archive at Washington University in St. Louis, research assistants were surprised at the many dunning letters they found in the files. During the decade of Blackside's explosive growth, dozens of long overdue bills from insurance companies, film labs, car rental companies, and utilities piled up. After running disputes over unpaid bills in 1973, '74, and '75, Marsh & McLennan threw up its hands and turned the whole affair over to Trans American Collections. Then ensued a series of registered letters from Blackside with photographs of collection agents, each more menacing than the last, like Mafia enforcers, saying, "Will you pay what you owe Marsh and McLennan, or will I have to knock on your door?" The Wash U college kids got a kick out of it in 2003, but Henry probably did not in 1976.

With the dunning documents were letters, sometimes sad, sometimes angry, always desperate, from individuals Henry had hired and never paid. Researchers found letters from a freelance writer who had worked on *Black Chronicles* years before, pleading for at least partial payment. Some were for as little as $30, long overdue to a negative cutter, and as large as $10,000 to a writer. When after many months Blackside finally paid part of what they owed Bobby Shepard for his work in New Haven, he endorsed the check and scrawled "I will never work for you again" on the back. In every single case Henry wrote back to the supplicant (but never to the collection agencies) with a personal letter, sometimes with a small check in partial payment, explaining his cash-flow troubles, asking for patience.

Steve Fayer recalled that at the time, "We were battling the IRS over unpaid payroll taxes. Henry prided himself in being the great rebel; that was part of why we weren't paying taxes. . . . After five years of that, in '77, I finally thought I had all the back taxes paid. Then the IRS knocked on the door, literally with a padlock, and said, 'We're going to padlock the place.' It turned out Henry had sent the forms but had never actually sent a check." Henry wrote a check.

Steve said, "Henry's position was 'White businesses must be getting away with this all the time. Why can't I? I busted my balls putting this company together and nobody is going to tell me how to run it. I started this company so I would never have to take orders from another white person.' Nonpayment of his personal taxes was also an issue, perhaps a protest against the war in Vietnam and American racism."

Meanwhile, Mark Harris was traveling around the country directing *Tax Talk,* a Blackside film for the Internal Revenue Service.

Bill collection was not always bureaucratic. Henry had never paid off Dwight Williams for work in New Haven on *Kinfolks,* so a couple of years later Dwight sent a representative. Judy Richardson was working the morning reception shift at Blackside and remembers, "I get this call . . . and he says 'I want my money. You tell that didadidadi that if I don't get my money I will do something to his other leg, and I am sending some-body up for it.' So in walks this . . . young black woman with really *really* itty-bitty short shorts, really short shorts, and *really* high heels. Very nice child. She just walks up the stairs . . . and she says 'Hiiiiiiii, I'm here for Dwight Williams's check.' I said, 'I have it right here.' Of course, Henry did understand that Dwight was really serious; there's a part of Dwight that's definitely really street."

Blackside now stored its growing array of expensive film equipment at Metropolitan Storage, a massive brick warehouse on Massachusetts Avenue that had once served as a Cold War fallout bunker. Access to the gear required two keys, one at Blackside and the other in the hands of the facility manager, only available when payments were up to date. Romas remembered that more than once he had to return from the vault empty-handed, until Henry paid the bill.

Together, Henry and Steve thrived creatively, but by 1977 Fayer be-came exhausted by "attempting to figure out how many years of unpaid taxes BSI owed, why the bank was not foreclosing on the unpaid loans," and a dozen other frustrations with Hampton's management style. He had been through the thick and thin of the company's amped-up incuba-tion, but "had my final big-time disagreement with Henry that autumn, and quit. I no longer felt an obligation to protect the man from himself." In their final meeting, Henry looked Steve straight in the eye and said, "You'll be back."

With Fayer gone, Henry was without a professional film writer, but he still had a dozen projects in the pipeline and a powerhouse staff—Orlando Bagwell, Jackie Shearer, Romas Slezas, Mark Harris, Henry Johnson— to produce them. Blackside never missed a beat, fighting the good fight to put African Americans on screen and behind the camera. In 1978, Henry got the contract to do all the training films for the 1980 National Census, the largest civilian training program ever done by anyone at anytime in the United States.

Romas was by then Henry's most reliable producer, directly overseeing the majority of Blackside projects. Henry always turned to him when films by other producer-directors ran off the tracks, and Romas would again and again wrestle them back in line with clear guidance that did not destroy anyone's ego, a skill that Henry had not yet mastered. He was the always professional go-to fix-it guy.

By the beginning of 1978 Blackside could boast sales of $500,000 a year, and was on the way to doubling that. Henry's life and work were taking on all the sheen of the American computer-startup-in-a-garage trope just gaining traction on the far side of the continent in Silicon Valley. Starting with no documentary experience whatever, Henry Hampton had built the most important African American documentary company in America, even if it was for the moment mostly making training and promotional films and the occasional animated TV commercial.

But he said, "I've tried over the past ten years to generate income from commercial clients, and you bang your head for years and end up with a five-thousand-dollar shoot. It doesn't take a great deal of brilliance to figure out that whether it is racism or problems of being new on the block, it is not going to happen . . . and you end up being almost as dependent as if you were working for somebody. You have to do these idiot lunches and you have to turn into a sycophant. And what you get to do is a dancing toothbrush."

Henry Hampton, giddy with success but stuck in an endless eddy of sponsored projects, had grown tired of other people's meager visions.

CHAPTER THREE

America, We Loved You Madly

1978–82

Despite its wide, sympathetic, and often heroic coverage of the civil rights movement, TV was by the 1970s still mostly "of the whites, by the whites, and for the whites." The lack of black perspective was striking once you noticed it despite the presence of a few black producers, fewer black correspondents, and *Julia,* the first sitcom with a nonstereotyped black lead actor, Diahann Carroll, as a more or less race-agnostic middle-class nurse.

In one of his very smart pundit pieces for *Say Brother,* Henry—boyish, beardless, suave—had hailed what he called "black television," a new era that began after the assassination of Dr. King and the riots that followed. He noted that a few broadcasters embraced the public interest by offering blocks of airtime and services to black writers and producers. But most of these shows soon withered. "Some lacked the necessary skills . . . some were simply axed because we didn't riot last summer. . . . Perhaps a few failed because they were too honest with those who sponsored them."

Henry continued, "It is important to distinguish between what black-controlled programs are trying to do and just what white producers and sponsors have discovered is *saleable* about black America. *Julia* is the answer of General Foods and CBS to the challenge of relevant programming. . . . I cringe at the program *Julia,* even though tens of thousands of black people watch it and enjoy it faithfully, because rather than creating possible models for young black and white Americans . . . *Julia* seems to offer the unreal fantasy of 'going white.'"

He saw potential. "Black television . . . might finally be able to create the mixture of TV programming that is intellectually attractive yet flavorful enough for a substantial audience, a true instrument of communication . . . as a mirror of what black America might become and the log of where we have been."

The ideas behind what would eventually become *Eyes on the Prize* had waited patiently in Henry's project queue since 1965 while he took care of other business for a dozen years. He now believed he had the skills and confidence to take a stab at something big, but who would take Henry's vision seriously? Blackside, despite its growing portfolio of government and corporate films, and the credibility of *Code Blue* and *Voices of a Divided City*, had thin experience in big documentaries. It was a small colored film company, based in Boston, a network TV backwater, not in Los Angeles or New York, where the prime-time mojo was.

But then in late 1978 he got an unexpected call from Capital Cities Communications, a nationwide media corporation wanting to polish its diversity image in preparation for FCC license renewal. Cap Cities, on its way to merging with ABC Televison, was inviting minority producers to propose projects. They asked Blackside to develop a major television project of its choice.

Alex Haley's best-selling *The Autobiography of Malcolm X* and his *Roots* had given black history new allure in the mainstream, and ABC's melodramatic adaptation of *Roots* reaped a ratings bonanza in 1977. The network had good experience with their long-running *Close-Up!* documentary series. When Cap Cities asked Henry what program he would produce if he had enough money, "It took me about ten seconds to say I would do the television history of the civil rights movement."

Henry imagined a massive twenty-six-part series of half-hour programs chronicling the southern movement from 1954 to 1965, laying out for the first time a schematic of the epic in his mind. Even in its original conception, Henry's story plan had the core values that set it apart from all that had come before and most that would come after. This series about African Americans would be produced largely by African Americans, led by an African American executive producer. Most important, he wanted to show "southern African Americans' *strengths,* not their weakness, the active role that black Americans played in shaping their own destiny that had not been shown in scholarship or in film." It would be told from the point of view of ordinary people, mostly black, who had lived the history. African Americans could claim a unique story, but in Henry's hands it would be broadly aimed at *all* Americans of all color and class, and it would resoundingly celebrate the glorious, fumbling, maddening progress of multicultural constitutional democracy. It would be messy history.

He christened the series *America, We Loved You Madly,* homage to Duke Ellington's farewell salute to his audience at the end of each concert: "We love you madly!" Henry's strengths were many, but clear and concise titling was not among them, and he found himself having to explain the "mad/love," "angry love affair" double entendre to puzzled listeners.

For years, filmmakers had dreamed of an epic civil rights history; it was the Holy Grail, the Dream, the Unified Field Theory of historical documentary makers, and surfaced regularly in proposals to the National Endowment for the Arts, the National Endowment for the Humanities, PBS, and the commercial networks. Jack Willis had done the exceptional *The Streets of Greenwood,* but most independent producers tackling the movement had gone down in defeat.

He wrote, "There has been no serious inclusive television project that focuses on the little-known participants and major issues of post–WWII civil rights activity," and added, "They have always been done by whites who depicted black folks as poor, downtrodden and brutalized primitives . . . but it was the *strength* of blacks that made the civil rights movement happen, with support from some whites." Henry was quick to acknowledge that eventually a white Congress and white president, Lyndon Johnson, would ally themselves with the movement, but he refused to embark on a tale of "white people to the rescue," amid victimhood of "the long-suffering blacks."

The seminal version Hampton had conjured up for Cap Cities would be a privileged inside view of the power of local people, not just their leaders in the southern struggles. He was determined also to look at dangerous work in the isolated rural South, far from the spotlight on charismatic leaders like King, underreported, unnoticed, and unfilmed, and the exhausting months and years of on-the-ground community organizing that lay behind the movement's great battles. Here was a chance to set the myths straight, to raise a praise shout to the courage of "the fan ladies, the ordinary world parishioners." This would be Henry's fanfare for the common man (something he himself never was).

And perhaps he might even bring Howard Thurman's insights—Jesus could transform the lives of those on the bottom rungs of society's ladder: the despised, rejected, wretched, and powerless—to commercial television.

"They gave me $350,000 and I began work." The first order of business was to invite a hundred guests to a celebratory gala launch party on February 8, 1979: Derrick Bell, Ruth Batson, Henry's Unitarian mentor Jack Mendelsohn, WGBH general manager Henry Becton, MIT president Jerome Wiesner, Noam Chomsky, congressman Mel King, respected civil rights journalist Paul Good, activists Mike Thelwell, Bob Moses, and Julius Lester, comedian Dick Gregory, psychiatrist Alvin Poussaint, filmmaker Topper Carew, and pretty much everyone who was anybody in Boston's black, progressive, and media communities.

The experience of black America may have made for a bit of good television by 1979, a few documentaries were out there, but civil rights was not a natural ratings driver. Commercial TV in the United States was (and remains) an enterprise powered by advertising; TV demanded millions of eyeballs, or better yet, tens of millions. The top-rated shows that year were all white: *Happy Days, Laverne & Shirley,* and *Three's Company.* The top TV advertiser that year was the shampoo and laundry soap company Procter & Gamble.

The meetings with Cap Cities began. Henry Johnson remembered, "They all had suits on. One of the guys was named Andy Jackson and he was a tall, thin black man with—I don't know how to say this—it almost looked like he had a conk. He had long hair combed across. But it was a strange look for a black person at a time when all of us had long Afros. But obviously it suited him well in the business he had chosen." Andy got along well with Henry; both of them were pilots. Johnson said, "As a thirty-year-old, I didn't know that many fifty-year-olds. Charlie Keller was white and had white hair, curly, looked kinda like the guy on *Mad Men.*"

Henry delegated Romas Slezas to oversee all the other projects already in the Blackside pipeline while he turned his attention to *America, We Loved You Madly.*

And in a wise move that would enrich Blackside for decades to come, he once again brought in the smart and well-liked SNCC veteran Judy Richardson, who at the time was working on police brutality in New York as information director for the United Church of Christ. Judy, the daughter of a Tarrytown, New York, United Auto Workers organizer and a former jazz singer, had dropped out of a four-year scholarship at Swarthmore in 1963 to join the movement. She'd been through some of SNCC's roughest battles in the South, where she served on the organization's full-time staff in Mississippi, Georgia, and Alabama, working closely with James Forman, Fannie Lou Hamer, Stokely Carmichael, John Lewis, Ruby Doris Smith, Julian Bond, and a host of local organizers. Judy had been jailed several times, once for (inadvertently) kicking a white policeman in the balls during a sit-in. She was the real deal.

She said, "So I come in as the associate producer, having had zilch, zed, nada experience in film." For starters Henry paid her fifty bucks to do a chronology of the civil rights movement (no such time line existed in 1979) on oversize architect's drafting paper, and told her she would have to work as the receptionist for the first month because the money had not yet come in.

Steve Fayer reluctantly agreed to return from his oceangoing gig, but only as a freelance writer, unwilling to endure once again the rigors of being Henry's employee and financial minder (Henry still owed him thousands for previous work, and was paying it off at five hundred dollars a month). And Henry lured Madison Davis Lacy, one of the country's few black documentary producers, to help out on writing.

Plans for the original twenty-six-week series concept soon shrank to a single two-hour prime-time documentary special. Henry told Judy, "Nothing takes more than six months."

In 1979, few scholars and journalists had begun the challenging work of finding and interviewing the movement's foot soldiers. Henry knew that historian Howard Zinn was starting to do serious history through the eyes of common men and women rather than the elite leaders, raising the questions of who gets to tell popular history and what exactly *is* popular history. Charles Payne (*I've Got the Light of Freedom*), John Dittmer (*Local People*), Clayborne Carson (*In Struggle*), and other pioneers of "new history" were just beginning their research in the South. Believe it or not, twenty-five years out from the *Brown v. Board of Education* case no one had yet written a good comprehensive history of the whole civil rights movement. Henry's vision of a people's history on television was stepping out in advance of the work-in-progress scholarship. Undaunted, his team set off on their own to research and develop his concept pretty much from scratch, and base the film on what they found.

Neither Henry nor anyone else at Blackside had ever done a historical documentary. He said, "We were amateurs," when it came to prime-time television. The Internet, cell phones, Google, YouTube, and even Post-its as we know them did not exist. No one had a computer or fax machine. Library card catalogs, paper archives, newspaper morgues, letters, postcards, phone calls, and face-to-face talking were the tools of research.

And virtually everything in print and film focused on the leaders, especially Martin Luther King and his very articulate advisors. Judy Richardson recalled, "There's nothing there at that point to look at. I mean there's the *Montgomery to Memphis* documentary, which is all King, King, King."

They began to locate and preinterview civil rights veterans around the South, one by one. Judy Richardson did most of the personal contact, because she had an irresistible winning manner and came with strong movement credentials from her SNCC days. How could anyone *not* talk with Judy Richardson? "Henry figures that nobody we're trying to interview knows Blackside; but maybe they'll talk to us because maybe they'll know me."

Judy dialed all over the country, but failed to turn up much on the local people that she knew were so important. "At some point I find Jo Ann Robinson, because I'm reading King's *Stride Toward Freedom*. It's *finally* the name of a woman, so I called her. She had never been contacted before by *anyone, nobody* had done an interview with her. . . . She starts telling me about the Women's Political Council of Montgomery . . . and I get so excited!" It was a breakthrough: the most important woman organizer of the Montgomery bus boycott was an unknown, proof of concept that a fresh story *could* be told by locals.

Then Henry sent Richardson and Henry Johnson on a quick trip gathering audio preinterviews to show Cap Cities that they knew what they were doing. In Los Angeles they sat down and talked with Myrlie Evers, Medgar's widow. Judy was transported: "It was one of the first times I realized *what this could be,* because I asked her to describe a mass meeting. At that point I'm thinking I had romanticized it all, I had made it up in my mind. She describes it the way I remember my own experience in the movement, the exhilaration of it all. I started to tear up. I think OK, this is real, it's real for her, it's real for me . . . *it's almost like being back in the movement.*"

Then, with enough preinterviews in hand, Henry himself set off to write the required film treatment, leaving Judy and Wally Terry, a leading black reporter at *Time* magazine, to continue research. Steve Fayer remembered that Henry "kind of separated from the company, got an apartment in D.C., living large like a big-time producer." Judy Richardson recalled, "Young Henry Hampton . . . He was *very* bright, *very* smart, and he could write well. He waited till the last minute to do things." On the day before the treatment was due, Henry returned and announced ruefully to his startled staff that he had not finished it; in fact, he had not even started writing it.

Romas Slezas went home in disgust. Fayer said, "I remember Henry standing at the blackboard ready to chalk it out . . . I think with tears in his eyes." Henry and Steve Fayer churned out the entire fifty-page treatment for the original two-hour project in a single day that stretched into an all-nighter.

"We *had* to write the treatment. Henry and I, sitting at opposite ends of the second floor at 501 Shawmut, wrote the treatment, and Howie and Jackie Shearer were passing me information with little pieces of paper tucked into the books. We both had IBM Selectrics. I knew some of the history just from being alive during that period . . . I knew that there was a statue of Vulcan in Birmingham, Alabama, so that would be my lede. That's the only thing I know about Birmingham, so I open up on this statue. Both Henry and I were chain-smokers and coffee drinkers, and we kept ourselves fueled all through the night, and we got it done."

They got the structure right on the first try. The basic content of the original two-hour *America, We Loved You Madly* was nearly identical to the six-part *Eyes on the Prize* six years later. It began with the 1955 Emmett Till murder, flashed back to the 1954 *Brown v. Board* school desegregation case, then charged ahead through the Montgomery bus boycott and the Little Rock school crisis, the sit-ins, the Freedom Rides, the riot at Ole Miss, the Albany Movement, the Birmingham Children's Crusade, the murder of Medgar Evers, and Mississippi Freedom Summer, to the climactic confrontation at Selma—all the battles that would become the basic canonized chapters of movement history. The treatment Steve and Henry wrote featured lots of American flags, and a logo with swaths of red, white, and blue.

The central narrative armature cobbled together that long night would never change as Henry's civil rights enterprise lurched onward over the coming years. Sifting through material at the Blackside archives decades later, I was astonished to see that, in broad strokes, Henry Hampton made his civil rights series *twice*, once at two hours in 1979, and again at six hours in 1985. The redundancy in research, planning, and production is mind-boggling. Of the original thirty-five interview subjects slated for

America, We Loved You Madly, thirty-three of them would appear years later in *Eyes on the Prize.*

The very capable Charlie Cobb, an old friend of Judy's from the SNCC staff, joined the team. Together with Henry Johnson, they did extraordinarily good and thorough preproduction research, preparing big binders with thousands of facts, archive clip logs, and preinterviews for the shows. Research notes on Till, for example, were extremely thorough, at a time when only one meager book on the subject existed, and that was about the trial: "Till's father hanged for murder and rape in Italy July 2, 1945 at Age 24. War Dept said 'cause of death was willful misconduct.' *Life* magazine on 10/10/55: Till's father had been killed in France 'fighting for the proposition that all men are equal.' T's father was a badass. . . . And Till's mother may not have been the most admirable mother of the year, either . . . she gets into hassles with Negro orgs about her percentage of the take. White orgs say Till is alive, charge this is hoax created by the Jewish-inspired NAACP to implement racial hatred. Money Miss pop 55 now." Crisp research, not always flattering to the movement, pervaded the enterprise.

Almost from the git-go, their zeal to make a commercial television hit began to chip away at their zeal to tell simple honest history. The four lively half-hour acts, marked out by commercial breaks every fifteen minutes, quickly acquired an on-camera presenter. At one point it was to be the wildly popular comedian Mort Sahl, then Dick Gregory ("the Black Mort Sahl"), and then several different white correspondents, all written into various script drafts at various times. In their desire to satisfy the network, the team began spicing up the stories, amped up some flowery writing, and peppered the history with hints of solving cold cases that would help boost ratings. Bit by bit, *America, We Loved You Madly* edged away from simple faith in letting ordinary people do the storytelling, and began to bend toward the familiar network template in which commentary explained nearly everything.

And Henry Johnson became concerned that they were trying to do so much in such a short schedule. True to his conviction that "nothing takes more than six months," Hampton had set out a schedule that called for shooting to wrap by late June 1979, and completion of an assembly edit only two weeks later, and a rough cut two weeks after that, lightning speed for a two-hour film.

• • • • • •

After two months of preparation they were at last primed and ready to begin filming. In February 1979, Orlando, Romas, Jean-Philippe Boucicaut, Judy Richardson, and soundman Charles Blackwell fetched the Blackside camera, lights, and sound gear from the Metro Storage vault and set off to the South. Henry originally wanted to pile his crew into a Winnebago, but in the end they traveled by commercial jet and rented vans.

The first stop was Montgomery, Alabama, birthplace of the movement. Montgomery was by 1979 an ordinary southern city, with decent race relations. This was Haitian Jean-Philippe's first time in the South. "We went to a store that was owned by some Chinese, a soda place. That's the first time I heard a Chinese with a southern accent." J-P loved the people and the food, but the folklore of violence trumped all. He said, "That was the scariest place for me, because of the stories. Charles was afraid to be there, and he started making me nervous. You know, the crew would go to a bar . . . He was afraid to go, he would stay in his room. . . . I remember Henry Hampton being very quiet."

Henry had convinced the elegant and wry Julian Bond, former SNCC director of communications, to do the on-camera stand-up pieces, introducing places and themes, guiding viewers through the story. Hampton's original faith in having the everyday troops do the exposition had waned, and he had accepted that the complexity of the history required a lot of concisely written explanation. And neither Cap Cities/ABC nor any other network would air a prime-time documentary without commentary, preferably delivered on camera with the suave authority of a *60 Minutes* correspondent, which Julian Bond could easily have been (except that *60 Minutes* didn't hire its first full-time black correspondent, Ed Bradley, until 1981).

Bond remembered meeting Henry for the first time on the set in Montgomery. They had similar backgrounds, and both were urbane, well spoken, and unafraid of quiet eloquence. Hampton struck him as "a serious guy. He carried himself well, in serious ways. He was courtly. I assumed he had lengthy and deep experience in documentary, and assumed he had all the money in the world. But I had no sense of the grand sense of the series." He thought Henry would be on the set directing at every location, but nearly all their interaction was by telephone and Bond seldom saw Hampton again.

They filmed black citizens who had walked to work all year during the 1955–56 Montgomery bus boycott; Judy Richardson remembered most of them as not terribly interesting: "Yeah, I walked." They rented an old municipal bus, and under Romas's direction Orlando filmed an elaborate reenactment scene in which Julian explained on camera the routine process by which black citizens of Montgomery had to pay the driver the same fare as whites at the front door, then get off, reenter through the rear door, and find a seat in the back of the bus, what Fayer called "a legislated insult." They filmed at King's Dexter Avenue Baptist Church with Judy Richardson holding up big hand-lettered cue cards for Julian.

The crew drove across the South in rented vans, while Henry hopscotched ahead in his little plane, meeting them at each location. Back in Boston, Steve Fayer madly revised stand-up copy for Julian and dictated it over the phone. Bond delivered lines on the spot where King gave his "I have a dream" speech, at the segregated section of Arlington National Cemetery, on the Pettus Bridge, and driving an old pickup truck in the Mississippi Delta. And decades before reenactment entered mainstream documentary, they planned the staging of a black family in period costume arriving at a hotel for colored, with Julian, svelte and slender with a big Afro and smartly tailored three-piece suit, shadowing them as he explains the action to the camera: "Host in late '50s model automobile with black family, pulling up in front of a black motor court with a name like the Ebony Motel. All exit the car. Host remains at car, turns to camera as family moves toward building. . . . 'In the years of segregation black folks needed a guidebook to their own country, *The Negro Motorist Green Book.*' . . ."

And finally in Montgomery, Judy Richardson's newfound friend Jo Ann Robinson, sitting relaxed on a lawn in the sun, guided them through the intricate organizing process by which tens of thousands of black citizens brought down the system of bus segregation.

The crew drove deep into the Mississippi Delta to the tiny town of Money, on an oxbow of the Tallahatchie River, where J. W. Milam and Roy Bryant murdered Emmett Till in 1955.

By the time Blackside arrived, only a few dozen people still lived in Money, and they did not share Henry Hampton's obsession with the murder of Emmett Till, nor his interest in the expansion of democracy. Rumors spread quickly that a "nigger movie crew" had come to town. Till's relatives avoided them, and when the crew did track them down, they were scared to talk. While Orlando and Henry were mounting a camera on the pickup truck, a little white boy came up and asked Jean-Philippe Boucicaut what they were doing. With his lyrical French Caribbean accent Jean-Philippe began to explain the film, when the kid interrupted, "'Are you the *foreign* nigger?' I started laughing, and that's when he got mad."

Bryant's dilapidated little store was still open for business in 1979, opposite the old cotton gin on Money's only street. With Henry directing, Orlando and Jean-Philippe set up the camera to film Julian's stand-up. J-P remembered, "We started shooting and all of a sudden six pickup trucks show up, with guns in the back. These white guys wanted to know what we were doing . . . I don't know what the answer was, because I was so scared, but they told us, 'You better get out of town.' We packed up and they escorted us out of town, three pickups in front of us, three behind. I remember rednecks. I'd seen them in movies before, but in person, it was like . . . gosh. Even O was nervous."

The white men ushered Henry and his crew two miles out of town and told them not to come back. J-P said, "But Henry was determined." It was movement strategy, and it sometimes became Henry's strategy, that the harder they resist you, the harder you push. So they went looking for the murderers Milam and Bryant themselves, driving around the county's back roads searching for the house where they had heard one of the men had moved. They never found the house or either of the killers.

The next day, they tried again without success to interview Till's frightened relatives, who again wanted nothing more than for the film crew to simply go away. Henry and most of the crew departed, leaving Orlando and Jean-Philippe to get additional visuals. They found the spot where the killers had thrown Till's body into the Tallahatchie, and began shooting evocative shots of the river. J-P remembered, "It was just the two of us . . . no fixer. It was really quiet. We didn't really know what we were doing, I guess." A Mississippi state trooper drove up and said, "You'd better get out of here," and escorted them to the county line. Orlando said, "Henry had a small plane at a little airport that could take us out."

Several months later Henry dispatched Orlando and white veteran investigative reporter Paul Good to confront Roy Bryant in his store. "Henry had this reporter, this investigative guy, who was just crazy. He wanted me to walk into the store with the camera rolling. I said, 'Look, I'm down here, but I'm not going to get killed.' We staked it out, and wired up the reporter with a radio mic so that if something happened we could walk in with the cameras. He goes in, starts to talk to this guy, and the guy throws him out." The guy was, in fact, the wrong guy, the new owner of the store; Bryant had moved away years before, and as it turned out, Milam was on his deathbed in Texas.

Blackside left Money, Mississippi, empty-handed except for a few nice landscape shots. For the launch of an audacious prime-time television program, these were lean pickings.

But they did record a few good tales on that trip.

Look magazine reporter William Bradford Huie gave his account of how Till's acquitted murderers, knowing they could not be tried again, had confessed their version of the whole grisly story to him in exchange for four thousand dollars cash in a bag, veiled as an "advance against film rights." Huie had published J. W. Milam and Roy Bryant's version of events, but had never gone on camera. Orlando shot the interview and remembered, "Henry really connected with Huie, allowed him to talk in ways he had never talked before; he's a natural storyteller. It was here that I realized we were doing something different." Henry was supremely comfortable with white people, even white people talking about the murder of black people.

Huie said of the killers, "They had inherited a way of life. They were told that for a young black man to put his hand sexually on a white woman was something that could not be allowed. . . . So they thought that they had to make an example of a young man like Emmett Till. . . . See, these men lived in a sea of black people. They ran little stores and lived in the back of the stores; you'd have to go to South Africa today to find anything like it."

Bill Huie told Henry, "Milam was startled at . . . the fact that young Till didn't appear to be afraid of him. Now he'd gone and gotten him out of bed and had him in the back of a truck and J. W. Milam . . . was utterly startled when he found Emmett Till talking back to him, showing absolutely no fear of him at all, telling him he's as good as he is."

According to Huie's account, "They did not intend to kill him when they went and got him. . . . Young Till never realized the danger he was in. . . . But J. W. Milam looked up at me and said, 'Well, when he told me about this white girl he had,' he says, 'my friend, that's what this war's about down here now.' And he says, 'I just looked at him and I said, boy, you ain't ever going to see the sun come up again.' He says, 'When we got down to the side of the river . . . I pulled out my .45 . . . God, you could knock a lizard's head off with forty feet with that darn thing . . . I told him to drop his clothes off.'"

They did a couple dozen interviews in all, many too spartan even by the standards of 1979 television, two or three rolls of 16mm film for each person. They recorded legendary organizer Bayard Rustin, mastermind of the March on Washington, with one roll only—eleven minutes—which today would barely count as warm-up chitchat. Major storytellers like John Lewis, Ernest Green of the Little Rock Nine, and Huie warranted four rolls each, about forty minutes. In Mississippi, Orlando, Henry, and Judy did the most extensive interview ever filmed with Amzie Moore, the towering and fearless local black organizer who had worked with Bob Moses in the earliest days of voter registration in "the heart of the iceberg."

Cap Cities/ABC executives were well aware in the lingering glow of the 1974 Watergate scandal that sharp investigative reports could boost ratings. Memos urged researchers to go after "never-before-aired" material and exclusive, long-buried scoops. They got Henry to send the Blackside team to investigate a rumor that Jimmie Lee Jackson's murder by a state trooper in Marion, Alabama—pivotal to the Selma movement—had been aided and abetted by the white surgeon who treated Jackson: "death by surgeon's scalpel." First, "The sources all shut up, and then the story collapsed," said Fayer. Henry's crew came away with only a stiff interview with a different doctor, a shot of Jackson's grave, and one of his jail cell.

But in Marion, Henry and Orlando shot a fine-looking interview with voter registration organizer Albert Turner. As with so many aging witnesses, leaders and foot soldiers, this would be the last interview ever filmed with Turner. (Thirty years later, two graduate students of mine at Berkeley would use that 1979 Blackside interview in their documentary about Turner's son, who had been elected mayor of Marion. Free from the scourge of legal segregation, Marion and other poor black communities now endured the scourge of toxic dumping—"environmental racism"—which Turner Jr. had to navigate.)

By the fall of 1985, long after the deadline for completion of principal photography had passed, Henry and the team were apparently under pressure from the network to shoot more and better material, and were planning new replacement dramatized stand-ups, "Hosted by James Earl Jones," voice of Darth Vader in the recently released *Star Wars* movies.

Word came that a competing civil rights project by a white producer was running off the rails before even leaving the station. The *America, We Loved You Madly* team pressed on. Suspecting that black companies might be held to a higher standard than white companies, producer Henry Johnson sent memos trying to force professional business practices onto the creeping disorder at Blackside.

All the while Henry's partner Romas Slezas, now back in Boston, kept the company's several "industrials" and the enormous census project on track. Blackside's contract summary for 1979 shows a whopping $2,191,000 in production. Cash flow had rocketed twenty-five-fold from $8,000 a month to $200,000 a month. But Romas heard unsettling tales from the ongoing civil rights field production, "stories coming back that it was a mess, nothing was happening."

The archive footage research ranged beyond the usual American sources, with transcripts of interviews with Bull Connor and George Wallace coming in from the BBC and Swedish television. But many of the trails went cold. As it turned out, they couldn't locate some crucial pieces of the visual storytelling. Dr. King's electrifying earliest call to arms at Holt Street Baptist Church on the first night of the Montgomery bus boycott had apparently not been recorded; the "lost speech" was indeed lost, as was teenage Elizabeth Eckford's famous long walk through the white mob toward Central High in Little Rock.

Johnson placed classified ads in forty southern newspapers, including black papers, asking for home movies and snapshots. Fearing that white southerners with promising material would be put off by the name "Blackside, Inc.," he listed the company as "BSI." Judy Richardson filed requests with the FBI for surveillance photos. Neither effort turned up new material. And some of their new footage was still held hostage at the lab because of unpaid bills.

Henry's editors worked at lacing together interviews, host stand-ups, and meager archive footage according to Fayer's well-structured script, filling in blank black film leader as a placeholder where they hoped missing material would later be inserted. Early on, Cap Cities was impressed: John Toutkaldjian sent a memo to Hampton just before Christmas 1979 saying he was "impressed with the organization," but when

Charlie Keller saw a 20-minute interim cut, he told Fayer they "did not have a television show."

In truth Blackside was naive, said Fayer. "Few people in television cared about colored people and nobody cared about civil rights, and it was no help that we didn't really know what we were doing." Cap Cities was commercial TV, and commercial TV had in mind the attention-getting drama of "the story behind the story," not Henry's notions about "the responsibility of the government to its people and vice versa," and "honoring people on the bottom rung of the ladder."

Judy Richardson and Romas Slezas agreed: "We were amateurs." Hard as it is to believe today, no one anywhere, amateur or pro, had yet worked out the infernal calculus of making a complex major historical TV series, and few understood how hard it was; the closest thing was the patriotic World War II clip show *Victory at Sea* series that had captivated Henry and me as kids in the 1950s. The widely acclaimed individual one-hour *CBS White Paper* documentaries were the model, but Blackside had no idea how to make a "white paper." And no American producer had ever made an analytical historical television series of linked programs. The Blacksiders were pioneering, and all true pioneers are amateurs.

The tortured memos from that winter of 1979–80 hint that Blackside was running scared in the end, trying to simply salvage some history along the way as they puffed up the shows with drama at the expense of story. Story chronology was a particularly thorny issue, because the two-hour program made bold attempts to dance fluidly back and forth between the 1979 present and many different points in the 1960s civil rights past. The fractured order in which the Till narrative unfolded was a particular concern for the network executives, who sent a memo demanding the editor "move it up into proper chronological position." Till chronology would be a running issue inside the Blackside story factory for much of the next decade.

Surprisingly, Henry never called on the one professional who might have wrestled all the narrative, production, archive, schedule, and budget threads of *AWLYM* into submission—Mr. Fix-it—Romas Slezas. As time and money began to run out, Romas, balancing his responsibilities on five other BSI projects, lost all patience with Henry's inability to convert his vision into practical guidance for editors and directors. The disorder was, at least, quite egalitarian: payroll records show that all the staff earned about ten dollars an hour, and Henry, the boss, earned about twenty dollars.

But Henry Johnson said, "The problem at that point was: I was using my own American Express card for a lot of the travel, and sometime during the summer I stopped getting paychecks." Fayer, concerned about the cost drain, said to Henry, "Don't spend the last of the company's money to keep the ABC project going."

And everyone hated the title, except Henry, who loved it. *AWLYM* was even a lousy acronym. In October 1979 Judy Richardson produced a now legendary memo with names of twenty-two freedom songs, including "This Little Light of Mine," "We'll Never Turn Back, "We Shall Overcome," and "Keep Your Eyes on the Prize," pleading that any one of them would be better than *America, We Loved You Madly*. Not long after, for the first time one of the many revised script drafts appeared with the title *Eyes on the Prize*.

No copy of the *America, We Loved You Madly* work in progress survives, but it is obvious from memos that it was no lost masterpiece. A year after the original delivery date, Cap Cities executives came to Boston for a rough cut screening, to which Henry invited the entire office staff. It was by every account a disaster, a rambling patchwork of clips, amateurish dramatizations, stand-ups, interviews, title cards, and blank spots. Julian Bond didn't quite work. The film was not fluid.

Judy Richardson said, "They were increasingly unhappy with what we were doing, but we didn't *know* what we were doing. . . . The screening was horrible . . . and we were still trying to figure out what the stories were." Steve Fayer had to endure every filmmaker's bad dream of saying what his film had failed to say. "I felt I had personally failed . . . sitting with Cap Cities Charlie the white guy, trying to explain, 'This is a privileged view into this community.'"

Romas said, "They were attentive and watched it . . . sort of shaking their heads. There was nothing there, just some interviews and big long sections of blank film leader. In my professional experience, I had never seen such an embarrassment. Right after the screening the . . . executives went off into a room with Henry; everyone else went home, knowing what was coming."

Years later, Henry's friend Bob Hohler put it charitably: "It became very clear that Cap Cities and Blackside were about two very different kinds of television. Cap Cities wanted riveting, exposé material." Steve

Fayer said, "They had wanted us to make news—to reveal the story behind the story. But we had faith in the history. The history *was* the story.
We tried to tell them: no one had ever tried to see it through the eyes of
ordinary citizens."

Cap Cities/ABC put *America, We Loved You Madly* out of its misery.
Henry joined the growing list of television producers defeated by the civil
rights movement.

In years to come a million reasons floated in Blackside folklore: *AWLYM*
wasn't King-centric enough; it had no investigative scoops; they were
softball players in a hardball game; it was overly dramatic; it wasn't dramatic enough; they hadn't found a "new thing" to Cap Cities's liking; Cap
Cities were a bunch of lowbrows; it was their nickel; ABC wanted something really entertaining like *Roots*. Or Henry and crew were just lousy
filmmakers.

To his great credit, Henry never defended the quality of the Cap Cities
film to me or anyone else, but simply said, "We weren't ready to do it." And
looking back now, it seems obvious that the network expected something
Henry simply could never deliver. Henry and the execs had probably been
talking past each other, like future divorcees.

Not long after, I survived a near identical creative wreck on *Close-Up!*
at ABC (by then merged with Cap Cities) and joined Henry in the exclusive, bitter club of independents fired by their network execs. I spent the
summer of 1982 following a tough wheat harvest boss and his combine
crew northward across the Great Plains from Texas to Montana. I envisioned a grand, imagistic *Moby Dick of the Plains,* but ABC actually
needed a hard-hitting report on commodities pricing and farm foreclo-
sure. They fired me after fine cut, and I then had to endure the humiliation of sitting in a hallway at ABC headquarters on West Sixty-sixth
Street listening as they re-edited my film behind a closed door.

When networks and independent filmmakers like us court each other,
we leap at the assumption they want us to make a film of our own devising,
with our own sensibility, values, and cinematic chops. We (and perhaps
they) believe in our hearts that the network philistines have finally abandoned crass commercial infotainment, risen above ratings, at last embraced honest cinema art—*our* brilliant cinema art. When will we learn
that as soon as a network executive says, "We want *your* vision," as they

said to Henry, it's time to reach for your pistol. They are truly skilled in the news business, the entertainment business, the prime-time business, while we often fancy ourselves not beholden to any business at all, only the art of film and our noble calling of The People's History. If everyone could agree from the beginning that they don't want to make our movie, that they want us to go out and gather material for *their* movie, no problem. They may serve the commercial monster, but they know what they are doing.

It gave Henry and me a common enemy to snarl about over dinner for years to come. We were in good company: the acclaimed director Marcel Ophuls was enduring his own creative crash with ABC at the same time. At least my wheat harvest film got broadcast, but not until the ABC staff editor had to excise every single image of the harvest boss, my Ahab, star of the show; he got himself busted in Texas smuggling fifty pounds of narcotics in the backseat of his light plane two weeks before the broadcast date. (*That* would have made excellent television.)

Romas Slezas took the hard view of Hampton's role in the failure. No stranger to upheaval, he looked back at Blackside's revolutionary first decade and said, "A revolution is one thing, but running the country after the revolution is different . . . and because Henry had spent so much of his energy on Cap Cities doing whatever he was doing, he didn't mind the store and wasn't selling." Henry was a stunningly effective pitchman, but by 1980 it was a year since he had pitched a new project, and the Blackside pipeline was running dry.

The sad and angry Blacksiders had given a year of their lives to *America, We Loved You Madly* and had nothing to show for it.

Romas, with a young family to support, left for a high-paying steady job in high tech. Steve Fayer, who had quit once before, left in a fit of anger. Henry Johnson "knew he was going nowhere fast" and joined the westward migration of promising young black filmmakers to Hollywood, where he would become a major film and television producer. There, Johnson, in fact, helped to invent the viable "black television" that Henry had championed in his *Say Brother* commentaries. Judy Richardson and Madison Davis Lacy headed for Los Angeles together to work for Topper Carew's new black company, and Howie was by then in New York. Carol Munday had peeled off long before when "the burden of poverty became too oppressive," to take a steady job at *Say Brother*.

Orlando Bagwell stayed longer than anyone, loyal to the man who had given him his first real break, but finally split with Henry over budget in late 1980, following the others to a new career in Hollywood. At their final parting, Henry told him, as he had told Fayer, "You'll be back."

Cap Cities was not the only reversal. The socially inspired government contracts that had sustained so many small documentary companies began to dry up for good under the newly elected Reagan administration.

Blackside limped along with a new business plan despite a "net loss and $1,560,049 owed to 130 different angry creditors." Hampton applied for a high-level security clearance so that he could do more secret work for the Pentagon. "If no corrective actions are taken, the company will cease to operate within 60 to 90 days," said the annual report. Yet with his company collapsing around him, Henry found a way, perhaps out of desperation, to go on a Caribbean vacation with friends on Virgin Gorda.

When the board of directors held their annual meeting at a Chinese restaurant in 1981 to dicuss selling the building, there was no mention whatever of *America, We Loved You Madly* in the minutes. The civil rights history was gone from the institutional narrative, exiled to the Island of Lost Films. By the end of 1982 Blackside was down to a single employee, "bitter, lonely, depressed, and abandoned" Henry Hampton, alone in his office at 486 Shawmut Avenue.

Some of the big steel cans of civil rights film ended up locked away in Henry's mysterious garages up on Fort Hill in Roxbury, and Judy Richardson had taken the John Lewis interview with her, fearing it might be misused in the future by persons unknown. The rest of the film was sequestered down at the massive brick Metro Storage building next to the Charles River in Cambridge, with its big sign on the façade:

METROPOLITAN
STORAGE WAREHOUSE
FIRE PROOF

Here in the boneyard it sat. Viewed from across Massachusetts Avenue, with its sign half obscured by another building, the repository of Henry's dream was labeled in six-foot-tall bold, block letters:

RAGE WAREHOUSE
IRE PROOF

CHAPTER FOUR

Last Visionary Standing

1983–85

If Henry had dragged *America, We Loved You Madly* over the finish line, a piece of well-meaning junk consigned to the 2 A.M. broadcast slot it surely deserved, he might have spent the rest of his career as just another embittered B-list corporate/industrial filmmaker. ("You can always go back to medical school.") Failure stinks, but at least when the network killed the show, Henry got his scorching lesson in how not to make a television series about civil rights.

Today the Ford Foundation considers Henry Hampton "one of the great visionaries," and, preposterously stubborn visionary that he was, I doubt he ever seriously considered abandoning the civil rights concept. Terminator-like, driven by his epiphany on the bridge in Selma, his adopted kinship with Emmett Till and Uncle Mose Wright, his determination to exercise his privilege and ability for good work, he could not let the civil rights documentaries die.

Both tempered and energized by defeat, Henry understood that his passion to bring filmmakers, historians, journalists, and activists together for an epic journey through the "expansion of democracy," and "the responsibilities of government to its citizens and vice versa," would never fly on commercial TV. But maybe it could be produced independently in the nonprofit sphere, free from the demands of for-profit broadcasting.

As it turned out, back on October 18, 1979, three months *before* the Cap Cities project crashed, while he was still enduring ever more demanding script notes from the executives, Henry had quietly, without telling anyone, submitted a proposal to PBS for a multipart civil rights series entitled *Eyes on the Prize: America's Civil Rights Years.*

American television had been resolutely commercial from the start, its first-ever U.S. telecast in 1941 sponsored by the soap maker Procter & Gamble. America is the only industrialized nation that had only commercially sponsored broadcasting long before public broadcasting. It treated viewers more as customers than as citizens. As for-profit television became increasingly deregulated, disconnected from the public interest, and in the end driven almost entirely by ratings and ad sales, the presentation of an occasional excellent documentary was a lucky bonus, not a goal. It seemed to confirm a haughty but prescient warning by the BBC's eccentric founder, Lord John Reith, who said in 1934, "Broadcasting is too important to be trivialized and vulgarized by market forces." Reith considered public broadcasting "one of the supreme cultural creations of the twentieth century."

With pivotal early help from the Ford Foundation, our own PBS was a creation of the 1960s, established by Congress as an alternative to for-profit networks, which had by then become primarily a delivery system for advertising. LBJ's special assistant, the former pastor-journalist Bill Moyers, explained to the president that this new, publicly supported venture would give worthy television programs immunity from the poison of short-term ratings. The public air was suddenly alive with independent fervor and creative hope. For those of us just beginning our documentary careers in the early seventies, the promise of public television was intoxicating. Here was a government-supported commercial-free enterprise dedicated to the arts, culture, and political discourse, sworn to seek out and support bold voices and ideas, free from corporate and commercial dictates. The same year Cap Cities sponsored *America, We Loved You Madly*, the public agencies PBS and CPB had funded my film *The Day After Trinity: J. Robert Oppenheimer and the Atomic Bomb*, a 90-minute history-heavy documentary that could never have attracted a commercial network. By the early eighties Fred Wiseman had turned out enough idiosyncratic PBS documentaries to be well under way on his "50-hour movie about life as it existed during my lifetime." And Ken Burns was making the first installment in his own 50-hour movie about life as it existed before his lifetime.

Hard to believe now, but PBS in those days was *the* thing, hip, smart, and cutting-edge, still willing to take risks with new forms and experiments like *The Great American Dream Machine, Signal to Noise, An American Family, The Electric Company, Say Brother,* or *Sesame Street*'s droll avant-garde visual haikus. Public television attracted a lot of the best and the brightest, and was edging toward multiculturalism before Americans knew the word. Orlando remembers how people were awestruck when he told them he worked for WGBH.

· · · · · ·

In 1982, Hampton's basic ingredients for a massive civil rights series were still there for the taking, none yet successfully claimed by any other documentarian: the grand Shakespearean drama, larger-than-life and smaller-than-life characters, the troves of news film, the surviving storytellers, the moral power, and the messy history. Cap Cities may have sacked Henry and taken the last of their money with them, but he still owned rights to the interview footage stashed in storage on Mass Ave.

With support and advice from his friends, he began to raise little bits of money to jump-start a reimagined *Eyes*. Henry said, "It was the African American spirit that drove this enterprise." Chief among his boosters was razor-sharp and courtly Ruth Batson, African American professor of psychiatry at Boston University School of Medicine, president of the New England Regional NAACP, and director of Boston's Museum of African American History. Ruth Batson was a thoroughgoing grown-up, with the institutional management savvy that many guessed Henry lacked. Henry always said Batson "was the one you really wanted to have on your side."

Hampton worried that funders would get wind that his first try had crashed. And he worried that people would question a black man setting out to do a sober and considered history of the civil rights movement, free of liberal tropes. His company was on the verge of bankruptcy, hounded by creditors. He worried that other, more credible producers were developing their own competing civil rights projects (unaware that PBS and NEH were turning them down). If any funder had checked—apparently none did—they would have discovered that Hampton's company, in fact, had a record of expensive failure in historical filmmaking.

Around this time his former employer, the Unitarian church, was arranging for successful white executives to mentor emerging black enterprises, and assigned Michael Ambrosino, the amiable, churchgoing founder of PBS's flagship science series, *Nova*, to help Blackside. Mike and Henry immediately hit it off. "I didn't know he had polio, so it was surprising to see him come lumbering in on his brace." Ambrosino himself had worn a 15-pound leg brace as a polio-stricken teenager. And they were both pilots and dedicated golfers.

Ambrosino probably knew more about documentary series production than anyone in the country in 1983, and was widely respected and influential within PBS, one of the few execs I never heard anyone complain about. Orlando said, "At WGBH he was the only guy I really liked."

Mike helped keep Henry's struggling little company afloat by connecting him with a few new corporate clients for whom "hiring a minority business was a plus." When Henry explained his new project, *Eyes on the Prize,* it was clear that the series was going nowhere and was draining Henry's own money. As always, Henry was loath to fall into the "no excellence without a white partner" trap, but he and Mike really admired and respected each other and it was clear that the consummate insider could help the consummate outsider navigate the byzantine halls of public television, so Ambrosino signed on as consulting executive producer.

Henry had coaxed Romas Slezas and Frank Galvin back to edit a smart 38-minute pilot on a pair of ancient U-matic three-quarter-inch tape decks. Now, spending the last of his own money and throwing the company further into debt, he created a new 8-minute sample reel out of the Montgomery bus boycott footage from *America, We Loved You Madly,* braiding together some of Julian's stand-ups, a few good interview bites, a lively a cappella version of "Keep Your Eyes on the Prize," and an array of hot newsreel footage. The sample was clunky but powerful, and got people's attention.

Ambrosino remembered, "We stayed true to the message of the series: the Montgomery bus boycott was created and sustained by the average folks of Montgomery who were bold, courageous, and powerful. Like the series that we hoped would follow, the promo's story differed from the public myth that the citizens of Montgomery were at loose ends until Martin Luther King Jr. arrived." Ambrosino's understanding of how Henry wanted to do history from the bottom up was fueled by Mike's friend and neighbor, historian Howard Zinn.

Ambrosino's main job was to anoint Blackside with credibility at PBS. "We attended the annual PBS meeting together and made a joint pitch to the assembled stations. PBS stations had previously funded black programs mostly out of guilt and then threw them away by scheduling them on Saturday or Sunday mornings in ghetto TV times. I told them that *Eyes on the Prize* would be real prime-time material."

Over the next two years Hampton wrote, typed, xeroxed, and mailed proposal after proposal, each painstakingly customized for the intended executive at CPB, NEH, NEA, PBS, and dozens of foundations. Without ever mentioning the late *America, We Loved You Madly,* he could now spin that project as the "formative stages of *Eyes on the Prize,* which has been in development for five years," and write, "We have in past years spent more than $230,000 in the identification, logging, and organizing of stock footage and other visual archival materials. . . . Our research has included identifying and interviewing more than 60 movement participants." It took nerve, chutzpah, and a bit of genius to write, with a straight face, "My attempts to get the *Eyes on the Prize* series produced have been actively under way for five years," which was technically true, but glossed over the inconvenient fact that another television network had lost a quarter million dollars on the effort.

Depending on the potential funder, he described the project as "personal stories of five people in the center of key events in the civil rights movement," "thirteen 1-hours . . . focused on the triumphs, tragedies, pain, and humor of black and white Americans on the move towards justice and equality," or "a two-hour special," or "six programs," or "14 programs." On paper the new series was sometimes "primarily for a black audience," sometimes for blacks and whites. It was sometimes to be narrated by Gordon Parks, sometimes by Julian Bond. As before, "At its center, *Eyes on the Prize* will remind us of the sturdiness of the brand of democracy we practice."

Despite a dramatic shift in the cultural winds that brought Ronald Reagan to office in 1980, multiculturalism and second-wave feminism were entering the national conversation, establishing small footholds in public television. Henry's first stealthy submission to PBS, back when Blackside was still fully staffed up on the doomed *America, We Loved You Madly,* could accurately note with pride, "Exec producer Henry Hampton and Producer Henry Johnson are black . . . anticipated project staff and crews in the field will be 75% minority, 50% women. Blackside is currently employing 28 people . . . 50% are women, and 50% are minority." And he notes that on screen, most of the storytellers are black and "many women are featured." He could also write, "Blackside is one of the oldest minority-owned production firms in the country . . . having just celebrated our 15th year," though when he wrote that particular proposal the company was, in actuality, on life support with little to celebrate.

The curse of commercial funding—you have to do what they say—is also its blessing—they give you all the money. Henry now figured he had to raise a million dollars. The total budget varied from $350,000 to

$1,200,000, depending on the specific proposal and potential funder. Gone was the amateur fantasy of doing the project in six months; all the submissions called for a one-year schedule.

Free from the hyperventilating demands of network TV, Hampton could focus once again on the local organizers and complex untold stories that had originally drawn him to the history. The persuasive pitching style he had honed in the years of selling to corporations, ad agencies, and government bureaus could now be put in service to the cause of history. I've seen him mesmerize a room full of very smart rich people by treating them as intellectual equals, his voice so restrained that he was often hard to hear, inviting the whole room to lean forward in rapt silence. Finally liberated from adspeak in 1982, he laid out his case to potential donors the same way he would lay it out to Batson, Ambrosino, Bagwell, or any other peer, as a piece of smart, important, and riveting television. He knew perfectly well that some issues, like armed self-defense, would scare some funders, but he never compromised content solely for funding. He was far more worried about scaring away viewers.

He feared that the movement's gains were in real jeopardy under Ronald Reagan. "We are aware of the danger of presenting history that may not have been fully settled into clear perspective, but I think the risk is worth it. Our times seem to be ones of retreat from the dearly won gains of earlier generations. That is why the lessons of these voices are so important."

Donations dribbled in. Henry said, "It died a thousand times, but each time somebody would send me a check for a hundred dollars, or some kid somewhere would send me twenty-five dollars." Thirty-seven foundations turned him down: Aetna, Pew, MacArthur, and the National Endowment for the Humanities, soon to be joined by the charitable arms of General Motors, Equitable Insurance, TRW, Coca-Cola, Coors, IBM, Chrysler, Philip Morris, and Chase Manhattan. Henry's sister Judi, by 1984 Mobil Corporation's first full-time media spokesperson, tried to get her employer to have a look. Mobil, too, joined the club of companies and institutions declining to fund *Eyes on the Prize*.

Ambrosino and Henry did "Oreo Cookie chats with rich ladies . . . and we'd get pledges of a couple thousand dollars here and a couple thousand there." Over the coming decade Henry would do hundreds of these dog and pony shows.

Among the myriad frustrations of raising big documentary money is that so many different funders each give you so little; dozens of foundations make tiny grants, each requiring its own special proposal, meetings, phone calls, schmoozing, contracts, accounting, reporting, deliverables, final reports, credits, and thanks. What we desperately want is one single, big, fat check. Henry had gathered just barely enough small contributions to keep *Eyes* in development, when the clincher finally came from PBS vice president Barry Chase. Henry wrote in his daybook on January 30, 1983: "Phone call. Barry. $250,000 is assured . . . Sue Weil . . . must raise additional $250,000."

Now Madison Davis Lacy worked behind the scenes to help Hampton crack the foundation system. When he set up a meeting with Ford Foundation lawyer and longtime civil rights activist Lynn Walker, Henry insisted they fly down to New York in his plane. Davis Lacy, an air force veteran, said that when they headed into the traffic pattern toward New York, it was "rush hour in the air; planes above us, planes below us, Henry on the radio squawking with air traffic control. At one point he had to deal with a map and said, 'You take it, just keep it on the straight and narrow.' It was the scariest thing I've ever experienced." Arriving at the Ford Foundation's monumental glass edifice in midtown Manhattan, Davis Lacy realized that Hampton had never been there before and was intimidated. "Floored by the setting, which tells you a lot. He should have been an insider." In time, he would be.

The Ford Foundation had funded the NAACP's early *Brown v. Board of Education* legal work and CORE's organizing in the South. By 1983 the timing was perfect; Ford saw the potential of bringing scholarly work to millions through the broad reach of the media, and was beginning to explore television as a tool for social justice through "public education." (As a tax-exempt foundation they could not call it "advocacy.") Lynn Walker pushed through a major Ford grant for *Eyes,* and soon shepherded Hampton and Davis Lacy to a meeting at the Revson Foundation headquarters in Detroit, where she "got a little bidding war going; Hampton was floored by the amount of money they were discussing."

Soon the *Eyes on the Prize* bank account swelled with additional grants from business executive Stanley Goldstein, Polaroid, and Lotus Development, while Tom Layton of the Gerbode Foundation spearheaded San Francisco fund-raising. They resubmitted to the NEH for the third time, and finally won a grant. Henry now had about 70 percent of the money in hand. By the time it was over, forty-one major funders and hundreds of small donors would support *Eyes on the Prize*. The final cost would climb above two and a half million dollars.

Having lost his shirt, his dignity, and very nearly his company making the series the wrong way in 1979, Henry Hampton now set out to make it the right way in 1983.

Eyes on the Prize may be a grainy old fossil of a movie, but you can learn a lot from fossils if you understand where they sit in the layers of rock and how they got there.

Would things be different this time around? There was bad news and good news. As a force in mainstream American politics and discourse, the civil rights movement had peaked a decade before and the country had turned rightward. On August 3, 1980, Ronald Reagan had launched his presidential campaign at the Neshoba County fairgrounds in Philadelphia, Mississippi, near the spot where Klansmen murdered Andrew Goodman, James Chaney, and Michael Schwerner, and declared, "I believe in states' rights." Reagan added that Jefferson Davis, president of the Confederacy, was "a hero of mine," the Voting Rights Act of 1965 was "humiliating to the South," and he was perfectly comfortable in his vocal opposition to establishing a national holiday in Martin Luther King's name.

Back when Henry made his earlier attempt, no one in the English-speaking world had ever completed a serious multipart series following a continuously linked historical story, other than boilerplate WWII clip shows. But by now, Jeremy Isaacs at the new British outfit Thames Television had perfected the basic mechanics of intricate television history in the majestic twenty-six-part *The World at War*. It was the most expensive documentary series ever made, with Sir Laurence Olivier reading some of the greatest narration ever written. French television had created their five-part tragic narrative *La Guerre d'Algérie;* and WGBH, with some French and British talent borrowed from *The World at War,* had in 1983 just released its own hugely successful elegy *Vietnam: A Television History.* (Unbeknownst to Henry, the success of that series had set PBS on the hunt for a domestic issue equally suitable for a multipart series. Network executives saw civil rights as an obvious possible choice, but they were unsure how to proceed or who should tackle the topic.)

So this time Henry could learn from three successful models for sweeping historical narrative on TV. He was particularly inspired by the searing *Vietnam* series, and saw that the eloquently crafted horror of that project could be bent to the warmth, purpose, and nuanced triumph of civil rights. The bitterly calm storytelling of *Vietnam*, requiem for a war that we lost in nearly every way, could serve to tell the story of a different war, which we seemed to have won in nearly every way.

By 1983 the post-Watergate clamor for game-changing investigative scoops, which he could not deliver to Cap Cities, was fading. And for the first time, many scholars and journalists were digging into "history from the bottom up," doing serious work locating and interviewing the hundreds of unknown local people who were the movement's backbone.

And perhaps most important, Henry cleared the decks, at last putting aside industrials, commercials, corporates, and dancing toothbrushes to devote 100 percent of Blackside's resources to the new incarnation of his dream. All chips in. When he first considered the *Eyes on the Prize* reboot in 1980, the company's annual report showed thirty-six different projects in the pipeline, but now in 1983 there was only one: *Eyes on the Prize.*

This time Henry knew he needed adult supervision, and made it official by creating the nonprofit Civil Rights Project, Inc., as an umbrella for fundraising and a steward of the archives and new historical material *Eyes* would generate. Ruth Batson and Michael Ambrosino anchored the new culture of responsibility, and Henry added Peter Karoff, founder of The Philanthropic Initiative; Rev. Jack Mendelsohn, a feisty player in the "Unitarian Mafia"; the poet Sam Allen; and Bob Hohler, who had marched shoulder to shoulder with him in Selma. He brought in a number of rising early players among Boston's high-tech start-ups, and a national advisory board that included civil rights luminaries Mary Francis Berry, Peter Edelman, Vernon Jordan, John Lewis, and Eleanor Holmes Norton. The inclusion of high-profile partisans like these would have raised eyebrows in a more traditional journalistic institution or at a network news operation, but they emblazoned Blackside as the genuine article when it came to civil rights.

Steve Fayer said, "Henry called me in the summer of 1983. . . . He told me he wanted to resurrect the civil rights series. I told him to save his money. And I think my exact words were 'Henry, you haven't learned it yet; nobody gives a shit about colored people any more.' (I might actually have said 'niggers.') Somehow, I don't know how, he talked me into working on it again."

In the sweltering basement at the otherwise empty office at 486 Shawmut, he pounded out treatments with Davis Lacy and Judy Richardson. Steve said, "We were walking with ghosts, trafficking in spirits that summer." Through all the myriad proposed new incarnations of his dream, the greatest change was that Henry was now *really* committed to serve the history— not the network, not advertisers, not false constructions of drama, not committees of executives—or die trying.

As the stuff of history, the civil rights movement and its heroes had stood the test of time, to be embraced, in word if not in deed, in 1985 by liberals, radicals, and many conservatives, but as lived experience the movement was slipping away. In his introduction to the opening treatment, Steve Fayer described the new 1980s context: "Half our audience was not yet born when these events unfolded . . . and there are some who are still convinced that gradualism and enduring patience would have liberated black Americans and the white South itself from the laws and local custom that were strangling progress and opportunity. . . . It is also difficult for many younger black Americans today to understand why those who came before would have played the game so long, why they would have tolerated lifelong injustice and indignity without resorting to the southern courts or calling in the police, or turning to force of arms to secure rights guaranteed by the American Constitution. . . . Millions lived outside the law's protection. Parallels to other societies can never be exact; but the Jews in Germany after the passage of the Nuremberg Laws would have understood Jim Crow . . . as do blacks in South Africa today. It would not be overly optimistic to hope that the viewers of this series will come to the realization that the participants in the Civil Rights Movement were American patriots, brothers and sisters in idealism with those who fought another revolution two hundred years ago." With those smart and honest lines, *Eyes on the Prize* laid out its mission statement.

Blackside still had $40,000 in lab bills left from Cap Cities, and Ambrosino counseled patience until 100 percent of the money to complete *Eyes on the Prize* was in the bank. But Henry knew that delay might mean defeat, so he plunged into the new series in April 1985, fearing that if he did not start, the momentum would be lost and the rich materials of history would slip away. Some archive footage had already been lost in a fire at the National Archives. Amzie Moore, Jo Ann Robinson, and Bill Huie had already died; who would be next? No gala reception this time.

CHAPTER FIVE

The Revolution Will Be Televised

Summer 1985

When a critic from *Variety* asked Les Blank how he prepared for shooting his dazzling films about southern music and culture, Les said, "Well, I just go down there, I get drunk with the people, and I make the film." What a series *Eyes* would be if we'd done it that way. But we didn't; it was the most excruciatingly well-prepared television I've ever worked on.

Among Henry Hampton's great strengths was his ability to inspire skilled people, no matter where he found them, to rally around the grand arc of a grand true story. He would within the coming year lure thirty remarkable folks to the new Blackside. His first hire was thirty-four-year-old white senior producer Judith Vecchione, a brilliant choice to be his second-in-command, chief of staff, and producer/director on two of the programs. She and Henry immediately respected each other, and she said, "He was smart, honest, ready to take on the whole thing. . . . I knew instantly I wanted to join." Judith told him, "I didn't see this as a story of 'other/black people,' but a fundamental American story for everyone, whether they knew it or not. It's my history too."

Though she had limited civil rights movement experience, collecting supplies in New York for southern activists and covering the New Haven Black Panther trials as a journalist, Judith was a rising star in documentary who brought everything the old, original Blackside team lacked: deep experience in producing complex and sustained historical series for national broadcast, the standards of blue-chip journalism, and unbending discipline. She had been part of the first class of women ever admitted to Yale College, a human rights action of a different sort. Graduating in linguistics in 1972, Judith had gone directly into WGBH, worked on Watergate news coverage, *Nova,* and *Frontline,* and most important had produced and directed two programs in the landmark *Vietnam: A Television History.* If needed, she could be a strategic go-between to WGBH or the PBS network itself. Now she took the risk of leaving her steady, full-time job at the most important public television institution in America to join a tiny black film company across town with a little-known black executive producer.

Judith was among the new Blackside producers who had come of age in broadcast television, where every project is locked into an airdate, where you take care of business or you don't survive, where producers and executives smack disciplines on each other to ensure that the thing is completed to length, on time, on budget, and then racks up awards. Over the next year and a half, Judith would be tough and, if necessary, combative, unafraid of a fierce fight with Henry or anyone else. The series might never have achieved its long leap from Hampton's brain to twenty million TV screens without her resolve. Before it was over, many weary Blackside veterans credited Judith Vecchione with keeping the careening enterprise on track to the end.

Fortunately for all of us, Henry unleashed all his considerable persuasive powers on Orlando Bagwell, who was by then nicely settled with his wife, Rosa, and two kids, Jaffar and Cira, in Los Angeles, living the dream of a young Hollywood cinematographer. He had knocked around as a set electrician, a grip on *Repo Man,* then shot a couple of music videos for Chaka Khan, and was now a rising player in the giddy world of 1980s black Hollywood. He was in the union, making real money. "I was in that weird bubble. . . . It was a new time when black film was coming in, hip-hop film was coming in. I could work fast. I had a good crew. People are paying attention to me."

He had just shot one of Shelley Duvall's quirky *Faerie Tale Theatre* dramas, starring Elliott Gould as a frog prince, when suddenly one day, "Henry Hampton called and asked me to come back to Boston and direct on *Eyes on the Prize.* That call changed the whole course of my life, because I could have stayed in L.A., and I probably would have made a decent living. I was on that verge of stepping over into the other side." Making the next leap from crew to director in hypercompetitive Hollywood, with its veiled currents of racism, might be problematic. "It's OK to be an electrician, but they don't see you as a director."

Orlando did not at first accept Henry's summons, not sure he was up to the critical thinking involved in directing a major documentary, knowing he was not a good writer. After long discussions with Rosa, Orlando made the wrenching decision to once again cast his fate with Henry Hampton and commute from L.A. to Boston. "I only remember the awesome sense of responsibility."

Few could resist the Hampton force field. Judy Richardson, without whom the new series could never have been made the way it was, also returned from Los Angeles. Over the next decade, Judy would be our most vital link to lived experience in the movement of the 1960s, "Blackside's moral compass." When Henry asked the reluctant Steve Fayer, who had written many of the new proposals, to return once again as business manager, Steve said, "'Fuck that' . . . but Henry came back and says, 'You're going to be the series writer,'" to which Fayer, thank God, agreed.

Callie Crossley came of age in the Jim Crow South, a teenager in Memplis when King was killed there, and in 1985 had a secure position on the career track at ABC News in New York. She had just finished a Nieman journalism fellowship at Harvard when Henry and Judith summoned her about a possible producer job. But she felt the interview went badly. Months later she was off in Africa and received a telex message: "Callie Crossley, Hotel Intercontinental, Nairobi, Kenya, July 11, 1985, Blackside would like you as co-producer on 'Eyes.' School starts 22 July. Welcome aboard. Henry Hampton."

Callie called her parents from Nairobi and told them she intended to quit her secure network producer job for a series on civil rights. "I was going to do this project, you know, black woman with a good job, and they said, 'You're going to go to do *what*?' I had never in my life done anything that risky."

Henry's choices were bold and occasionally mystifying, and they seemed clearly aimed at avoiding the same old roster of high-paid lifers who had made the same old documentaries under the same old structures for decades.

Jim DeVinney, a journeyman white producer of children's films, had no movement experience whatever. Jim had grown up in a Catholic working-class family in Fort Wayne, Indiana, supporting himself as the night news cameraman at a local station, "but so apolitical that I wasn't even aware of the Vietnam War." He was happy to admit his puzzlement at why out of all that hyperskilled documentary talent in America, Henry had chosen him. Like Callie, Jim had never done a one-hour documentary, had never written narration, had no documentary archive experience, and he had, in fact, told Henry in his interview, "'I don't know how to do it.' But I think he liked my background in children's programming and thought I could help in the education component of the shows." Henry also knew that if *Eyes* was to appeal to middle-class white people in the heartland, he needed a white middle-class midwesterner on staff.

With Jim, Callie, Orlando, Judith, Steve, and Judy Richardson on board, Henry now had his core team.

In July 1985 the new staff gathered for an intense ten-day "civil rights school" in borrowed rooms at the PBS flagship station, WGBH, the destination to which every worthy documentary maker of the 1980s sooner or later made their pilgrimage. "School"—literally: professors, lectures, and thousands of pages of assigned reading—was an ingenious invention of the Vietnam project, a way to reconcile the competing and often contradictory demands of rigorous history and riveting television. An esteemed professor's academic book may be read by 1,000 scholars and 100 policy makers, a very popular author's nonfiction hit may reach 100,000 readers, and a good television maker's show may be seen by 10,000,000 citizens, but none alone can fuel a robust national conversation without the other. The creative and intellectual tensions Henry and Judith fine-tuned at school that summer became the gold standard for a new kind of television-making process, a fixture on every Blackside project for the next fifteen years.

They knew that SNCC had convened a nearly identical symposium back in 1964 to prepare for its Mississippi Summer Project, with historians, psychologists, academics, labor leaders, government officials, Ella Baker ("the Godmother of SNCC"), Bob Moses, and Martin Luther King, under the title "Understanding the Nature of Social Change." It was not the last time Henry would take a page from the movement's playbook.

I was a late arrival at *Eyes on the Prize*. The year before, I had seen a small article in the Corporation for Public Broadcasting newsletter with the picture of a friendly-looking black man, and I cold-called Henry Hampton. He answered the phone himself, struck me as a serious fellow, and politely listened while I pitched myself as a great addition to his team. Hearing other phone lines ringing unanswered in the background, I guessed correctly that there was not yet any team. A year later, by the time he suggested we discuss my directing and producing episodes of *Eyes*, I was prepping for work with the *Top Gun* special-effects unit, and I had just signed on for a year as director of photography on Michael Ambrosino's new global science series, *The Ring of Truth*.

On a July 1985 trip to Boston for preproduction meetings with Ambrosino, I stopped by the *Eyes* school just to stay in touch with Hampton.

Slipping into the back row of a darkened screening room at WGBH, I arrived just at the moment they were watching Alabama state troopers bludgeon my old SNCC boss John Lewis. Long-simmering memory welled up, came roaring back, and I decided on the spot, in the dark, that I had to work on *Eyes on the Prize.* Sign me up.

Later that day Henry and I met for the first time over drinks at the Copley Plaza, and I was instantly taken by his welcoming warmth, wit, charm, world-class smarts, and most of all by his deep and original understanding of civil rights history. I explained my work directing the atomic bomb documentary, which he had seen and liked, and a few hour-long documentaries for ABC and HBO. I asked if he had any sort of opening left and he said, "I'll find something; how about if we make you series producer?" As it turned out, Judith Vecchione and I would together fill the gap left by Romas Slezas. I would be Blackside's floating fix-it man, consigliere, and lead cinematographer. That night at a noisy Beacon Hill *Eyes* cocktail party overlooking lights along the Charles River, I walked out onto Ruth Batson's deck, lit a cigarette, and told a startled Michael Ambrosino I was quitting his *Ring of Truth* to work for his friend Henry Hampton.

The next morning, back at WGBH, after calling school to order, Henry introduced me to his surprised production staff as the new member of their team.

Each of us received a copy of the giant time line Judy Richardson had laid out on architect's blueprint paper a few years before. Hampton would not repeat the mistake of going it alone as he had before, when the young Blacksiders had tried to cowboy their way through *America, We Loved You Madly,* with little help from advisors or academics. Now, highly regarded scholars Clayborne Carson, David Garrow, Darlene Clark Hine, William Strickland, J. Mills Thornton, Harvard Sitkoff, Steve Lawson, and Aldon Morris joined other academics, producers, directors, researchers, and activists—three dozen in all—for a crash course in both the scholarship of civil rights and the disciplines of filmmaking. The historians, who typically worked in relative isolation except for encounters at academic conferences, found themselves thrown together in a rough-and-tumble symposium on the questions of what actually happened in the southern civil rights movement, what it all meant, what mattered most, and how to get it seen and understood by ten or twenty million television viewers two years in the future. They were apparently delighted and surprised to be part of the formative process, more accustomed instead to being summoned by filmmakers for fact-checking and sign-off, often as a kind of cover after all the important storytelling and editing choices had been made long before.

Henry and Judith brought to *Eyes* a special breed of historians who were all invested in "people's history," the growing fresh discipline of new social history. They studied slave narratives, labor union documents, pioneer women's diaries, local movement strategies, and the like, shunting aside the sturdy but narrow Great Men approach to history. Their exploration of the American saga through the eyes of the broad and diverse population rather than through the eyes of the powerful elites had found wide popular success with *A People's History of the United States* by Howard Zinn. Since his 1974 bestseller, *Working,* oral historian Studs Terkel had become the low priest of American working people. Stanford historian Clay Carson had been friends with Stokely Carmichael and Bob Moses of SNCC back in the day, and in 1981 published *In Struggle: SNCC and the Black Awakening of the 1960s,* one of the first and finest books examining the movement's foot soldiers. Clay said, "You can *always* tell history from the top down . . . but all *Eyes* advisors pushed the bottom up perspective."

Judith Vecchione convinced Henry that contrary to the common practice of the time, the experts would never appear on screen as talking heads. It was here, in person at the planning sessions and later at rough cut screenings, that the academics brought their decades of scholarship to bear, rolled out their troves of research and analysis, and had their say in shaping the story. This allowed the *Eyes on the Prize* films when they reached the screen to stay completely in the moment, never breaking out of the movement's steadily advancing 1960s present tense with commentary from an authority analyzing events twenty years after the fact.

Many filmmakers had until then viewed scholars as pests, not allies. We documentary directors often held professors in mild contempt: priggish, nitpicky, boring, elitist, droning, cinema philistines who ground everything to a full stop whenever they meddled in our artistic process or popped up on screen.

But on second thought, why would you *not* seek wise counsel from someone who had spent a lifetime studying the subject? While producing *The Day*

After Trinity: Robert Oppenheimer and the Atomic Bomb, I had been won over by working with Stanford historian Barton Bernstein and then Tufts professor Martin Sherwin, who would go on to share a Pulitzer Prize with Kai Bird for *American Prometheus,* their biography of Oppenheimer. Marty and Bart taught me more about Robert Oppenheimer in a day than I would have struggled to learn on my own in a month, and much I could never have learned. And scholarly history and documentary making are a two-way street. Sherwin's book on Oppenheimer cites numerous quotes from *The Day After Trinity,* just as dozens of books would someday quote from *Eyes on the Prize.* We and the scholars stand on each others' shoulders.

Henry and Judith made serious efforts to bring in older conservative southern historians to push us out of our own ideological comfort zone and ensure that the southern voice would be heard. Of particular concern to me was that this television series about poor undereducated people in the rural South was being made almost entirely by well-off hypereducated people in the urban North. The setting at WGBH, just across the Charles River from Harvard, was culturally and geographically about as far from the Mississippi Delta as you could get.

Joining the academic historians in school were many of the selfsame civil rights movement players whom they studied: former attorney general Ramsey Clark, Rev. C. T. Vivian, Rev. Fred Shuttlesworth, *New York Amsterdam News* reporter James Hicks, SNCC's Julian Bond and John Lewis, Ernest Green of the Little Rock Nine, Bobby Kennedy's chief negotiator Burke Marshall, and Judge Constance Baker Motley. Vincent Harding, undisputed wise elder among the advisors, friend of Howard Thurman's, advisor and speechwriter to Dr. King, brought a grandeur born of deep experience to the proceedings. Vince was equally a master of the long Quaker silence and of the bracing secular sermon, in which he could rise to the power of an Old Testament prophet.

As the most respected thinker among the consultants, Harding shared honors with the brilliant and sometimes unknowable strategist of SNCC's Mississippi voting project, Bob Moses himself. No one could match Bob's pure intelligence, and his calm, measured speech caught the attention of the yakety-yakking Blacksiders. Llew Smith said, "What I remember most was Bob Moses . . . this is the whole *under*history, that doesn't exist in the books. I have no reference book for this; *he* is the source. Mississippi was *way* more complex than Americans suspected. Mississippi was the land of mystery."

We were getting to know each other. Jim DeVinney, oldest of the producers at forty-five, struck me as confident and self-assured, but he was, in fact, intimidated, a reticent outsider working with a tribe of chummy insiders. "I got to Blackside and I thought, 'I'm not in Indiana anymore.' At school I tried to be invisible. . . . The white side of me was not in sync with all this. Sometimes when I saw white people behaving badly in the footage I would feel defensive. The staff all knew the subject matter so well . . . They were so intellectual. I had never seen anything like it. At school most days I felt very stupid, but I sure felt the power of Odetta's singing."

Henry brought in Guy Carawan, the white folksinger who had woven together religious, labor, and protest songs to coin "We Shall Overcome," and Odetta, the diminutive black woman with the voice of a lion. Jim had never before heard a freedom song. "One day I was in the front row. Guy Carawan was standing off to one side with his guitar and Odetta was right in front of me. When she opened her mouth it knocked me back in my chair. I had never heard anything like it. An hour later we were all standing singing 'We Shall Overcome,' and I had my arms crossed, holding hands with Odetta on one side and Julian Bond on the other."

What exactly *was* the history, and *how* exactly could we get it on screen? Thousands of successes and failures in the long continuum of liberation struggle lay spread across myriad states and towns from the early days of the republic to the present. We had to chapterize it, bound it, discard nearly all of it, impose an orderly television narrative on it. For ten days the scholars, activists, and filmmakers debated, cajoled, ranted, and coaxed into being the practical framework for *Eyes on the Prize*. What is the prize? Whose eyes? What is nonviolence? What is the force? Who are the carriers of this force? Are we giving whites too great a place in this series? Blacks? Men? Can this series keep alive the transforming vision of the movement? Should it? How do we present Malcolm X? By choosing certain events over others, are we distorting? Can we northerners depict the true South? All cautioned against the danger of leaving viewers thinking that everything ended happily in 1965. And Vincent Harding insisted that our work was invaluable, because a new movement "must happen every generation." Clay Carson said, "This is not about how we got things changed in the past, but about how we get things changed *any* time. The viewer must understand this as a *vision*, not just a bunch of laws and programs." Without ever saying so, we could present the civil rights movement as an operating manual for successful social change in the future.

This raised the question: Is it the job of historical television to drive partisan social movements? Henry was conflicted: his mission as passionate African American activist was often at war with his mission as sober African American producer of documentary journalism. All Blackside's effort was directed at presenting accurate nonpartisan history. But were we kidding ourselves? Our national advisory board members were almost entirely veteran civil rights activists, with a stake in the history. Prue Arndt, Henry, and Judith had been active in CORE. Judy Richardson and I had actually been on the SNCC payroll and gone to jail for the cause, as had editor Chuck Scott. Can you trust the partisans themselves to write an honest history of a partisan struggle?

We spent the next decade sorting that one out, with Henry Hampton often taking the Jesuitical, antipartisan stance, insisting on balance. But we understood that many radical transforming movements throughout history have failed, their vision crushed by oppression or neglect, in part because storytellers of previous movements had failed to keep alive the vision and the operating strategy.

All of us in the room knew that if we succeeded this would be the first, the last, and, for the moment, the definitive series about civil rights, and the zeal to get it right was electric. In a brilliant tactic, Henry and Judith did not reveal which specific stories any of us would be working on. So the staff all paid manic attention to everything in school, directing micro and macro focus to every bit of the history, knowing Hampton could and would demand that any one of us make a film about any one of the topics. Crack student Llew Smith said, "I never wrote so fast in my life."

The entire century-long evolution of documentary film can be seen as a struggle to explore race and ethnicity. White male hegemony was nothing new, and from the beginning of filmmaking nearly all the power, expertise, and technology were in the hands of Europeans and Euro-Americans. Time will tell if *Eyes on the Prize* marked a real change. From the Lumière brothers filming in Asia only a few years after they invented movies in 1895, through *Nanook of the North, Chronicle of a Summer, Night and Fog, Ethnic Notions,* all the way up to *The Act of Killing* and *O.J.: Made in America,* the history of our art form is marked out by pivotal works that address encounters and collisions between the majority and minority, oppressor and oppressed.

We were all in consensus with Henry's obsession to "honor the foot soldiers, the fan ladies, and the ordinary world parishioners," doggedly organizing, marching, demonstrating for months and years. He later wrote of
"the energy and the courage of the people who moved out of those fields
and came forward to confront what were terrifying circumstances. I
wouldn't have had the guts. You could find yourself dead, overnight, bang;
your family cut up, burned. It was a horrific thing."

Henry Hampton transformed the convenient abstraction of hapless victims into a tangible flesh-and-blood army of political actors; that was the genius of his vision. Henry said, "They were not just people marching around
waiting for the white folks to come and save them. They were the people who
led into the streets." He intended to put them on camera rather than those
who wrote about them. We were out to subvert the popular master narrative,
and if we could subvert the prevailing white gaze as well, so much the better.

He said, "Everybody needs history, but the people who need it most
are poor folks, people without resources or options. There are missing
pages in our history."

Hampton was our visionary and now bit by bit was becoming a better
executive producer, developing that mysterious talent for herding the
world's real-life disorder into orderly films. And he was slowly getting up
to speed on herding his disorderly producers.

Judy Richardson had pitched Henry on having an all-black production unit, fearing that if whites had a major role and the series was a hit, it
would once again invite suspicion of white excellence at the expense of
black excellence. Judy said, "I would not have found a problem with an
all-black staff. . . . As long as you have a lot of different inputs and you
have the academic grounding, then what a *statement* it would have been
for an all-black team to have done an amazing, wonderful job.

"I grew up in a world where it was assumed that you could not be excellent without some white person involved. Everybody wanted to have
white doctors, white attorneys, white dentists," and, one assumes, white
documentary producers. Henry countered that because both whites and
blacks benefited from the civil rights movement, because both were involved on all sides, and both whites and blacks would make up our audience, the filmmaking operation had to be racially integrated, and he
could keep the "whitewashing" in check.

He insisted on a bold multicultural, multiethnic, collaborative production process of his own devising, in which each film team would be led by one woman and one man, one white and the other black. The "salt-and-pepper" teams would consume great volumes of Blackside's time, money, and anxiety, but gave most of us confidence that we were honestly giving each story our best pluralist shot. In short, no single filmmaker—black, white, male, female—could comprehend the whole. And is not the conundrum of race a problem of white America as well as black America? No team would get to the heart of the whole story, but to the multiple hearts of the story. This unique Hampton-devised process, in play for the next ten years, became known and was hotly debated as "the Blackside Method."

Henry said it was better to work together than apart. For him, diversity in the teams trumped the powerful statement that an all-black production would have made. "This is a new version of this stuff, that's the gift we want to give to people . . . and it wasn't just to say a black point of view or a white point of view." He was the executive producer; he prevailed. In the end, the *Eyes on the Prize* staff would be roughly half white, half black, half men, half women. (This same debate had flared inside SNCC years before, and the organization finally chose the opposite path, redefining itself as all black.)

And years later many of us finally realized that Henry *wanted* combat, so each production team would be one strong man and one strong woman. His friend Bob Hohler recalled, "Henry knew full well that excellence comes from the healthy abrasion of good minds."

Every new person came with his or her own life experience. Orlando's associate producer, Prue Arndt, brought the unique perspective of having grown up in a white pro-integration Jewish-Quaker-Unitarian household in the Black Belt South, enduring hate mail when her parents took a stand against segregation, always aware of an undercurrent of barely suppressed violence. "Even as a child you could see how distorted things were, and had a visceral understanding of it. There's something about that that's hard to convey . . . within the discourse at Blackside. Knowing when you're eight years old that a black older man of seventy is calling you 'Miss,' and knowing that you're more powerful than that person; it's wrong in the scheme of things, you're not sure why."

Judith's associate producer, Llew Smith, had just finished grad school at Howard and a year of study in Nigeria, planning to be a history teacher, but "was stuck in D.C. selling furniture and Thorntons Chocolates, doing a bit of TV work and writing plays for the Howard Theatre Workshop. . . . We were all hustling." He saw a little story in the *Washington Post* about the Blackside series, cold-called, and got the job. "It was unique at Blackside that Henry was willing to take risks with people who were not skilled." Judith made clear in Llew's job interview that "he was going to be the backstop, the person on the team who dug deep on every word and picture to be sure the editor and I weren't getting carried away with telling a good story that wasn't supportable. Was he ready to spend those hours in the library? He was completely convincing when he said yes, and he proved quickly how much more he could do."

Running throughout the films by stealth, ever present in the six shows but seldom spoken out loud, would be four strong themes.

First, the liberation of African Americans in the South rose from below and from inside southern black communities, more than from above or from the outside.

Second, the struggle could only have resolved itself peacefully in a pluralist constitutional democracy, as southern blacks at last gained full citizenship in their own nation, in a constant tug-of-war between federal, state, and local authorities.

Third, the victories of the classic civil rights movement were all achieved through the strategic and tactical (though not always philosophical) force of nonviolence. Court cases, nonviolent direct actions, boycotts, and massive voter registration campaigns all forced the judicial, legislative, and administrative branches of government to affirm rights long promised but long denied.

Fourth, the complementary but competing strategies of SCLC, CORE, the NAACP, SNCC, and local people themselves led to serious backstage rivalries, often coalescing into an uneasy united front in times of crisis. The same sort of factionalism could divide or unite white segregationists. This was the messiest part of the messy history.

We were not working in a vacuum. Everyone in school that summer of 1985 knew that we were launching *Eyes on the Prize* at a time when blacks in South Africa were not citizens of their own nation, protected by few constitutional rights, their nonviolent action barely effective, and their activist factions in conflict. Henry and I often talked about this, and on a good day he said it made him proud to be American. On television we watched the brutal dramas in Cape Town, Johannesburg, and their townships as a ghoulish inverse of the American story, cautionary tales of what could happen to freedom fighters under a fiercely repressive regime in the absence of constitutional protection by their federal government. We noticed also that in contrast to the civil rights movement in the American South, fair numbers of South African whites openly embraced the anti-apartheid struggle.

I thought it was a mistake, but Henry insisted that our cinematic style would be antistyle, the deliberately unadorned braiding of four simple ingredients:

- Archive footage from the period
- Interviews with people who were there
- Narration, thoroughly fact-checked
- Music from the period

That was it; nothing daring or experimental, no genre busting, no avant-garde, no reenactments, no postmodern mirrors upon mirrors, no animated scenes, no presence of the filmmaker, no on-camera commentator, no fracturing of time, no original music, no twenty-twenty hindsight, no fancy dancing. It had in it a touch of the Book of Common Prayer, simple, clear, easily accessible to all, and you didn't have to learn Latin.

Henry's aesthetics flew in the face of the times; in 1985 the country was riding "the third golden wave" of bold experimentation in documentary, and his kind of austere nonfiction storytelling had fallen on hard times. Everyone else was rushing headlong into documentary territory that mixed every device, style, snap, and irony under the sun: Errol Morris's brilliant metaphysical reenactments, Les Blank's pleasure-soaked music films, Lourdes Portillo's wry investigative surrealism. The French New Wave theorists and the Maysles brothers' acidy *Gimme Shelter* were fresh in our memories, with Marlon Riggs and Michael Moore crouching in the wings. A bustling anarchy of style reigned everywhere but Blackside. Everyone had their secret sauce, but not us.

On the feature-film side, a new wave of black independent filmmakers—Charles Burnett, Reggie Hudlin, Julie Dash, Pearl Bowser—were churning out original work about the African American experience, just before Spike Lee exploded onto the scene. Henry went down to New York to check out the scene, but was apparently not persuaded that any of its artistic maneuvers could serve *Eyes on the Prize*. No *auteurs* for him.

I proposed to frame it all with evocative images we would shoot in the Deep South, echoing Faulkner and Walker Evans: the kudzu jungles, dolly shots at dawn through crumbling plantation ruins, mist on the great river, dusty streets, cotton fields in the blazing sun, two-lane blacktop in the moonlight, haunted landscapes as in Donald Brittain's *Volcano* or Alain Resnais's *Night and Fog*. Henry didn't buy it.

His approach to history on film seemed breathtakingly spare, at a cultural moment when innovations in history telling, like John Adams's opera *Nixon in China*, were turning heads. Henry and Judith wanted no artifice interfering with audience comfort or with the story's simple power; the *form* of *Eyes on the Prize* would be in no way disruptive as it laid out a clearly disruptive history. The only thing bold or stylish about *Eyes* was the integrity of story itself, and therein lay the wisdom of the choice. With narrow rules and vocabulary, we denied ourselves the temptation to obscure actuality with virtuosity. Tom Shales, in his 1987 *Washington Post* review, would write, "The series is so well made that most people will be too engrossed to notice it is a precise working model of the artful documentary."

Not appreciating that Henry had really thought this through, I argued for elaborate elliptical story construction that would jump from the Jim Crow era to the present, back to the movement, do some time travel to show how the DNA of civil rights informed the women's movement, and then leap to a present-day epilogue summing up what had changed since the sixties. Steve had done some nice time hopping in his original script by setting black activist Unita Blackwell's interview about being denied the right to vote in 1962 amid the bustle of her present-day mayoral office. (Years later Orlando and Noland Walker would subtly marry past and present with a masterstroke in their film *Citizen King*, when Taylor Branch says of Martin Luther King's arrest in 1963 in Birmingham, "This is somebody that's going to have a national holiday named for him. This is another nigger going to jail.")

Hampton understood that we would have our hands full simply wrestling the sprawling historical content into clarity, and would have gone crazy trying to wrestle any sort of sprawling style at the same time.

· · · · · ·

America may someday find peace with its racial legacies, but in 1985 the trauma and triumph of civil rights were still raw and even contested. The "I have a dream" speech had not yet snuggled up in the national consciousness with the ring of a familiar anthem. So Henry and Judith expected the series would be controversial and highly scrutinized on both the right and the left.

Veteran CBS producer Robert Northshield said in school that the civil rights movement was one of the very few stories he covered where he knew there was a right side and a wrong side. One could argue that virtually *all* mainstream civil rights journalism, like most serious environmental journalism, is in some sense advocacy; for better or worse, the skinheads and toxic dumpers seldom get a hearing. But Henry insisted that the important and measured voices of segregation and states' rights would have their say. *Eyes on the Prize* would include interviews with several southern sheriffs, segregationist governors, and the head of the Citizens' Council. We tried without success to secure interviews with the Ku Klux Klan and even with men who had murdered civil rights workers. Allowing segregationists to articulate their resistance also had a narrative function, as Judith put it, "To make it emotionally, dramatically clear what was at stake for the activists, you needed to understand how dead set the white supremacists were on winning, emphasis on 'dead.'"

At school Judith looked us all in the eye and said, "Don't make a claim because it is politically correct or because you were there" in the movement in the 1960s. That took nerve because so many of us had been there, but it was absolutely necessary.

As documentary makers, partisan or not, all we bring to the table is true testimony and real evidence; that is what makes us different from fiction filmmakers, and for that we ask our audience to trust us. Like law and science, documentary begins with evidence, then heads into rhetorical constructions that should retain the truth of things but sometimes do not. The journalism-based ethical standards of the *Vietnam* series, which flowed directly from the British news protocols and *New York Times* standards, were brought intact to *Eyes* by Judith Vecchione and archive supervisor Kenn Rabin. The evenhanded *Vietnam,* an equally raw story, had come under merciless attack from Accuracy in Media and other conservative critics just the year before, prompting a two-hour rebuttal narrated by Charlton Heston in prime time on PBS. But Judith and the other producers of *Vietnam* were able to effectively defend their work because they had been inflexible with accuracy, ethics, and record keeping during production. "We weren't going to fail because we took short cuts in our scholarship," remembered Judith.

Henry loved to quote Daniel Patrick Moynihan's declaration "You are entitled to your own opinion; you are not entitled to your own facts." *Eyes* would maintain zero tolerance for factual inaccuracy. I had first seen this discipline during a stint at ABC News in 1982, where I was handed a thick "News Department Standards and Practices" book on my first day in New York. After years of seeing routine petty fudging in documentaries on the scent of a good story—cheating a shot, reordering words, shortchanging a contrary voice—I found ABC's hardball attitude bracing.

Judith and Henry laid out three basic journalistic principles that would underlie *Eyes on the Prize*.

- Every assertion of fact, no matter who said it, would be confirmed from two primary or secondary sources, with strict record keeping throughout in a "fact book" for each program.
- Every film archive image and sound would be what it purported to be, certified genuine, with all sources meticulously recorded.
- The people appearing in the films would have no editorial control, and we would not show any work in progress to subjects before broadcast.

Because many of us had come from activism and organizing, with commitment to involving communities in shaping their own narrative, the prohibition against showing work in progress to people in our films was a new and not entirely welcome idea.

Even interviewees' stories would be fact-checked, and in the end it meant we lost some riveting tales when Blackside researchers discovered they were simply not true. (As we later learned, a few falsehoods may have slipped by.) It is a problem documentarians often face: Can you let someone claim as fact something that you know is false, but they believe is true? Clay Carson found factual errors when he edited a scholarly edition of Dr. King's autobiography, cases when King could not have been at an event he describes so clearly, and Carson decided to let the conflations stand—with appropriate critical comment—because the book was all King's words, not his own. We decided differently because we were framing all the *Eyes on the Prize* interview stories with fact-checked narration, and felt interviews should approach the same high standard.

With Henry's backing, Judith intended the rules to be taken literally, and made it clear in school that she was quite ready to police them herself if we didn't. The landscape of high-profile documentaries was soon to be dotted with factually suspect films made by directors bent on getting to the "greater truth" with lesser evidence or outright fraud. Richard Bernstein put it well in the *New York Times:* "When artists, intentionally or not, distort the known facts to get an effect, either political or commercial, they are on the wrong side of the line between poetic truth and historical falsification. Artists who present as fact things that never happened, who refuse to allow the truth to interfere with a good story, are betraying their art and history as well."

I was surprised that Henry himself said little during these school sessions. He graciously introduced each speaker and then stood off to the side and let the discussion unfold, occasionally reining in egos, encouraging skepticism, keeping it civil, making it work. He sometimes seemed bemused by what he had unleashed.

Hampton finally announced work assignments during the last hour of the last day, twelve stories spread over six episodes.

- Episode 1: Judith Vecchione and Llew Smith
  - Introduction to the segregated South
  - The murder of Emmett Till 1955
  - The Montgomery bus boycott 1956
- Episode 2: Judith Vecchione and Llew Smith
  - The Little Rock school crisis 1957
  - James Meredith at Ole Miss 1962
- Episode 3: Orlando Bagwell and Prudence Arndt
  - The sit-ins 1960
  - The Freedom Rides 1961
- Episode 4: Callie Crossley and Jim DeVinney
  - The Albany, Georgia, movement 1962

I would serve as director of photography and series producer, responsible for the minimalist visual style and, together with Steve, Judy, and Henry, story continuity across all six shows.

Before bidding farewell to the professors, we joined hands and sang "We Shall Overcome." As a journalist I felt a little squeamish and Judith seemed the same, conflicted about really belting it out. And Jim DeVinney remembered, "Henry seemed uncomfortable that we were doing that, as though it was a violation of journalistic ethics. I didn't care. I was in the midst of a profound conversion."

CHAPTER SIX

Mother Ship

Summer 1985

In the last days of summer 1985, the *Eyes* crew, now twenty strong, settled into the five-story brick walk-up that would be home for the duration. Henry had been prudent to launch *Eyes* at the genteel suites of WGBH rather than at Blackside's office in the South End, a few blocks from the abandoned hotel that served as a set for the gritty TV drama *St. Elsewhere.*

The building at 486 Shawmut Avenue would one day be described as "a mandatory destination for American documentary makers," and "world headquarters of an authentic new secular televangelism." Today it's a high-end condo in a trendy upscaling district. One apartment where our editors worked in 1985 was listed by Sotheby's for $1,200,000 in 2014. But back then it was just another old tenement on a backwater street in a sketchy neighborhood, with trash piling up on the street, "Pussy" graffiti next to the front door, and prostitutes on the corner after dark. The place was over a struggling dry cleaner, in a limbo land bordering Roxbury on one side and the slowly gentrifying sections of Tremont Avenue on the other. You could get black coffee, beer, excellent empanadas, and BBQ nearby, but no cappuccino. The neighborhood was quite wonderful once you got to know it, but Henry knew that those of us from out of town might feel uneasy on Shawmut Avenue, and had briefed us, "If you see anyone who makes you uncomfortable, it's OK to cross the street."

I had been back in California shooting Toys "R" Us commercials, flew to Boston, and went to 486 for the first time on foot at about ten at night. As I got nearer the address I noticed a black man in a hoodie following me. I crossed the street and he crossed to my side. I quickened my step and so did he, and when I moved all too fast the last twenty feet toward the door, so did he. Suddenly realizing he had a scared white guy on his hands, he said, "Hi, I'm Ron, Henry's carpenter." He let me in with a chuckle, pointed me up the stairwell toward Orlando Bagwell's apartment on the top floor. Orlando extended a warm greeting to me, his new assigned roommate. Henry lumbered up the five flights and popped in with a big grin and bear hug. He joined us for beer and some excellent chicken Orlando had cooked with his mom's recipe.

We could hear Ron hammering away.

Next morning it was quickly clear that Blackside world headquarters was hardly world class, still cluttered with cardboard boxes from the Cap Cities fiasco, dozens of tantalizing film reels marked "Dr. King's speeches," a forgotten Blackside educational film about birth control. There was sawdust everywhere. The phones didn't quite work. Henry's bachelor sense in décor and housecleaning carried over from his home up on Fort Hill to the office on Shawmut. Newly hired archive researcher Laurie Kahn showed up with a door from home, put it on two file cabinets, and that was her desk for the next two years.

Judith had taken the job without ever seeing the building. "I showed up the first day in a mostly white dress and strappy sandals, and apparently Henry thought I'd take one look at the second floor and just quit. That never occurred to me, but it was *filthy*, layers of dust, beyond revolting. The bathroom on the second floor was just disgusting, cracked floors, peeling paint. Henry told me to pick out tiles and paint, and he'd have his friend the handyman fix it up right away. So I picked out some handsome tiles, white with a pattern of thin straight gray lines forming squares, and the guy put them in without lining up the gray lines. The room looked higgledy-piggledy forever. But at least it was clean. I still have one of those tiles in my office, to remind me that no good deed goes unpunished." It was not the last collision between Judith's sense of order and Henry's disorder.

She was clearly a tough nut. I felt like an idiot floundering around in her subject areas (school desegregation, the Till case, the Montgomery boycott), but when she showed up the second day in an embroidered Grateful Dead jacket I knew we would get along.

Over the next fifteen years, "moving to Blackside" became a rite of passage for hundreds of young documentarians. With each new project, a new flock arrived, abandoning secure jobs, boyfriends, and girlfriends; some, like Orlando and me, parking wives and kids back home in California to join Henry's quixotic missions. The flood of eager applicants grew so fast that Henry and Judith were never able to read all the the résumés, including one from Jill Lepore, a junior in English at Tufts ("typing speed: 70 words/minute") who would one day be a premier writer of American cultural history. She would have been a great catch.

Now the preproduction scramble was on. We could sit around and talk these films to death, but now each team had to deliver a synopsis, a list of participants, and a new twenty-five-page treatment. When Meredith Woods showed up to start her internship, "the mood in the building was a flurry of prep for interviews, a frenzy of paper deadlines."

I did not yet know Henry that well, but I could see that he was already overstretched. Sara Chazen, his hardworking secretary by day, aspiring young actress by night, had a screaming argument in his office the day I arrived. I sent memo after memo to Henry about budget, the editing schedule, the shooting schedule, the Blackside infrastructure, and the ongoing remodel. "Last thing you need right now is to begin building more walls. Sooner or later the staff is going to revolt at working in a facility constantly under construction. Get the fucking heat installed." This was only the first week.

With discipline that would mark all his years at Blackside, senior archive supervisor Kenn Rabin laid concrete plans, issued memos in September calling for us to complete all our shooting by Thanksgiving, screen fine cuts by the end of February, and deliver broadcast master tapes on June 22, 1986, only nine months away. Judith distributed a memo allocating thirty-four rolls of film to do fifteen or twenty new interviews on each new program, at about twenty-five minutes per interview.

It seemed that all we did was work. Few of the producers and staff had ever before embraced such intense research and study, ranging over hundreds of books, unpublished PhD dissertations, articles, movies, documents, and hundreds of phone calls. Callie said in the beginning, "We didn't do anything except try to figure out how we were going to tackle those initial story lines that Henry had put forward. . . . And discover who was dead and who wasn't." The ratio of primary research material pages to film treatment pages could be a thousand to one. Clay Carson said, "What we historians do is cut down fifty thousand documents to eight hundred pages, and then documentary makers come along and cut the eight hundred pages down to a twenty-five-page treatment."

Henry was all over us in his quietly insistent manner: "In three sentences tell me what your film is. What is your story? Where is the conflict? Why will I care? Who's in your movie? What's at stake? Do you believe in it? What is this story driving toward? Where is the payoff? What will make a seventy-year-old white lady in Peoria care about this film?" He was never shy about saying, "I don't get it."

Henry was a liberal Democrat who truly loved this country despite its horrific flaws. But he knew he had a lot of left-leaning skeptics making his films. As the stories developed he constantly saved us from our own ideological narrowness, insisting that we hear from the opposition, dig for complexity, and not slap yet another smiley face on the movement. And from the start he demanded that we deploy a lot of American flags on the screen, in part to reassure skeptical conservative viewers and partly because he so believed in America.

Clay Carson countered, "Perhaps the most significant area of disagreement concerned Hampton's determination to view the civil rights movement as a patriotic story of America's realization of its ideals. He clearly wanted white viewers to react positively to the series. I was more inclined to tell a more balanced story that reminded viewers that King and many other activists applauded the passages of civil rights but continued to insist that more radical changes were needed."

A film treatment is a long prose description of the film-to-be as it will appear on the screen, written scene by scene like a short story. Henry required each team to do a new treatment rewrite that this time would actually emerge as a finished film if all went according to plan.

Henry scheduled a treatment-writing class with Fayer as instructor. "He said, 'I want you to talk to them about dramatic structure in documentary film. I think it's good that we get on the same page about storytelling.' I ran down to the BU bookstore and bought every book on film and scriptwriting that I could find. The thing that saved me was the screenwriter's book with . . . the man up the tree. I have people calling me up to this day: 'I got my man up the tree and now what?'"

The Fayer parable involved chasing the protagonist up a tree (establishing a predicament with something at stake) in the first act, then throwing rocks at him (raising the stakes and introducing jeopardy) in the second act, and then rescuing him from the tree at the end of the third act (resolving it all with action). Fayer knew perfectly well that forcing rowdy unplotted history into the three-act cookie cutter could devolve into a numbing formula. But his articulation of traditional dramatic levers would be a serviceable organizing plan for the *Eyes* films and dozens more.

The problem in documentary is how to impose orderly dramatic structure onto disorderly events, to reconcile the unending tension between life's herky-jerky realities and our apparently hardwired desire for the comfort of satisfying narrative. We all knew that it also opens a door to a Faustian bargain: making messy history unmessy in exchange for holding viewers.

The treatment offers a way to map it all out. In his "Notes on Dramatic Storytelling" memo, distributed on *Eyes on the Prize* and every Blackside project afterward, Fayer wrote, "Know the climax before you write a word on paper, the moment at which all the problems are resolved. Everything leads to this moment, it is your destination, and if you lose sight of it the ending may not be as sharp and forceful as it should be." This reverse engineering would work because fortunately for us, Henry, Judith, and Steve had chosen a dozen battle stories each blessed with a resolute landing, whether for good or for ill: lunch counters were finally desegregated, marchers finally made it all the way to Montgomery, Chief Pritchett outfoxed Rev. King in Albany, Georgia, Freedom Riders finally pushed through to Jackson. Around those very solid narrative anchors we could deploy reams of political nuance, racial heat, and dramatic ambiguity while keeping the audience comfortably grounded. The trick was to not confuse an ending with a happy ending.

Henry and Steve established early on that they would construct each episode not around abstract themes, but around the emotional surge of one or two big campaigns with the themes cleverly baked in: the battle of Montgomery, the battles of Selma, Birmingham—willful people forcing something to *happen* in a specific place at a specific time. Henry said, "Focus on small battles in big wars," with the best available heroes and villains. The forward narrative motion on screen through each hour would rest on overtly dramatic struggles: the courageous stand of Emmett Till's uncle Mose Wright, Jo Ann Robinson's organizing in Montgomery, James Bevel launching the Children's Crusade in Birmingham, local SNCC organizers taking on Lyndon Johnson, and ordinary people facing down the troopers in Selma.

This was, after all, prime-time television. There would, for instance, be no filmed exegesis on the philosophies, strategies, and tactics of nonviolence, but there would be a filmed *story* exploring the *practice* of nonviolence on the first Freedom Ride, in 1961. We would create no cinema essay about the long history of racial murder, but rather a film story of the Emmett Till trial in the context of lynching.

By choosing to do a thorough and well-crafted job on only twelve stories in six programs spanning eleven years, Henry took heat for leaving

out the other ten thousand stories of civil rights. Digging through old production memos, I found long lists of important chapters considered but
abandoned early on: George Wallace defiant in the schoolhouse door in
1963; the blind, white rage unleashed against blacks in St. Augustine, Florida, in the spring of 1964. Several times we discussed with Henry the need
for a section on Robert Williams and the armed Deacons for Defense, and
a "getting to know the racists" sequence. We should have done more with
Little Rock organizer Daisy Bates or Al Lowenstein, who recruited thousands of white students to go south; Ella Baker or Gary Thomas Rowe, the
FBI's informant and provocateur in the Klan. Today these would go onto a
documentary's companion Web site or as DVD bonus extras.

Henry's presence warmed the building, the daily grin, the daily laugh, the
daily dark humor about the "Blackside Death Watch": Which important witness to civil rights history is today sick, fixing to die, or dead? Callie complained, "The first phone calls we made were to people who were saying, 'I'm
not talking to you people. You don't know what you're doing.'" Slowly word
spread up and down the civil rights trail that this new team *did* know what
they were doing. Judy Richardson once again opened many doors.

Henry read the new treatments from his new producers, and he could
not hide his disappointment. When he and I drove Ruth Batson to Logan
Airport, on her way to Africa, he voiced his concern to her, and when we
stopped for a nice Brazilian dinner in East Cambridge, he said, "Birmingham is a piece of shit, and Mississippi is badly written." I had to agree that
after all that work the new treatments were wanting for well-drawn characters and riveting forward motion, but I felt that the expository and dramatic missteps were easily remedied. He was clearly despondent that his
people were missing the point of long-form documentary structure. After
supper we went back to the office and got ourselves reenergized by watching the original *Eyes on the Prize* sample reel, and then deflated again
when we reviewed the producers' notes on which of the aging warriors
they had counted on to tell the story had died.

Feeling all too shaky after weeks of preproduction in the office, we
needed a kick in the pants. So we blasted right out of the gate, to film the first
interview of our reinvented *Eyes on the Prize* with SCLC's Andrew Young.

Hampton and I flew down to New York and slept a few hours at the
Sheraton. I loaded "Eyes on the Prize Camera Roll #1, October 11, 1985"

into Orlando's Arriflex SR camera. We met Callie Crossley and the rest of the crew, Bob Richman and Felipe Borrero, at Judy Richardson's old United Church of Christ office up on Madison Avenue. Henry was a nervous wreck, because a couple of suits from CPB and PBS had tagged along to sit in, and because he was worried Callie would blow it, worried I couldn't make it look good, worried Young would blow us off, that PBS would take the money back, worried about everything.

Andrew Young had been Martin Luther King's levelheaded lieutenant colonel, playing a role in every battle and every newsreel over twenty years; he was everywhere, enduring repeated beatings, tear gas, and jail, finally in the end standing so close to Martin that he was splattered with blood when the assassin's bullet hit. His boundless energy, warm good humor, intellectual chops, and devotion to moral citizenship had gotten him elected to Congress and then appointed ambassador to the United Nations by his fellow Georgian Jimmy Carter. He had been president of the National Council of Churches, and when he spoke with us in 1985, Andy was in his second term as mayor of Atlanta. One of his two bodyguards stood behind the ladies from PBS, the other outside the door. He greeted us like relatives. I asked him if it was fun being mayor of Atlanta, and he said, "I love it; you can do anything you want."

Every major television series has a couple of elders who lived through decades of a particular history—Henry Kissinger did it in *Vietnam: A Television History,* Floyd Dominy did it for me in *Cadillac Desert,* and Andrew Young did it on *Eyes on the Prize.* Before the camera rolled he warned us, "Martin taught me that with journalists you talk about what you want to talk about, not what they want to talk about, so good luck!" He was a warm, precise, and funny storyteller, comfortable in his own skin and in his own unhurried Georgia speech. Callie, the company firecracker, was sharp and professional, with well-formed questions that she asked in smart order.

Andy and Callie talked about Emmett Till, about Montgomery, Birmingham, Mississippi, and Albany, Georgia, but mostly they talked about Selma. In that very first interview he described a little scenelet that would be one of the final moments in the final show of *Eyes on the Prize,* as thousands of white and black demonstrators from Selma approached George Wallace's State House in Montgomery. It involved a sniper.

"John Doar came to me and said, 'Look, we understand that there is a plot on Martin Luther King's life,' and said, 'We can't search every house in

Montgomery. We'd like for you to drive him . . . to the capitol, not let him walk through this entire town.' Well, we normally didn't discuss things like that with Martin. We usually just told him we thought that he needed to ride and didn't tell him the reasons. And he said, 'No.' He wanted to walk in with everybody else. And so finally then we told him what the situation was, and he said that he didn't care. He still wanted to walk.

"Now Martin always wore the good preacher blue suit. I figured since we couldn't stop him from marching, we just had to kind of believe that it was true when white folks said we all look alike. So everybody that was about Martin's size and had on a blue suit, I put in the front of the line with him . . . and, of course, I had on my blue suit. And we all just lined up. But there were some very important people who felt as though they were being pushed back. But all of the preachers *loved* the chance to get up front in the front line with Martin Luther King; it's amazing how many people will risk getting shot just to be on television . . . but I don't think to this day most of them know why they were up there!"

We all had a good time. As the conversation evolved, I could see the tension drain from Henry's body, and he began to smile. We shot an extravagant five rolls of film, a little less than an hour. Flying back to Boston with the boss, I remember thinking, "This is actually going to work, and it might even be great."

Eyes on the Prize was launched.

CHAPTER SEVEN

Not the Other Man's Country

Fall 1985

Filming Andy Young had forced self-confidence upon us, planted the Blackside flag, made the new series real. Now we had to churn our way across the country, revisiting the civil rights players and their movement nearly in its entirety. Callie remembers thinking of them, "It feels as though they lived for someone to take care of their story. . . . It's the last chance, and *we can't mess up these people's story.*"

I had somehow ended up as Blackside's affirmative action point man for hiring minority field crew. It became immediately clear how most film schools and unions had faltered in training black film professionals, and were now trying to catch up. Among the hundreds of really experienced sound recordists and camera people in the country, I could find only a handful of African Americans, nearly all of whom had worked for Blackside before. One guy sighed, "Henry Hampton, he's the only brother who hires black crew. I worked on that Cap Cities original. I love the brother, but he still owes me money from 1978."

Sekou Shepard came on as our soundman, his twin brother Bobby Shepard as our second cinematographer. The Shepards had both joined the Marine Corps after high school in 1964 as an alternative to the bleak prospects in West Harlem, at a time when white college students were doing everything possible to avoid the draft and stop the war. They both survived fierce combat tours in Vietnam. Bobby rose to sergeant, then decided not to pursue a military career and ended up in the excellent minority training program at WNET in New York, which eventually landed him on Hampton's ill-fated film in New Haven. Bobby had sworn he would never work for Blackside again, so when I first asked he politely declined. But in the end he could not resist the movement's aura, and Henry convinced him to help us out on *Eyes.*

My good friend Michael Chin, our first camera assistant, had worked before for Blackside, and like the Shepards, he knew what he was getting into. Mike had never met Henry but heard on the street that "he had all these big ideas . . . but he always paid his bills late . . . but he had grand ideas, a *real* vision."

Mike had studied photography and printmaking at San Francisco State, and had been an activist-artist during campus ethnic studies upheavals in the late 1960s. His first film experience, in Harlem with the original Blackside back in the late 1970s, had made a deep impression. "It was sort of like imprinting, you know when birds come out of the shell, and wake up. I woke up and it was: *Blackside!!!*" He met Orlando Bagwell when they were loading 16mm film magazines together in a back room at Smalls Paradise, and worked with O and Jean-Philippe Boucicaut on Henry's nuclear defense and aircraft carrier films in 1981. He'd done *The Day After Trinity* with me, and shot Wayne Wang's now classic low-budget feature *Chan Is Missing*. When I told *Eyes* production manager Jo Ann Mathieu we had hired an Asian camera assistant, she thought I said "Haitian," happy to have another crew member from the African diaspora, and was surprised when Mike Chin walked into the office.

Henry cranked up his old fantasy of barnstorming across the South in a Winnebago packed with cameras, food, sleeping bags, and crew. Cooler heads prevailed, and in the end we were the most pedestrian of documentary crews: flying economy class on Delta; driving rented vans; sleeping in Ramada Inns, Holiday Inns, Quality Inns, Rodeway Inns, Comfort Inns, Days Inns; eating at Denny's, with a coat-and-tie dress code for the men, skirt and blouse for the women.

By the end I would log 106 flights in "the Hampton Air Force," often falling into exhausted sleep before takeoff. More than once I woke up jammed into a seat having no idea where I had come from or where I was going. (Snapping awake clueless goes with this job; I dozed off at the viewfinder during a numbing interview with the chief interrogator at Guantánamo, and against the blade of a parked bulldozer during a lull on a forest fire shoot in Montana, but never more than on Blackside shoots.)

I set out with Judith and Llew; the other producers would rotate in to meet us on the road to shoot material for all the six episodes.

We gathered seventy-nine interviews on film for *Eyes I*, most of them during that long journey through the Black Belt that fall of 1985. Our crew more or less followed the route of the 1961 Freedom Rides, from the Virginia/Carolina tidewaters down through Georgia, Alabama, and into

Jackson, Mississippi. What a month it was, a blizzard of impassioned stories from the foot soldiers and the great commanders: Georgia Gilmore in Montgomery, Diane Nash in Chicago, Dave Dennis in Mississippi, Assistant Attorney General Nicholas Katzenbach, Alabama governor John Patterson, James Bevel, Melba Pattillo Beals of the Little Rock Nine, Chief of Police Laurie Pritchett in Georgia, and Sheriff Mel Bailey in Birmingham.

Even the most mundane interview setup had a physicality about it: load a few hundred pounds of gear into the vehicles at first light, carry it all into a home, an office, a church, marshal the lights and sound equipment and camera, shoot, wrap, load out, grab a bite, on to the next location, repeat, repeat, repeat, and back to the hotel just before the coffee shop closed at 10 P.M., check the day's headlines (What new catastrophe has befallen South Africa? Reagan bombed Gaddafi?), fill out the camera reports, call home, sleep.

Fancying ourselves "the Henry Hampton All-Stars" on the road, we called it "the Fourteenth Amendment 1985 World Tour," because every question in every interview had deep roots in that fundamental of American equality, the Fourteenth Amendment to the Constitution. It granted birthright citizenship and equal protection under law to all Americans, but most specifically to Americans of African descent newly freed from slavery. (Some of the events we covered were only ninety years away from slavery.) We fought a Civil War over it, ratified the amendment in 1868, and we have been struggling ever since to fulfill its promise, in large part because of a feedback loop in which southern white political power excluded blacks and thus ensured the continuance of southern white political power. At the core of our interviewing was the vexing question of who is responsible for protecting those Fourteenth Amendment citizenship rights: Is it the city, county, state, or the United States itself that decides how people are treated and mistreated, included and excluded?

First stop was Charleston, South Carolina, October 25, 1985, where we picked up Richard Chisholm and a local all-white crew for the first interview, leaving Llew Smith, who was black, back at the Ramada Inn. Vecchione was hoping that without a black person in the room, Thomas Waring, a white moderate, retired newspaperman, would give a more candid account of white southerners' resistance to school integration. But Waring was tepid and just not very interesting, papering over the ferocity of white resistance with phrases like "a great tribute to the underlying good will between the races." Huh? Somehow the old resistance got lost in a fog of revisionist politesse. Waring did introduce the startling fact that in 1959 the local government in Prince Edward County, Virginia, chose to shut down the entire county school system for five years—all schools at all levels, white and colored—rather than educate white and black children together. White kids went to hastily organized private academies supported by state tuition grants and county tax credits, while black children simply had no schooling at all for the next five years, except for a few educated out of state by the Society of Friends.

Llew Smith rejoined us that afternoon for desultory, awkward interviews with Harry and Eliza Briggs, two of the original black petitioners in the *Brown v. Board of Education* desegregation case. Llew had a frustrating time with them, but did elicit a powerful sense of determination from these parents who, upon seeing their children's future slip away, refused to give up the legal fight despite endless threats and bribes from local whites. The white and Negro schools were separate but clearly not equal: the black school had sixty kids in a dilapidated one-room wooden schoolhouse. "All parents had to go in the woods and get wood to give heat for the children." Whites rode the bus to their two-story brick school, passing black children walking on foot six miles in the morning and back home after class.

Much of the "New South" in 1985 was still culturally and socially conservative in the extreme, especially for those of us from libertine San Francisco and hip New York. That evening Judith and I had a long, nervous discussion because our soundman Sekou Shepard arrived from New York with a "goddamned gold earring." Hard to believe now, but we feared that a suave black man showing up in rural Alabama with one gold earring would not put the locals at ease. He might as well have come in a bikini. She politely asked him to stash it away for the duration.

We flew over to Topeka, Kansas, for more lukewarm *Brown v. Board* interviews with the child herself, Linda Brown, now grown, and her mother, now aged. Interesting material, but slim pickings to show for the first couple of long hard days on the road, and we were still all thumbs as a production team.

Undaunted, Judith was bubbly and working nonstop with pen and legal pad—on the plane, at the hotel, in the van. She could be astonishing in her precision as she guided an interview subject to say exactly what needed to be said and nothing extraneous; the only other director I've worked with who comes close to such economy is Ken Burns. She was soon off and running with a great shooting ratio. Judith had wisely assigned Llew to conduct some of the interviewees, but sometimes couldn't restrain herself from backseat kibitzing. Her zeal to get the story right with exact economy came across as whispered badgering, and putting Llew forward as the interviewer sometimes took on the appearance of an awkward ploy. But Llew quickly proved he had the chops and Judith soon sent him out on the road solo to do interviews.

Evenings back at the motel we absorbed the TV news of the day: Jews and Palestinians, the disinherited of the Middle East, were slugging it out again over the hijacking of the cruise liner *Achille Lauro.* As Mike and I had in years past and would for years to come, we caught *Monday Night Football* in the motel, sometimes the newly launched *Cosby Show,* or pro wrestling, unloading and reloading film magazines as we watched. I found myself paying attention to how the cinematographers lit black people and white people in Budweiser commercials.

We pushed through seven cities in our first three days.

Blacks had resisted segregated travel in the South for decades, even back in the days when Frederick Douglass rode the railroad, and the truly organized modern movement had first coalesced in resistance to segregated buses in Montgomery, Alabama, in 1955. With his young wife, Coretta, Martin Luther King had settled there after grad school in Boston, hoping for a quiet place to finish his dissertation, improve his preaching, and give parishioners pastoral counseling with their family problems. But he quickly found himself active in a flurry of church and civic politics, just at the historical moment when years of local NAACP organizing culminated in Rosa Parks's arrest for refusing to give up her seat to a white man. King, the new preacher in town, found himself willingly dragooned into leading the boycott.

Over the coming decade, Henry Hampton and Orlando Bagwell would champion the breadth and power of King's leadership and oratory in half a dozen films, searching at every turn for nuance and complexity beyond the popular image of moral heroism. Henry would be the first filmmaker to look seriously at King's opposition to the Vietnam War, and at his fight for economic equality. It all began here, grounded in the local community, in the 1955 Montgomery bus boycott, the first African American mass uprising to succeed when all others before in the South had failed.

On October 30, 1986, we touched down in Montgomery, one of those small cities still blessed with a humane little airport where you actually walk down off the plane onto the tarmac, into the cozy terminal, and out to the street. A former white segregationist named Fitzgerald, booked into our schedule, had canceled on us the night before. In the preinterview he had told Llew Smith on the phone, "The reason black people sat in the back of the bus was because they had miserable jobs in dirty places and smelled bad; that's why they sat in back." Llew was then faced with a dilemma: in allowing the segregationists to really speak for themselves, how much bullshit could we tolerate? Judith and Henry had both insisted that we never push back, but racist fantasy had its limits. Smith challenged Fitzgerald: "Wait a minute. Weren't they forced to sit in back by the laws of segregation, because they were black?" Llew Smith figured it had pissed Fitzgerald off, so he canceled.

Our researchers had scored a coup by convincing the white former police officer who booked Rosa Parks to give us his first-ever interview. After we arrived at Montgomery police headquarters and were chitchatting with the thirtysomething receptionist, I was surprised that she had apparently never heard of the Montgomery bus boycott, clearly had no idea who Rosa Parks was, and was vague on Martin Luther King. In the end it mattered little, because after two more hours of polite waiting in the lobby in our coats and ties like so many eager missionaries while the receptionist gave increasingly odd excuses, it became clear that the detective, too, was blowing us off.

We'll never know, but that Montgomery police officer may have thought we were out to kill the messenger or put the white sinner in the stocks. Few would speak with candor about the culture of segregation, and who could blame them for not rushing to dredge up insults from the wrong side of history? In documentary it seems few people other than recovering drug addicts and reformed South African bankers are eager to talk honestly about their formerly acceptable outrages.

There remains a strong film to be made about segregationists, especially those conflicted native white southerners who supported the movement but did not speak out; we did not make it. In his later series *Africans in America,* Orlando did a fine job unpacking the psyche of slave owners and exploring how slavery in its way could seem like a *really* great deal for white people who could manage to avoid thinking about it too deeply. Under both slavery and Jim Crow, dirt-cheap labor gave whites freedom at the expense of blacks' freedom.

Back in Boston the Blackside home team did a marvelous interview with aging Virginia Durr, one of the few Montgomery whites who openly supported the boycott. With her husband, attorney Clifford Durr, and E. D. Nixon, she had bailed out Rosa Parks on the afternoon of the arrest. Durr, born in Alabama in 1903, described the system against which Negroes were rebelling. "If you are born into a system that's wrong, whether it's a slave system or whether it is a segregated system, you take it for granted."

Retired white newspaper reporter Joe Azbell told us, "Well, Montgomery in 1955 was a typical Southern city but much more segregated than most because we are the 'Cradle of the Confederacy.' And there was a great deal of talk of states' rights. . . . No black held public office, no black was on any committees whatsoever. . . . They had white toilets, men and women, and colored, men and women. It was a good deal for plumbers. . . . We had separate taxis; you had black taxis and you had white taxis, and the poor white guy that looked in the phone book and called a black taxi, he was told by the black taxi driver, 'I'm sorry I can't take you, you have to call a white taxi.'

"The thing that kept the whites going was segregation, it was the old way: Don't break the old way, don't break this fabric. Don't take this away, this old South . . . these things that we've always known, that we fought a war over."

Virginia Durr put it succinctly: "I think it was the desire to have somebody cook and clean up, and nurse the children, and do the work. You see, the whole thing about the system of segregation, you have to get to the bottom of it, from slavery on, the whole thing has been to have cheap labor. . . . The great desire of mankind is to have somebody else to do the dirty work."

It all may have started with Rosa Parks, but not when most people think, certainly not the day she was arrested. Later, in Detroit congressman John Conyers's office, Callie interviewed Rosa Parks herself, the dainty elder, barely audible, so slight in stature it seemed she might blow away. How could this birdlike creature have launched a mass movement?

She had guarded her privacy after the movement years and gave few interviews. So popular culture, with a mind of its own, stripped her of her lifelong history of activism and fury at American injustice, and created the legend of the simple, quiet woman who impulsively disrupted segregation on the spur of the moment. The *New York Times* had called her the "accidental matriarch of the civil rights movement," but there was nothing accidental about it.

Henry was determined to undo the inspirational fable of a "tired seamstress who just wanted to sit down." Her image as a prim lady perfectly suited for a test case was accurate as far as it went. *Eyes* could restore a full portrait of the granddaughter of a slave and slave owner, a tough and savvy lifelong activist who had been organizing for decades, worked to free black men falsely accused of raping white women, and was unafraid of associating with Malcolm X and later with the Black Panthers. Strains of black radicalism and protest ran through her life: the Scottsboro Boys, Marcus Garvey, sessions at Highlander Folk School, the social justice training center where "We Shall Overcome" originated. She had been schooled in a deep understanding of American citizenship and the rights that it guaranteed. There were close friends active in the Sharecroppers Union and Communist Party, midnight meetings with the "kitchen table covered with guns."

She was forty-three when she was arrested, and knew well that many blacks had been jailed for sitting in the wrong place on a city bus in Montgomery. Bus drivers carried pistols, and police shot a black man in 1950 for refusing to enter a bus by the rear door. She decidedly did not spring up like a "lightbulb moment," that favorite of American mythmaking, but had helped drive the NAACP's long effort to find a perfect test case. Rosa Parks's action was certainly disruptive both in the Darwinian evolutionary sense and in the way we now see "disruption" in high tech, a sudden explosive change, but it was embedded in a calculated decades-long organizing effort. Hers was a philosophy and strategy as patiently simmered as Martin Buber's, Martin Luther King's, or Henry Hampton's view of Christian social justice.

Henry would press us toward an understanding that, as his nephew Jacob remembered, "None of the important stuff happens when the event happens"; we should pull the planning, strategizing, and organizing out of the background and into the foreground. It was a kind of dogged organizing for social change that meant putting your own body in real jeopardy, and certainly required long-haul persistence.

In her soft little voice, Parks told us: "The front seats were occupied, and this one man, a white man standing. At this point the driver asked us to stand up and let him have those seats and when . . . none of us moved at his first words, he said, 'Y'all make it light on yourselves and let me have those seats.'" All the blacks except Rosa Parks gave up their seats.

She spoke to us with meticulous calm about how the same bus driver, Jim Blake, had ejected her from a bus twelve years before, and about her decade of working with local NAACP chairman E. D. Nixon of the Brotherhood of Sleeping Car Porters, "mayor of black Montgomery," who had soldiered on for years unheralded and ignored. Rosa Parks embodied the test case they had been looking for: middle-aged, religious, of good character, attractive, known and respected in the community for her political work, happily married, working class in income, middle class in demeanor, well educated and well spoken, sympathetic to a wide spectrum of black and white Montgomerians, and she had a clean police record. Rosa Parks was a living Sermon on the Mount.

The Montgomery bus boycott had been lying in wait for the proper trigger. Back on *America, We Loved You Madly,* when Henry, Judy, and Orlando had interviewed Jo Ann Robinson, English teacher at the local all-black college, president of the Women's Political Council, a real firecracker, she'd told them, "We had gone through it over and over in our minds, on paper, and even the courts came into an awareness of the fact that the women had planned this bus boycott." Sitting on a lawn, she explained the intricate plans already in place for months, and how she stayed up all night after Parks was arrested, typing and clandestinely running off 35,000 flyers on the school's mimeograph machine and distributing them through a prearranged phone-tree communication system within churches, public schools, men's and women's clubs, and the Women's Political Council.

"And one lone black woman who was so 'faithful to her white lady' . . . went back to work and took one of the circulars to this woman so she would know what the blacks had planned. When the white woman got it, she immediately called the media, and then following the television, the radios, and evening newspapers; everybody told those persons whom we had not reached, that there would be the boycott. So the die was cast."

At dawn on the cold, cloudy morning of December 5, 1955, Jo Ann Robinson scanned the streets, fearful that if it rained people would ride the bus. "But as the buses began to roll and there were one or two people on some of them, none on some of them, then we began to realize that the people were cooperating and that they were going to stay off the bus that first day.

"The spirit, the desire, the injustices that had been endured by thousands of people through the years, I think that people had reached the point that they knew there was no return, that they had to do it or die. It was the sheer spirit for freedom, for the feeling of being a *man* and a *woman*."

That night, after a day of boycott, thousands attended a mass rally (described in the white press as a "top secret meeting") at the Holt Street Baptist Church, to let the community decide whether to continue beyond that first day. Jo Ann Robinson said, "The church itself holds four or five thousand people. But there were thousands of people outside of the church that night. And they had to put loudspeakers so they would know what was happening."

Newsman Joe Azbell, one of the few whites present that night, told us, "The Holt Street Baptist Church was probably, in my lifetime so far, the most fired up, enthusiastic gathering of human beings that I've ever seen. That audience was so on fire . . . the preacher would get up and say, 'Do you want your freedom?' And they'd say, 'Yes, I want my freedom!' 'Are you for what we're doing?' 'Yes, go ahead, go ahead!'

"I've never heard singing like that. . . . (There was no one taking a tape of it.) They were on fire for freedom . . . a spirit there that no one could capture in a movie. And then King stood up. . . . It's been said that if he had said go tear up the town, they would have gone and torn up the town. But they were peaceful, they were. Even at that early first meeting . . . called for law and order . . . don't y'all do anything illegal now, y'all stay right. And then they got to singing again and the voices would come back, 'Yes, go ahead, Amen, tell Jesus, tell Jesus!'"

King, a newcomer in town and not entirely sure he was the right person to lead the boycott, prepared his speech in the car on the way to Holt Street. Unfortunately we had only the transcribed text of King's speech that night, not a recording. "I want it to be known that we're going to work with grim and bold determination to gain justice on the buses in this city. And we are not wrong. . . . If we are wrong, the Supreme Court of this nation is wrong. If we are wrong, the Constitution of the United States is wrong. If we are wrong, God Almighty is wrong!"

Later, Rev. Ralph Abernathy would describe to us the singing that night: "The fear that had shackled us across the years all left suddenly when we were in that church together. And I can tell you the name of the first song that we sang, and it was 'Leaning on the Everlasting Arms.'"

Jo Ann Robinson explained the unanimous vote to continue the boycott. "They had been touched by the persecution, the humiliation that many of them had endured on buses. And they voted for it unanimously, and that meant thousands of people." And, not for the first time, the newborn movement could count on the media to spread its word. Azbell said, "I went back and I wrote, on the editorial page the next day, in a special column, I wrote that this was the beginning of a flame that would go across America."

Henry and crew had done one of the last film interviews with black Montgomery organizer E. D. Nixon back in 1978, before he passed away. Now we filmed Rufus Lewis, one of young Rev. King's senior parishioners. As director of a black funeral home in 1955, Lewis had access to cars and set up the boycott transportation center. He worked out the intricate scheduling of hundreds of private vehicles and Montgomery's eighteen black-owned taxi companies to get tens of thousands of black citizens to and from work for over a year without their using buses.

Virginia Durr told us, "It didn't take long for white housewives to wonder 'Where's my cook? Where's my maid?' and began driving their own cars to pick up the help.

"The strange thing that happened was a kind of a play between white women and black women. The mayor issued advice saying that if the white women of Montgomery would stop taking their maids back and forth, the boycott would end because then they would have to walk in the rain. . . . Some of them said, 'Well, if he wants to come out and do my cooking and laundry and nurse the children and clean up, he can,' because her whole life was built on this maid."

Georgia Gilmore, a black maid who walked three miles a day month after month, explained to us the role of the black radio station, the first media to report Mrs. Parks's arrest. Llew Smith and I had gotten completely drenched in a torrential Alabama cloudburst while loading our equipment into her modest home, and I sat behind the camera in her living room shivering in soaking wet clothes, enjoying the fresh rain smell, hoping she would not notice the little pool of water around me on her rug. "Well, you know a lot of times some of the young whites would come along and they would say, 'Nigger, don't you know it's better to ride the bus than it is to walk?' And we would say, 'No, cracker. No, we rather walk.'"

Virginia Durr's brother-in-law, Supreme Court justice Hugo Black, got wind of the action and told her, "'When you get back to Montgomery, you tell your friend Dr. King to take those children off the streets and those people off the streets or they're gonna be massacred.' So when I went back to Montgomery, I . . . spoke to him and said I had a message from . . . Justice Black and I told him what he'd said. And he looked at me and he said, 'Mrs. Durr, you tell Justice Black that I feel exactly the way he does. I'm terrified those people are going to be shot down and massacred.' But he said, 'There's something more important than that.' And he said, 'The only way they're ever gonna become able to be men and women in their own right and stand up to the world is to lose that fear.'"

The bus company was soon losing thirty thousand fares a day, testament to the massive economic power of its second-class citizens, who provided two thirds of the company's income. Police took to stopping carpool drivers for hundreds of minuscule or imaginary violations; they served up seventeen tickets in two months to the obsessively law-abiding Jo Ann Robinson herself, and fines strained the movement's meager treasury. Night riders dynamited the homes of E. D. Nixon, Martin Luther King, and four other ministers. Police jailed King (the first of his thirty arrests) and twenty-two other ministers, and the Alabama White Citizens' Council drew thousands of white Montgomerians to the largest pro-segregation rally of the century, featuring Senator James Eastland of Mississippi, who pledged to "utterly destroy" any whites who did not support segregation. The Klan marched in full regalia through downtown and through black neighborhoods.

Henry was determined to communicate the often forgotten fact that the mammoth yearlong project was launched and sustained entirely by thousands of *local* citizens, and not a single leader from the outside. Martin Luther King himself was at the time a completely unknown twenty-six-year-old Black Belt preacher. (King and Abernathy did accept informal strategy advice from the Fellowship of Reconciliation's Bayard Rustin, but had to keep him out of sight because of Rustin's reputation as a homosexual Communist. For some supremacists the only thing lower than a nigger was a nigger fag, and below that a nigger fag Communist. Rustin slipped in and out of Montgomery, crouched on the floor of a car, or posed as a reporter from *France-Soir* and *Le Figaro*.)

Financial support from northern whites, particularly Unitarians and Quakers, rolled in. With their oratory, King and Abernathy fueled the nightly mass meetings, inspiring everyone to fight on. Slowly national press took notice and ramped up its attention to what was developing into the country's first truly mass movement against segregation. At one point, thirty newspaper, radio, and news film reporters covered a mass meeting, filing stories in India, France, England, Germany, Japan, and the Netherlands and to the *New York Times,* which described King as "inscrutable." Blackside researchers would track some of these down thirty years later.

The boycott stretched into a second Christmas season. Jo Ann Robinson told Judy Richardson, "In thirteen months, the bus company had completely been put out of business. There was no transportation at all for anybody, white or black, and whites constituted about a third of the riders anyway. Half of them had stopped riding, before many weeks after the beginning of the bus boycott, out of sympathy."

Legal bus segregation by race was doomed. In archive footage these cooks, maids, nannies, laborers, and janitors whom Henry so revered, tens of thousands, walked for more than a year, yet the white city government and bus company met none of their modest demands, until the Supreme Court declared Alabama's state and local segregation laws unconstitutional, and the boycott organizers declared victory on December 20, 1965. As Henry often quoted Douglass: "The limits of tyrants are prescribed by the endurance of those whom they oppress."

Blackside researchers found news film of the victory celebration that night, Ralph Abernathy raising a praise shout for the victorious community. "This show, is *your* show . . . the show of Negroes all over America . . . this show is the show of all freedom-loving people all over the world." The movement had crafted a strategy, as King said: "Christ showed us the way, and Gandhi in India showed it could work."

I had a hell of a time keeping Rufus Lewis in frame as he described the victory, waving his arms and hurling his body to and fro with joyful abandon. "When the bus boycott was over, the blacks got on the bus to sit on the *front* seat *just to show off.* And they had a lot of fun, sitting on the front seat, riding up to the college, or riding away from the college. *Nobody* sat in the back then; *all* of them sat on the front. It was a *jubilation.* It was a *joy!*"

King said the victory would benefit all races, not just colored. "In the long run, it is more honorable to walk in dignity than ride in humiliation.

So . . . we decided to substitute tired feet for tired souls, and walk the streets of Montgomery."

Sitting on the grass in 1979, Jo Ann Robinson told Henry, Orlando, and Judy, "We felt that we were *citizens*. We felt that we were somebody, that somebody had to listen to us, that we had forced the white man to give what we knew was a part of our own citizenship . . . we had won that. And if you have never had the feeling that this is not the other man's country and you are an alien in it, but that this is *your* country too, then you don't know what I'm talking about. But it is a . . . hilarious feeling that just goes all over you, that makes you feel that America is a great country and we're going to do more to make it greater."

These lines moved Henry Hampton more than any other in *Eyes on the Prize,* and in years to come he often folded Jo Ann's words into his own speeches and essays about the painful notion of being "immigrants in our own country."

It led to formation of the Southern Christian Leadership Conference, and marked the start of Dr. King's meteoric rise to his not always comfortable role as leader of America's civil rights movement. His picture on the cover of *Jet* was soon eclipsed by his picture on the cover of *Time* magazine in February 1957, the first of five such celebrated appearances.

The Montgomery story in *Eyes* would in the end be whittled down by the frustrating demands of screen time to a shadow of what it could have been, still strong but a shadow nonetheless. Except for the underlying story of her lifelong organizing, editors had little choice but to simply consign most of Rosa Parks's backstory to the Blackside archive.

In 1985, the only people I saw riding buses in Montgomery were black.

A few years later, I saw a giant picture of Rosa Parks, serene and austere, covering the outside of a city bus in Palo Alto with the words "Think Different" and a big Apple logo: the perfect postmodern hall of mirrors. She was now in service to a brand of computer. Did Steve Jobs or the people at the Chiat\Day ad agency in Santa Monica have any idea what Rosa Parks was really about? Were they indifferent to the decades of tireless work and political savvy, or was she once again simply the meek seamstress who decided on the spur of the moment to upend segregation? Soon buses with Cesar Chavez, Nelson Mandela, the Dalai Lama, Mahatma Gandhi, and Martin Luther King himself popped up, posthumously contracted by the Silicon Valley corporation as emblems of "disruption." No one had the nerve to put Jesus or Malcolm X on the side of a "Think Different" bus.

· · · · · ·

It was on to Little Rock, Arkansas. In September 1957, after making an inflammatory speech the night before court-ordered school integration was
to take effect, Arkansas governor Orval Faubus deployed the Arkansas National Guard around prestigious Central High School with orders to admit
only white students. Next morning the troops confronted a mob of a thousand. By turning away the eight black students who arrived, the governor
was using Alabama state forces to prevent enforcement of federal law. One
black teenager, Elizabeth Eckford, arrived by herself and was quickly surrounded by the enraged whites, saved only by an anonymous woman who
emerged from the pack and managed to get her safely onto a city bus before
fading back into the crowd. The mob then attacked black reporters.

Hampton and his advisors wanted to remind Americans, who had
surely forgotten, that the governors of Alabama and Mississippi, claiming
the legal doctrines of "nullification" and "interposition," had aggressively
and unapologetically blocked enforcement of federal law that had been
unanimously settled in the *Brown v. Board of Education* desegregation
case. He also wanted to articulate how Eisenhower and Kennedy were
willing to deploy thousands of heavily armed federal troops to assert the
supremacy of the federal government over the state government.

Judith conducted a masterful interview with the courageous federal
judge John Minor Wisdom, who sat on the southern Fifth Circuit. Talking
of Governor Faubus, Wisdom told us, "The doctrine is that a state may
interpose itself between the national government and some action that is
sought to be imposed upon the state by the federal government. The supremacy clause, which provides that in case of a conflict between the
nation and the states, the law of the nation prevails, makes *hash* of the
doctrine of interposition and any lawyer worth his salt knows that." President Eisenhower agreed and said of Little Rock, "This blot on the honor of
our nation will be removed. . . . Mob rule will not be allowed to override
the decision of our courts." At the request of Little Rock's mayor he placed
Faubus's guardsmen under federal control, and also ordered a thousand
regular army paratroopers of the 101st Airborne, with a helicopter overhead, to escort nine black students to high school the next day. Governor
Faubus, seeing northern soldiers in his capital city for the first time since
the War Between the States, said, "We are now an occupied territory . . .
what is happening in America?"

We sat down with white public relations executive Craig Rains, who had been on the student council at Central High back in '57. After Eisenhower sent soldiers to his school to control the mob, "My first thought was not that we were going to have to go to school with blacks, that didn't bother me, but that we were being told by the federal government to do something and we didn't have any say-so in."

Rains said he had ushered the first disoriented black students to the school office, and began to change his position on the state's right to deny equal education. "And I also developed a real dislike for the people that were out there that were causing problems. It was very unsettling to me."

Rains talked about Minnijean Brown, Melba Pattillo Beals, Ernest Green, and the other black students. "So one day I asked Ernest if he'd come join us for lunch. And he got his tray, and came over and sat down with us. And then I realized it was very awkward to talk with him. Because I began to realize that I didn't have anything in common with him, other than we were in the same school. I couldn't talk about things that you do after school, 'cause I didn't know whether the black kids did the same things we did; I mean, that's how segregated we were."

The 101st Airborne soldiers occupied Craig and Ernest's school his entire senior year, protecting the Little Rock Nine from white violence, to the fascination of the national press. At my middle school in Sacramento, California, we knew their names and followed the events on television and radio day by day; young Henry Hampton did the same in segregated St. Louis. Rains, like 100 percent of the white southerners we interviewed, still carried resentment at the way the northern liberal press had often failed to report on moderate white southerners, and how the northerners saw what local whites considered "the state's right to decide" as the state's right to oppress.

Elizabeth Eckford, who had been caught alone in the white crowd on the first day of school, had become very reclusive in the intervening years since 1957, moved to Canada, and refused to be interviewed in 1985. But Henry had filmed a fine interview with Ernest Green for Cap Cities and later we would interview another of the nine, Melba Pattillo Beals.

We were foraging, slowly weaving together old and new anecdotes from different points of view, conflicting shreds of history and memory, bits of newsreel film, documents, snapshots, songs, confirmed facts for narration, all the ingredients of a nonfiction television show. Movies are shot out of order, one tiny piece at a time, so in the heat of production you have little sense of the whole that will eventually coalesce. We were shooting *six* movies out of order. Assembling them from chaos to coherence would mean reverse engineering tens of thousands of little pieces of raw film over weeks and months to form a documentary. (Imagine an ultra-slow-motion video of a porcelain vase arcing through the air and shattering on the floor. Now run the event backward in ultra-slow-motion reverse: a million unconnected little fragments rise up with excruciating slowness, and at last magically unite into a magnificent vase floating slowly up into the air; so it is with assembling a documentary.)

But what if there is no news footage? How much of white resistance and black resolve was out of the camera's view? Were not most of the tears shed in private? How many martyrs died alone in the woods at night? In cases where there was no filmed record, all we could do was gather as many participants as possible and edit their bites to refract the event from multiple points of view.

For example: A police captain spirited the nine black students out a back door when the mob surrounded Central High on the first day of school. They were then escorted back into the school two days later in a regular army caravan armed with machine guns, under the gaze of news cameras, and began a long painful school year like none other in American history. Each black student was assigned an individual soldier, but still they faced relentless harassment and isolation in the face of segregationist resistance, with all cameras barred from the building. Here's how they recounted it for us:

Craig Rains: "I remember lunch was particularly interesting, because I had the same lunch period as the blacks did. There were a group of white boys, they would taunt the black students. And they had to be very subtle about it, because the 101st was standing maybe twenty feet away, at the door to the cafeteria, but the taunts could be heard by the black students."

Ernest Green: "Every time we went to lunch, we were always hassled and heckled by a number of white kids. Part of it was the attitude at that time that somehow we were supposed to be so stoic that we weren't to retaliate to any of this. For a couple of weeks there had been a number of white kids following us . . . continuously calling us 'niggers, nigger, nigger, nigger,' one right after the other."

Melba Patillo Beals: "There was this huge cafeteria . . . you're going to get food splattered on you, you're going to get tripped . . . you were always going to get heckled."

Craig Rains: "Minnijean had been getting more than her fair share of taunts because she would talk back. The other black students kept to themselves, and as the Bible says, they would turn the other cheek. Minnijean would snap back at people and so that caused her to become a target."

Melba Patillo Beals: "She was a big black woman, tall, pensive, thoughtful, and creative. Minnijean was under a great amount of stress because both of us were big. . . . I could see day by day a little bit of her being chewed away . . . every day a little bit of her automatically telling herself, 'No, I can't hit back . . .' And yet, going further out in the edge just like all of us were."

Ernest Green: "We were standing in the lunch line, Minni, myself, two others I think. And there was this white kid behind Minni, and this fellow couldn't have been more than five feet four. He was going to 'nigger' her to death. . . . And he reminded me of a small dog yelping at somebody's leg. And she had just gotten a bowl of chili from the cafeteria and . . ."

Melba Patillo Beals: "She just couldn't handle it anymore . . . and I could just see her little head click, she consciously said to herself, 'No, Minnijean, if you do this you know you won't be here,' but then this was a time of the year when we *all* didn't want to be there."

Ernest Green: "And before I could even say . . . 'Minni, why don't you tell 'em to shut up?' . . . without even blinking an eye, Minni turned around and took that chili and dumped it on this dude's head. He was standing there, the last 'nigger' coming out of his mouth with chili rolling off his face."

Craig Rains: "She just proceeded to dump it on top of this fellow's head . . . and a lot of people started cheering and laughing, but immediately the troops came over to make sure nothing was going to happen, and got her out. We thought it was kind of funny at our table."

Ernest Green: "Silence. I mean . . . all the kitchen help in the cafeteria were black. And some of them we knew, because they either went to churches or lived in the same neighborhood that many of us did. It was just absolute silence in the place. And then the help, all black, broke into applause. The rest of the white students, there was just absolute silence. Nobody knew what to do; I'm sure it's the first time a white kid had seen somebody black physically retaliate against somebody white. . . . And it was a good feeling to see that happen, to be able to let them know that we were capable of taking care of ourselves."

Craig Rains: "The chili wasn't that hot apparently, but we had seen her do some things that we did not think were good for the situation that was going on."

Ernest Green: "And, with that, the school board suspended Minni."

Melba Patillo Beals: "She found a way out; and I was so jealous."

Craig Rains: "The White Citizens' Council would bring things to school and pass them out, and it was really hate literature. When Minnijean . . . was kicked out of school following the chili incident, they brought cards and gave them out that said 'One down, eight to go.'"

Not a single second of this event was on film, only their testimony to us, which Judith and her editor, Dan Eisenberg, fashioned into a riveting sequence.

The kids made it through the whole year, all the way to graduation in June 1958. Ernest Green remembers applause for the dozens of students who walked to the podium before him. But, "When they called my name there was nothing, just the name and there was this eerie silence. Nobody clapped. But I figured they didn't have to 'cause after I got that diploma that was it. I had accomplished what I had come there for." After the last day of school, Melba Pattillo Beals "came home and by myself I walked to the backyard and burned my books and I burned everything that I could burn and I just stood there crying, looking into the fire."

After Orval Faubus finally closed down all the high schools in Little Rock, black and white, to prevent integration, citizens elected him for a third term. Inspired by "what we saw in Little Rock," college student Joe McNeil and three others staged the first sit-in of the modern civil rights movement in Greensboro, North Carolina.

On the fortieth anniversary of the crisis President Bill Clinton, Arkansas native, ceremoniously opened the doors of Central High and welcomed all of the Little Rock Nine. As it turned out, federal courts would adjudicate school desegregation in Little Rock for nearly sixty years, the legal battles grinding on until 2014, when they finally ended with an ambiguity that satisfied no one. Little Rock's Central High, today about half black and half white, is peaceful.

We had our pictures taken, like tourists, in front of the school, and headed for Georgia.

• • • • • •

Deciding whom to interview on camera for *Eyes* in 1985 had been easy: Judith Vecchione said, "Ask yourself, Whose story is this to tell?" and look for the good and reliable storytellers with direct experience. Then split it between the leaders and the foot soldiers on both sides of the struggle, not the experts who wrote about them. Stick to the mandate, "If you weren't there, you can't be in the movie."

The articulate college-educated leaders were, of course, magnets for us, and if Henry, Judy, Vincent, and Clay hadn't hounded producers about the local people, we could have gone on interviewing Andy Young, Virginia Durr, and Bob Moses all year. It resembled the disconnect between SNCC's determination to let local leadership rise from below and the hyperabundance of hyperarticulate leaders inside SNCC. But Hampton, the scholars, and Richardson knew that was a trap that would land us right back in the same old picture, showing few strong men and precious few women at the top winning liberty for all the downtrodden at the bottom.

Producers had been prepping their interview questions for weeks. Judith said in her clear memo: "Strip out all the non-essentials. . . . Be thoroughly versed in the story, more than anyone who's ever interviewed this person before. Don't bait and switch. We do not pay for interviews. Above all, don't let them ramble." It would be surgical, or at least clinical. It is a fact that historical documentary interviewers seldom discover new information, but rather elicit a superb telling of tales we already know from academics and journalists who had done the research long before, in as few takes as possible.

Judith and Henry extended the original meager film allotment of twenty-five minutes of stock per interview to a less meager forty minutes, partly to create at least a bit more historical record beyond what would be used on screen in *Eyes*.

For the story of the Albany, Georgia, movement we flew the storytellers, who were now scattered around the country, to Atlanta and put them up overnight in a Holiday Inn where Mike and I had set up an improvised ministudio in a hotel room. I rigged lights until ten, hit the sack, was just falling asleep when Henry called from Boston, excited about a 15-minute TV microspecial on Martin Luther King he wanted to pitch to PBS.

On the evening before our interviews Albany's white former police chief Laurie Pritchett, now in his sixties, was having supper in the hotel coffee shop when he spotted former Albany activist Dr. William Anderson and thought, "I know that black man over there; I arrested him once." Laurie walked over and introduced himself; the two men began chatting and shut down the bar hours later.

Pritchett had indeed arrested Anderson more than once, together with thousands of other Albany blacks willing to accept jail time as they attempted to transform their 100 percent segregated hometown. Anderson explained, "Going to jail was one of the most feared things in rural Georgia. There were many blacks arrested in small towns in Georgia who were never heard from again."

Movement strategists had high hopes that the Albany campaign would follow close on the heels of the successful Montgomery movement and Freedom Rides. But Chief Pritchett had been locked in a stalemate with SNCC's Charles Sherrod for months (Pritchett told Sherrod, "It's a matter of mind over matter: I don't mind and you don't matter"). When SNCC's efforts to organize in Albany stalled, the local leaders convinced Dr. King to drive over from Atlanta for a mass meeting.

Suspecting that King, no longer an unknown, might come to town, Pritchett read his writings about Montgomery, familiarized himself with the strategies of Gandhi, and even gave his officers workshops on how to deal with classic nonviolent tactics. He vowed, "We're going to out-nonviolent them," and kept federal intervention at bay by avoiding the public police violence against demonstrators that had been common fare elsewhere in the South.

But Pritchett sent busloads of his detainees to jails in surrounding counties, where other lawmen and jailers doled out very rough treatment. Back in New York we had interviewed Wyatt Tee Walker, SCLC executive director, who said that Pritchett himself "was non*brutal* rather than non-violent. I'd say he was slick. It's bizarre to say that . . . a law enforcement official of a segregationist system could be nonviolent, because nonviolence works in a moral climate and segregation is not a moral climate." Sitting with us in 1985, Chief Pritchett struck me as a smart, cagey, and decent fellow who back in the 1960s had clearly understood that integration was coming, whether he liked it or not.

When King arrived in Albany for the evening meeting on December 14, 1961, Dr. Anderson put him on the spot by asking him from the pulpit to stay overnight and join the sit-in the next day; King agreed and immediately found himself in the Albany jail with Ralph Abernathy and several hundred others. The two SCLC leaders refused to pay their bail or fine and vowed to stay in jail until Albany was desegregated.

But within four days a mysterious black man arrived with a thousand dollars in cash and paid their fine. Rev. Abernathy later told us, "Some person unknown to me paid the fine and that messed up my plans and the plans of Dr. King. When Mr. Pritchett came down and unlocked the door, he said, 'You may go now,' and Dr. King asked why, and he said, 'Somebody has paid your fine,' and we do not know to this day who paid the fine." Once in a blue moon on the road, the producers beat the academics and came up with a nice new tidbit of history. Jim DeVinney asked Laurie Pritchett about the unknown fine payer. He replied, "It was a matter of strategy. I knew that if King stayed in jail, we'd continue to have problems, so I talked to some people, I said, 'We've got to get him out, and once we do, I think he'll leave here.' And arrangements were made; frankly, I don't know who the man was that paid the bond."

"But it was done at your request?"

"Yes, it was done at my request. And it sort of surprised Dr. King—this was one time, the only time I've ever seen when . . . he didn't know which way to go." King was arrested twice more and finally left town depressed, with Albany nearly as segregated as when he arrived. But SNCC, so tied to local people and the local movement, soldiered on without him. Sherrod said, "Don't get weary . . . victory is not to the swift or to the strong. We didn't stop a beat. King left, but we kept moving."

Now it was on to Birmingham—"Bombingham"—driving past the fifty-seven-foot-tall cast-iron statue of Vulcan, Roman god of fire, reminder of the town's former blast-furnace glory, which had inspired Fayer through that long night of treatment writing years before. It was hard not to notice his enormous cast-iron bare butt mooning the surrounding suburbs. This was once a thundering steel town, one of the most racially divided cities in the country, now settled into being nice enough but a little dreary by the time the Blackside crew arrived in 1985. Andy Young had set the tone by telling us how in 1957 two KKK men had stopped a random young black man on the street, beaten him, then taken him to their office, castrated him, and dumped him on the highway. The castrators were caught only because two younger Klansmen vomited during the ritual and then told their wives, who went to the police. Fifty-nine bombings of black churches, homes, and businesess had rocked the city, all unsolved.

Ralph Abernathy said, "Probably in the whole state of Alabama where I grew up we had less than five black doctors . . . we didn't do anything but dig ditches and work with some white supervisor. . . . We could not sit on the grand juries. We could not sit on any jury, period. There were no black judges . . . we in the midfifties were where they are at this particular hour in South Africa . . . the worst city this side of Johannesburg." With a population of more than a quarter million in 1963, Birmingham had not a single black police officer, firefighter, bus driver, or downtown sales clerk. James Bevel told us, "In Birmingham most adults felt that segregation was permanent. That it was just that way. That was a permanent system."

Wyatt Tee Walker, the wily and fiery SCLC strategist, had laid out the basics of the 1963 Birmingham campaign. He had a spikiness about him, playing James Brown to Andy Young's Sam Cooke.

Walker said, "I wrote a document, probably seven or eight typed pages, called 'Project C.' . . . My theory was that if we mounted a strong nonviolent movement, the opposition would surely do something to a) attract the media, and b) induce national sympathy and attention to what the everyday segregated circumstance of a black person was like living in the Deep South. . . . Dr. King's feeling was that if nonviolence wouldn't work in Birmingham, then it wouldn't work anywhere. And I think we were fearful that probably King, Abernathy, Shuttlesworth, Walker, and maybe Young would not get out of Birmingham alive. I know when I kissed my wife and four children good-bye in February and went to Birmingham, I didn't really believe I'd ever see them again."

Henry had learned that if you look behind any one of the iconic southern confrontations, you will find local leaders of astonishing courage who labored in obscurity for decades at great personal risk, long before the high-profile leaders and press arrived. Many of these, like Birmingham's rough-and-ready Rev. Fred Shuttlesworth, were ministers of the Gospel, sustained by deep empowering faith in God. Shuttlesworth was fearless, a former moonshiner, truck driver, and cement worker. He had led the initial boycott, been arrested thirty-five times, beaten many times over, and chain whipped in front of his young daughter when he attempted to enroll her in a white elementary school. Public Safety Commissioner Bull Connor's men had arrested Rev. Shuttlesworth and three other ministers for vagrancy in his own house. His church had been bombed twice by the time white militants bombed his home.

"The Klan set . . . sixteen sticks of dynamite right at the head of my bed . . . the corner of the house, and I was in the bed at the point of the blast. . . . It blew the wall away, it blew the floor out from under my bed. The springs that I was lying on, we never found them. There I was lying on the mattress. I knew the relevance of Moses's statement when he said, 'Underneath are the everlasting arms.'"

It was a miracle he had survived to appear in *Eyes on the Prize*. Shuttlesworth, barely five feet tall, took command the moment he walked in. He cut right to the matter at hand, the movement's unending balance between confrontation and persuasion. "America, look at your promises, and look at how you're treating your poor Negro citizens. You ought to be ashamed of yourself. But you know, you can't shame segregation. . . . Ball teams don't strike themselves out; you gotta put 'em out." We all knew that tacked on the wall of Henry Hampton's office were the words of Frederick Douglass: "Power concedes nothing without a demand. It never did and it never will." Fred put it more directly: "Rattlesnakes don't commit suicide."

So it was in Birmingham, with the archracist Bull Connor stepping right up in the role of public rattlesnake. Shuttlesworth threw himself into the fight, was blown off his feet by a fire hose, and "thought I was dying for the third or fourth or fifth time. And God seemed to speak to me and said, 'Not yet.'" Seeing Shuttlesworth heading for the hospital, Bull Connor said, "I wished they'd carried him away in a hearse."

With the church in America today so polarized, fractured, and ill attended, and sometimes more associated with the contraction of democracy rather than its expansion, we often forget that our civil rights movement was rooted almost entirely in fundamentalist black churches in the South. It was driven by parishioners, deacons, theologians, and ministers of astonishing eloquence, seldom plagued by religious doubt of any sort. The Sermon on the Mount was their guiding text. They were steadfast in their beliefs, the religious opposites of Henry's ever-questioning Unitarians, who were equally committed to the same cause. Our Christian intellectuals have now mostly withdrawn their gifts from political action. The church-based civil rights movement was an outlier among most twentieth-century postcolonial and liberation struggles exploding around the same time in Algeria, India, and sub-Saharan Africa, nearly all of which were secular.

Having survived successive attempts to kill him, Rev. Shuttlesworth said, "I'm happy to be used by God. This was a divine interjection, or interference in human affairs. God always has to use men, and in every situation there *is* a man. . . . Here I am. This is my duty. If God is with me, how can I lose, leaning on the everlasting arms."

Coming out of what Henry called "the morass" in Albany, Georgia, with King's image somewhat on the wane, but having learned the financial power of a bus boycott in Montgomery, SCLC's initial tactical weapon in Birmingham was their plan to completely end black patronage of downtown stores. By pinpointing specific retail targets, they would force business leaders to open employment to all and to integrate public facilities. King had said, "The purpose of . . . direct action is to create a situation so crisis-packed that it will inevitably open the door to negotiation." Andy Young told us that the economic boycotts and marches "essentially stopped the black community and white people of good will from buying anything except food and medicine. . . . That was basically a workable plan in any community. The profit margin in most businesses is ten or fifteen percent, and if you take the black community in the Black Belt out, you could cut the profit by fifty percent. You could stop business in almost any city in America with an organized effort and daily demonstrations."

Massive sit-in demonstrations began in April 1963 with kneel-ins at white churches and sit-ins at Woolworth's lunch counter, but soon stalled because organizers had only a finite number of citizens willing to face jail.

I had last seen Ralph Abernathy in Selma in 1965, thundering the "rousements" from the pulpit before a march. But when Rev. Abernathy shuffled into the parsonage for our interview in Atlanta, he greeted us so haltingly that I hardly recognized him. He was only sixty years old but seemed a hundred, slow of speech, so frail he might just die on us right there from the heat of the lights and the strain of the interview. Were we too late?

"Where do I look?"

"You look at me."

"Oh, good."

" 'Cause I'm the prettiest one in the room."

"Oh, I agree with that. And your name again is?"

"Callie Crossley."

Callie remembered, "I thought it was magical from the beginning, because he *was* the civil rights movement, and just as close to Martin Luther King as one could get. And so in him you saw the whole history of the movement." Abernathy had spent his adult life at King's side, at every station of the cross: Montgomery, Albany, Birmingham, St. Augustine, Mississippi, Selma, Memphis. Ralph and Martin were inseparable, known in the movement as "the twins." Abernathy had gone around the world with King on the peace tour with religious leaders in 1968, and only a few months later was standing next to Martin on the balcony of the Lorraine Motel in Memphis when the bullet tore through King's neck.

Rev. Abernathy said, "Bull Connor discovered that we drew strength from each other, because I always carried in my inside coat pocket a small Bible, and I always said my Psalms, the twenty-seventh number of the Psalms. Every time we were arrested, Martin would say, 'Ralph, read your Psalms.' . . . We would always fast during our stay in jail, and we would always have devotional services each morning . . . especially in Birmingham."

In the softest, most calm and pastorly voice I have ever heard, he said, "'The Lord is my light and my salvation, whom shall I fear? The Lord is the strength of my life; of whom shall I be afraid? When the wicked, even my enemies, came up on me to eat up my flesh they stumbled and fell.' . . . I would've fainted unless I believed to see the goodness of the Lord."

Then quietly, "We had a good time. We had the assurance that we had the power, even though the policemen had the guns and the billy clubs."

Callie and Ralph talked for what seemed like hours, transporting us into reveries of a long-ago time and place, with a little churchy flirting thrown in. He seemed to me a Baptist Yoda. As cameramen do sometimes, I checked out of the muggy outside world around me and lost myself to the dreamscape inside the viewfinder: the warmth of the old pastor's measured voice, a little private church service.

She said, "OK, we got the spirit from listening to you talk about it, and I wondered if you could just sing a little bit of that first song, that first meeting in church."

I believe I could hear every one of Rev. Abernathy's sixty southern years layered in his voice as he sang:

What a fellowship, what a joy divine,
Leaning on the everlasting arms.

What a blessedness, what a peace is mine,
Leaning on the everlasting arms.
Leaning on Jesus, leaning on Jesus, safe and secure from all alarms.
Leaning on Jesus, leaning on Jesus, leaning on the everlasting arms.

But Callie made little progress in getting clear, clean answers to her carefully ordered questions, and sometimes just had to let Ralph roam through his memories. It was one of the few times I saw any Blackside producer let a subject meander off topic, because Ralph was, after all, Ralph Abernathy. Callie remembers, "Yeah, he was a humble guy. The very end, talking about the march on Washington, and I could literally see him go back to the day, and the moment."

Closing his eyes, he transported us all back to August 1963, the evening after the March on Washington, speaking barely above a whisper, Callie leaning in to hear him, Sekou lifting both hands to press headphones to his ears. "Where two hundred and fifty thousand people had sat that day there was nothing but the wind, blowing the leftover programs and scattered litter across the way, across the reflecting pool the wind was moving and blowing, and blowing, and keeping music. And we were so proud that no violence had taken place that day. This beautiful scene of the wind dancing in the sands of the Lincoln Memorial I will never forget. This was the greatest day of my life."

After a very long few moments of silence, the crew offered a gentle collective praise shout, but in my heart of hearts I worried it would never fly on TV. He was too old, too slow, too halting for prime time; we *were* too late. In the van after the interview Callie said to Jim, "Damn, that was a waste of time. . . . I don't know what we'll do with that." That night I broke the news to Henry that Abernathy was moving, but "must have been on quaaludes."

Years before, I had learned a lesson from my friend David Webb Peoples, who labored alone in a darkened room as an editor, shaping raw film into movies: film crews are often unable to separate their own deeply felt experience in the field from what they actually captured on film, and we forget that what we perceive as riveting may be simply boring, and what we perceive as boring may be riveting. It seemed Abernathy had been both. Dave's mandate to field crews was: "Never confuse a good film with a good time." In those days, long before Peoples wrote *Blade Runner* and *Unforgiven,* he was stuck year after year cutting documentaries in the basement of a trucking company in Emeryville, California (the same basement where Errol Morris made his first film). Again and again he found himself saving directors who came back from location convinced they had gathered great material when they had, in fact, simply had a great time.

The director and crew would fly around in helicopters, eat glorious meals in Paris and Bangkok, fall in love with a production assistant, savor a long lunch with Gloria Steinem, collapse under the spell of men like Ralph Abernathy, and know the sublime existential jolt of risking their lives to get a shot without getting shot. On location they believed they lived more in a day than most people—certainly editors—live in a month. But then someone—the editor—had to tell them when it was all bullshit; the jolt existed only in their minds, not on the screen.

On the other hand, I had learned over the years to never confuse a *bad* time with a bad film. We remember the crew underpaid and overworked, falling out of love, eating lousy meals, enduring the ramblings of a feeble old preacher, only to discover weeks later that the footage contradicts the experience, especially in the hands of a fine editor.

Sure enough, back in Boston a month later, Callie would recognize the grace and power we hadn't appreciated in Abernathy's magical delivery. She correctly pointed out, "His affect is just slow; he's a slow talker." Though he seemed at death's door, old Ralph had effortlessly outfoxed our impatience and cynicism. "We didn't know what a treasure we had at the moment. We got back to Boston and realized it. This fritter was worth begging for."

SCLC's Young had explained to us their strategy for mass demonstrations that would transform law and custom in Birmingham. Wyatt Tee Walker explained the meticulously planned tactics.

"We could take three hundred and march them at ten or twelve a day, with the presumption that something would happen, and it surely did, which would in turn—people admire heroism, and then they imitate it— would create a groundswell of support in a community. . . . I targeted three stores. And since the 16th Street Baptist Church was going to be our headquarters, I had it timed how long it took a youngster to walk down there, how long it would take an older person to walk down there, how long it would take a middle-aged person to walk down there. Under some subterfuge, I visited all three of these stores and counted the stools, the tables, the chairs, et cetera, and what the best method of ingress and egress was."

Agitated in his chair, Walker continued, "In addition to that I spent time with the lawyers, to be absolutely familiar with the laws of the City of Birmingham, Jefferson County, and the State of Alabama, so that we could anticipate what the legal moves would be.

"One of the basic tenets of the nonviolent philosophy is that it is the kind of struggle in which everyone can participate—young, old, children, adults, blind, crippled, halt, lame, whatever—because it is a moral struggle. Six days in the Jefferson County Jail would be more educational to these children than six months in the segregated Birmingham schools."

It was clear that Henry had been right that the movement's complex planning was impressive and virtually unknown to most Americans, certainly to me.

Birmingham's black community was not at first united behind SCLC's plan, and the local black paper, *Birmingham World,* editorialized that the desegregation battle should be waged in the courts, not in the streets. When sit-ins to desegregate public facilities failed to generate much press and faltered because black men and women could no longer afford to go to jail, SCLC hit on the controversial idea of sending children and teenagers into the streets. James Bevel, one of the movement's most brilliant young tacticians, explained it to us.

"So a boy from high school, he gets the same effect in terms of being in jail and putting the pressure on the city as his father, and yet there is no economic threat on the family because the father is still on the job. OK . . . so the high school students were our choice, and we brought that to them in terms of, 'You're adults, but you're still sort of living on your mamas and your daddies, so it is your responsibility, in that you don't have to pay the bills . . . to confront the segregation question.' We went around and started organizing the queens of the high schools, the basketball stars, the football stars. . . . The students they have a sort of community they'd been in for say, ten, eleven, twelve years since they were in elementary school, so they had bonded well. So if one went to jail, that was a direct effect upon another one because they was classmates. We had . . . to help them overcome the crippling fears of dogs, and jails, and to help them start thinking through problems on their feet."

The mercurial Bevel, whom King called "one of my wild men," was a navy veteran and Gandhian, and wore a yarmulke on his shaved head in solidarity with victims of the Holocaust. He trained youngsters in the techniques of nonviolence, shepherding them in groups of fifty from the 16th Street Baptist Church down to City Hall for the purpose of praying and discussing race with the mayor. They were all promptly arrested and taken off to jail.

Andy Young talked about King's dilemma in 1963: "We had about five or six hundred people in jail, but all of the money was gone and we couldn't get people out of jail, and . . . the black business community and some of the white clergy were pressuring us to call off the demonstrations and just get out of town. We didn't know what to do. And he sat there in Room 30 in the Gaston Motel and he didn't say anything. He listened to people talk for about two hours. And then finally he got up and he went in the bedroom and he came back with his blue jeans on and his jacket, and he said, 'Look,' he said, 'I don't know what to do. I just know that something has got to change in Birmingham. I don't know whether I can raise money to get people out of jail. I do know that I can go into jail with them.' And not knowing how it was going to work out, he walked out of the room and went down to the church and led a demonstration and went to jail. That was, I think, the beginning of his true leadership."

Former Birmingham sheriff Mel Bailey joined us for an early breakfast of eggs, sausage, biscuits, and gravy cooked and served by inmates in the old Birmingham City Jail, where he had locked up King, Abernathy, and thousands of demonstrators, some as young as eight, in 1963. With evident historical pride, jailers showed us the dingy cell where King, in response to a published plea from local white clergy asking him to wait, had written his now famous "Letter from Birmingham Jail" on scraps of paper smuggled to him by a janitor. He proclaimed, "'Wait' has almost always meant 'Never' . . . justice too long delayed is justice denied."

Jim DeVinney interviewed Sheriff Bailey, by 1985 in his ninth term. "This mounted into hundreds and thousands just almost in hours, required school buses to move them. . . . They were in the yard like cattle and being herded into buses . . . to get them in shelter, get them in safe and secure places, boys and girls. At one time I had here in this building on the seventh and eighth floor, over twelve hundred male juveniles, black, on top of our regular complement of probably near a thousand."

Henry had a particular fascination with men like Bailey, who along with Selma's Wilson Baker and Albany's Laurie Pritchett, was one of the few southern lawmen who tried to minimize violent conflict between demonstrators, white supremacists, and on occasion their own rogue officers, and who actually met, often secretly, with black ministers and leaders. He was also one of the few who would sit down and talk with us in 1985.

Mel Bailey, who struck me as a rational man in an irrational system, had the unenviable job that spring of dealing with the Children's Crusade of strong-willed young demonstrators on the streets of his city, while at the same time trying to contain the theatrical cruelty of Birmingham's proudly racist commissioner of public safety, Bull Connor. (Could any snarky northern satirist have conjured up a better name?) Connor had by this time ordered the Birmingham Fire Department to use high-pressure hoses against the middle-school kids attempting to go to City Hall and pray, blasting them off their feet and then stone skipping them across the wet pavement. In his *Eyes* interview Ralph Abernathy told us Bull Connor was "the most evil man I have ever had any dealings with," which is saying a lot, because Ralph had gone up against a lot of evil men ("but we changed him from a bull into a steer").

When hundreds of men, women, and children returned day after day to face the hoses, Connor then set police dogs on them, and the story went global, a front-page triumph for the movement, especially in the Soviet Union, Africa, and Asia. Henry Hampton later added: "Birmingham gave its future to Bull Connor and his dogs, forever freezing the city as a barbaric opposer of human rights." Two decades later, Blackside researchers would dig up those same attack dog photos and foreign headlines and put them on the screen, together with a clip of George Wallace saying he didn't care about the foreign coverage because "The average foreign man in Africa and Asia doesn't know where *he* is, much less where Alabama is."

Councilman David Vann told us, "It was a masterpiece in the use of media. In those days we had fifteen minutes of local news and fifteen minutes of national news, and in marching only one block they could get enough news to fill all the newscasts on all the television stations in the United States."

In classic Gandhian strategy, nonviolence depends for its success on the violence of others. But lawmen like Pritchett could outfox SCLC and SNCC by simply refusing to brutalize young demonstrators in public. Wyatt Tee told us, "I often wonder why Bull Connor didn't have somebody smart enough around him to say, 'Let the niggers go on to City Hall and pray' . . . after three or four days it's an old story. . . . Instead he was fixed on stopping us, and that became the flash point of the dogs and the hoses and of the national and international attention in the 1964 Civil Rights bills." Striding center stage on the street, barking orders, Connor asserted that the city "ain't gonna segregate no niggers and whites together in this town." President John F. Kennedy later said of him, "The Civil Rights movement should thank God for Bull Connor. He's helped it as much as Abraham Lincoln."

Worried that the South would be in even worse trouble if harm came to King, chief Laurie Pritchett told us he had driven over from Albany, Georgia, to Birmingham that spring of 1963 to talk Bull Connor out of his cartoon savagery. (Connor had filled the holes in all the city golf courses with concrete rather than integrate them.) "I told him that he had to guard Dr. King, that the Klan was nearby. . . . I said, 'He's vulnerable. If he's ever killed, the cities in this country are going to burn.' Connor said, 'I'm not going to guard him. If they want to kill him, that's up to them.' . . . I left. He didn't take my advice." Sheriff Bailey said, "I had many identified Klansmen call me and say, 'Sheriff, you just give us the word, we'll take this thing and handle it if you want, you won't ever know what happened.'"

Birmingham's recent contested 1963 election had left the city with two mayors and two city councils convening their own meetings, to which Sheriff Bailey had to report as the massive demonstrations grew. Birmingham in 1963 was, in the parlance of the day, a clusterfuck. The president had federal troops mustered just off stage, ready to restore civil order if the mayor and police couldn't. This was the magnificently messy history that Henry Hampton loved; from the beginning he understood that the Birmingham story was about far more than the lunch counters or attack dogs and fire hoses in those news photos. It was about governance itself.

Why was the resistance so fierce? Sheriff Bailey said, "Suddenly we have the Fourteenth Amendment, that . . . after a hundred years, brought on by the Civil War, suddenly must be complied with. *Equal treatment under the law?* They are *not* going to get equal treatment. What do you *mean*? Go to school with *my* little daughter?!?' Now *that* is why resistance."

The boycott was sometimes aided by black "enforcers" who would intimidate blacks trying to shop downtown. Black crowds facing the police and fire brigades at Kelly Ingram Park sometimes hurled rocks and bottles at the police. Though Henry Hampton was loath to venture into the sticky, awkward fact that the pushback against white state power was not always nonviolent, he welcomed the inclusion of a scene in which James Bevel borrowed a bullhorn from the astonished police and quickly calmed a riot.

As the world watched, demonstrations effectively ground all civic function to paralysis. Negotiations stalled. National and international outrage at the spectacle of extreme violence unleashed on child demonstrators finally forced the parties to the bargaining table. David Vann told us, "The ball game was over once they brought out the hoses and dogs." After thirty-eight days of negotiations with "Shuttlesworth and Vann going at it," the city government changed its racial discrimination laws, but not before the white firefighters refused orders to use hoses again on children, the police refused to attack marchers after church on a Sunday, and the Kennedys deployed three thousand troops of the Second Infantry Division. A massive bomb hit the Gaston Motel, where King was staying, triggering a full-scale fiery riot as blacks fought back at attacking Alabama state troopers, destroying half the police cars in Birmingham. Finally, it was over, though actual desegregation would take years.

Then the resounding and peaceful March on Washington, with MLK's stirring "I have a dream" speech, crowned 1963's summer triumph. But two weeks later, in a uniquely horrific act of vengeance, Klansmen detonated a huge bomb directly under the Sunday school in the 16th Street Baptist Church, movement headquarters, killing four little black girls. On my way to Mississippi with a contingent from college back in '63 just after the bombing, we spent the night at the white YMCA and in the morning asked directions to the 16th Street Baptist Church; the desk clerk replied, "You mean that church the niggers bombed?" It had sheets of plywood nailed over the gaping cavity blown open by the bomb.

On the day the Blackside crew arrived in 1985, news came on the local Birmingham television station that "Dynamite Bob" Chambliss, convicted in 1977 of bombing the church, had died of natural causes.

In years to come, Birmingham would name its new county courthouse in honor of Sheriff Mel Bailey, its airport in honor of Rev. Fred Shuttlesworth.

CHAPTER EIGHT

What Have I to Fear?

1985–86

O ur daily coat-and-tie drill was fun, like playing dress up. I was also enjoying the "Sir" and "Ma'am" routine, sweet tea, BBQ, and people taking time to visit, the courtesy and gracious cultural furniture of the South. On to Nashville, Tennessee, one of several cities laying claim to "the buckle on the Bible Belt." Will Campbell, Waylon Jennings's white "bootleg pastor" and sometime tour-bus cook, entertained us on the porch of his log cabin in the rolling hills outside town with a shot of homemade corn liquor before filming. His farm was a few miles from the thundering new mile-long Nissan truck factory.

Rev. Campbell, long known as a renegade, had been one of the few white southern clergy to fight openly for racial equity, the only white person at the founding meeting of the Southern Christian Leadership Conference back in 1957. He had helped the Freedom Riders, accompanied the Little Rock Nine on their first attempt to enter Central High, attended the Till trial, and he had ministered to a grand dragon of the KKK because "Jesus died for the bigots as well." Will's rhythm of speech, relaxed and literate, was remarkable. I remember little of what the minister said; what I remember, as a Californian, is the comfortable southerness of it all: the succulent warm air, the smooth moonshine, the squeak of his handmade rocking chair, and most of all his ambrosia voice. It was a visit untroubled by expository content; I could have sat there all day and listened to the man just talk about anything, recite the Sermon on the Mount or the Nashville phone book.

Tired of enduring airport after airport, we took to driving from city to city, and it was during these long evenings on the road that Sekou and I really got to know each other, and he told me about his year in Vietnam protecting the perimeter of Da Nang from rocket attacks, the time he met Malcolm X, and a little more than I wanted to know about every one of his former girlfriends. Across the Black Belt (which we finally learned was named for its rich black soil, not its people), nothing had changed and everything had changed in the twenty years since I drove those same roads during the movement's heyday. In the mid-1980s most of the South was still thinly populated, rural in the extreme, only a few people per square mile, little farms and hamlets scattered along lazy miles of two-lane blacktop. And then rising up out of the tropical green appeared dowager cities like Birmingham and then glistening glass towers and suburbs of newly imagined metropolises like Atlanta, with their centers almost as dense as Manhattan. Atlanta had by 1985 a huge and powerful black upper-middle class and business elites unthinkable when I had lived there in 1965.

Over the countryside hung a legacy cloak of unease that we northerners, so steeped in Boston research and folklore of long-ago southern furies, could not shake off, especially at night. Passing one evening through Cullman, Alabama, known throughout the region to have been a "sundown town" where blacks shouldn't be seen after dark and certainly not mixing with whites after dark, Judith Vecchione looked around the van at me, Llew Smith, Mike Chin, and Sekou Shepard and said, "We better not get stopped by the police." Our anxiety was unfair to the southerners of 1985.

I remembered a long and to me frightening drive across Georgia with SNCC's Stokely Carmichael and Ivanhoe Donaldson through a moonless night in 1964. On the way out of Atlanta we stopped at a little corner store that displayed, incongruously, an advertising poster for Royal Crown Cola featuring our colleague Julian Bond, who had done some moonlighting as a model. Stokely stocked up on comic books, which he read in the backseat all the way to Montgomery, giving us a running commentary, his buoyant Trinidad/Bronx voice filling the darkness. After hours at the wheel I wanted to stop and take a leak next to the road, as any civilized Californian would do. Ivanhoe said, "No. What if a state trooper comes drifting around that corner?" I really had to pee, trying to hold it until we got to a safe haven, just as *The Negro Motorist Green Book* instructed back in the day. I had no lived experience with the humiliations of segregation, no security guard had ever followed me through a department store because of my color, no bank manager ever denied me a loan; I had never been the victim of anything because of my race. The closest I ever came as a grown man to the experience of being black in the South was the simple petty indignity of nearly wetting my pants before we got to a black roadhouse.

· · · · · ·

If you have little interest in the mechanics of 16mm documentary film-making on location, you might skip the next few pages.

Although analog videotape was commonplace by 1985, it was finicky, bulky, unreliable, lacked high definition, and without the skills of a good engineer it could have the tinny look of a 1970s soap opera. More important, archivists in those days had no reliable way to preserve videotape over the long haul, so over time it became unplayable, and after enough years the images could simply evaporate as the tape grew brittle and the iron oxide molecules demagnetized, relaxed back to the entropy of their natural state, or sloughed off into dust. Historical filmmakers took a terrible hit in the mid-1970s when TV stations and networks began shifting away from 16mm news film, which can last a hundred years, to "electronic news gathering" on perishable three-quarter-inch videotape, reliable for ten or fifteen years at most. Stations quickly discovered the enormous cost savings to be had by simply erasing yesterday's news and reusing the videotape for today's news. We learned the hard way on the *Cadillac Desert* series in 1996 when the only available footage of Jimmy Carter's 1976 inauguration was fuzzy, muddy three-quarter-inch videotape from ABC. But the original 1948 uncut rushes from Robert Flaherty's *Louisiana Story* in the Museum of Modern Art archive remain tack sharp and brilliant to this day. Henry Hampton understood that the *Eyes* interviews would become part of the permanent record of American history, not to be trusted to the volatile videotape of the time.

Reliable high-definition all-electronic digital video capture was ten years in the future. So we recorded our civil rights stories on 16mm negative film in the nearly square, old-fashioned 4:3 aspect ratio, its underlying technology dating from 1895, with cameras that had been greatly refined but fundamentally unchanged from their introduction in the late 1940s.

Shooting 16mm color film was complex and artisanal, like fine carpentry or cheese making, only much more expensive. To purchase, expose, develop, print, sound synchronize, and edge code one 400-foot 11-minute roll of Kodak 7291 negative film and make it edit-ready cost about three hundred dollars in 1985. One roll in its distinctive metal can weighed a couple of pounds. Today that same eleven minutes of interview, shot as a brilliant HD or 4K digital file, a few trillion trillion trillion reoriented electrons, costs and weighs almost nothing. We shot about eighty hours for all six hours of *Eyes on the Prize*, more or less a thousand pounds of 16mm film. Every can of film, especially the miniature 3-minute spools in their jewel-yellow Kodak boxes, were packets of pure potential, all single-use future tense, like a stick of dynamite or a blank check.

Few were better positioned to destroy a day's work than Mike Chin and the other camera assistants, who had to load and unload each roll of film into and out of the camera magazine in total darkness with both hands inside a double-layered, double-zippered black nylon and rubber "changing bag," threading the film by touch through a little maze of rollers, retainers, loops, and latches, which were different for every camera. Remembering changing bags, Fred Wiseman said, "People wondered what you're doing in there with your hands inside a black bag on your lap." What we were doing was maintaining total darkness. When I worked in the darkrooms at a giant Berkey Photo processing plant, it made perfect sense when a half dozen blind men tap-tapped their way in and out at the shift change.

God help the assistant who let a speck of dust into the bag, mixed up two types of film, let even a hint of light in, failed to run a scratch test, failed to seal the magazine with tape, or didn't check for lint in the camera gate before and after every setup. It demanded manic attention. As a young assistant I once—you only do it once—committed the sin of "talking while loading," got distracted, and opened a can of exposed film to the light, just as novice Orlando Bagwell and novice Mike Chin on their first job together, a film about the Cotton Club, in 1976; they got to talking and Orlando flashed a roll of film. He remembered. "Mike shot me that Cheshire cat grin, and I snapped the magazine closed." It was no excuse that the underpaid, sleep-deprived assistants worked sweatshop hours long into the night while the rest of us went to the bar and to bed. Theirs was a thankless, all-defense profession, in which you seldom get noticed unless you screw up; no one ever comes out of a movie and says, "What great camera assisting!"

Mike Chin was way overqualified to be working as my assistant, so on some of the interviews we traded roles: he shot and I loaded magazines for him.

Our assigned shooting ratio was so low that in order to squeak out enough film stock for maybe one extra response per roll, I would usually stop the camera while the interviewer asked each new question. Sekou recorded sound separately on the Nagra IV quarter-inch magnetic tape recorder (sometimes called "the Nigra"), a museum-quality 17-pound Swiss machine, brushed aluminum, beautiful to look at and touch, probably one of the finest achievements in a century of analog sound technology. It would soon and suddenly vanish into obsolescence, replaced by charmless digital recorders. The Nagra had no safeguard against recording over previous material, and once—another thing you only do once—sleep-deprived Sekou recorded a sit-in interview over the preceding Freedom Ride interview. The honor code of documentary sound recording demanded that if you accidentally erased audio you'd cowboy up and tell the producer, which Sekou—an honorable man if ever there was one—immediately did. We set the lights and camera back up and redid the interview.

Since the dawn of sound recording, the industrialized global North and even much of the rural South have been drenched in a relentless base level of background noise: the hum of trucks on a nearby highway, car alarms, sirens, jets, light planes, helicopters, ringing phones, chain saws, construction equipment, the geese next door, the buzz of fluorescent lights, buses, barking dogs, honking horns, church bells, and a constant, low infrastructural droning so universal we don't even notice it, but the recorder does. Years later, looking at the archived transcripts of our interviews, I found Sekou's notes: "Please Mr. Editor, please please forgive the sound problems we had at this location." Even over thirty years of filming in Yosemite National Park, I've never located a truly quiet place for an outdoor interview.

All this can make it hard to record more than a few minutes at a time without stopping to wait for a plane to pass. Judith Vecchione perfected the tactic of using a real or imagined airplane passing overhead during an interview to say that the audio was no good and elicit a second and often better response to her question. The sound guys would usually unplug the refrigerator to quiet it, and then put their car keys inside so they could not leave without turning the fridge back on.

On the road that fall, we did not actually see any of our interviews until a month later. We had no video monitor, no playback, no nothing except our eyes to the viewfinder, praying we had captured a good image. The enterprise relied on unforgiving discipline, confidence that the assistant was running a clean camera, and dead reckoning with a couple of light meters to get the exposure and color right. We sealed the cans of exposed film with "Do Not X-Ray" tape and shipped them by Trailways bus or Federal Express every day to the lab in New York for processing in machines with a quarter mile of film threaded over a thousand individual rollers in six chemical baths, four separate washes, and two drying stacks. A lot could go wrong.

It was always an act of faith, high flying without a net as we waited for an early-morning phone message with the "negative report" from New York. Very little could be done after the fact to salvage a bad shot in those days before digital color correction. The photographic sin was irredeemable. Each of us knew that sooner or later we would get the dreaded "We have a problem" call from the lab or director: something was out of focus, underexposed, overexposed, shaky, scratched, light struck, flashed by X-rays, or just simply blank. When the cost per minute of digital capture shrank to almost nothing in the late 1990s, and much of the on-set control disappeared into software, so did much of the discipline. Was our filming any better because of the discipline? Perhaps.

Because there was no way then to electronically import still images directly into the editing room without first putting a dog-eared coffee-stained hard-copy photograph or document in front of a camera, we captured all the archive photos onto film in the old-school way, on a tripod, doing the zooms and moves by hand.

The pressure was not eased by the fact that Sekou Shepard and I had chosen the *Eyes* shooting trip for one of our many mutual attempts to quit smoking.

Before hitting the road, I had written a pompous memo to Henry about how we needed to honor the history and the people by "breathing new eloquent life into that stale corner of cinematography." We pulled off a few good ones, but *Eyes on the Prize* has a lot of mediocre shooting, because interviewing actually *was* a stale corner into which neither I nor anyone else had put much artistic thought. We were just beginning to learn from cinematographers Buddy Squires and Kyle Kibbe, whose painterly interviews became their signature contribution to the films of Ken Burns and Lourdes Portillo. Blackside's cinematography never really hit its game until Mike Chin and Bobby Shepard shot elegant portraits in the Chicago Black Panthers story for *Eyes II* a few years later. It wasn't until the nineties that most of us had cooked up our own special style, and documentary interview photography evolved into the high, flamboyant art it is today.

In the 1980s we worked with Lowel tungsten lights and a couple of FAY lights that looked and acted exactly like car headlights except that they generated more heat. On interviews we had to open the doors while changing film every ten minutes to cool down the room. Light or no light, story is everything. More often than we like to admit, light matters little; powerful content trumps a beautiful picture every time. Orlando remembers filming Montgomery organizer Jo Ann Robinson back in 1979 under harsh noonday sunlight in what must be the most unattractive interviews in all of *Eyes on the Prize,* but one of the strongest.

"It's a terrible, terrible setup, the worst setup you could ever have. Judy . . . wanted to sit down in the middle of this field, like kind of girl talk, and it was just terrible—but when Jo Ann opened up *it didn't matter.* I remember sitting behind the camera and thinking, 'Something's going on here.' Judy had a relationship with her that was trusting."

For reasons I never understood, we erased ourselves from our documentaries sometime in the 1960s and adopted the interview convention that made Ralph Abernathy or Virginia Durr appear to be conversing with an offscreen phantom, a correspondent, or with nobody at all. You never saw or heard from the filmmaker, that gracious bully in the room who is controlling every detail of the process; go figure. Hence, our instructions to interview subjects—"Be sure to include my question in your answer"—became the bane of documentary interviews; many people simply can't do it, or come back with a version of "In answer to your question about the boycott . . ."

We had practical concerns: Keep track of screen direction, so that people engaging on opposite sides of an issue in your film will be facing each other on opposite sides of the screen. (The Interrotron was ten years in the future.) Find large quiet locations, seventy-nine of them. Except for the director, keep the crew out of the interviewee's eyeline. Ask people to bring some alternate wardrobe, including "something slightly darker than your skin," which would automatically adjust to complement the dozens of skin tones in this series about race. Keep the atmosphere in the room quiet and civilized. Shoot three frame sizes so the editor can cut from one to another. No zooms while the person is talking.

We purged every interview location of any visual cue that might distract or take us out of the 1960s, swept locations clean of knickknacks, nameplates, posters, family photos, and even books with legible covers. (*Eyes* had no problem with the occasional American flag in the background; no surprise.) It was Judith's idea, and a good one, because it allowed our films to remain suspended in time past. And we tried to keep the backgrounds slightly out of focus—a tough feat in small-format 16mm—so that all attention went to the speaker's face.

We had forty minutes of film for each interview, laughably low by today's standards or even the standards of 1985. (Hopping back and forth between California and the Black Belt, Mike Chin and I were at the same time as *Eyes* doing what must be the longest interview with the highest shooting ratio in documentary history, seventeen days with psychologist Bruno Bettelheim for the BBC, discussing disturbed children, autism, and his time in Dachau and Buchenwald. We had spent one hour with Ralph Abernathy.)

Today, fifty years after the movement, thirty years after *Eyes,* the pristine 16mm original negative of every frame we shot for *Eyes on the Prize* and dozens of other Blackside documentaries—a singular record of the American experience—is archived in a climate-controlled vault at the Henry Hampton Collection in the Film & Media Archive at Washington University in St. Louis. It is exquisitely organized, cataloged, and managed by professional archivists, is accessible to the public, and is used every day by scholars and filmmakers. Archivists are transferring interviews from acetate-based film stock to more permanent polyester-based and digitizing them one by one.

Our interviews with many of these people would be their last, for some it was the only interview they ever gave, and others who told their tales for *Eyes on the Prize* never lived to see it broadcast. We joked that an interview appointment with Blackside marked you for death.

Much of the story remains untold. I wondered about interviews we should have done but couldn't, or didn't because of cost, or maybe we were just too frazzled: Bob Zellner of SNCC; Jim Zwerg and William Barbee, savagely beaten at the Montgomery bus station; Annie Lee Cooper, who sank her teeth into Sheriff Clark in Selma; archsegregationist Lester Maddox. I wondered, too, who among our cast may have revised, embellished, or even invented a bit of their own history.

• • • • • •

I phoned in a production report most nights, checked in with our other camera guys Tom Kaufman and Bobby Shepard. My motel phone rang near midnight more than once, with an amped-up Henry on the line pitching a half-hour animated version of *Eyes on the Prize,* an *Eyes* comic book, an MTV *Eyes on the Prize* video with Public Enemy, or a celebration of a tiny new grant. I had hoped and expected that Henry would be on the road with us, it would have been fun, but he believed his producers should do the work on their own, without the boss looking over their shoulders. And there were too many demands back at headquarters. He and Judy Richardson threw themselves into securing interviews with the big fish: Harry Belafonte, Assistant Attorney General Nicholas Katzenbach, and Alabama governor George Wallace. Justice Thurgood Marshall had already politely turned us down, as had senators John Stennis and Strom Thurmond.

In the thick of production, we still did not have all the money. In a weak moment I had agreed to do southern fund-raising for *Eyes on the Prize.* On my days off on the road, I went from nostalgic interviews with movement veterans to numbing meetings with friendly state humanities council representatives in Georgia, Mississippi, and Alabama, trying to convince them to give us money to tell the story of a very uncomfortable time in their own history. To their credit, Alabama and Georgia joined New York and California with public money to fund *Eyes on the Prize.* I took particular pleasure that a tipping point had clearly passed when the state of Mississippi, which had put me in jail years before, granted taxpayer money to help pay for a television series about why they had locked up hundreds of civil rights workers.

Travel in the South in the 1960s, by car, bus, or on foot, was ideological in the extreme, rooted in elaborate protocols of the spatial relationship between white bodies and black bodies . . . whites in front, blacks in the back, blacks stepping off a narrow sidewalk to let whites pass, separate waiting rooms in bus stations, separate restrooms at filling stations, separate motels, separate state parks.

The first Freedom Riders' bus was attacked and firebombed by Klansmen in the quiet little town of Anniston, Alabama, on May 14, 1961. The riders might have all burned to death inside had not a state investigator on board, E. L. Cowling, pulled his pistol, shown his badge, and forced the attackers to release the doors before the gas tank exploded. Later that same day the black and white riders in a second bus pulled into the Birmingham station determined to get off the front of the bus and enter the white waiting room. They were met by reporters and a white mob one thousand strong. Bull Connor, alerted by an FBI informant, had arranged to withhold police from interfering for fifteen minutes while whites beat the journalists and riders with pipes and baseball bats. Some riders were maimed for life. Connor said policemen were unavailable because it was Mother's Day, and "they were busy visiting their mothers." The badly injured riders called off their plans to travel all the way to New Orleans.

Alabama governor John Patterson had been furious because he thought the Kennedy administration was encouraging Freedom Riders to stir up trouble in Alabama and then asking Alabama to protect the troublemakers. Attorney General Robert Kennedy had dispatched his assistant, white Tennessee native John Seigenthaler, to negotiate with Governor Patterson, and Siegenthaler succeeded in getting the severely injured first wave evacuated on a plane from Birmingham to New Orleans.

Hearing the news, Fisk University student Diane Nash and a cadre from the Nashville student movement decided they had to step forward.

She told us in 1985, "You know, if the Freedom Ride had been stopped as a result of violence, I strongly felt that the future of the movement was going to be just cut short, because the impression would have been given that whenever a movement starts, all that has to be done is that you attack it; massive violence and the blacks would stop." Nash explained to John Doar, the Justice Department's man on the ground in Alabama, that the new wave of students had already signed their wills, adding, "We know someone will be killed, but we cannot let violence overcome nonviolence."

Orlando was conducting the interview. Diane said, "When the buses were burned in Anniston, on Mother's Day, . . . it was our fight, every bit as much as theirs. It was as though *we* had been attacked. And a contingency of students left Nashville to go and pick up the Freedom Ride where it had been stopped. Now, that was really one of the times where I saw people face death. Because nobody went and joined the Freedom Ride without realizing that they might not come back."

Then, suddenly, quietly, Diane Nash began to sing:

What have I to dread, what have I to fear,
Leaning on the everlasting arms?
I have blessed peace with my Lord so near,
Leaning on the everlasting arms.

After a couple of dozen cities on the road, we got our rhythm. And once in a while a little story in an interview took on the power and economy of a parable. In Nashville, we wrangled through all the usual hassles, loaded equipment, made it to the hotel, and finally got some late supper. Next morning we planned to put the Freedom Ride narrative on hold and mop up a couple of sit-in stories. Orlando, who was famous for putting interview subjects at ease with his good advance work, said he couldn't join us for dinner that first night because he had to meet with the next day's subject, sit-in veteran Leo Lillard. Prue and I offered to join him for moral support, but Orlando wanted to go alone and talk through the project with Leo, who had been cagey and cautious on the phone.

After a long aimless night drive around Nashville, Leo finally brought Orlando to some other guy's little house, and to Orlando's consternation they did nothing more than watch *Monday Night Football* for an hour, nibbling on snacks and sipping beer. "And I've got to get up early and shoot the next morning. When the game is over I say to Leo, 'You know, we haven't talked at all. . . . Let me stop for a minute and tell you the context of this film: we're doing the sit-in movement and I'm really glad to meet you. And the other part of this project is that we're going to do the Freedom Rides, when they are stopped and Diane and the SNCC students decide they are going to pick that ride up and go on into Montgomery and Mississippi.'

"And this guy, who's not talking at all—we're in his house—says, 'Oh, I was on that ride.' I looked at him, I said, 'What do you mean, you were *on* that ride?' He says, 'Yeah, I was on that ride, you know, with Diane. I volunteered for that ride.' And he starts talking and telling me about it. And I said to myself, 'He was on that fucking *ride*.' And *now* I understand why Leo's brought me here." Freddie Leonard had been a young black Freedom Rider in 1961, but was not in any of the books, never showed up in any of the research, and was certainly not on our shooting schedule.

Knowing that we had no archive footage of the Montgomery attack because the mob had once again first attacked newsmen and smashed cameras, Orlando said to Freddie, "'Well, I'd really like to interview you,' and I can see him start shaking. 'I can't do an interview; I'll *never* do an interview,' said Freddie. And then I start to calm him down and start talking about how the interview's going to be fine, and we'll come to *his* house. . . . Because he was scared shitless. I said, 'We're going to come with some cameras and set up, and he said 'Cameras?!' He goes into this whole thing about how he's not going to do it, but by getting Leo to come to his house, that's what got him to do it. That was a strategy on the spot."

We were behind schedule by the time we got to Freddie Leonard's modest home the next day, and Prue was doing her best to keep us moving quickly. Freddie, muscular and looking far younger than his forty-some years, sat in the kitchen with Orlando while Mike, Sekou, and I set up equipment. Orlando remembered, "That whole scene was so tense. I'm watching this guy sweating bullets, sweat dropping from his face. His wife says, 'You should have a glass of beer,' so she pours him a glass of beer and he doesn't drink it. He is just frightened."

Sekou later told me that when he saw that Freddie was so nervous he held out a pill, explaining it was Valium and would calm him down, and said, "Take this," which Leonard did. It was a Tylenol.

"So I said, 'Look, Freddie, when we go out there the lights are there, the camera is there, but you are looking at *me*. It's only you and me talking.' And when he sits down he is incredibly nervous, still sweating. And I ask him one question about arriving at the bus station, and once he goes into the space, he just *goes,* he's just *there,* at the bus station in Montgomery in 1961."

Freddie Leonard told us: "And then all of a sudden, just like *whoosh!* Magic. White people. Sticks and bricks. 'Nigger! Kill the niggers!' We were still on the bus, you know. But I think we were all kind of deciding, 'Well, maybe we should go off the back of this bus,' because we kind of knew that if we had gone off at the back of the bus that maybe they wouldn't be so bad on us. They wanted us to go off the back of the bus. But we decided—no, no, we'll go off the front and take what's coming to us.

"We went out the front of the bus. Jim Zwerg was a white fellow from Madison, Wisconsin—he had a lot of nerve. And I think that's what saved me, Bernard Lafayette, and Allen Cason, 'cause Jim Zwerg walked off the bus in front of us, and it was like they were *possessed*; they couldn't believe that there was a white man who would help us; and they grabbed him and pulled him into the mob, I mean it was a *mob*. When we came off the bus, their attention was on him. It's like they didn't see the rest of us, for maybe thirty seconds, they didn't see us at all. And we were held in by this rail, parking lot down below, cars down there. And then when they did turn toward us, we had a choice, about ten or fifteen feet below."

President Kennedy's representative John Seigenthaler had raced to the bus station in Montgomery just as the Greyhound carrying John Lewis, Jim Zwerg, Freddie Leonard, and twenty other riders arrived. Once again, by prearrangement, city police protection had suddenly vanished, while the crowd of white men, women, and children set upon the riders with fists and baseball bats.

Seigenthaler said, "As I came down the far side I saw this anthill of activity. The Freedom Riders emerging from the bus were attacked, were being mauled. It looked like two or three hundred people, just all over them. There were screams, shouts; as I drove along, I saw two young women who were Freedom Riders being pummeled to one side. There was a woman who was walking behind one of these young women, she had a purse on a strap and she was beating her over the head, and a young, skinny blond teenager in a T-shirt was sort of dancing backward in front of her punching her in the face. Instinctively, I just bumped up onto the sidewalk, blew the horn, jumped out of the car, came around, grabbed the one who was being hit, took her back to the car. The other young woman got into the backseat of the car, and I opened the door, pushed this young woman, and said, 'Get in the car.' And she said, 'Mister, this is not your fight, I'm nonviolent, don't get hurt because of me.'

"I *almost* got away with it, if she had just gotten into the car . . . but that moment of hesitation gave the mob a chance to collect their wits and one grabbed me by the arm, wheeled me around, and said, 'What the hell are you doing?' And I said, 'Get back! I'm a federal man,' turned back to her, and the lights went out. I was hit with a pipe over this ear and literally don't remember anything that happened; they kicked me up under the car."

Freddie Leonard and the others were still hemmed in by the railing back at the bus station. "We could stand there and take it or we could go over the rail—so over the rail we went, me and Bernard Lafayette, and Allen Cason, who always carried his little typewriter, always had his typewriter; over the rail we went, on top of a car, hit the ground, took off, ran into the back of this building. It was the post office and the people were in there carrying on the business of the day just like nothing was happening outside. But when we came through there, now mail went to flying everywhere 'cause we were *running*."

In the edit, Seigenthaler picked up the story: "I woke up a half hour later. I was wearing John Doar's shirt. . . . I had borrowed his shirt from him. The shirt was drenched with blood and my first thought was 'Poor John; I've ruined his shirt.' The officer who was beside me was a lieutenant. He had my notebook which had all sorts of phone numbers in it, like Fred Shuttlesworth, Bull Connor, the White House, the Justice Department, Governor John Patterson, and he told me, he said, 'Well, you've had some trouble, buddy, is there anybody I can call for you?' And I had enough wits about me to say, 'Yes, if you would call, Mr. Kennedy.'"

While Seigenthaler was out cold and Leonard raced through the post office to safety, the segregationist state director of public safety, Floyd Mann, sprinted into the mob, stood over the riders who had been beaten unconscious, and fired his pistol in the air, forcing the mob to scatter before they could kill anyone. City police were nowhere in sight. Ambulances refused to pick up the injured. Mann sent for a hundred state troopers, who managed to get the remaining riders to a nearby black church.

Leonard said, "Later we heard the news about Jim Zwerg, about John Lewis, about William Barbee. William Barbee was damaged for life, Jim Zwerg for life. It's amazing that they're still living. . . . I think what saved them was this fellow who was in the crowd shot a gun in the air, and if it was not for him . . . all of us would be dead."

It did not occur to me until years later that Orlando was far too modest to remind us all that he knew exactly what it was like to be attacked from behind by racist thugs in a mob intent on death.

The Freedom Riders made their way to the First Baptist Church. Martin Luther King and Fred Shuttlesworth joined those who took refuge with fifteen hundred parishioners. When darkness fell, a white mob of three thousand surrounded the church. The archive footage in *Eyes on the Prize* shows King and Abernathy calming the crowd while outside outnumbered and ill-trained federal marshals were trying to hold their ground. The crowd burned cars, hurled rocks and bottles through the church windows, and tried to set it afire.

When church leaders stepped out front, Wyatt Tee Walker told us, "The tear gas was flying and a brick flew over Dr. King's head, then a tear

gas canister came and Fred picked it up and threw it back at the mob."
King and Shuttlesworth went to the basement, with tear gas drifting in, to
phone Attorney General Robert Kennedy in Washington. Robert said he
had sent the FBI, and King talked to President Kennedy. Armed black
cabdrivers were on their way to attempt a rescue when Governor John
Patterson finally declared citywide martial law, and at 4 A.M. National
Guardsmen led the Freedom Riders to safety.

Undaunted, Leonard, Lewis, Nash, and the bandaged riders who could
still walk climbed back onto the Greyhound, under federal guard, bound
for Jackson, Mississippi, where they were immediately jailed, convicted,
sentenced, and on their way to prison the next day.

Freddie Leonard said: "In the penitentiary, Parchman, we were only
allowed one book, that was the Bible. So we did a lot of singing, praying
too, but a lot of singing. And those folks just couldn't understand how we
could be *happy* singing. So they would say, 'Shut up! Shut up!' And . . . we
could hear the women on the other side, they'd sing to us and we'd sing to
them. So they came through and said, 'Well, if you don't shut up, we'll
take your mattresses.'

"So we start singing again, freedom songs: 'Freedom's coming and it
won't be long.' They came through a cellblock—Stokely Carmichael was
my cellmate—I told Stokely, 'I'm not letting my mattress go.' Everybody
peacefully let their mattress go, but I remembered the night before when
I had to sleep on that cold steel. So they came in to take my mattress. . . .
They drug me out into the cellblock, I still had my mattress, I wouldn't
turn it loose, and one of the inmates—they would use the black inmates
to come and get our mattresses, I mean the *inmates,* you know? And there
was this guy, 'Peewee' they called him, short and *muscular.* They said,
'Peewee, *get* him! Peewee came down on my head, man, wamp, wamp . . .
He was crying. Peewee was crying. And I still had my mattress. Do you
remember when your parents used to whup you and say, 'It's going to hurt
me more than it hurt you.' It hurt Peewee more than it hurt me."

As a camera operator you learn over the years to hold back emotion; we
get paid to record with detachment, not to participate. If you laugh when
the whole crowd is laughing, you'll jiggle the camera; if you cry when everyone else is crying, you can't focus through the tears. Dancing can be a
problem. So you train yourself to detach. But here with Freddie, the whole
crew choked up. Orlando said, "After the interview, his wife told him, 'I
never knew you did that.' 'Yeah,' Freddie said, 'I kind of put it behind me.'

He'd never told his wife, his kids, no one, only Leo. . . . These are simple people; they have their life and they work hard every day. And this moment in his life is not like any other moment he's ever had . . . that's why I'm surprised he never shared it. No one had come and inquired and wanted to know.

"I'm thinking God touched us, because . . . we opened this door that had been there all along. . . . It was affirmation that you could take every bit of archive footage that we all had seen before and you could put a different voice behind it, and it all had new meaning. People like Freddie Leonard gave it new meaning, and suddenly the whole thing was fresh. And we knew that when we walked out that door. Holy shit: This is it! Oh, I *get* what we are doing now; I really get it now."

Henry had sent us out on a quest of his own devising, but never really told us exactly what the quest was. We had been floundering along getting decent stuff, but here with Freddie Leonard we finally understood what it could be: a deep journey back in time with men and women who had been waiting years to tell their tale.

CHAPTER NINE

Mississippi Goddamn

1963, 1964, 1985

People like myself was born on this river. It's the Delta. . . . It's history. We came up out of slavery and this is where we acted it out, and we love the land. This is Mississippi." So said Mrs. Unita Blackwell in *Eyes on the Prize* in 1985, over Orlando's handsome panoramas of the grand Mississippi River, Father of All Waters.

The serene beauty of Mississippi was lost on me when I had first arrived as a voter registration worker twenty-two years before, in 1963: mist on the river, the woods so fragrant after a rain, and people visiting on porches in the little hamlets. For us back then, those ambling two-lane roads through piney forests and green tunnels of kudzu were where Emmett Till, Andy Goodman, Mickey Schwerner, James Chaney, Louis Allen, and countless unknown others were murdered.

When our flight from Nashville touched down in Jackson in the fall of 1985, it was the first time I had returned since jumping bail in 1964, and the sight of that Mississippi red clay along the runway suddenly made me anxious.

By 1985 segregation by law was a thing of the past, and time had blunted the sharp edges of segregation by custom. Because the only Mississippi I had ever known was under the naked racial codes of the old Jim Crow, I was surprised to find a black manager greeting us at the front desk of the Holiday Inn. (The nationwide New Jim Crow of black incarceration was in '85 still out of sight and out of mind for us.) Though most of the black people were still poor, and most of the poor people were still black, Mississippi by then had more black elected officials than any state in the country—not so much because white voters had come to Jesus, but because black people could finally vote.

That was beyond imagining in the fall of 1963, when fifty of us from Yale had first invaded the state for a couple of weeks to work on voter registration after President Kennedy and Medgar Evers had been shot. For weeks the *Yale Daily News* ran headlines about us, and lavished contempt upon the benighted state, noting that the thirty-hour drive from Connecticut to Mississippi was "arduous, worthy of the evil to which it leads." But op-eds questioned our "missionary zeal" in setting out to reform Mississippi when racism festered in our own backyard up north. Young Barney Frank and young Joe Lieberman were in our group. Many among the volunteers were beaten or arrested. Not long after, in June 1964, I left college for good to work full time in Mississippi.

It had been an easy choice. We were too young to have fought the good fight against Franco's Fascists in the Spanish Civil War, so we had to settle for reading Hemingway and Orwell's vivid accounts. When we were infants, our fathers, mothers, aunts, and uncles had with quiet conviction stepped up to beat the pants off the Nazis in World War II, and a few, with equal conviction, had served hard time in American prisons as conscientious objectors. So what was our generation's just war? Civil rights.

What little we knew about Mississippi we learned from Faulkner's *Intruder in the Dust* in our freshman English class, until we saw news film of the riots at Ole Miss, the sit-ins, and the Freedom Rides. In the dorm rooms we heard tales about this thing called SNCC, about Bob Moses, Stokely Carmichael, Sam Block, and a white college kid named Dennis Sweeney careening through the Delta woods at ninety miles an hour with the Klan shooting at them. These guys were only a year or two older than us but already living legends, right up there with Odysseus and Achilles, authentic in a way we doubted we could ever be.

By the timing of our birth we had been spared the barbarism of World War II. Prosperity reigned and except for those couple of days during the Cuban Missile Crisis, it was a fine time for most Americans to be American. But it was surely an odd time to be in the all-male, virtually all-white Ivy League, trudging through snow in our coats and ties, cloistered from the great waves of social change poised to break over the nation. Striding across Yale's Old Campus in his Navy ROTC great coat, our fellow freshman John Kerry was alive with purpose and already senatorial at nineteen. But as a public school boy from the Central Valley of California, I felt ill at ease and a little stupid among the governing class.

Rev. William Sloane Coffin, our fire-breathing chaplain of the Social Gospel at Yale, had all but convinced us that the authentic life of purpose lay in the Peace Corps, or better yet, in the southern freedom struggle. And starting with my nursery school teacher, all the black people I had ever really known in life had been authority figures, mentors, and role models, not my equal but my superior. Contrary to Henry and Judy Richardson's fears about "no excellence without white people," I came of age suspecting there could be little excellence without black people. For as long as I could remember, our parents had taught us that white privilege demanded a stand for tolerance and justice, so all I needed was a trigger. We knew that SNCC and CORE were moving into the more isolated counties of the rural South, in a narrowly focused effort to gain voting rights. Governor J. P. Coleman had stated flatly that Negroes were not fit to vote. The state was almost half black, with no black officeholders.

Then, in the fall of 1963, Allard Lowenstein, the charismatic, bug-eyed Pied Piper who in his lifetime inspired thousands of young people, including Dennis Sweeney, to join progressive causes, barnstormed through New Haven with a plea that SNCC needed students from elite colleges to draw fire and publicity in Mississippi. As Henry Hampton and Martin Buber would argue: If we didn't do it, who would? Al himself had shown astonishing courage in smuggling anti-apartheid activists out of South-West Africa only a few years before. It came down to us as a simple challenge: we could hang around Yale and read more Kant, Thucydides, and Homer, or risk our lives in a great battle for democracy in the jungles of Mississippi. Wrestling with less flamboyant racism, police brutality, and de facto segregation in our northern hometowns surely could wait, I thought. We sensed that we, too, had a stake in the struggle, that blowing open American racial codes would benefit whites as well as blacks.

Then Bernice Johnson Reagon and SNCC's Freedom Singers came to New Haven and set us on fire with a song we'd never heard before, "Keep Your Eyes on the Prize." That sealed the deal.

Driving across the state line into Mississippi back in 1963, I in my nineteen-year-old imagination thought we might as well have entered the Belgian Congo. The idea that by crossing a state border we had lost some protection of the law was a novel experience for white college kids, but well known to Henry Hampton and every young black person of the Till generation. We seemed in ways to have left the twentieth century and United States itself, entering a nation within the nation, lost in time, provincial in the extreme: every license plate had the county name on it—Lauderdale, Choctaw, Jefferson Davis, Lowndes, Tallahatchie, Neshoba. Throughout the southern border states legal segregation may have been in the throes of slow death by then, but Mississippi was different. Ten years after the *Brown v. Board of Education* school desegregation ruling, not a single black student had entered a white school in Mississippi, and restrooms, drinking fountains, lunch counters, and bus stations were still emblazoned with "Colored" and "White" signs, in open defiance of federal law. The Citizens' Council had masterfully engineered widespread white resistance; the state remained segregated.

My first image of Mississippi, vivid to this day, is of an old black man the stature and stoop of my own grandfather, in frayed overalls, pacing along behind a mule and plow in a gentle, warm rain, with hundreds of gently sloping rows of black soil behind him and hundreds ahead, mist rising off the furrows.

A few weeks before we arrived, E. H. Hurst, a Democratic member of the state legislature and author of a book in which he compared black people to chimpanzees, caterpillars, and cockroaches, shot and killed local NAACP leader Herbert Lee in broad daylight in front of a dozen witnesses in Liberty, Mississippi. Lee was working with Bob Moses on voter registration. Persons unknown then murdered the only black witness, Louis Allen, when he agreed to testify against Hurst. Voting, justice, and citizenship itself were fantasies for nearly all blacks in the state. Dr. King told a rally in Jackson that at the current rate of registration, "It will take 135 years for *half* the present Negro population to become registered voters."

"I guess our courage came . . . because we didn't have nothing; we couldn't lose nothing. But we wanted something for ourselves and for our children. And so we took a chance with our lives," said Mrs. Blackwell in her soft, unhurried way.

In 1985, Orlando was directing the *Eyes* episode about the 1963 murder of state NAACP chairman Medgar Evers and about the huge 1964 Mississippi Freedom Summer Project.

We scheduled interviews with the White Citizen's Council's William J. Simmons, and with Erle Johnston, former director of the Mississippi State Sovereignty Commission, both of whom we assumed might not be comfortable with nonwhites in the room during an interview. Back in Boston, Hampton and the staff had done a lot of to-ing and fro-ing over whether it would be justified for the resolutely multicultural/multiracial Blackside to arrive on location with an all-white or all-black crew, as they had back on *Voices of a Divided City* a few years before.

Many of the white Blackside staff thought it hypocritical for us to ever send in a segregated crew on these films about integration. But Prue Arndt, a white southerner herself, knew that talking with a white southern interviewer and white crew might be the only way to generate a fluid and candid conversation. So she volunteered to convince a number of them to go on camera, and she conducted interviews with several once powerful leaders of segregationist institutions.

We never hid our interest in civil rights, but these were tough choices. Callie, Orlando, Judy, and most of the black staff argued it was more important for people, whatever their race or politics, to feel absolutely comfortable talking to Blackside, to speak their truth, not ours. It was simply foolish to dismiss white supremacists as stupid or uneducated, and Henry understood the danger of compressing all the myriad varieties of white racism and privilege into one demon archetype. We should give them a safe venue in which to be their true selves, honest selves, best selves, and not have to edit their own speech for fear of offending someone in the room. Their comfort trumped our politics. Callie said, "Crap, leave the black people home, or leave the white people at the hotel." In school Jim DeVinney had asked, "How do you film the Klan?" to which Henry shot back, "Get a sheet."

After months of trying, we hadn't convinced anyone from the Ku Klux Klan to go on camera, and as it turned out we never could. But to their credit, Simmons and Johnston agreed to talk about segregation and the civil rights movement. We hired a local white sound recordist to replace Sekou Shepard for the day, and a local white camera assistant to replace Mike Chin. Prue and I felt just plain rotten, as though Jim Crow were still in force, when our all-white crew pulled away from the Jackson Holiday Inn, leaving Sekou, Michael, and Llew standing there at the loading area. Chin hollered after us, "Don't leave me here in the yellow zone!" They had a leisurely lunch at the mall, on the clock, and Sekou said, "It was the only time I ever got paid for not being white."

Our first interview was a boring bust, Erle Johnston watering everything down to mush, including his explanation that most Mississippians believed that citizenship alone should not guarantee the right to vote. I thought he was kind of a snake, opting for benign amnesia, but he did articulate the pervasive fear of racial intermarriage, and the power of the Citizens' Council network back in 1964.

William Simmons had been chief spokesman for the Citizens' Council, a more veiled and gentlemanly white separatist alternative to the Klan, and Hampton really wanted to get his testimony. The council was formed in 1954 and successfully organized fierce economic reprisals and political leverage to keep the races separate. In most of Mississippi virtually all the white business class were members. (The Klan served as a paramilitary rearguard force, often prodded by white political leaders.) The council had paid all the legal defense costs for the two trials of Klansman Byron De La Beckwith, their member who murdered Medgar Evers. They had published a children's book explaining how heaven was segregated into white and colored sections.

Simmons looked like a tall, lean Colonel Sanders, and spoke to us with consummate, well-educated southern grace, forthright and courteous in his condemnation of "the overweening power of the federal government . . . forcing the compulsory mixing of people who had two completely separate ways of life." He said, "There was concern about interracial dating, to be perfectly frank," and, "When the civil rights workers invaded the state in the summer of 1964 to change us, presumably into their own image, they were met with a feeling of some curiosity, but mostly resentment. They fanned out across the state, made a great to-do of breaking up our customs, of flaunting social practices that had been respected by people here over the years. That was the time of the hippies just coming in; many had on hippie uniforms and conducted themselves in hippie ways. . . . Also, the arrogance that they showed in wanting to reform a whole state in the way they thought it should be created resentment."

The business about hippies was news to me, since we had jumped through hoops back in 1964 to be well-groomed, well-mannered youngsters—nice shirts, crew cuts, no sideburns, no shorts, no tennis shoes, and certainly no dope. If there was weed, free love, or tie-dye, I never heard about them. But we certainly could have been considered arrogant, the latest in a long line of white northerners arriving to tell white Mississippians how to manage their affairs.

"Black people have had voting rights in this state all along," Mr. Simmons explained. "They had to meet certain qualifications. . . . The objective of this student invasion was to eliminate all of the qualifications, to have mass voting, and it was frankly to advance black political power. It was a very racist objective, and, as such, it was opposed." He certainly had the part about mass voting and black political power right.

"And then later, as the long hot summers began with the rioting in Watts, Chicago, Cleveland, Rochester, New York City, the feeling began to be: 'Well, why, why, why are these people coming to Mississippi to try to change things when their own backyard is blowing up?'" He had made a lot of northern civil rights workers squirm back in the day by deriding us as hypocrites, noting that in the "integrated" North, Harlem was the "largest *segregated* Negro community in the world," while "white liberals may invariably be found inhabiting the suburbs." That was hard to dispute, and, in fact, some of my black friends back in Sacramento had been skeptical about the Mississippi Project. Simmons would be one of the few segregationists willing to speak with some honesty in *Eyes on the Prize* about their fierce defense of what most Americans by now in 1985 considered a century-long moral catastrophe. Even fewer were willing to articulate that it was a struggle over power.

Would a more rousing and productive conversation have boiled up that day had Simmons known that I, his cameraman, had begun my adult life as an outside agitator in Mississippi? Probably. But would it have put Simmons ill at ease? Was it dishonest? Orlando, Prue, Henry, and I had decided long before that that was a different film for a different time. I now regret that decision, since outside agitators were the topic at hand.

Orlando's Mississippi segment was about power, pure and simple, and the violent white resistance to sharing power. Who will rule? Everything else was froth. The film had its roots in the interview he and Henry had done back in 1979 with Amzie Moore, grandson of a Mississippi slave. Amzie had since died, so theirs remained the only in-depth film interview ever done with him.

Moore had been, in Bob Moses's words, "a taproot for his people" in early days of voter registration, a self-educated veteran whose World War II hitch in the segregated army had opened new worlds to him. Sitting at home in the tiny delta town of Cleveland, Mississippi, not far from Money, Amzie told Henry, "I sailed through the Atlantic Ocean to the Rock of Gibraltar . . . the Mediterranean, got to the Suez Canal and took a right turn . . . 104 miles to the Gulf of Aden . . . from the Mediterranean of the Great Sea to Alexandria, Egypt, to Port Said; we saw the old civilizations. If you'd follow the Mediterranean Sea up a piece and turn left, you would come to the boot, Italy, and that's where the great Roman

Empire had its foundation. . . . You leave Calcutta, you leave Egypt, you can go down the Red Sea and through the Suez Canal, you can hit the Indian Ocean, you can go up the Gulf of Said. . . . You are going to find black people all the way over." He had wrenched free his mind and psyche, found air to breathe beyond the suffocation of Mississippi segregation. To Henry's everlasting credit, he allowed that 1979 conversation with Moore to roam far beyond the narrow topics of the moment.

Amzie had disguised himself as a cotton picker to help search for Emmett Till's body in 1955, and his gas station on Highway 61, "the Blues Highway," was a safe house for movement people passing through. He and Medgar Evers chipped away at civil rights for decades in isolation, until Bob Moses, the mysteriously compelling Harlem-born, Harvard-educated math teacher, arrived on a solo trip back in 1960 to see if SNCC could gain a foothold in "the heart of the iceberg."

Bob told us, "Amzie understood that the vote and the subsequent political action would actually unlock Mississippi. He wasn't distracted at all about integration of public facilities . . . he didn't want the legal procedures that he had been going through for years . . . it was not going straight to the heart of what was the trouble in Mississippi. Somehow, in following his guidance there, we stumbled on the key." The key was the vote.

The very idea of voting was foreign to most black Mississippians when Bob first arrived. Amzie told Henry and Orlando back in 1979, "Listen, for a long time, I had the idea that a man with white skin was superior, because it appeared to me that he had everything. And I figured if God would justify the white man having everything, that God had put him in a position to be the best. But when SNCC came, it didn't seem to matter what these white people thought. When SNCC moved, SNCC moved in SNCC's way. Sometimes they put all nine or ten leaders of SNCC in jail. It didn't seem to bother them."

Two other local men Moses worked with were gunned down. Bob himself had been beaten bloody and arrested. Then late one night on a road near Greenwood, whites fired machine-gun rounds into the SNCC car, blowing out the windows and windshield, wounding the driver, Jimmie Travis, in the neck and barely missing Bob, who managed to grab the steering wheel and bring the car to a stop. That story made its way up to our dorm rooms at Yale.

And in 1985 Unita Blackwell told Orlando that when Bob Moses came, "That's the first time in my life that I ever come in contact with anybody that tell me that I had the right to register to vote. . . . And they said, just try to encourage people to go and try to register. And that was my start of going around here to my neighbors and friends and asking them . . . would they come go to the courthouse and try to register to vote. . . . And for the whites, they understood it even larger than that, in terms of political power, but we hadn't even heard the words 'political power.'"

After the Simmons interview Prue and I had thanked our white crew, picked up Mike, Llew, and Sekou at the Jackson Holiday Inn, and headed over to Tougaloo Southern Christian College, a nineteenth-century black school on the grounds of the old Boddie Plantation. Tougaloo had been a safe haven for the Freedom Riders, and I had gone to SNCC staff meetings there back in the day. I did not learn until years later that Tougaloo faculty and staff, drawing on a long southern tradition, had quietly spread word that their campus (and our meetings) was guarded by armed local black men. Like so many historically black colleges, Tougaloo had lost enrollment after the 1960s when African American students gained access to the University of Mississippi or the wherewithal to study out of state. Now in 1985, like the aging SNCC veterans, it showed a patina of wear.

At Tougaloo we reunited with Orlando and all sang freedom songs with civil rights workers, now in their fifties and sixties, at a Mississippi Freedom Democratic Party reunion. Mike and I climbed around in the balcony of the beautiful old chapel to set up lighting for Orlando's interview with Annie Devine, a genuine movement *griot*. In 1963, Devine had quit her job selling insurance—much movement business had been done through the network of black insurance brokers and taxi companies across the South—to become a cofounder of the Mississippi Freedom Democratic Party with Victoria Gray, Fannie Lou Hamer, and Unita Blackwell. I had not seen her since 1964, and Blackside researchers had not been able to preinterview her, but were counting on Devine to explain exactly what the Mississippi Freedom Democratic Party was.

Mrs. Devine was indeed a lovely elder, but arrived seeming a bit confused and agitated about being interviewed. From the moment she settled into the warm light in the sanctuary, Orlando and Judy Richardson knew they had a problem. No one had told us that she was struggling with Alzheimer's; she could not really understand his questions. Orlando gamely went through the motions, never missing a beat as he swatted away mosquitoes, gently grasping for a lucid moment, to no avail. He soldiered on, with grace and respect for Mrs. Devine, knowing we were too late, knowing that her stories would go with her to the grave. After fifteen minutes of trying, he finally said, "Thank you so much for being with us. Now, that wasn't so bad, was it?" We had shot barely one roll; to save money we never developed it, and the sealed can sat for years unprocessed in a refrigerator at Blackside. Its frost-fringed label in Mike Chin's handwriting stared out to remind us every time we opened the freezer just how perishable this messy history was—"Mrs. Annie Devine 11/9/85."

(And a couple of years later, on *Eyes II*, after five tries, Henry finally secured an interview with Muhammad Ali, and ran up against the Champ's advanced Parkinson's disease. In 1997, I confronted the dementia problem in what turned out to be the last interview Barry Goldwater ever granted. We had come to his home in Arizona to discuss John Wesley Powell, the first white man to go down the Colorado River; Goldwater thought at first that we were discussing General Colin Powell.)

Voting in Mississippi in the early 1960s required all citizens to fill out a twenty-one-question registration form and then, to the satisfaction of the white registrar, write out an interpretation of any one of the 285 sections of the state constitution. Failure excluded a citizen not only from voting but from juries as well.

Bob Moses told us in his interview, "The '63 Freedom Vote was a way to raise the consciousness of black people. Eventually people were going to be electing black people to office, but it wasn't a thought in their mind at that time. So what you had to do was to begin to prepare them, so that they could begin to think that someday a black person would run for governor of Mississippi, for lieutenant governor of Mississippi. That they would be responsible for putting the state together."

So what, exactly, was the Mississippi Freedom Democratic Party? The same illusive political concept that made the MFDP hard for us to explain in Mississippi in 1964 came back and made it hard to explain on television in 1985. At its core was the conundrum of activists trying to change the system both from the outside and from the inside at the same time. No ploy like it had ever been tried before in America.

It was in essence a mock vote, hatched in response to SNCC and CORE's excruciatingly slow progress in the dangerous business of actually registering rural voters. The strategy seemed simple: in a massive drive first tested with the college students in the fall of 1963 and then launched in full force during the summer of 1964, northern volunteers working with local people would collect unofficial one-page "Freedom Registration" forms from thousands of disenfranchised blacks across Mississippi. The freedom voters would organize the selection of local black (and a few local white) "freedom delegates," who would present themselves to the Democratic National Convention in Atlantic City in late August. By creating a shadow voter registration system, open to all, outside segregated state control, it would demonstrate to the nation that the state's black citizens would vote en masse if they could.

Success assumed that Lyndon Johnson's Democratic Party, sympathetic to civil rights in an election year, would award seats at their convention to the freedom delegates and reject the all-white official Mississippi Democratic Party delegation. The radical push from below would shame the liberal reformers at the top into purging the segregationists and embracing the truly democratic MFDP, all on prime-time national television.

Pitching this phantom parallel political instrument to poorly educated Mississippi sharecroppers who in 1964 had no experience with the two-party political system, voting, political conventions, or even full citizenship was hard. But Moses was nothing if not patient. "A lot of what turned out to be organizing turned out to be patience. . . . I mean you can't force people to move, right? But just the presence of the organizer and the knowledge that the organizer is there and committing himself to something which people want to do. . . . They all agreed that they do want to register to vote."

Victoria Gray, who had run for the U.S. Senate on the MFDP ticket, joined us the next morning in warm conversation on camera. I remembered that back in 1964 she had stylishly coiffed straightened hair; today in '85 she sported a big stylish Afro. Mike shot the interview while I loaded magazines for him. She described the sudden explosion of hope with the arrival of the movement in Mississippi. "People had made a discovery . . . that there is a way out of much that is wrong with our lives. And so we can't get past these people at the state level because they've locked us out, but we just knew that once we get to the national level, with all of the proof that we have been locked out, and the fact that we've had the courage to go ahead and create our own party then. . . . We felt like we were going to get that representation that we'd been denied for so long."

• • • • • •

Orlando interviewed SNCC's Hollis Watkins about the party, knowing now after Mrs. Devine's noninterview that a narrator would probably have to do basic exposition about the MFDP in *Eyes on the Prize*. Hollis was one of the few SNCC staff who was still as fit and trim as I remembered him in his youth.

Within SNCC and CORE many had questioned the wisdom of flooding Mississippi with hypereducated college students, 90 percent white, who would interact with equally smart but undereducated local laborers, cooks, farmhands, and maids serving white people by day, organizing for freedom by night. Hollis was concerned that white students would overshadow local grassroots people, make them feel that "'Well, since they are more educated than I am, then maybe I should listen to them, do what they say,' and fall back into the same rut they were in before we started the grassroots organizations."

From the beginning Henry Hampton had been keenly averse to making a "white people to the rescue" film, and wanted to tamp down the notion of heroic summer volunteers shouldering the burden to help befuddled local black victims. Bob Moses told us that before the 1964 Summer Project, "We met for months over this question. By and large most of the staff did not want to do it. . . . But the local people by and large wanted the students. . . . Mrs. Hamer, an excellent case in point, she wanted the students to come . . . and so we were at loggerheads." Polls at the time showed that two thirds of Americans nationwide opposed the Summer Project.

Within Blackside in 1985 opinions differed on how much to focus on the Summer Project and its mostly white volunteers. Richardson was "a little irritated at putting white folks in front," but Henry believed that "white people have got to see themselves" on the screen.

Mississippi organizer Dave Dennis had been arrested thirty times. Sitting under an oak tree draped with Spanish moss on that cool morning at Tougaloo in 1985, he told Orlando, "I don't think that anyone had in their minds that it was gonna be a clean summer, without the racists being able to take their toll on someone. We hadn't expected it to happen so soon, and we didn't expect it to happen so close to the family." If one major goal of Mississippi Freedom Summer was to make the state's private violence public, grisly success came within the first days, near the little town of Philadelphia, Mississippi.

The White Knights of the Ku Klux Klan, a particularly virulent splinter group around Meridian and Philadelphia, met regularly in a room of the Neshoba County courthouse. On June 16, 1964, the meeting formally marked Meridian project director Michael Schwerner, "the Jew-boy with the beard," for elimination. Klansmen set out to murder him during a voter registration meeting at Mt. Zion Methodist Church, the center of fruitless voter registration activity in all-black Longdale, and soon to be the site of a summer Freedom School. When Schwerner did not appear, they beat two elderly black deacons nearly to death. Not satisfied with violence against black men, they then visited violence upon their sacred black space, poured gasoline across the floors, and burned the church down to its foundations.

Two days later Schwerner and his local black coworker James Chaney drove with Andy Goodman, a white New York volunteer on his second day in Mississippi, to inspect the church's ruins. The State Sovereignty Commission had passed the license plate number of Mickey's car to the Neshoba County sheriff, and at four in the afternoon Deputy Cecil Price, a member of the White Knights of the KKK, pulled them over and took the three to jail in Philadelphia. They were released at 10 P.M. and never heard from again.

Cleve Sellers, Donna Moses, and a number of CORE and SNCC workers spent the night searching for the missing workers, escorted by men from the local community. Volunteer David Crittendon and local organizers from Meridian joined the search and ended up in a high-speed chase, pursued by white men in pickup trucks.

Had only Chaney alone, a black Mississippian, vanished that night, few outside his community might have heard about it. But the disappearance of two young white college kids from New York sparked immediate attention on TV and radio around the country. President Johnson deployed four hundred sailors from the Meridian Naval Air Station to search the woods and swamps, with the help of FBI agents flown in from other states. As the search for the bodies droned on across the landscape of northeast Mississippi, the FBI came up with the corpses of eight other unidentified murdered black men whose killings had gone unreported and unsolved.

CHAPTER TEN

Crossroads

1964

Because I had canvassed for votes the year before in Meridian, I was assigned there to gather MFDP Freedom Registration signatures right after the young men disappeared. I joined about thirty-five volunteers from the North already at work, together with twice as many local people. Preston Ponder, Roscoe Jones, Sue Brown, Catherine Crowell, A. C. Henderson, and other local black organizers made all the decisions, and were in charge of work schedules, mass meetings, transportation, and liaisons with local churches and with the state project headquarters in Jackson. Among the volunteers were a divinity student from Minnesota; a classical musician; a Stanford medical student; Jan Goodman, who was a manager from the Girl Scouts in New York; and Susan Brownmiller, a young writer who was using her vacation time from *Newsweek* to volunteer (the magazine prudently took her name off their masthead).

(Both Brownmiller and Goodman had years of organizing experience in New York CORE and political campaigns. When they arrived, a project leader asked to see the new volunteers, and as they proudly raised their hands, he said, "Shit. I asked for volunteers and they sent me white women.")

We had several New York schoolteachers, and three Unitarian ministers, Rev. Dan Lion, Rev. Arthur Wilmot, and a Rev. Motley. Though I didn't figure it out until I met Henry Hampton years later, the ministers arrived bearing printed materials about racial equality that Henry had created working for the Unitarians in Boston.

I had just turned twenty, and went to the South not as a revolutionary, but as an evangelist for the simple democratic principles I had learned in Mr. McClellan's social studies class at Sacramento High School. We had to cover our own travel and living costs, and each of us brought the required five hundred dollars cash in bail money, mostly raised from our home churches. We northerners in the Meridian office were foot soldiers, pounding the city streets to register freedom voters, or teaching in the Freedom School. Like most soldiers in most wars, we were rank beginners.

Meridian was a midsize dairy and timber town just south of Philadelphia, Mississippi. We worked in six bustling rooms of an old doctor's office above the only black drug store and taxi company. To reach the stairs up to our office you had to pass the taxi dispatcher, who sat at his desk with a shotgun across his knees. Mickey and Rita Schwerner had the place beautifully fixed up, a library with several thousand donated books, art supplies, a mimeograph machine, a nice big room for meetings, and friendly blue curtains. Everyone assumed Mickey and the other guys were dead, despite claims from the Citizens' Council and Klan that it was all a Communist hoax and the kids were dining with Fidel Castro in Cuba or with the beatniks in Greenwich Village.

Dave Crittendon, a black music student at Juilliard, and I stayed at the home of a local family, Mr. and Mrs. Harris. I slept in what had been Mickey Schwerner's bed, in the back of the house. This was the home where Medgar Evers stayed when he was in Meridian, and on the first night the lady of the house showed me a pistol and ammunition under the bed. I did not yet understand that SNCC and CORE organizers were quite comfortable in the knowledge that local black Mississippians had always been well armed and were not about to give up their weapons now. Medgar had a gun with him the night he was killed. Henry Hampton did not want to go there in *Eyes*.

As we had been trained, we never stood near the windows, and seldom turned on the lights after sundown; it was better to fumble around in the dark than to present a clear target. We never traveled alone, never without a full tank of gas, and never drove home or to the office when we were being followed. We disabled the dome lights in our cars, carried dimes in our shoes for pay phones, and slept in the back of the house as far from the street as possible. Some nights I'd be awakened by headlights of cars circling the block. As directed, we had our photos developed out of state.

I saw my first cockroach, smelled my first curling iron, ate my first pigs' feet, and had my hair cut by a black barber baffled at how to navigate his first encounter with the wispy hair of a white person.

The office was alive with optimism. James Chaney's little brother, eleven-year-old Ben, was there most days. Energetic second and third graders had great fun climbing all over us white guys, shrieking with glee, pounding us with their little fists. One afternoon a black man in his thirties came in to thank us for what we were doing and started to cry uncontrollably; I didn't know what to do.

As he explained on camera, Bob Moses and others saw a benefit beyond voting in bringing white volunteers to a state where the codes of interaction between black and white were rigid: "It was a closed society. . . . I think part of the difficulty was people thinking that they had to do something on a grand scale, particularly the volunteers, but just their very presence in the black community made a difference. . . . It was not possible for white people to actually live in any kind of normal day-to-day association with black people in the black community. And so what we were trying to do with the students was to open up the black community, to make it a place in which black people could feel that they could invite whomever they pleased into their home. . . . People could serve whom they pleased in their own little coffee shop. White people were welcome in the black community even if black people were not welcome in the white community."

Howard Thurman had written: "In the section of the country where there is the most contact between Negro and white there is the least real fellowship . . . the intimacy of the servant and the served . . . all normal contacts poisoned."

Mrs. Unita Blackwell had worked in the white folks' kitchens, the white folks' homes, where the family would seat themselves for dinner and then ring a little bell to summon the black maid, who carried the food to their table. She told Orlando what an experience it was to have white volunteers come into her own crowded home, serve themselves from a big pot of pinto beans, and then take a seat on the floor. "We were sitting there laughing, and I guess they became very real and very human, we each to one another. . . . We wasn't a closed society anymore. . . . That was the freedom summer."

We did indeed live very comfortably black and white together that summer, though some cultural precincts remained off-limits; the black staff would occasionally go to a local juke at night, but we never went. During all that time in the South I never heard a note of delta blues or country music, never set foot in a white church, and never had a real conversation with a white Mississippian.

• • • • • •

On June 23, 1964, a Chocktaw hunter found the burned-out hulk of the National Council of Churches station wagon registered to Mickey Schwerner in the muck of the Bogue Chitto Swamp, fifty miles north of us.

Every night two of us did the graveyard shift in the office, with the lights off for safety, enduring for a few hours the low-level terror many local black organizers had to endure much of their adult lives. In those days before speakerphones, voice mail, or answering machines, the telephones were reserved for emergencies, so we had to answer every call. As soon as night fell the phone began to ring, and when you picked it up you could hear that echo-in-a-submarine ambience of a tapped line; after a few moments a southern white voice might say, "We know you're there. . . . We're on our way to burn you out," or "We're coming over to shoot you." The phantom on the line might spin the cylinder of a revolver into the phone; it sounded exactly like the cute little clicking of numbers on my iPhone today.

Most jarring were the little kids, with their ten-year-old-child versions of the gracious southern speech I later so admired in William J. Simmons, bellowing, "Nigger, nigger, nigger, shit, shit, shit, you nigger shit, you nigger-loving shit," then passing the phone to a younger playmate. "You nigger-loving SHIT SHIT SHIT!" We could never tell exactly who it was listening on the line, but assumed the FBI, State Sovereignty Commission, Klan, Meridian Police Department, and maybe the Citizens' Council all had their own wiretaps—a party line if ever there was one.

SNCC and CORE were the only civil rights organizations willing to organize aggressively in rural Mississippi, deemed too difficult for the return by SCLC and the NAACP, who were skilled at court battles and strategies for big cities like Birmingham. CORE's state director, with responsibility for Meridian, was an intense young guy from Louisiana, Dave Dennis, who worked closely with Bob Moses and had mentored Mickey Schwerner. Over the course of Freedom Summer, Dave had begun to seriously question nonviolent tactics in the face of unapologetic murder, calling it in private "a waste of good lives." He, like many others, questioned the value of flooding the state with white college kids, but accepted us as necessary elements of the apparatus and treated us with respect.

Twenty years later, he was still wound up like a spring when we interviewed him at Tougaloo. Orlando asked him about the decision to bring hundreds of white students into Mississippi that summer. "Most of the students . . . were from the large universities, from families who were politicians, bankers, lawyers . . . and we felt that by bringing in those particular people that the attention of their parents and relatives, from the various different other parts of the country, would be on these areas."

We had been willing bait that summer, big visible targets, knowing that we, with our attitude, privilege, and connections would attract a particular ferocious anger from local whites and a lot of attention from national media. The intent was to swing press focus quickly and decisively toward civil rights by bringing the violence out of the alleys and backwoods and into the shame of a national spotlight. We understood the strategy, and we certainly understood that local black activists and SNCC and CORE staff had already worked for years under threat of death. Bob Moses said, "We weren't asking the volunteers to do anything we ourselves wouldn't do."

Our job was to be white, showing that blacks and whites could work together in Mississippi, and taunting the local white vigilantes into action. My overriding memories of that summer are suffocating humid heat, joy, and fear. The fear was jumpy and ever present, but untroubled by doubt. What a blessing it was to discover at that young age what I was willing to die for, in a heartbeat, without pause or ambiguity. Years later, Henry told me he had the same new sensation of freedom when he walked toward the bridge in Selma, terrified but free of doubt.

After a couple of weeks canvassing the dusty streets of Meridian, I went to work in the county's rural farming areas, east toward the Alabama border and up north along the Neshoba County line. By then some of us had cultivated a peculiar faux-southern accent in the ridiculous hope that we might pass as locals. I'd head out early every morning with James Chaney's classmate George Smith, Sam "Freedom" Brown, and Freddie Watson, young black men from Meridian who knew the country roads, and Dave Kotz, a sophomore from Harvard. Because SNCC and CORE lacked enough two-way radios to go around, we scouted out black roadhouses with pay phones so we could check into the Meridian office exactly on schedule every three hours.

We had a rough time gathering signatures on the MFDP Freedom

Registration forms from sharecroppers, knowing that our mere presence on their front porch stoked well-founded fears of trouble. The conversations were warm but all thumbs, as they struggled to get past the awkward business of simply shaking hands with well-dressed white strangers, and we struggled to articulate our common mission across the great gap of race and culture. We had barely a vague glimmer of each other's lives, and no experience in each other's shoes. We may have been the Target of the Month, but they surely knew that Dave Kotz and I were just passing through, that we would retreat back to faraway safety in a few months, leaving them alone out there on the farm at the mercy of the local deputy. What sadism might be visited upon them for talking with a couple of northern organizers? Anchored to family, home, community, and often to debt, they did not have the option of retreating. And among the very few lucky enough to own land, many had risked it all as collateral to bond civil rights workers out of jail.

A older farmer so poor his house was insulated with cast-off newspapers said to us, "I pay my taxes, I know right from wrong, and I want to vote," but were they signing those Freedom Registration forms because they wanted full citizenship, or because they had spent their lives reluctant to say "No" to a white man half their age? We never really figured out how to unpack the MFDP's challenge to the upcoming Democratic convention in a way that could be clear to people who, in Amzie Moore's words, considered voting "something that white people did." But all our fumbling explanations could not defeat the local people's clear-eyed understanding that this was the moment for change and for freedom, and hundreds signed the MFDP registration form. What courage that took.

Cloudbursts—thunder and lightning all around and the fresh smell of ozone; I had never seen such thunderous cloudbursts—could turn a thinly graveled road slimy with red mud in a few minutes, "snotty," the locals called it, and more than once we slid into a ditch. The air in eastern Mississippi that summer seemed to me, a boy from the arid West, like a mix of pure oxygen and steam. Amzie Moore said, "The weather is so hot you can almost see it. If the wind doesn't blow every once in a while, you look like you might be getting yourself ready to be burned to death."

We covered about fifty miles every day, usually singing freedom songs in the car, "freedom high," and on Sundays we made our pitch in rural churches if the minister would risk inviting us. The passion of a preacher in a backwoods church, rising to the old hoop-and-holler style—"Start low, build slow, move higher, strike fire"—was something I could never have imagined growing up on those Unitarian sermon/essays back in California. Once, a Mississippi pastor suddenly called on me to shout out witness for freedom. Never in generations had anyone in my lineage ever shouted out witness for anything in church, but I stood up and stumbled through something about "so long as any man is in chains, I am not free," praying that my mere presence as a white person in their church would trump my fumble-bunny rhetoric.

To the local black folks we may have represented hope wrapped in danger, but to the local whites we were a different sort of threat. The last northerner to force change onto Meridian, Mississippi, was General Sherman, who burned most of the town to the ground in 1864 and left behind a conquered people.

The White Knights of the KKK blanketed our area with leaflets warning of "the long hot summer promised by savage blacks and their Communist masters. . . . Pray for our persecuted people. Destroy these agents of Satan. . . . Communists are anxious to . . . expand the issue into a bloody revolution. We Knights are working day and night to preserve Law and Order here in Mississippi, in the only way that it can be preserved: by strict segregation of the races, and control of the social structure in the hands of Christian, Anglo-Saxon White men. . . . We are deadly serious about this business . . . we are not going to sit back and permit our rights and rights of our posterity to be negotiated away by a group composed of atheistic priests, brainwashed black savages, and mongrelized monkey worshippers. Take heed, atheists and mongrels, we will not travel your path to a Leninist Hell, but we will buy YOU a ticket to the Eternal if you insist. Take your choice, SEGREGATION, TRANQUILITY AND JUSTICE, OR BI-RACISM, CHAOS AND DEATH."

The Klan flourished in that rural triangle where we worked, between Meridian, Jackson, and Philadelphia, drawing in county sheriffs, city police, preachers, and businessmen. Meridian boasted 250 Klansmen, and the imperial wizard himself had issued a communiqué commanding each one in our area to "prepare himself and his unit for effective combat against the enemy."

The *Neshoba County Democrat* newspaper advised in an editorial: "Outsiders who come here and try to stir up trouble should be dealt with in a manner they won't forget." Even the staid *Meridian Star*, with particular scorn for northern churchmen taking part, editorialized about "the student volunteers—the beatniks, the wild-eyed left wing nuts, the unshaven and unwashed trash, and the just plain stupid or ignorant or misled—go on meddling and muddling with things about which they know nothing and which concern them not. . . . God help the United States."

No wonder they were gunning for us.

I saw very little actual violence in the South, but violence always hovered. The hassles were mostly trivial: Driving back from the little town of Whynot with white Rev. Dan Lion at the wheel, black Dave Crittendon next to him, and me in back, a state trooper pulled us over for no apparent reason other than that we had a black man in the front seat and a white man in the backseat, blacks and whites wrongly arranged. When Rev. Lion took out his license, which in those days bore the bold designation "Clergy—Reverend Felix Danford Lion," the trooper, in a cleverly petty dig at the outside agitator, said, "OK, Felix, just wanted to see what you are up to," and sent us on our way.

We were obsessive in obeying traffic laws, mindful of arrest for "driving while organizing." Headed out to the hamlet of Zero at six in the morning through the utterly deserted streets of Meridian, I stopped at a red light. A cop pulled me over in the next block for running the red light and took me to the courthouse, where the desk sergeant booked me into a cell before releasing me a few hours later on ten dollars' cash bail. White teenagers smashed out the rear window of another team's car as it drove by them. That afternoon another car came back to the office with a bullet hole in the front window. White taxi drivers with ax handles surrounded Joe Morse and Dave Crittendon and smashed Joe's camera.

Three white men approached us at a railroad crossing—exactly the sort of hot, dusty place you could imagine Robert Johnson trading his soul to the devil in exchange for the blues—and threatened us with a baseball bat. When Rev. Lion tried to introduce himself, the guy with the bat shot back that he didn't give a shit who he was, reverend or not, and that we'd better get out of town fast. Dan replied that we were doing voter registration work and it would be a federal offense for them to interfere. The man laughed, and said they would kill us, and we couldn't do much work if we were dead.

One sticky afternoon George Smith, Dave Kotz, Freddie Watson, and I had actually gotten about a dozen signatures on MFDP registration forms from people in a barbershop and a café in the tiny crossroads town of Lauderdale. We were explaining voter registration to three black women sitting on a cabin porch shelling peas into their aprons when a red sheriff's car pulled into the gravel driveway, blocking our car. A constable in a Smokey Bear flat hat got out, walked up to us, and said, "You two white boys are under arrest." He was unmoved by my explanation that we were protected under federal law, instructing citizens in their right to vote, and simply said, "Get in the car," which I did. He ordered George, Freddie, and Dave to follow in our National Council of Churches car. I asked him, "What are the charges?" to which he replied, "That's for the judge to decide."

Constable Gray got on the radio and called in, "Mission accomplished." As we drove, he asked me, "How much do the Communists pay you to come down here? You come down here to marry niggers, don't you?" I did my college best to explain that we believed in equal rights and voting rights for all under the Fourteenth and Fifteenth Amendments to the United States Constitution and various federal statutes and that we were instructing Negro citizens under the First and Fifteenth Amendments. He must have thought I had flown in from Mars or from hell itself. He should welcome those poor, uneducated black women, those mammies in their bandannas, as his equals? The sun will rise in the West? It was fifty years ago, but I have a vivid memory of looking over at this peace officer twice my age, who as far as I knew was delivering me to be killed, and understanding that I, a kid from California, was upending the only social order he had ever known. It might have taken a superhuman leap of faith for him to willingly share power with an illiterate black sharecropper who didn't even understand voting. You want me to allow this person to rule over me?

Watching the pines fly by the window, looking over at Constable Gray, I suspected for the very first time in my life that maybe no one is born evil, that he and I might just as easily have reversed roles had we been born and raised in each other's worlds. Neither of us got up that morning determined to be an asshole; he got up to do what he believed was right, and I had done the same. And at that moment I believed unflinchingly, with a pang of regret for him, that whatever happened now, he would lose this fight. I thought, "These guys haven't gotten the news."

Constable Gray asked who was our leader, and who were the "local niggers" we worked with. I dodged the question, but suddenly remembered the signed Freedom Registration forms in the other car, with names and addresses of local people, about to fall into the hands of the sheriff, the Klan, the Citizens' Council, and the State Sovereignty Commission.

The justice of the peace's office turned out to be Lauderdale's only gas station; Judge Henry Hatcher was the station owner and mechanic. The scene was what we might now call Cormac McCarthy Gothic: doomed flies struggling on the flypaper, cigars, grimy socket wrenches, the smell of oil in the blistering heat, unshaven Judge Hatcher in his Hawaiian shirt, all of us dripping sweat. Hatcher asked Dave and me, "How much are they paying you to come down here and marry niggers?" A small crowd of whites had begun to gather, a nicely coiffed white lady from the little beauty shop next door, two more deputies. I guessed they and Hatcher surely knew the men who had murdered Goodman, Schwerner, and Chaney, and they certainly had read the Klan warnings about us. Hatcher said, "You're a bunch of agitators . . . Why don't you go home and worry about your own states?" Another deputy arrived and produced Robert Richardson, a black barber, and Hatcher said, "We take care of our colored people, don't we, Robert." Looking at the floor, Richardson answered, "Yes sir." After hushed discussion with Constable Gray and the other lawmen, he charged Dave and me with trespass, but wouldn't tell us whose property we had trespassed on.

"Take 'em away, boys." Into a new squad car I went in handcuffs, down the highway and then a sudden turn onto a gravel road. We were headed, as it turned out, not to a lynching, but down the back way to jail in Meridian. The jailers booked me and Dave, going out of their way to be courteous, and released our local black coworkers George and Freddie. What we did not know was that the county was by then swarming with federal agents on the Philadelphia murder case. Sheriffs and police knew perfectly well they were now under the eye of the Justice Department, that the FBI had informers undercover inside the Meridian police department. By triggering the reluctant J. Edgar Hoover's deployment of so many overt and covert agents to the area, putting the local police on good behavior, Andy Goodman's death may have saved my life.

I added my name to the graffiti scratched on the cell wall. It had been movement strategy to flood the jails, stay behind bars as long as you could stand it, "jail/no bail." SNCC and CORE people did months of hellish hard time alone, enduring beatings, in Parchman penitentiary and wretched little county jails far from the media's view. But since the Philadelphia disappearance, project field offices now bailed people out as quickly as possible. When we failed to check in by phone on time, our office had started calling jails and hospitals, found out what had happened, and posted bond later that day. By then the charges had expanded to include felony trespass and malicious mischief.

Only after I got out of jail did George tell me that he, Freddie, and Dave, following in the rental car, had eaten as many Freedom Registration ballots as they could stomach, torn the rest to tiny bits, and stuffed them under the ashtrays. Our contacts were safe.

That day's events went into the files as two of the thousand civil rights arrests in Mississippi that summer, the vast majority unfolding in little towns across the state where there were no news crews. Blackside researchers combed those same files two decades later. These encounters between individuals—sharecroppers, volunteers, CORE and SNCC workers, sheriffs, farmhands, lawyers, ministers, judges—were the core fabric of the Mississippi movement, but they were outside the frame, neither filmed nor photographed. Unlike the thousands of demonstrators and brash cops in the streets of Birmingham or Selma, they left few bread crumbs for later historians and documentary filmmakers. Blackside would struggle with that problem years later.

I phoned my parents in Sacramento on the tapped phone, sitting at what had been Mickey Schwerner's desk, with some of his papers still there in front of me. Then, since the whole summer enterprise rested on getting national press attention, I called a reporter at the *Sacramento Bee,* and the next day's Sacramento paper headlined "Capital Youth Seized in Mississippi." The article included my folks' names and address, and they immediately started getting hate calls; what terrible pain I caused them that summer. A southern man called late one night, saying that their son had been killed in Mississippi.

Our arrest got a few lines in the next day's *New York Times*. Constable Gray and I had both fulfilled our duties, he by getting one outside agitator out of town, and me by generating a couple of sentences about Mississippi into the national press. Mission accomplished. We felt good that night at a mass meeting, a little cocky at having gotten our stripes and lived to fight another day, as the crowd sang freedom songs.

State of Mississippi v. Jon Else would drone on for the rest of the summer, with the DA adding a second felony trespass charge, letting our attorney know he was pressing for trial and one year in the county jail, and then upped that to ten years in state prison. One of the movement's most durable strategies was to never let the violence or intimidation scare you away; bring in more people. Out on bail, Dave and I went back to work in Lauderdale, now with Dave Crittendon and Henry's Unitarian colleague Rev. Dan Lion. After our arrest it was harder to convince people to put their name on a Freedom Ballot. We couldn't convince any of the black farmers to put us up overnight; "You don't want to get caught here at night." Whites with baseball bats again threatened us and we dutifully went to the gas station and reported it to the local law enforcement authority, Judge Hatcher, who said, "You should expect that sort of thing if you keep coming back into town and trying to turn the niggers against the whites. I know how to handle my niggers."

At dawn on August 4, 1964, we got a call from CBS about a rumor that the bodies of Goodman, Chaney, and Schwerner had been found. For forty-four days it had simmered as the perfect crime: Sheriff Lawrence Rainey had held the three men in jail long enough for the preacher Edgar Ray Killen to gather a posse of Klansmen in Meridian, then released the boys into the moonlit night. Deputy Price and a dozen Klansmen had stopped their station wagon on a remote stretch between Philadelphia and Meridian, shot the two white boys in the head, and savagely beat Chaney before they shot him three times in the chest. Then, around midnight, with the help of local farmhands, they buried the three fifteen feet down inside an earthen dam on the Old Jolly Farm, but not before driving over them with a bulldozer. As far as anyone knew, it was the first time since the Civil War that black men and white men had been buried together in Mississippi. The newsreels Orlando and Jeanne Jordan used in *Eyes on the Prize* are ghoulish, with Price and Rainey themselves, in uniform, moving the body bags containing the young men whose murder they had planned and perpetrated.

That same afternoon we heard that the wire services were reporting American gunboats had exchanged fire with North Vietnamese ships in the Gulf of Tonkin, half a world away. No one knew it, but the American war in Vietnam had begun. Plans for the evening mass meeting went ahead, and I got the job of picking up the visiting singer, Pete Seeger, at Meridian's only colored hotel, the Beale. I knocked, Pete answered the door, invited me in, and as we exchanged a little small talk I realized he hadn't heard the news of the day. When I explained that the bodies were likely found, and that the United States was in an armed conflict halfway around the world, he fell silent.

How on earth could Pete Seeger, a forty-five-year-old white folk singer from Dutchess County, New York, stir the people of Meridian that terrible night, awash in the awful news? Somehow he did it. Somehow deep inside he found reserves of energy, compassion, good jokes, and his thundering banjo to bring us comfort and even to forget our troubles for a little while. He was, after all, one of the few white men in America who could really sing freedom songs, not by imitating black singers, but by unleashing his own split tenor power and singular harmonies. Mostly, he did it for the kids; romping around with his banjo, Pete had little Ben Chaney and his friends prancing, clowning, duckwalking, and running all around that Mt. Olive Baptist Church basement as he gleefully belted out his version of the South African tale of "Abby Yo Yo," in which a little boy charms an evil giant with his ukulele. A crew-cut fellow in suit and skinny tie, surely an FBI agent, watched from the back of the room, not singing. At some point Roscoe Jones walked over to Seeger with a note, and Pete made the official announcement everyone knew was coming.

A couple of days later, we joined a long convoy of locals driving up Highway 16 to Longdale for a memorial at the ruins of Mt. Zion Church. As newsreel cameras captured a scene that Henry and Orlando would use a quarter century later, we gathered around the rubble—Mrs. Chaney and Ben, Howard Zinn, Roscoe Jones, Preston Ponder, local people, about fifty of us. An old woman broke the silence with a soft "Amazing Grace" and extended her hand to Bob Moses. They stood together clasping hands as one by one we joined the song. Price and Rainey watched stone-faced from the tree line. Next to me I could hear the NBC camera purring. Bob talked about the three young men with his usual melancholy calm, unblinking, and then, Zinn recalled, "with bitterness, surprised everyone by referring to a headline in that morning's paper which read: 'President Johnson Says Shoot to Kill in Gulf of Tonkin.' Then Bob said, 'This is what we're trying to do away with, the idea that whoever disagrees with us must be killed.'"

At the Mississippi Freedom Democratic Party state convention in Jackson a few days later, with all its trappings and pageantry of mainstream politics, caucuses from every single county selected delegates to go to the Democratic National Convention in Atlantic City. They nominated black pharmacist Aaron Henry for governor and white Tougaloo chaplain Rev. Ed King for lieutenant governor, both Mississippi natives. Ella Baker, the "Godmother of SNCC" rose to proclaim, "We who believe in freedom cannot rest until it comes!" I had stood in wonderment at so many orators that year, but none like this regal little woman I'd never heard of, Miss

Baker, thundering about why political power mattered. "Until the killing of a black mother's son becomes as important as the killing of a white mother's son, we who believe in freedom cannot rest!"

The memorial service for murdered James Chaney looms large in movement history and in *Eyes on the Prize*. Goodman's and Schwerner's families had wanted their sons interred next to Chaney in the same cemetery, but Mississippi segregation law would not allow it, enforcing the distance between black bodies and white bodies even in death. So on the afternoon of August 7, Chaney's family laid him to his final rest in a Negro cemetery just south of town. Around dusk, hundreds of Meridian's black folks made the long walk in silence from their neighborhoods toward First Union Baptist, and we from the office joined them. Years later, in an out-of-body experience, I would see myself in an archive newsreel Kenn Rabin and the researchers dug up for Prue and Orlando, a skinny, wired-up twenty-year-old in line outside the church in a sea of black faces. We were nearing the end of a very long, hard summer, and I was ready to escape the South with all its fear, death, and feudalism.

No white citizen of Meridian came to the service, and only one white minister, Rev. Clay Lee, spoke out against the crime.

Inside the church with five hundred people under the blistering newsreel lights, Mrs. Chaney sitting next to little Ben in the front row, the pastor began, "We have come here to proclaim to the world that all men might know that life has conquered death, that love has conquered hate, that freedom is conquering slavery's darkness." Really? We sang a weary "Rock of Ages," suffocating in heat and humidity. A second sweat-soaked minister in his preacher blue suit plodded through the Twenty-third Psalm. Rev. Ed King later remembered the tenor "was so cautious a stranger might have thought the victim had been killed in an auto accident." Dave Dennis, who had buried his friend Medgar Evers only the year before, waited his turn to deliver the eulogy, becoming more and more angry as the preachers droned on. He told Orlando in 1985 that the national CORE people had asked him to keep it cool and make sure his speech was calm.

Judy Richardson and Orlando had worked late the night before his interview to devise an order of questions for the famously mercurial Dave Dennis. (He had stood up Judy on *America, We Loved You Madly* back in 1979, and never showed up for an interview I was to shoot for *Soundtrack for a Revolution* in 2008.) Fearing Dave might run off the tracks, Judy counseled, "Don't ask Dave Dennis about Ben Chaney until the very end."

On screen in *Eyes* you can watch the scene I'd witnessed in the church that evening in 1964. Walking to the podium in his worn denim jacket, Dave Dennis seemed already world-weary at twenty-eight. Standing a few yards behind him as he started talking about James Chaney in his steady, quiet way, I could feel resolve rising in the church. Dave said, "I'm not here to do the traditional thing most of us do at such a gathering. . . . What I want to talk about is what I really *grieve* about. I don't grieve for Chaney because . . . I feel he lived a fuller life than many of us will ever live. I feel that he's got his freedom and we are still fighting for it."

More camera lights came on.

> But what I want to talk about right now is the *living dead that we have right among our midst,* not only in the state of Mississippi, but through-out the nation. . . . I blame not just those individuals who pulled the trigger or did the beating or dug the hole with the shovel . . . but *I blame the president on down in the government of the state of Mississippi.*

Dave reminded us that the men who murdered Emmett Till were walking the streets that very evening.

Orlando later noted exactly when "Dave moved toward the zone and abandoned his prepared remarks" that night in 1965, and he finally asked him about Ben.

> I looked out there and I saw little Ben Chaney, things just sort of snapped and I was in a fantasy world, to be sitting up here talking about "things gonna get better," and we should do it in an easy manner and nonvio-lence and stuff like that. In this country you cannot make a man change by speaking a foreign language, he has to understand what you're talk-ing about. This country operated then and still operates on violence. Eye for an eye, and tooth for a tooth, that's what we respect. . . . And there was no need to stand in front of that kid Ben Chaney and lie to him.

In the *Eyes on the Prize* black-and-white newsreel you can see as his measured speech suddenly lurched into fierce anger, his voice rising in pitch, and Dave Dennis began barking out the raw realities we had all held barely in check through all the tensions of that summer.

Well . . . I'm sick and tired of going to funerals! I've got a bitter vengeance in my heart tonight, and can't help but feel bitter, you see, deep down inside, and I'm not going to stand here and ask anybody not to be angry tonight. You see, I know what's gonna happen. *I feel it deep in my heart! When they find the people who killed these guys in Neshoba County, you've got to have a jury of their cousins, their aunts, and their uncles, and I know what they're going to say: "Not guilty!"*

The collective soul power in the church was now a rising wave, cresting with "Amen" and "Say it!" as Dave shouted out that the newly passed Civil Rights Act guaranteed *no* voting rights, and therefore had no effect on all-white jury selection in Mississippi. Only political *power* could stop racist violence.

Unless we as individuals stand up and demand our rights in this dad-blasted country, you see . . . tomorrow, baby, it could be you or your child . . . and what are we going to do as people . . . as a result of what happened, for what this guy died for and the other people died for? We're going to come to this memorial here, say, "Oh, what a shame," go back home and pray to the Lord as we've done for years. We go back to work in some white folks' kitchen tomorrow and forget about the whole God-blasted thing, you see.

The audience started clapping.

Don't applaud! Don't get your frustration out by clapping your hands. *Each and every one of us as individuals is going to have to take it upon YOURSELF to become leaders in our community. Block by block, house by house, city by city, state by state throughout this entire country. . . .*
  Don't *ask* if I can become a registered voter. *Demand! Say, "Baby, I'm here!"*

And then with sudden calm:

I look at the people of gray hair down here, the tiredness in the face, and I think about the millions of bolls of cotton that you picked . . . for ten dollars a week, twenty-five dollars a week, or whatever you could get to eat.

Overstepping now all the traditions of praise, lament, and consolation we expected in a eulogy, rising to the white-hot fury of an Old Testament prophet, accuser, and judge, his hands whipping the air, his eyes burning with rage, barely restraining himself from cursing in church:

For the whites . . . those same ones you cook for, wash and iron for, who come right out and say, *"I can't sit down and eat beside a nigger . . ."* I'm *tired* of that . . . I'm *tired* of him talking about how much he *hates* me and he can't stand for me to go to school with his children. But yet, when he wants someone to babysit for him, *he gets my black mammy to hold that baby! And as long as he can do that, he can sit down beside me, he can watch me go up there and register to vote, he can watch me take . . . public office in this state, and he can sit down as I rule over him just as he's ruled over me for years!*

There it was. This summer was no longer about persuasion in the beloved community, it was about *power* in a democracy, the demand for power Henry Hampton understood in Frederick Douglass.

Don't just . . . say that you've been to a nice service, a lot of people came, there were a lot of hot-blasted newsmen around. . . . *I'm going to tell you deep down in my heart what I feel right now: If you do go back home and sit down and take it, God damn your souls!*

He had kicked down the door, thrown a challenge to all of us: fight the fight or go to hell. No more business as usual at the funerals of black men. Then he turned, faint and weak, and literally collapsed into the arms of Ed King amid the crowd's weeping, cheers, and applause.

Rev. Ed King preached, calming the crowd. "My white brothers have killed my black brothers. . . . Bloody Neshoba has had the red blood of black men and the red blood of white men enrich its soil. . . . If we can die together in Mississippi, surely we can find a way to live together."

We sang "Oh Freedom" and the most powerful "We Shall Overcome" I'd ever heard. I was really rattled, and looking down at Ben Chaney myself, I was possessed on the spot with a realization that I, too, had anger in my heart that night and could not yet leave the South and its struggles. I stopped Dave on the street outside and told him, "I can't leave, I have to stay," and headed over to my night shift at the office with Crittendon. I realized only years later that those words might have been exactly what Dave Dennis *didn't* want to hear: more white people staying in the movement in Mississippi. Perhaps Dave's cry for black political power had backfired. Fifty years later, in 2014, he did confide to me, with the warm knowing chuckle, that that might have been true, but it was OK.

On my last day in Meridian in 1964, a few of us from the office walked over to the courthouse to see Deputy Price, Sheriff Rainey, Pastor Killen, and a half dozen Klansmen arraigned on federal charges of violating the civil rights of Goodman, Schwerner, and Chaney by killing them. There they were, joking around, dipping Red Man chewing tobacco, looking for all the world like B-movie rednecks with nothing to fear. I looked over *Life* photographer Paul Reed's shoulder as he snapped that iconic "Red Man Redneck" photo.

Even after they had been charged by the Justice Department, Price and Rainey remained unrepentant, still wearing their guns and badges and informing the new movement office in Philadelphia to say that anyone attempting to register to vote would be arrested. They were never charged with murder, a state crime, but in 1967 an all-white jury in federal court convicted seven of them, including Price, Rainey, the former sheriff, the incoming sheriff, a Meridian city policeman, and the imperial wizard of the Klan, on federal civil rights charges stemming from the murders. Mississippi's "cold case" law reopened the case against Killen, and he was convicted of manslaughter in state court forty years later.

That summer I saw only a tiny slice of Mississippi for a short time, and couldn't know what was happening elsewhere as the complex drama unfolded. I was a speck in the southern galaxy, a small part of something strange and probably important that I did not completely understand. I would have to wait for Orlando Bagwell, Henry Hampton, Clay Carson, Prue Arndt, Steve Fayer, and *Eyes on the Prize* to fully untangle it. Despite it all, during the 1960s I never lost faith that change could be achieved within this democracy's bruised and battered constitutional system by using that system's own values, and I don't think Henry did either.

Eighty thousand Mississippians had signed MFDP Freedom Ballots and selected sixty-four black and four white delegates to unseat the regular

Mississippi delegation at the Democratic convention in Atlantic City, New Jersey, in August 1964. So much was at stake: the whole strategy of a self-reliant local Mississippi movement aided by northerners was now airlifted onto the national political stage. Fortunately for *Eyes,* television networks anointed the convention with wall-to-wall prime-time coverage, preserved on kinescope recordings. Could a revolutionary rural black delegation force the Democrats to expel the entrenched all-white state delegation in favor of mostly poor but very savvy black Mississippians in their cheap suits and home-sewn cotton dresses? Bob Moses told us, "They had not been through book learning. What they knew about was life. They had lived it to the full and they knew about life in Mississippi and the relationship to politics. . . . We were challenging them not only on the obvious racial grounds, but on the existence of a whole group of people who are the underclass in this country, white and black."

When movement leaders launched the Summer Project, they had read signals from party leaders that President Lyndon Johnson would likely welcome Mrs. Hamer, Mrs. Devine, Mrs. Gray, and Mrs. Blackwell, and send the segregationists packing. In Moses's words, "People felt that the Democratic Party would actually embrace them, but I think there was a lack of real understanding of the depth to which the local Southern politicians were entwined in the Democratic Party." The Democratic Party was, in fact, an amalgam mainly of white southerners and working-class northerners.

That summer Republican Barry Goldwater was churning up his presidential campaign on a staunchly anti-Communist, states' rights platform.

It was nothing if not messy. The moral force of the Mississippi Freedom Democratic Party was no match for the reality of Democratic Party power politics; the outcome was not what we had envisioned when it all began. Lowenstein and Moses's dream of internal reform was quickly on the rocks. (Allard Lowenstein himself, who had little use for revolutionaries or local leaders, had long since fallen out with SNCC.) When Fannie Lou Hamer began her now famous plainspoken plea for simple justice before the convention on national television—"Is this the land of the free and the home of the brave? I question America!"—Lyndon Johnson's aides adroitly cut off her testimony by suddenly calling an emergency press conference for Johnson to announce a minor judicial appointment. Today no one remembers what LBJ had to say, but a lot of people remember Mrs. Hamer shut down in midsentence. Later that night the networks did broadcast a bit of her impassioned plea, but it was too late; its real airing to a national audience would come a quarter century later in *Eyes on the Prize.*

The liberal forces couldn't deliver. In a compromise brokered by Hubert Humphrey, Bayard Rustin, Martin Luther King, Joseph Rauh, and Walter Reuther, the Democrats refused to let the MFDP delegates represent the state of Mississippi, offering instead two seats at large on the convention floor. They did not consult the MFDP delegation. To those political insiders steeled in the ways of brass-ball politics, it was a significant first step forward toward inclusion, but to those from Mississippi who risked their lives to go there, it was an insulting token, a dismissal of everything they had fought for. In a six-hour meeting, Fannie Lou said she might not understand how politics worked, but "We didn't come all this way for no two seats."

With "borrowed" credentials, weary Annie Devine, Victoria Gray, and Fannie Lou Hamer made one last desperate attempt to force their way into the all-white Mississippi delegation's seats, to no avail. Under the gaze of news cameras, police ejected them from the convention hall.

Mrs. Blackwell told Orlando and Prue in 1985, "The compromise did not say anything to me . . . two seats at large could be anywhere. It could be at large in Hawaii or anyplace and that's what it said to us. . . . It was some kind of political ploy that they understood, but for us, for Mississippi, we had been done wrong. Our rights had been taken away and you just couldn't issue some two seats at large to correct that. . . . They knew about those kind of things, but we didn't; how to sit in the rooms and negotiate away and say, 'We'll take the best of this, a piece of that.' I guess they thought it was something, but it didn't mean nothing to us."

To a person, the men and women of SNCC and CORE left Atlantic City feeling baffled and betrayed by the politicians' action. And by refusing to embrace the Mississippi Freedom Democratic Party, mainstream leaders had inadvertently given local whites in Mississippi license to go after the agitators and organizers with brazen ferocity. Most of the northern volunteers left and took the national media with them, and a cloak of isolation once again descended over Meridian. Within weeks night riders sprayed Mrs. Chaney's house with gunfire and bombed it with a Molotov cocktail, burned four more backwoods churches in Lauderdale County, and finally persons unknown torched the office where we had spent so many night shifts listening to empty threats on the phone. After heated internal discussion, some of the SNCC and CORE staff now began carrying guns.

In his conversation with Orlando under the oak tree at Tougaloo twenty years later in 1985, Dave Dennis said, "Frankly, within a year's time the people who played those leadership roles from our side were gone, and you can't blame them for leaving . . . there was just so much you could take . . . we had put so much faith and confidence and hope in this country . . . and the country had said, 'I am sorry I'm going to tell you, my most loyal subjects, most democratic people, that we're not going to let you in.' Students went home. . . . This country was never the same again, and never will be the same again . . . and that tore everybody apart. I know it ripped me apart."

Back in 1964, trying to explain to my sympathetic and terrified parents why I had dropped out of college and was heading for Mississippi to take the place of a young man who was murdered, I said, "This is our Spain." Most of us had read *Homage to Catalonia,* George Orwell's droll account of his fighting as an anti-Fascist volunteer in the Spanish Civil War in 1937, and believed that our struggle in Mississippi was the moral equivalent of his. Orwell himself would have chuckled at how we romanticized his tale of slogging through mud and shit in freezing-cold trenches, how we ignored his grumpy account of comic opera fratricidal factions within factions in the Popular Front against Franco, and how we forgot that he got himself shot.

Flush with youthful passion, sailing off over the horizon in 1964, we felt, as Orwell's ragtag soldiers must have felt, that the black/white partnership in Mississippi was "a state of affairs worth fighting for." On the Greyhound bus heading out to fix Mississippi in 1964, having just left my mother—sure her son was going to die—weeping at the kitchen table, how could I have forgotten that theirs was in the end a lost cause. In 1964, the Fascist Franco still ruled Spain, and virtually every anti-Fascist fighter was either dead, jailed, or blacklisted. Backed by Mussolini and Hitler, the bad guys won the Spanish Civil War because they were stronger. Perhaps evil triumphs when good men do nothing, but in the end Orwell barely escaped into France, with little choice but to leave his friends who had given up everything for the cause to die in Spanish prisons. But he sure spun it into an inspiring story.

And then, sure enough, as SNCC veteran Charles Cobb has pointed out, "Southern struggle had become romanticized—rugged, ragged SNCC and CORE shock troops bravely confronting white supremacy, especially police and mad-dog sheriffs."

By any reasonable political metric the convention challenge failed, and sent SNCC into a tailspin of soul-searching and despair. But in the mysterious ways of postmodern media politics, the high-profile Philadelphia murders and Fanny Lou Hamer's plainspoken eloquence on TV had set the stage for change that would come only a year later with the 1965 Voting Rights Act. Those Mississippi images kindled and then fueled a wave of empowerment, which LBJ would finally embrace with his words "Their struggle must be our struggle . . . and we *shall* overcome."

It would drive Henry Hampton's life mission, and Orlando Bagwell's film two decades later. And most important, Mississippi, so long in isolation, would at last become part of the national conversation, with tens of thousands of black Mississippians brought into a system of political power for the first time in the twentieth century.

By the end of summer 1964 I was still out on bail, chain-smoking, fifteen pounds lighter, thoroughly radicalized, "purely and simply infuriated" by what I had seen in the Deep South.

On a late September afternoon, with my college buddy Damon Rarey at the wheel, we ever so gingerly drove out of Jackson on Route 20, crawling along toward Vicksburg just below the speed limit, worried about a last-minute bust on the way out of state. As soon as we crossed the Mississippi River onto the swampy, scented plains of Louisiana, Damon slammed his old Dodge into high gear and we were on our way west at 90 miles an hour, sleepy little towns flying by, the Beach Boys blasting on the car radio, California ahead and Mississippi receding into the night. On the road at last, I was now a fugitive from Mississippi law, but didn't particularly worry about it, since the point of the whole affair had been to get us out of the state. They convicted me in absentia and then pretty much lost interest. After a couple of weeks reunited with my parents in Sacramento, I headed south to begin my new full-time job in the Atlanta SNCC office.

At Henry Hampton's suggestion in 1985, I checked with an attorney before returning to Mississippi to work on *Eyes*.

While I was shooting in Selma later that fall of 1985 for *Eyes on the Prize*, Orlando interviewed Unita Blackwell next to a cotton field in Mayersville, Mississippi, the heart of the delta. When she, a maid with an eighth-grade education, had led voter registration drives in her hometown in the 1960s, the local sheriff arrested her a dozen times. Now, in 1985, in her third term as mayor of Mayersville, the first African American woman ever elected mayor in the state, Mrs. Blackwell served on the Democratic National Committee, held a master's in regional planning from the University of Massachusetts Amherst, and was a MacArthur Fellow.

As was his way, Orlando took a long walk with her before they sat down in front of the camera. She talked quietly about politics, power, the river, and the land itself, the work done and the work still to be done. When traffic noise interrupted the interview for the third time, Mayor Blackwell picked up the phone, dialed 911, and told the dispatcher to have the sheriff stop traffic on her block so that she could continue the interview about why a previous sheriff years ago wouldn't let her vote.

CHAPTER ELEVEN

Emmett Till's Hometown

Winter 1985

The job of gathering enough material to do the Till story now took us to Chicago. Landing at O'Hare, with freezing night wind blasting in off the lake, the shrill clang of northern voices at the baggage claim set us on edge. Our flight was late, one of our fifteen equipment cases got lost, somebody screwed up the rental cars, the cops at curbside bullied us, Mike Chin was muttering about the "goddamn ugly Bauhaus buildings." When we finally got the vehicles and the gear to the hotel, around one in the morning, there was no place open for food.

Blackside field management was seldom smooth. Henry and other Boston producers hired the smartest young researchers in America, right out of Harvard, Tufts, Northeastern, and Boston University, but then to save money they pressed these same young scholars into service as production managers, a down and dirty practical job for which the kids had little experience, interest, or aptitude. Often they just didn't button things up—car rentals, plane tickets, hotels, schedules, meals. That meant short rations and short sleep on location. Mike remembered, "There would always be something; there wouldn't be a car, there wouldn't be a hotel, the day would go long . . . we'd exchange those looks in the van, like 'Maybe these people know something we don't know. Maybe there is no hotel at the end of this road.'"

Henry's fixation with Till's killers had almost gotten the better of him again that fall and he told me, "We should just go down to Money and walk in on Milam and Bryant with a hot camera rolling, ambush those guys," forgetting that it had not even come close to working the first time he sent Orlando to try it in 1979. It was a mad idea, not least because Milam was by then dead, and Bryant had moved away and refused to be interviewed or even photographed. The caper would have left us either empty-handed or dead, but I had to admire Henry's grit. I came to suspect that what he really wanted was to come face-to-face with the killers of young Till, look them in the eye, and put them on national television.

By 1985 Mose Wright, Till's uncle who had bravely identified the murderers, had passed away. Milam had gone to his grave without ever giving
a television interview. Most of Till's relatives were no more interested in
talking to us than they had been interested in talking to Orlando and
Henry years before.

The Till family had moved to Chicago during the Great Migration,
and it was from Chicago that fourteen-year-old Emmett had returned to
Mississippi for summer vacation in 1955. We had asked every single Mississippi native of the "Till generation" how the news of his killing had affected them. Unita Blackwell said, "That's the strangest thing I suppose
for a lot of people to understand about us, that we always knew that death
was always near. . . ." Rosa Parks herself, then an obscure NAACP organizer in Montgomery, no stranger to the murder of young black men,
said, "I couldn't be any way than very upset, very devastated that in the
United States of America a child could be just taken out and killed."

And it was in Chicago that Mamie Till had insisted on an open casket
for her son.

In a hotel room at the Chicago Radisson, we interviewed Emmett
Till's cousin Curtis Jones, a working city policeman who traded Marine
Corps stories with Sekou while Mike and I set up lights. Jones described
going to church with young Emmett to hear their great-uncle Mose
Wright preach, and then into the little crossroads town of Money. Emmett
showed the local boys pictures of black kids and white kids in his Chicago
high school class before going into Bryant's store to buy candy from Mrs.
Bryant. "So he told the boys . . . gathered round this store, there must have
been round about maybe ten to twelve youngsters, that the girl was his
girlfriend. So one of the local boys said, 'Hey! There's a girl in that store
there. . . . I bet you won't go in there and talk to her.' . . . So he went in
there to . . . get some candy. When he was leaving after buying the candy,
he said, 'Bye, baby.'

"And the next thing I know, one of the boys came up to me and said,
'Say, man, you got a *crazy* cousin, he just went in there and said "Bye,
baby" to that white woman.' And that's when this man I was playing
checkers with, I guess he must've been around 'bout sixty or seventy, he
jumped straight up and said, 'Boy, y'all better get out of here,' he say 'that
lady'll come out of that store and blow your brains out.'"

Four nights later twelve-year-old Curtis Jones was awakened at three
in the morning in his Uncle Wright's three-room house, and watched as

two armed white men struck down his aunt with the butt of a shotgun and took his cousin Emmett away into the night. Jones asked his uncle, "Ain't you going to call the police? He told me that 'If I call the sheriff they was going to kill everybody in this house.' . . . I realized that . . . it was possible that he wasn't coming back." I had heard Henry quote Howard Thurman's assertion that at the extreme end of everyday life in the black South was the task of simply not being killed.

Emmett Till's cousin Wheeler Parker, and Emmett's mother, Mamie Till, both later appeared in Stanley Nelson's 2003 documentary about Till. In 1985, Parker turned us down, and Judith Vecchione feared that Mrs. Till would embellish the story. But Henry, Judy Richardson, and Orlando, keenly sensitive to the role of black mothers in the southern story, tried to convince Judith to do the interview. They argued that Till's mother should emerge as a more powerful persona, the archetype of black mothers who said to their sons, "Don't do this or you will get killed," in an attempt to inoculate them against constant threat. Orlando said, "I remember having that conversation and saying, 'Judith, you seem to feel that because she has a closeness to it she's not going to tell you the truth? But why do you think people on the other side or who are distant from it and have another way they want to frame the history wouldn't? It's all about their perspective on the truth.' I remember having this really deep conversation with her about how she thought Mamie Till would get too emotional. Yeah, so, what's wrong with that? That's her son; that's real."

Judith was adamant that she wanted to bring force to Mamie Till's character through archive footage of her at the time in 1955, not with a new interview.

So Curtis Jones and reporter James Hicks would be the only two claiming direct participation who would appear in our film about Till.

In Chicago we also picked up the Nashville sit-in story that Orlando had introduced with Leo Lillard and Will Campbell weeks before. At Nashville's historically black colleges, young student leaders Marion Barry, James Bevel, Bernard Lafayette, John Lewis, Diane Nash, and their slightly older mentors Rev. C. T. Vivian and James Lawson had been running nonviolence workshops in preparation for what was to have been the nation's first sit-in at a segregated southern lunch counter.

One could divide the methodology and results of historical documentary interviewing technique between the crisp but kindly deposition style of Judith Vecchione and the talk-therapy style of Orlando Bagwell. She had perfect pitch for expository intellectual content, he for emotional content, and both were invaluable. Orlando is the best interviewer I've seen in action, with Judith, Barbara Kopple, and Ken Burns close behind, and Errol Morris on a remarkable planet of his own. Their attitude and mechanics differ wildly. Many filmmakers view the person being interviewed as a commodity, a slightly baffled but exhaustively researched "talent," from whom we must extract exactly the precise information we need. At its worst, I've seen it unfold like an ever-so-polite Stasi or *60 Minutes* interrogation, until the producer has checked every box on the list.

Researcher Laurie Kahn, who got to see all the Blackside producers at work in the field, said, "Judith was the surgeon: precise, efficient, getting exactly what she needed on a very low shooting ratio. Jim and Callie were 'hail fellow well met,' much more loose. Orlando looked through their eyes into their soul and got them to tell stories they had never told before." Not until years later did I understand the otherworldly patience that allowed Orlando to liberate those pent-up soliloquies, coaxing reluctant storytellers to exit the present moment and return into the movement days, if only for an hour or two. Nobody paid Orlando overtime for talking long into the night with Freddie Leonard, or strolling along the river deep in conversation with Unita Blackwell. And the SNCC personnel we interviewed may have connected with Orlando because they sensed that had he been born ten years earlier, he himself could easily have been a leader in SNCC.

By the time we met Diane Nash in Chicago, she was in her fifties, rivetingly smart and still radiant with the beauty that had gotten her into the Miss Illinois pageant back in the day. She had not only been a leader of the Nashville movement, she was the young woman who had led the second wave of Freedom Riders in 1961 after Klansmen burned the first bus in Anniston, Alabama. Historian David Halberstam described her as "bright, focused, utterly fearless, with an unerring instinct for the correct tactical move at each increment of the crisis; as a leader, her instincts had been flawless, and she was the kind of person who pushed those around her to be at their best, or be gone from the movement."

After playing a leading role in the 1965 Selma struggle with her husband, James Bevel, Diane Nash retreated from view. As far as we knew, she had not been interviewed for television in twenty-five years. As we had so many times before after pulling in late to a city, the crew went off to load magazines and phone home while Orlando headed down to the lobby to meet Diane.

Orlando said, "We talked for a long while and then she said she was going home and I said, 'How are you going to get home?' and she said, 'I think I'm going to walk.' I said, well, 'Where do you live?' She said, 'It's nice out.' I didn't realize how far it was and we walked all the way there and we talked the whole way . . . mostly about the movement and about herself. And it never moved into a kind of weird conversation, but I could tell that she appreciated this, that she could trust me.

"And so when she sat down in the chair the next day . . . at that moment she was back there. . . ." In his fine book *The Shadows of Youth,* Andrew B. Lewis would later credit Blackside with "resurrecting Diane Nash."

She had first gone south from Chicago to study English at Fisk University. "I didn't have an emotional relationship to segregation. I understood the facts, and the stories, but there was not an emotional relationship. When I actually went south, and actually saw signs that said 'White' and 'Colored' and I actually could not drink out of that water fountain, or go to that ladies' room, I had a real emotional reaction."

In the nonviolence workshops, "We would practice things such as how to protect your head from a beating, how to protect each other. If one person was taking a severe beating, we would practice other people putting their bodies in between that person and the violence . . . not striking back if someone struck us."

Then on February 1, 1960, four students in Greensboro, North Carolina, beat them to it with the first lunch counter sit-in, and the floodgates were open. By summer's end a surge of sit-ins at lunch counters and restaurants would engulf seventy-eight southern cities, including St. Louis, Missouri, where young Henry and Judi Hampton joined the demonstrations. Suddenly the sit-ins were national news, sparking sympathy picket lines at Woolworth's and other major chain stores across the country, including my hometown of Sacramento. Within months, fifty thousand protested at lunch counters in a hundred southern cities.

(Historian Clay Carson has pointed out that the sit-ins, a key part of the greatest social transformation of the past century in America, were first launched not by anyone from the Ivy League, but by students from little-known black colleges in the Deep South, who were by most academic standards ill prepared and undereducated. The young Martin Luther King probably would not have gotten into any of the hundred highest-rated undergraduate programs in the country.)

The Nashville students quickly went to work, first negotiating with downtown store managers to quietly remove the "White" and "Colored" restrictions, and then when the stores declined and reasoned talk led nowhere, they sat in on February 13, 1960, and refused to leave. Nash remembered, "And the first sit-in we had was really funny, because the waitresses were nervous. And they must have dropped $2,000 worth of dishes that day. I mean, literally, it was almost a cartoon. I can remember one in particular, she was so nervous. She picked up dishes and she dropped one, and she'd pick up another one, and she'd drop it and another. It was really funny, and we were sitting there trying not to laugh, because we thought that laughing would be insulting, we didn't want to create that kind of atmosphere. At the same time, we were scared to death."

Local white minister Rev. Will Campbell warned John Lewis that the city police would stand aside and let whites beat up the group, but they decided to go and sit in anyway at the Woolworth's lunch counter. Whites beat up young women, "put lighted cigarettes down their back, in their hair, really beating people." Police finally arrived and arrested all the protesters, but none of the whites who attacked them. The *Eyes* archive newsreel footage of the attacks is jarring: calm black and white students enduring repeated blows from young whites, with astonishing nonviolent discipline, as the police stand by. Adding insult to injury, the thugs plastered the victims with eggs, coffee, ketchup, mustard, and cigarettes. The old black-and-white film fails to accurately render the mix of condiments and blood.

"It was like wall-to-wall terrified," said Diane. "I can remember sitting in class, many times, before demonstrations, and . . . the palms of my hands would be so sweaty, and I would be so tense and tight inside. I was really afraid. The movement had a way of reaching inside me and bringing out things that I never knew were there, like courage, and love for people.

"The day that the police first arrested us . . . they announced, 'OK, all you nigras, get up from the lunch counter or we're going to arrest you.' . . . So they repeated it a couple of times, and nobody moved. And, of course, we were prepared for this. So they said, 'Well, we warned you . . . OK, everybody's under arrest.' So we all get up and marched to the wagon. . . . And then they turned and they looked around at the lunch counter again, and the second wave of students had all taken seats. . . . They said, 'Well, OK, we'll arrest those too.' . . . Then the third wave. No matter what they did and how many they arrested, there was still a lunch counter full of students."

John Lewis added, "I had no way of envisioning myself in jail, and how that would be. You know, it was like somehow, a wall here, the end of life, that I couldn't see behind. . . . When it was time to go jail, I was much too busy to be afraid. . . . Growing up in the rural South . . . To go to jail was to bring shame and disgrace on the family. But for me it was a holy crusade, it became a badge of honor."

To ramp up the pressure, the Nashville movement called on blacks and sympathetic whites to boycott the downtown shopping district. Leo Lillard had told Orlando, "The boycott was a perfect time to say, 'Stay out of town.' And Nashville as a whole, black and white, did stay out of town because the white folks didn't go downtown because of the potential violence, 'the riots' as they saw it. . . . Although there were some black folks who went to downtown to try and break the boycott, and we had to send some education committees downtown to convince them that that was not the thing to do. And we didn't hurt them, but we did kind of snatch their bags and tear things away from them . . . and say, 'Stay out of town.'" Henry Hampton would resist including this in the film, fearful that the acknowledgment of forceful coercion would undercut our narrative of nonviolent struggle. But in the end Orlando prevailed, convinced Henry that this was exactly the awkward history we were after.

Henry and Orlando wanted to show that economic coercion worked when Christian persuasion and petition could not. Nashville's downtown businesses suffered mightily as the sit-ins, pickets, and boycott ground on, but the sides stalled at impasse. Then at 5:30 A.M. on the morning of April 19, 1960, a thundering explosion rocked downtown Nashville. Persons unknown had thrown a huge dynamite bomb into the residence of Alexander Looby, the highly respected black attorney who represented the students, destroying the home and blowing out all the windows across the street at Meharry Medical College, alma mater of Henry Hampton's mother and father.

Looby was a conservative Lincoln Republican, no revolutionary troublemaker. The bombing of his home solidified the black community and even enraged a segment of the white community. Within hours hundreds of students set out from the Tennessee A & I campus on a silent march to

City Hall to confront the mayor. Students in suits, ties, and dresses, from Fisk University, Meharry, Pearl High School, and other schools joined the crowd, numbering four thousand by the time they approached City Hall.

Nash told us: "We marched silently. And the long line of students must have continued for many, many blocks, miles, maybe. . . . We had sent telegrams ahead of time, telling him that as a result of the bombing . . . we felt we needed to talk to the mayor." White construction workers, not knowing quite what to do, watched quietly as thousands of hushed black students walked past. In assembling the story from these interviews and news footage of the day, Orlando, Prue, and the editor, Jeanne Jordan, understood the power of silence and let the archive film play with only the sound of shuffling feet.

Will Campbell said: "There was the white mayor who came out there and who with considerable prodding from that brilliant and beautiful twenty-two-year-old leader named Diane Nash, who kept pushing him, 'You are our mayor, sir, do you think that segregation is morally defendable?' And he eventually had to say, 'I do not.' Now that, in my judgment, was the turning point."

Diane Nash told us: "So we met him on the steps of City Hall, and confronted him with what his feelings were as a man, as a person . . . as opposed to just his being a mayor. And I have a lot of respect for the way he responded. He said that he felt like it was wrong for citizens of Nashville to be discriminated against at the lunch counters, solely on the basis of the color of their skin. . . . One of the things that we were able to do in the movement, that we learned . . . from Gandhi's movement, was to turn the energy of violence that was perpetrated against us into advantage."

Mayor Ben West went before television cameras and urged Nashville's businesspeople to end segregation.

Diane was our last interview in Chicago. Now we headed back to the Mother Ship on Shawmut Avenue.

CHAPTER TWELVE

Hunter-gatherers

Winter 1985–86

L ike farmers or ranchers, fiction filmmakers carefully cultivate what they want, while documentary makers are hunter-gatherers, foraging across the landscape for whatever is available. That fall of 1985 Blackside gathered both a set of recollections on film and a trove of archive material— fractured elements which we would fuse into coherent story on film.

Historians are limited by their sources, and documentary makers are limited by their footage. While we were whistle stopping around the South and Midwest, archive supervisor Kenn Rabin and his crew in Boston stayed on the hunt for newsreels, outtakes, still photos, vintage sound recordings, kinescopes, government films, corporate films, educational films, cartoons, songs, snapshots, posters, home movies, and newspaper headlines. These would be braided together with the interviews we shot in the field, in Blackside's spare film architecture of eyewitness accounts, archival images, songs, and narration, nothing more.

Rabin, a moonlighting fiction writer like Steve Fayer, had apprenticed at Bill Moyers's shop and come to Blackside from the *Vietnam* series, where he had quickly established himself as one of the country's foremost historical film specialists. Henry, as was his way, had invited Kenn for a job interview not at our office in the gritty South End, not up in Roxbury, but at a high-end French restaurant a couple of blocks from Harvard Square, next door to the Orson Welles Theater, the premier cineaste shrine of North America. Kenn remembered that Hampton in that first meeting was able to clearly convey with very few words his own authentic passion as well as the gravity and soaring potential of *Eyes*. "He was a benevolent version of Jim Jones; he had me at 'Hello.'"

With the bearing of a friendly badger, Kenn was deliberate, pleasantly but not obsessively detail oriented, and clear thinking, a rare combination at Blackside. He was joined by archive researcher Laurie Kahn, who had come from NPR and WGBH.

Henry knew that viewers would be ready to dismiss our shows if the visuals were the same old timeworn, iconic clip-show stuff: attack dogs and fire hoses, "I have a dream," maids and janitors with picket signs, "just one damn march after another." He wanted new stuff, better stuff, unlikely stuff, especially images that flew in the face of the King-leads-downtrodden-to-freedom narrative. Starting with the thick old research notebooks his team had compiled for Cap Cities back in 1979, the researchers now set out to amass the best civil rights archive ever assembled under one roof.

News film was the movement's megaphone. The partnership—or codependence—between the movement and the media endured for a decade, even as the battles became more complex, violent, and ambiguous in the 1970s. Because America's bittersweet love affair with civil rights coincided with the ascent of television news, a good deal of the movement's meat was preserved on reels of 16mm celluloid magnetic stripe sound film, the news-recording medium of choice from the mid-1950s through the mid-1970s. Tens of thousands of miles of the old news film lay in network vaults; you could actually go there and touch it with your hands, hold it up to the light, and see the image, a picture of Mose Wright or George Wallace. "The footage was on our side," said editor Chuck Scott.

We realize now that those combined network archives constitute probably the most complete 16mm sound film record of any social conflict in history. The visual and audio records of the great social movements of our twenty-first century, like the Arab Spring, or Black Lives Matter, are recorded not on physical film, not even on videotape, but by rearranging ones and zeroes on flash cards in cell phones and digital cameras and on servers. It becomes easier and cheaper every year, as Moore's Law pushes the cost of recording social turmoil to near zero. Will these ephemeral digital files survive for documentary makers of the future, at the mercy of molecular entropy or of whoever controls the cloud?

Permanent or not, millions of hours of mankind's collective audio-visual memory reside today on servers around the globe, and high-definition copies are available with a few clicks and a PayPal account. A ten-year-old with an iPad can download footage of Bloody Sunday in a few seconds. Back in our pre-Internet, prevideo, precloud, pre–search engine, mail-a-check-ship-a-film *Eyes* days, the archive riches were cataloged on dog-eared 3x5 library cards and paper "dope sheets." Kenn, the only one among us comfortable with computers, had convinced Henry to spend a small fortune on a primitive DOS-based DEC computer, with Rainbow software, and a ten-megabyte hard drive on which they kept a database of information about the material (but not the media) that came in the door at 486 Shawmut. It was not until Henry's *Eyes on the Prize II* series in 1988 that he and Kenn acquired the first digital archive film catalog to became available, $7,000 for a set of ten CDs, and that was just the searchable database of metadata (dates, locations, reel numbers, and the like), not the actual media, which remained on celluloid in the archive.

The physical footage, if Kenn and Laurie could locate it, existed as old reels of 16mm film cached in vaults, television stations, and people's garages. They had to find it squirreled away all over the country: heavy, rusting film cans in the Mississippi State Archives, mass meeting tape recordings in some guy's attic in Montgomery, and decaying local news footage in a TV station closet in Birmingham (showing two competing, duly elected city councils trying to govern the besieged city during the 1963 crisis). Editor Dan Eisenberg found the first half of a shot in one archive and the second half of the same shot in another archive.

Every clip actually involved several separate cans of film because the magnetic sound, workprint, positive picture, and master negative each required its own reel. The workflow laid out by Kenn in his 1985 memo was daunting:

> Each archive clip has 16mm full coat, A-Wind optical liquid gate low contrast fine grain positive master, B-wind slop picture, all edge coded together. Negative cutter will cut the fine grains together to match the slop print in our picture-locked films. He will then have that reel of our fine grain 'in's' printed onto new color internegative stock. This will produce a B-wind color internegative, which will intercut with our B-wind camera original negative (new interviews). The selected footage will be to the right length and in the right sequence based on our workprint. . . .

I get confused even describing the process; actually herding it all required hundreds of hours of hand labor, mostly by interns and assistants hunched over files and editing benches.

A few big archives controlled a lot of the archived newsreels in 1985: Hearst, Universal, the Library of Congress, the National Archives, Twentieth Century Fox, Paramount, and the three major television network archives, ABC, CBS, and NBC. The insular world of old film had its legendary archivists, activists, and curmudgeons, like the cigar-smoking and aptly named Ted Troll, who ran the musty Hearst Metrotone News archive under the Brooklyn Bridge, the eccentric monks at Sherman Grinberg in New York, outtake aficionado Pierce Rafferty, and ephemera collector Rick Prelinger.

Once you finally located the stuff and booked time at an archive cubicle, watching mid-twentieth-century newsreels on a little film viewer (sometimes hand cranked) was usually great fun, an expensive documentary Easter egg hunt. Many of the early shots that Henry's researchers had located on paper were embedded in 8-minute weekly newsreels produced for theaters before the migration of news to television. (Newsreels for southern white theaters and southern black theaters were different.) A day at the archive always meant seeing a lot of beauty pageants, dancing elephants, Korean War skirmishes, house fires, fashions of the day on Broadway or Carnaby Street, glamour at the Oscars, Ban the Bomb marches, the latest jet fighter, and finally, if you were lucky, the joy of stumbling onto beautiful, fresh imagery from Selma, Montgomery, or Birmingham or of Martin Luther King and Diane Nash in their twenties.

For every complete news story broadcast, there exists somewhere in some vault many more minutes or even hours of outtakes, the film shot for the story but never used. Chuck Scott said, "The outtakes were what made *Eyes* possible." Occasionally you can get stuck with the outtakes only, because the edited story itself—the juicy bits—was lost. What was important to us in 1985 as we looked back at the movement from the distant shore twenty years out could be radically different from what was important to a harried news film editor in New York or Los Angeles only hours after the event in 1965.

Clay Carson and other scholars "questioned the tendency of filmmakers to view dramatic footage as good history, ignoring the way historical accounts generally focus on historical figures who produce the most enduring historical materials." Because the news films had usually been shot by white cameramen working for the nearly all-white networks, and edited in New York or L.A. with white male executives, white male correspondents, and a white male anchorman providing guidance, certain points of view—philosophical and physical—about the movement and its participants on all sides were baked in.

The mainstream media representation of the movement was very much part of the story Hampton envisioned, especially because in those days most Americans got their news from the daily paper and from the three big TV networks. Henry set out to unhinge the raw footage from its original framework of commercial television sensibility, to sample the imagery as an original text and give it new meaning not limited by how an anchorman interpreted it in 1965. In the *Eyes II* program about the 1971 Attica prison rebellion, editors included several false starts by one of the network's first black on-camera correspondents, overcome by emotion and tear gas.

Because Hampton so believed that the unspoken symbiosis between civil rights strategists and news producers was a critical part of the *Eyes* story, it is no accident that throughout *Eyes,* especially in Selma, you will find apparently incidental images of news cameras in action.

Eyes was limited by what the networks and newsreel companies deemed newsworthy, and by their blind spots. The major news film operations were headquartered far from the South, and until the civil rights movement became a ratings driver they had seldom deployed their cameras to cover people of color, poor people, and pretty much all people on the margins in America, except when they were in the wrong place at the wrong time doing the wrong thing. Coverage was almost never grounded in local communities. With some exceptions, as we shall see, the newsreel pool is precious and finite, like an old-growth redwood forest, but not always exhaustively researched. So throughout his career, Henry sent his people off the beaten path in search of more idiosyncratic footage sources.

At the Alabama state library Laurie Kahn listened to hours of state police tapes recorded in a van outside the churches where mass meetings were held. She stumbled across the moment when Ralph Abernathy held up the recording device he found hidden under the pulpit in Selma and preached to the doohickey. "Doohickey . . . I don't know who you belong to, or who may be listening on the other end . . . but tell them we will keep on marching till hell freezes over if that's what it takes!"

Some unique material was in the hands of individuals, including southern plantation footage at the Atherton, California, home of Harvey Richards, a quixotic millionaire who on his own shot film for SNCC in Mississippi in 1962, for Cesar Chavez and the California farm workers a few years later, and for the emerging environmental movement in the 1970s. Looking every inch the ordinary white gentleman, Harvey had filmed the only moving images we could find of blacks on Mississippi plantations in the early 1960s. He was one of those rare, prolific progressives with the money, time, and patience few others could muster to document labor, civil rights, antiwar, and environmental movements from the inside. And he had a garage to store it all in for twenty-five years.

Prue Arndt remembers when a fellow named Dan from the Mississippi State Archives came up to Boston on the train clutching 16mm cans. Callie and Laurie convinced Dwayne Syltie at a Birmingham TV station to let them into the back room, where they found rolls of 16mm film marked with masking tape, and they recognized the names from two competing governments in Birmingham. Actor Richard Beymer, who played the lead in the 1961 film *West Side Story,* had driven his Austin-Healey sports car from Hollywood to rural Mississippi in 1964 and shot beautiful film of the Freedom Schools with a hand-cranked Bolex camera.

One rich source of material was the All American Newsreel, which flourished from 1919 through 1963, devoted entirely to the achievements and activities of African Americans, with blacks in front of the camera, behind the camera, and speaking the commentary. As teenagers in the 1950s, Henry and his sisters had seen many of these weekly newsreels at the Comet Theater in St. Louis. Here were images not only of leaders, but of ordinary, hardworking, and prosperous black citizens, hard to find in mainstream newsreels.

Another wellspring of footage for Henry's projects over the next decade was the radical Workers Film and Photo League, dedicated to using film as a lever for social change, whose members covered actions, protests, strikes, and demonstrations in the 1930s that newsreel companies usually ignored. If you need fresh images of Great Depression hunger marches or the Scottsboro Boys, you'll find it in the WFPL collection at the Museum of Modern Art.

The 1963 March on Washington for Jobs and Freedom had received saturation coverage by news crews and was broadcast live by all three networks, but new and striking footage was hard to come by. Kenn knew that the United States Information Agency had filmed the event for foreign audiences, under the direction of the brilliant documentary maker James Blue. Blue deployed fourteen 35mm cameramen to cover people converging from around the country, preparations, and the event itself.

The March was undoubtedly one of the greatest films of the period, but had never been seen inside the United States. In setting up the USIA after World War II in the long, nasty shadow of domestic propaganda films in Imperial Japan, Fascist Italy, Nazi Germany, and the United States itself, Congress had wisely insisted on a legal firewall between the USIA's magnificent films about America—and there were many—and domestic American eyes. By law, agency documentaries could only be shown abroad. Laurie Kahn arranged to screen a print at the State Department but was told, "You can watch it but you can't use it; it's against the law."

But Blackside got its own law passed. Like a dog on a bone, Laurie managed to get a bill introduced by newly appointed Massachusetts senator John Kerry and Representative Barney Frank and passed by the House and Senate, allowing first-ever stateside use of material from *The March*. HR 4985 and S 2538 passed both houses, and President Ronald Reagan signed Public Law 99-369 in 1986, amending the 1948 United States Information and Educational Exchange Act of 1948 to allow anyone to view and use *The March*.

Footage from *The March*—tens of thousands of ordinary people arriving, crews making thousands of cheese sandwiches, setting up equipment, singing "We Shall Overcome"—forms the spine of the *Eyes* March on Washington sequence. Editors wove it together with Henry's old one-roll Bayard Rustin interview, King's famous speech (but *not* the words "I have a dream"), Ralph Abernathy's soliloquy about the wind blowing across the Washington Mall, and Jim Forman's and John Lewis's recollections of the controversy over Lewis's speech.

In Birmingham, Jim DeVinney found a newsman who had saved footage headed for the dump. After gleaning every single frame having anything to do with Malcolm X for his 1990 Blackside film *Malcolm X: Make It Plain*, Orlando was surprised at the Flaherty Film Seminar to see what was apparently the only contemporary eyewitness account of Malcolm's assassination, plucked from a Dumpster in New York.

On *Eyes II*, Blackside got a congressman to strong-arm a local Buffalo TV station into releasing film from the Attica prison rebellion, giving a sense of how fear invaded the nearby local community. They wrangled footage shot inside the prison from a TV cameraman who had absconded with scenes that contradicted the widely held public image of the insurgent inmates as crazed madmen.

Henry Hampton, center, marching in Selma, Alabama, 1965, with Bob Hohler, local organizers, and members of the Unitarian delegation.
(Thomas Adams Rothschild, courtesy Unitarian Universalist Association)

LEFT: Dr. Henry Hampton Sr. with baby Henry Hampton Jr., St. Louis, 1940, "born into the most privileged life a Negro boy could reasonably expect in segregated St. Louis, Missouri, in the mid-twentieth century." (Courtesy Judi Hampton)

RIGHT: Henry Hampton Jr., Judi Hampton, and Veva Hampton with a parish priest, St. Louis, 1948, after the family converted to Catholicism. (Courtesy Judi Hampton)

"Thar he." Emmett Till's uncle Mose Wright points at his nephew's murderers in the Sumner, Mississippi, courtroom, 1955, the same summer Henry contracted polio. (Ernest Withers/Getty Images)

LEFT: Seventeen-year-old Henry Hampton, trained by the Jesuit gentleman scholars of St. Louis University High School. (Courtesy St. Louis University High School)

RIGHT: Henry Hampton, captain of the New England Blazers wheelchair basketball team, mostly Vietnam veterans from the Brockton VA hospital, around 1972. (Courtesy New England Blazers)

Early Blackside crew Billy Jackson and Romas Slezas. (Courtesy Washington University)

Henry's friend Ted Landsmark attacked during the 1976 Boston busing crisis in Stanley Forman's Pulitzer Prize–winning photo. (Stanley Forman)

Orlando Bagwell and Henry Hampton in the early days of Blackside, Inc. Even the most mundane government training film had a stealthy social purpose. (Courtesy Washington University)

Henry Hampton interviewing William Bradford Huie in 1978 about the murder of Emmett Till. (Courtesy Washington University)

Orlando, Jean-Philippe Boucicaut, and Romas rigging the old pickup truck for Julian Bond, 1979. One of the little boys asked J-P, "Are you the *foreign* nigger?"
(Judy Richardson)

Julian Bond in Money, Mississippi, with Orlando behind the Arriflex BL camera, minutes before the Blackside crew was run out of town, July 1979.
(Judy Richardson)

"Band of brothers and sisters." Judy Richardson and Jean Wheeler (front row) singing freedom songs with SNCC staff in the Atlanta office, 1964. Back row: Mike Sayer, McArthur Cotton, James Forman, unknown, unknown, Marion Barry, Lester MacKinney, unknown, Mike Thelwell, Lawrence Guyot, John Lewis, Julian Bond. (Danny Lyon)

Eyes on the Prize staff around the big table at 486 Shawmut Avenue, "the abrasion of good minds." From left: Jeanne Jordan, Kenn Rabin, Laurie Kahn, Liz Carver, Orlando Bagwell, Dan Eisenberg, Chuck Scott, Viki Garvin Davis, Llew Smith, Judy Richardson, Prudence Arndt, Callie Crossley, Sara Chazen, Henry Hampton, James DeVinney, Judith Vecchione. (Jon Else)

The Blackside team in front of 486 Shawmut Avenue, spring 1986. Henry Hampton is at the extreme right, Judith Vecchione third from left in front row, Kenn Rabin third from right in second row, Steve Fayer fourth from left in back row. (Jon Else)

Rosa Parks in Detroit, 1985, "the accidental matriarch." There was nothing accidental about it. (Jon Else)

Mississippi organizer Bob Moses worked with Amzie Moore in "the heart of the iceberg." (Jon Else)

"What have I to fear?" Diane Nash in Chicago, 1985. (Jon Else)

Rev. Abernathy sings "Leaning on the Everlasting Arms." Mike Chin, Jon Else, Ralph Abernathy, Callie Crossley, 1985. (Jim DeVinney)

"Peewee was crying." Freedom Rider Freddie Leonard talks about his beating at the hands of an inmate in Mississippi's Parchman Farm prison, Nashville, 1985. (Jon Else)

"The Fourteenth Amendment 1985 World Tour." Prue Arndt, Orlando Bagwell, Bobby Shepard in New York. (Courtesy Washington University)

Judith Vecchione, Henry's second in command, chief of staff, and producer of the first two *Eyes on the Prize* episodes in 1985. (Jon Else)

Orlando Bagwell, well versed in the bizarre and sometimes brutal ways of race in Boston. (Jon Else)

"The Henry Hampton All-Stars." Michael Chin and Sekou Shepard in Alabama, 1985. (Jon Else)

Henry Hampton in his office at 486 Shawmut Avenue, fall 1985, "the greatest commune builder I have ever seen." (Jon Else)

Jon Else with sharecroppers near Toomsuba, Mississippi, 1964. Our mere presence on their front porch stoked well-founded fears of trouble. Among the few who owned land, many had put it up as collateral to bond civil rights workers out of jail. (David Crittenden)

Dave Dennis, who had buried his friend Medgar Evers only the year before, at James Chaney's memorial, Meridian, Mississippi, 1964. "If you do go home and sit down and take it, God damn your souls!" (The Image Works)

Governor George Wallace in his last term, Montgomery, Alabama, "a feisty dog barking at the sun to keep it from shining." (Jon Else)

Sheriff Jim Clark rousts Mrs. Amelia Boynton in front of the Selma, Alabama, courthouse, February 1965. (Jon Else)

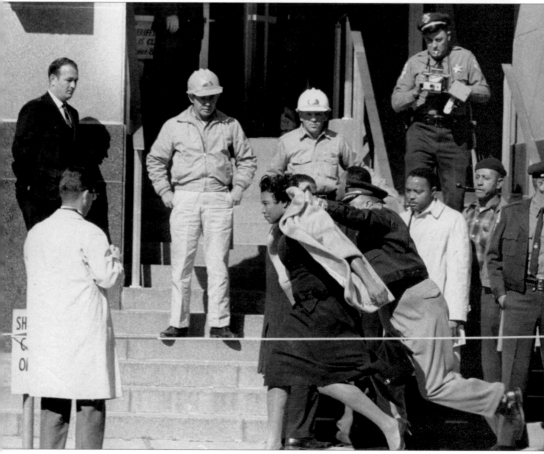

Henry interviewing Jesse Jackson for *Eyes on the Prize*, with Mike Chin behind the camera, 1989. (Courtesy Washington University)

Henry Hampton and Callie Crossley at the Academy Awards, Hollywood, 1988.

FOLLOWING PAGE: Henry Hampton recording *Eyes on the Prize* vocals at Roberto Mighty's studio on the night of "The Great Blackside Sit-In," 1986. (Jon Else)

Finding a citation on a film library card was no guarantee the material existed, because chemical degradation might have long since taken a toll; the reels of paper-thin audiotape might have fused into solid disks of acetate, or material might be simply misplaced forever. More than once, we were too late to the archive. I arrived at a local TV station in Jackson only to learn from the manager that they had just the week before taken a load of black-and-white 1960s news film to the landfill "because we needed the space for the new computers."

A nitrate fire at the National Archives vault in 1978 had destroyed nearly all of the Universal Newsreels from 1941 to 1945, and many of the Workers Film and Photo League films were lost in a storage fire, as was all of *Say Brother*'s first year. In 1979, at Ted Troll's shop, when I opened a can supposedly containing the only film record of J. Robert Oppenheimer and E. O. Lawrence working on the world's first cyclotron in 1939, it contained instead a couple of pounds of dry acetate flakes. Proper identification was a constant pitfall. Callie remembered "how many times our film researchers went to the archives and found many people mislabeled . . . If they didn't know who a kind of short and kind of round-faced black man was, they might just call him Martin Luther King." Researcher Sue Williams found a citation for "Negro man speaking"; it was Medgar Evers on the day before he was murdered. And Blackside researchers stealthily corrected the information and inked out antique racist terms like "pickaninnies" on the old cards from the 1950s.

Finally, if you live long enough, you create your own stock footage. Ironically, the only original interviews ever filmed with some now long-dead local southern leaders lay stacked in Henry's dingy garages up on Fort Hill, remnants of the *America, We Loved You Madly* project. Judy Richardson and Judith Vecchione went up to 88 Lambert, and Judy said, "I remember looking at Vecchione's face; she knew. These were cardboard boxes with unreconstructed 16mm." They cleaned them up and added them to our cache of stock footage.

Once discovered by the cameras in 1956, Dr. King was a newsreel magnet; no American since Franklin Roosevelt could consistently deliver oration that so deeply inspired so many Americans. News films of King's public persona were expensive but readily available to us. With *Eyes on the Prize* and *Eyes on the Prize II*, Henry redirected our understanding of King, giving him the screen time needed to understand Martin's enormous intellectual power and his later bold stands against militarism and economic inequity. (At the time in 1985, Taylor Branch had not yet published his majestic trilogy chronicling King's life, David Garrow had not written *Bearing the Cross,* nor had Clayborne Carson done *The Autogiography of Martin Luther King,* and Orlando and Noland's epic film *Citizen King* was still ten years in the future.) Much as Henry wanted to bring the foot soldiers to the forefront of movement history, Martin Luther King's superhuman eloquence was inescapable and irresistible. It was there right from the very start in 1955, soaring to preacherly heights in the text of his very first movement speech at Holt Street Baptist Church in Montgomery the night Rosa Parks was arrested. He had twenty minutes to prepare, and scribbled his final notes in the car on the way to the meeting. Even the written transcript showed the electricity of the moment, the crowd urging him on as he praised the height of Mrs. Parks's character, her Christian commitment and devotion to the teachings of Jesus. Then,

> There comes a time when people get tired of being trampled over by the iron feet of oppression. [*thundering applause*] There comes a time, my friends, when people get tired of being plunged across the abyss of humiliation, where they experience the bleakness of nagging despair. (*Keep talking*) There comes a time when people get *tired* of being pushed out of the glittering sunlight of life's July, and left standing amid the piercing chill of an alpine November. (*That's right*) [*applause*]

He reminded them they were not like their opponents, the Citizens' Council and the Klan.

> And I want to say that we are not here advocating violence. (*No*) . . . I want it to be known throughout Montgomery and throughout this nation (*Well*) that we are Christian people. (*Yes*) [*applause*]

He praised the glory of America, with all its faults, noting that behind the Iron Curtain, in totalitarian dungeons, they could exercise the weapon of nonviolence, the right to protest *for* right.

> And . . . If we are wrong, God Almighty is wrong. (*That's right*) [*applause*] If we are wrong, Jesus of Nazareth was merely a utopian

dreamer that never came down to earth. (*Yes*) [*applause*] If we are wrong, justice is a lie. (*Yes*) Love has no meaning. [*applause*] And we are determined here in Montgomery to work and fight until justice runs down like water (*Yes*) [*applause*], and righteousness like a mighty stream! (*Keep talking*) [*applause*]

There it was, a transformative gift to history, the very first civil rights speech the twenty-six-year-old King ever gave, the Ur-speech he conjured up before three thousand people on December 5, 1955, the first night of the boycott. But no recording could be found. The team had still photos of the overflow crowd and a written transcript of King's words, but no recording, despite reports that television crews had been present. Today many documentary directors would have an actor read the transcript.

But somehow after months of sleuthing, Llew Smith got the name of a local man who had recorded it on his quarter-inch Wollensak tape machine and promised to send it to Blackside. But the fellow promptly died and Llew ended up going to the widow's home and convincing her to lend him the precious recording. Then our researchers authenticated the words by comparing them to written transcripts and notes taken by reporters that night.

Any self-respecting social movement or corporation, like Greenpeace or Google, does an excellent job taking pictures of itself. The Ford Motor Company operated the largest film production operation outside Hollywood in the 1920s. The Citizens' Council produced slick weekly national television programs. The Student Nonviolent Coordinating Committee did a better job than anyone of photographing the rural movement in the 1960s. We made good use of Ford's huge archive on Blackside's *The Great Depression* and SNCC's archive on *Eyes*.

SNCC's in-house photo department was led by the mercurial Danny Lyon and Cliff Vaughs, inspired by the matchless verité style of Magnum photographers Robert Capa, Gordon Parks, and Henri Cartier-Bresson. I remember Danny as an intense white guy who seemed never to be in one town for more than half a day, and I remember Cliff, the black biker, who went on to work with Dennis Hopper on *Easy Rider*, for his refined elegant speech. These guys were hip, reckless, and they made sensational pictures, maybe because they loved being at the edge of danger. John Lewis refused to stand next to Cliff on a march in Selma, and I felt uneasy close to him at an antiwar demonstration in Oakland. SNCC used the pictures to great effect in photo-essay books and in their newspaper, the *Student Voice,* and we, of course, used them in *Eyes on the Prize.*

They did finally locate film of Elizabeth Eckford's walk through the gauntlet of screaming white women on her way to school in Little Rock, the footage that had eluded Henry Johnson back on *America, We Loved You Madly.* Powerful images we missed emerged years later in other documentaries: a genteel racist Citizens' Council film in *Soundtrack for a Revolution,* FBI evidence photographs of Goodman, Chaney, and Schwerner's savaged bodies. Some copyright holders, like *Jet's* and *Ebony's* Johnson Publishing, which owned the pictures of James Meredith trying to enter Ole Miss, refused to license anything to us. Some material, like Bull Connor ranting, "You will never whip these buds! I found out the hard way, you've got to keep the white and the black separate!" were hiding in European archives—the Swedish film crews did a particularly good job covering civil rights and Black Power in the United States and apartheid in South Africa. And the man who shot the graphic photos of the burning bus and beaten Freedom Riders in Anniston, Alabama, refused to release them to Orlando in 1985, because he still feared reprisals twenty years after the event; they appear in Stanley Nelson's 2010 *Freedom Riders.*

Some powerful material we simply decided not to use. Judith's researchers had unearthed a trove of startling racist Warner Bros. cartoons depicting Sambos, pickaninnies, coons, mammies, cannibals, minstrels, and Uncle Toms with grotesquely exaggerated "negroid" features, shuffling and vamping, the whole lurid package. But in the context of 1985, only twenty years out from the movement, trying to guide ordinary American viewers through this first television story of civil rights, Judith, Llew, and Henry chose not to put them on the screen. They were searingly instructive, but the risk of instantly alienating viewers with bigoted kitsch would have been too great. But by late 1987 the baseline of national cultural conversation about race had shifted just enough, in part because of *Eyes on the Prize,* that Marlon Riggs deployed them to powerful effect to show the murderous images in his brilliant film *Ethnic Notions.*

• • • • • •

At the core of the archive work was Henry, Kenn, and Judith Vecchione's demand—inherited from *Vietnam,* which had inherited it from *The World at War*—that every single image and sound had to be the real thing, certified genuine for time, place, and content. For those of us who came from the unpoliced world of independent film, this ethical true north in archive work was restorative. In that dangerous triangle between art, scholarship, and the temptations of ratings-hungry prime-time television, suspect evidence had no place.

Prue Arndt remembered, "There is something about the intellectual rigor of having to check to make sure that the recording of the Montgomery church service on the evening of the boycott really was the recording from that particular day, and not another day from a long year's worth of church meetings. That set a very high standard."

Judith Vecchione, our senior producer, had come to Blackside with "a reputation of being hard to work with," but Kenn and others quickly learned what that really meant was that she insisted on rigor. "Checks upon checks upon checks upon more checks," said Kenn.

My wake-up call about just how serious they were on footage accuracy came when I sensed they really did mean that *every* shot of feet walking in the Montgomery bus boycott film had to have been actually shot in Montgomery, and actually during the month in question. I thought they were joking. I realized the time and money it would take to comb the out-takes for the real thing, rather than just import a generic pair of feet walking in, say, Atlanta or Birmingham, or in Montgomery the year before. A foot's a foot, but not just any foot.

A shot that the audience would take to be in Birmingham in May 1963 had to actually be captured in Birmingham in May 1963. You couldn't snatch a close-up from one march and drop it into another march. "If we're going to be attacked, let's be attacked for the right reason, not for slipping in a cutaway from the wrong meeting in the wrong month," said Henry. The burden was partly a simple practical matter of making our work defensible to the harshest scrutiny, but also a deep sense that we were constructing a historical record, and, in the words of Albert Maysles, "To falsify history is a sin"; it violates audience trust, and we could not guess the downstream future consequences of our falsehood.

Archivists had to be on guard for counterfeit newsreel footage. On

Henry's later *Great Depression* series, producer Terry Rockefeller and researcher Cindy Kuhn discovered that the "newsreels" of hobos and bums showering praise on Upton Sinclair, Socialist candidate for governor of California in 1934, were, in fact, actors. Searching through outtakes, they found multiple repeated takes of each hobo interview, with offscreen directions from the director, and "Metro-Goldwyn-Mayer" clap slates. Louis B. Mayer was a chief supporter of Sinclair's Republican opponent, Frank Merriam. With Hampton's blessing, Terry used the forged footage, slates and all, and doubled their storytelling value by explaining exactly what they were, fake newsreels created by the opposition.

We all agreed that documentary is an expressive art given life by rhetorical maneuvers, but none of us accepted the "service to a higher truth" justification often put forward as a cover for archive trickery—the deceptive substitution of a more powerful shot for an accurate shot. In what critic Bill Nichols calls "the imbalance of power between filmmakers and both their subjects and their audience," the subjects and the viewers are most vulnerable to fraud.

My own articulation of documentary ethics evolved over the years at Blackside to the simple formula:

True=True
Real=Real

That is to say, any material, new or archive, that we want the audience to believe is true should be true, and everything that we want the audience to believe is real should be real.

By 1985 some imagery, like the Zapruder film of Kennedy's assassination, Hitler's salute, or dogs and fire hoses in Birmingham, had risen to icon status, genuine visual sacred texts of bad behavior in our age. On *Eyes*, Kenn and his crew unearthed all footage then available of the 1963 Birmingham conflagration. In 2005, Bobby Houston and Robert Hudson won the Oscar for Best Documentary Short Subject with their stunning *Mighty Times: The Children's March*, which chronicled those same events in Birmingham in spring of 1963. In an astonishing historical sleight of hand, the two California filmmakers had hired seven hundred extras in period dress, vintage fire trucks, German shepherds, dog wranglers, and actors dressed as Birmingham cops, demonstrators, and Klansmen. They reenacted the Birmingham, Alabama, campaign in Ojai, California, filmed it with vintage cameras and black-and-white film stock, and then, unbeknownst to the Academy of Motion Picture Arts and Sciences, spliced their fictional new material together with genuine news film from 1963 and interviews with the real James Bevel, Andrew Young, and others. Tell the Truth Pictures produced *The Children's March* for the highly respected Southern Poverty Law Center and HBO. Interestingly, Kenn Rabin had started working on the project as archive consultant, but removed himself midway through after requesting that the producers label the manufactured material on screen in all versions of the film.

It is a riveting short film, far more dazzling and entertaining than most of *Eyes on the Prize*. But once you set yourself free from the restraints of using the real and accurate footage, it's possible with enough resources, skill, and hard work to create something the audiences will mistake for a real documentary. *The Children's March* was masterfully and seamlessly made, a counterfeiting tour de force. Only after it won the documentary Oscar did members of the Motion Picture Academy begin questioning where that extraordinary archive footage had been hidden all these years. No filmmaker that I know of had any problem with the use of reenactments per se; the problem was that in the version screened by Academy members, they had no way to distinguish between genuine and reenacted footage. Reenactments have a long-standing, legitimate, and important place in documentary, unless they are foisted off on the audience as genuine archive footage.

When questioned by the press, Houston and Hudson never tried to hide their method, which they championed as "faux doc," and likened it to making biscotti: "We make a classic documentary using the archival record. We then make another layer of film. . . . The second layer of film fills in the gaps." But on screen the Academy had no reason to suspect the footage was not real.

I noticed that the producers had also—against Kenn Rabin's advice—freely spliced in shots of particularly ferocious white attacks on blacks from other cities in other years, as though they had occurred in Birmingham in 1963: the Little Rock school crisis in 1957, shots of the Watts Riot in 1965, archsegregationist Lester Maddox confronting blacks at his Atlanta restaurant in 1964. I took particular notice because I had been in Birmingham in 1963, and had, at some personal risk, testified against Maddox during his trial in 1965.

Jesse Jackson and the ministers of SCLC complained about "duplicity" in the film. Houston and Hudson argued they were making the documentary as energized as possible to engage a new young audience, and were technically within the Academy rules, which was true. The president of the Academy asked me to review archive footage in the film, which I did. Within hours I got a call from the *New York Times,* and found myself pulled into the controversy, explaining Blackside's documentary archive standards in the press and on NPR. It was even too much for Errol Morris, reigning master of fantastical documentary reenactments, who wrote, "It's a question about fraud." And as might be expected, the Blacksiders who had remained so resolutely Spartan in making *Eyes on the Prize* (which did not win an Oscar) found much to hate in *The Children's March.* Callie said, "The real story is powerful enough. You didn't need to jack it up if you had done what you were supposed to do. I just get furious every time I see it." Houston told me, "The audience doesn't care. The only people who care are documentary filmmakers."

They got to keep the Oscar, but the dustup prompted a debate within the Motion Picture Academy, which led to rules requiring more transparent disclosure of faux archive footage.

We were at that time all gaga over how movie music could send a documentary into the dramatic stratosphere, sometimes when there is not really much drama in the movie to begin with, like the empty-calorie rush of pure sugar. Apart from opening percussion by the Grateful Dead's Mickey Hart, *Vietnam: A Television History* is virtually devoid of music. In the music-drenched television landscape of the 1980s, that made *Vietnam* deliberately unnerving. In Rabin's words, the absence of music "raised the trust level." Former newspaper reporter David Simon, creator of *The Wire,* is most certainly right when he calls the manipulating emotional power of film scores "the most journalistically dishonest thing we do." Henry was suspicious of music's bullying capacity in film, and admired the spare soundscape of *Vietnam,* but knew from the start he would use vocal music of the 1960s in *Eyes.* How could we not? This series about freedom would rely on the bittersweet warmth and jubilation of freedom songs.

The music would be archival, just as the visuals were archival, and Blackside eventually licensed 140 separate pieces of music for the whole fourteen-part series. *Eyes on the Prize* was produced during the first golden

age of rap and hip-hop, with their own political verve, but just as we swept
the frame clean of visual references to the 1986 present, so we would insulate the sound track from present-day music. Why not? Producers had at
their fingertips a huge recorded trove of majestic freedom songs recorded
in the sixties in churches and meeting halls by devoutly religious people
alive with the fire of civil rights. (To understand what this means, stop
reading, download Betty Fikes singing "This Little Light of Mine" in church
in Selma, and listen to it loud on good speakers and luxuriate in its power.)

Among the movement's weapons—patient organizing, sustained direct action, court battles, Christian persuasion, voter registration, and a
willingness to get beat up or imprisoned—singing was certainly the most
fun. And for *Eyes on the Prize* it had the unbeatable combination of
earned emotional power *and* narrative exposition. You can see it on screen,
young women defiantly belting out "This Little Light of Mine" as police
chief Pritchett's men hustle them into a paddy wagon, parishioners shaking the rafters in Selma.

In a film, what could be stronger or more resolute than:

Ain't going to let Jim Clark
Turn me around
Turn me around
Turn me around . . .
Going to keep on walkin'
Keep on talkin'
Marchin' on to freedom land

Or with grim determination,

Paul and Silas bound in jail
had no body for to go their bail . . .
Keep your eyes on the prize, hold on . . .

Or the rollicking:

If you miss me from the back of the bus
If you can't find me nowhere
Come on over to the front of the bus
I'll be riding there

Judy Richardson said, "I don't know that you could have had a movement in the way that we had the movement without the music. Music took you outside of yourself. It made you feel that you were absolutely invincible." Henry said the singing would set your hair on fire it was so strong. I had felt the music's power myself again and again in the South back then, in SNCC's intimate "band of brothers and sisters" sessions, and in mass meetings in Mississippi and Alabama. The songs' unifying power was staggering. The first time I ever saw Martin Luther King was when he roused the crowd at a mass meeting in Meridian in July 1964; but what really fired us up that night was the singing, freedom songs, the heart and lungs of the people's movement, a thousand voices strong. With enough of that music, sung in congregational style with people who *really* knew how to sing, we would have walked into cannon fire.

Outside the crossroads hamlet of Causeyville, about ten miles south of Meridian, we planned a mass meeting to register freedom voters the night after King's visit. Night meetings were always dangerous, especially out in the rural woods, and we tried to avoid them, but sharecroppers and farmhands could only gather in the evening after work and chores. All that day we drove around the back roads reminding people to come to the church in the evening, and they all told us that deputy sheriffs had cruised around just ahead of us knocking on doors and telling them not to come, threatening that they would lose their jobs or be thrown off county welfare assistance.

When we arrived at dusk, carloads of local white men were parked on the gravel road nearby, and we already had a hundred local black people in the little wooden church, singing freedom songs. The pastor, courageous man that he was, knew perfectly well that the Klan had bombed and burned six churches where meetings were held in our county, but he was not intimidated. George Harris, one of the local organizers, explained the Freedom Vote to the assembled people. Others urged the crowd on and we sang and sang. Around 10 P.M., when it was time to go, George launched into "We Shall Not Be Moved." Outside, we could see the lights of cars now circling the church. Voices rose, with George and the minister urging us on, and when we began "We Shall Overcome," the cars swung around and stopped, engines revved, with their headlights shining in through the windows from all sides; the people went right on singing. We all hummed a chorus while the pastor offered a closing prayer, then cranked up to thundering full voice for a final chorus that rattled the rickety old building. Then the ushers threw open the sanctuary doors and the people walked right out into the night air, their fear in check, right past the stunned Klansmen, got in their cars, and drove away. Dave and I drove back out there the next morning to make sure the church was still standing.

In South Africa in the 1980s locally made songs, with "toyi-toyi" stamp dancing, likewise drove the anti-apartheid movement. I'm sure the environmental movement would greatly benefit from a few spectacular songs and the nerve to sing them loud and proud.

The *Eyes on the Prize* music policy, laid down by Henry and Judith and later overseen by music historian Rena Kosersky, demanded that music be used sparingly, to preserve force and surprise, and in any given scene we would use only music "which could have been heard at that place at that time." If we were watching a sequence in Albany, Georgia, in 1962, the freedom songs had to be from Albany, Georgia, in 1962.

The strict standards of the *Eyes* music enterprise barred us from deploying some powerful songs, like Joan Baez's haunting waltz, "Birmingham Sunday," written a year after the four young girls were killed; it is almost unbearably powerful in Spike Lee's 1997 *4 Little Girls*. Or later, when Henry and Steve Stept were doing a sequence about lynching in 1936, they did not use Billie Holiday's powerful anti-lynching refrain "Strange Fruit," because she did not release it until 1939. Maybe it was a mistake. We surely sacrificed emotional punch by the rigor, but we had a musical compass, believing we were leaving behind a more reliable history of the time.

Fortunately for us, freedom songs migrated easily from town to town and state to state across the region, even leapt across the ocean to the Caribbean and South Africa. They formed a vast musical archipelago, islands of song all connected underneath the surface in that ocean of protest. There were no written song sheets; everyone knew what to do. The song leaders or anyone else who was inspired would change the lyrics to suit the struggle at hand, so a single song could roll on for half an hour as new lines sprang forth. A core canon of about two dozen songs was sung virtually everywhere across the South, giving Blackside producers great flexibility. "Ain't going to let nobody (*or* George Wallace, *or* Laurie Pritchett, *or* Jim Clark, *or* Lyndon Johnson, *or* whoever was the local obstructionist in any one of a hundred towns) turn me around. . . ."

Henry dearly loved the music. But for a man so socially comfortable and blessed with such a resonant tenor voice, I was surprised to see that he was a shy singer. In those occasional times when Blackside meetings or screenings broke into song, you could see his mouth move, but I could barely hear him singing the words.

Henry had persuaded Bernice Johnson Reagon to come on as *Eyes* archive music consultant. She had been one of the original Freedom Singers who had inspired me to dump my college education and head for Mississippi back in 1963, and she had gone on to found Sweet Honey in the Rock. She, together with Guy and Candie Carawan, helped the producers, researchers, and editors, who were mostly newcomers to the movement and its music, understand the songs' roots in Africa, slavery, and the African American religious experience, and their extraordinary muscle as an organizing tool.

Henry, constantly on the road raising money, had specific archive headaches he did not need with footage of Diane Nash from the NBC documentary *Anatomy of a Demonstration,* which was tangled up in litigation. That 1961 film had sparked short-lived criticism from Tennessee politicians, but their lawsuit against the network refused to go away. And he was bedeviled with obstacles to the use of the Frank Sinatra song "High Hopes," recorded in 1960 for the Kennedy presidential campaign, about which Hampton's lawyer Mark Fischer advised: "Many unresolved issues . . . securing a master license and permissions of the volatile and litigious Frank Sinatra may not be easy." Fortunately, some people gave us music recordings and still photos for free, but in the end the rights to footage and music cost about $200,000 for the original *Eyes* series, chump change by today's standards but a fortune to Blackside. (A single feature documentary I shot about Tupac Shakur for Paramount/MTV in 2003 spent nearly $2 million on music alone.)

I had never heard the term "intellectual property" until *Eyes* was well under way, and it first struck me as preposterous. Was this a joke? But during the couple of years it took to make the series, America had become increasingly litigious in protecting the monetary value of archive material. The snag in using all that old music and news film was that neither PBS nor any other network would broadcast or distribute it without proof that all the intellectual property it contained was licensed, backed up by an "errors and omissions" insurance policy. So *Eyes* paid for it all, including a short portion of the "I have a dream" speech and a rendition of "Happy Birthday."

Rights purchase always comes at the end of a production, when we have spent all the contingency funds on extra shooting and editing, are almost out of cash, and exhausted. With *Eyes* still only three quarters funded, Kenn and Henry could have held off and later bought blue-chip "in perpetuity" broadcast licenses for all the material. But Hampton, under pressure from his harried staff, from a looming PBS delivery date, from his lawyers, and from WGBH, and from a thousand uncertainties, had little choice but to sign less expensive ten-year footage licenses for most of the newsreel clips and most of the music. And that would be only for domestic distribution, not international.

In essence, we paid to rent the footage, not buy it. Years later, when the nation's vast store of historical footage became mired in a vortex of corporate acquisition and copyright extensions, this fateful decision would prevent an entire generation of young people from seeing *Eyes on the Prize*. We built into each individual program a little ticking copyright time bomb that would wait patiently until its time came.

But that was all in the future. We had a series to finish.

CHAPTER THIRTEEN

True South?

1985

Mike, Callie, Sekou, and I had wrapped up principal photography on December 7, 1985, knowing we'd have to come back to Alabama for mop-up. We drove through "Bloody Lowndes" County to Montgomery, hopped a commuter jet, grabbed yet another hot dog in the Atlanta airport, and flew to Boston for a nice reunion dinner with Orlando at the Newbury Steak House. Richardson regaled us with stories about the early Black Panthers and about James Bevel's red "devil suit," complete with tail, that he wore in later years. Around midnight up in Orlando's apartment above the office, I copied the nauseating *Jet* magazine photo of Emmett Till's mauled face to 16mm film with Blackside's old Arri BL camera, trying to do it without looking through the viewfinder.

Henry had bought 486 Shawmut Avenue for a song decades before, when it was just another timeworn five-story walk-up on a backwater street at the ghetto's edge. While we had been away on location the locals had changed the graffiti from "Fuck" to elaborate spray-painted runes, glyphs, and pictures whose meaning I could not decipher, and the cops had pushed the prostitutes a few blocks east. Henry was still driving down from Roxbury every morning and parking his dark green Jag in front of the office, where the guys from the bodega-cum-numbers joint down the block kept an eye on it. Val Linson remembered that Jag was full of soda cans and papers. "It looked like he was living in his car." In defiance, Fayer parked his huge, ancient Buick across the street.

I loved crisp fall Sunday mornings in the neighborhood, music coming out of the Iglesia De Dios, black families in Sunday best on their way to church, yuppies in search of brunch. The sidewalks were actually covered with autumn leaves, just like in the picture books, and on a sunny early-winter day you could sense the ice and snow held at bay just over the horizon. We had a few homeless people, and were seeing more and more light and white skin in the neighborhood as gay couples and young professionals with two-hundred-dollar strollers moved in. Henry's activist buddy Royal Cloyd had rescued Boston's South End from total decay back in the sixties, and the area was now shedding its rough edges and working-class ethos as the new money pushed out the old community. By the time we wrapped up *Eyes* it would be easier to find croissants than empanadas, as nearby Tremont Street began its transition to a zone of hipsters, food-ies, and million-dollar condos.

Henry knew everyone in the South End. In those days this was still very much his turf, "the only more or less integrated neighborhood in Boston," a tough political city short on racial harmony. Boston struck me as a broad-shouldered place, Whitey Bulger's town, Malcolm X's town, the city of the bean and the cod, of Red Sox and Cardinal Law, not so many years removed from its own bloody school desegregation crisis in 1976. Hampton took seriously his responsibilities as a citizen of Boston, was well liked and well connected throughout Boston's business and po-litical class, as Henry Hampton Sr. had been in St. Louis. Together with his friend Ruth Batson and neighborhood organizer Rudy Rutledge, he spent decades fighting an uphill battle for affordable housing.

While we were off shooting, Henry had hired a couple of strapping neighborhood guys to clean up and haul truckloads of stuff to his garages up on Fort Hill, and now editing was well under way in the crowded war-rens of 486 Shawmut. Rain still dripped into the top floor, and I once found editor Chuck Scott working hunched over the Steenbeck editing console underneath a plastic tarp. The weather was turning bitter cold, and frigid ocean air found a way into every room on every floor through ill-fitting window frames. The old apartment building was so underwired that in any office you could run an electric heater *or* an IBM Selectric typewriter, but not both at the same time. Llew Smith did his xeroxing in an overcoat and fur hat. The phones still didn't all function. One visiting funder said it was "teeming with producers," and "nothing worked but the staff." Twenty-five of us on three floors still shared one single bath-room. The accounting systems were not ready to go when the project started and still weren't.

Henry had decided to remodel for *Eyes,* and the carpenters were still hammering and sawing. Prue Arndt said, "There were unfinished doors on sawhorses, and I thought, oh shit, I moved to Boston for *this*?" Produc-ers and editors complained, so Henry asked the construction crew to work at night, which only half solved the problem, because he and many others often kept working after a dinner break. Most nights I could hear him banging away at the typewriter in his office. Henry's friend Ditch, a nice guy in his fifties who lived upstairs and carried a pistol on his belt, served as night cleanup man.

When construction finally ceased, the makeover was rather nice: stylish oak molding and a nice new hardwood floor that made us feel like a grown-up film company. Key to the whole enterprise was Henry's socio-architectural mandate that every door in his company should be a glass door with a beefy oak frame, both sturdy and transparent in the literal and metaphorical sense.

The basic layout of the building had a lot to do with driving the social processes. Because getting from one place to another with his leg brace was difficult work, once Henry labored his way up the stairs to his office he tended to stay there. It meant that we would often gather around the Big Table on the same floor, which sat not in a removed conference room, but in the open main space at the head of the stairs, right in the thick of the action, our village square. This was the same table, now often piled with pizza boxes, at which he had beaten all those original Blacksiders at Ping-Pong years before.

The new bookkeeper, Irish Catholic native Bostonian Lorraine Kiley, arrived her first day in a business suit, found "a dozen people with their feet up on the big table drinking beer and thought, 'This is cool.'" She considered it a starter job right out of college, thought "public television documentaries would be the most boring thing I ever heard of," but ended up fighting the good fight to keep Blackside's finances rational for the next fourteen years. Her first office was literally a closet next to the bathroom.

Henry rented out a fourth-floor apartment to an immigrant Laotian (or Vietnamese, no one was quite sure) refugee family who spoke little English, and we marveled at the aroma of South Asian food filling the five-story stairwell. They, in turn, must have marveled at Callie Crossley coming up the stairs belting out "We Shall Not Be Moved." That creaky old stairwell telegraphed our comings and goings: Henry's thumping gait, Judith Vecchione's clicking heels, Inez Robinson bounding up the steps three at a time, Henry's warm, rowdy laugh ringing through the building. Accompanying it all was the soft, ceaseless patter of a dozen typewriters.

The place filled up with interns. Meredith Woods, who had worked on Ross McElwee's now classic film *Sherman's March,* was studying at Harvard, where she saw a notice tacked on a jobs bulletin board: "TV series on the Civil Rights Movement." She started at Blackside as an unpaid intern, transferring interviews from quarter-inch tape to magnetic film and doing the courier runs of color-coded rewrite pages to and from "the script factory" over at Fayer's place in Back Bay, while still managing her courses and work-study job on campus. Meredith, who had known the city only through Harvard, was "shocked" at the office: "I had never been to the *real* Boston." She wondered about Henry Hampton, the "mysterious person who ran it all but was always out raising money."

"I was like the little sister, watching everything." Operating the audio transfer system, she was the only person who "got to hear it all," every single interview across the whole spectrum of the whole civil rights movement, and was brought to tears as Medgar Evers's widow, Myrlie, described his murder. This eager young black woman who "wanted to see it all" so impressed Orlando that he convinced Henry to bring her on as a paid production assistant and researcher. Meredith would work with Bagwell and Hampton for the next fifteen years.

Henry's longtime attorney, Ike Williams, said, "He was the greatest commune builder I have ever seen. He did not want to be alone. Henry wanted to bring in everybody who had talent or will, and he didn't give a damn what they looked like, white or black, a long as they could put their shoulder to the wheel in the common cause. . . . But the net result of his enormous personal magnetism was that the floor still tilted into his office, even if his dream was to have this communal project." Henry held court, dispensed wisdom, listened carefully to advice, gave orders, doled out warmth, hired, fired, and oversaw the whole enterprise from his sunny corner office overlooking the corner lot at Shawmut and Wooster.

In a rolling chair he shuttled back and forth between the big funky old desk and a round table stacked high with manila folders, surrounded by more stacks on the floor. When she later took over, his new secretary, Valerie Linson, was impressed with the contradiction between the "great film impresario and the chaos of his office," and tried to impose order. Editor Jeanne Jordan, a Blackside veteran from the early days, a midwesterner like Henry, tried unsuccessfully all year to organize the papers and clean up the mess every time she went into his office for a meeting.

Blackside headquarters in 1985 was eerily like the Atlanta SNCC headquarters where I had worked as a low-level staffer decades before. Henry's operation was populated by energetic young people who would surely have helped lead the movement had they been a generation younger: most of the Blacksiders would have fit right in. SNCC headquarters at 8½ Raymond

Street in Atlanta was above a beauty shop, manned 24/7, with the SNCC print shop and photo lab in the basement. Blackside's publishing operation, too, was in the basement, and even the odd, skinny layout of the two offices was about the same. SNCC's and Blackside's quarters were both converted apartments in a marginal building in a mostly poor, mostly black neighborhood, with a couple dozen white and black zealots jammed together toiling into night. Both offices resonated with a funky aura of political-cultural fervor. We even, on occasion, sang the same freedom songs.

Blackside staff were mostly in their thirties, SNCC staff in their twenties; chairman John Lewis was twenty-three, and executive secretary James Forman seemed to me ancient at thirty-six, but like Henry Hampton at forty-five, capable of superhuman functioning. Though Henry was usually turned out in a Brooks Brothers suit, Blackside had no particular dress code, but back in the day many SNCC workers wore rough denim jackets or sharecropper overalls. Forman was the only man I ever knew who could with dignity wear a pressed white dress shirt, snappy sport coat, and tie with his frayed bib overalls and work boots. I and everyone else who ever worked in Atlanta remember James Forman, the boss, cleaning the restrooms on weekends, as Henry was known to do. SNCC had its iconic leaders—Moses, Forman, Lewis, Hamer, Carmichael. But both organizations were highly collaborative, and everyone's opinion mattered. SNCC even tried to operate by concensus, but Blackside was hierarchical, with Henry in solo—some said "dictatorial"—command at the top. Blackside was SNCC's documentary twin, a multiracial laboratory for setting the world right, often functioning at the edge of chaos. What could be more SNCC than Henry's stated mission, "the expansion of democracy," through documentary filmmaking?

And some of the same people, older and wiser, now even roamed Blackside's halls: historian Howard Zinn; Judy Richardson herself, who was just as funny and warm as on the day I first met her in Georgia in '64; Martin Luther King's advisor and now our de facto pastor, Vincent Harding; our song leader, Bernice Reagon; and one afternoon I found Bob Moses himself watching a videocassette outside Henry's office, unblinking as always. Coffee, cigarettes, and sugar had fueled the long nights at SNCC (we took particular pleasure in a local Georgia candy bar called the Snik Snak), but Blacksiders ate healthy. At both SNCC and at Blackside, it seemed that all we ever did was work.

But there were differences. No one ever went to jail for working at Blackside, close calls with the IRS notwithstanding. Federal marshals crashed one of our Atlanta staff meetings to serve subpoenas. Civil rights offices throughout the South could be burned, bombed, or shot up, so at the Atlanta office we tried not to sit near the windows. Julian Bond, who was SNCC's communication director and later Blackside's principal narrator, was "afraid that some nut would drive by and throw a bomb or start shooting . . . but mostly we were concerned about danger for our colleagues scattered around the South." In order to do all my West Coast calls, I often worked late at SNCC, and walked home to my apartment in the projects past midnight without really worrying or ever being bothered. The real unnerving danger was from large neighborhood packs of Atlanta's feral dogs that followed me. Neither feral dogs, bombs, nor gunfire were really a problem for Blackside. Nor did Blacksiders amuse themselves trying to figure out who was the FBI informant among us, as there surely was in the Atlanta SNCC office, though who it was remains a mystery.

It was in the Atlanta headquarters in 1964 that a friendly cameraman named Haskell Wexler, on his way from Mississippi back to Hollywood, parked his equipment in my little office. It had never occurred to me until lunch with Haskell that a person, a young person like me, might become a moviemaker: I told him, "I want to do what *you* do." That encounter in the SNCC office would in a roundabout way eventually land me in the Blackside office, where I was soon on the phone to Haskell asking if we could use that footage he had shot in Mississippi back in 1964.

Henry asked, with good reason, that producer/director Orlando Bagwell live in Boston for the duration, and set him up in the fifth-floor apartment. Orlando, who was three thousand miles away from his family, always made it a point to greet the little Lao kids in the stairwell on their way to school. Since I was commuting from California, O took pity and let me crash in his apartment's back room for a week or two every month, gracious in welcoming me in his home away from home. We all assumed his apartment was the Blackside crash pad, hostel, and interview studio; I didn't learn until years later that when *Eyes on the Prize* ran low on money, Henry asked Orlando to pay rent on the Spartan digs, as though working a million hours a week for starvation wages wasn't enough. And I was eating up all his Häagen-Dazs. Judy Richardson, commuting from New York, occasionally came and stayed; Orlando's young son, Jaffar, lived with him in the apartment during our second summer; and a mysterious sound editor showed up to bunk there for three weeks at the very end.

Orlando and I became close friends. For days at a time the two of us seldom left the building: get up, roll downstairs, work ten hours, go for a quick hike or a run around the neighborhood, phone our families back home, talk over supper, work a bit more, sleep, get up the next morning, and start all over again. For me the building became part haven, part prison. We called it "the U-boat," or on a really bad day we were trapped in "the slave ship."

Blackside and the movement also shared the common affliction of constant financial shortfall; simply keeping the doors open meant an unending money chase. In my job as SNCC northern campus coordinator in '65, I sent out mass mailings to our college support groups: "SNCC is flat, stone cold broke. . . . It costs $2000/day not counting bail to keep running. You in the North are the only ones who can see us through . . . we have nowhere else to turn." Clay Carson said that at both SNCC and Blackside "it was an experiment. You do what you need to and don't worry about the money." It was now part of my job at financially strapped Blackside in 1985 to help Henry raise money to chronicle events in that same financially strapped SNCC office twenty years before.

Eyes on the Prize production was in full swing, but Henry had not yet been able to secure completion funds. Even our beleaguered production manager, Jo Ann Mathieu, was in the dark about the exact amount of our shortfall. Mike, Bobby, Sekou, and I had not been paid; *Eyes* was spending money faster than the committed grants actually came in the door. It was dawning on me that we might never get ahead of the burn rate in any orderly way. We were heading into a dreaded documentary vortex: the more expensive a film, the longer it takes to raise the money, so it takes longer to make the film, so it becomes more expensive, so it takes longer, so it costs more, and longer, and more, and longer, spinning ever outward until something gives. I remembered what Bob Moses said twenty years before about SNCC: "We are in a boat with a hole in it in the middle of the ocean; we need to repair the hole, but to do that we need to stay afloat."

During the fall of 1985 editors Chuck Scott, Jeanne Jordan, and Dan Eisenberg and their assistants had begun cutting film on three of the shows, working with the meager stock footage that had come in so far. All six programs should by this time have been roughly assembled, but were still in bits and pieces. Over the next two months the braiding together of interviews, narration, archive footage, and songs would generate battles inside Blackside, a case study in the business of hammering thousands of pages of history and hundreds of hours of footage down to six hours of television without draining all the power. By that winter 486 Shawmut Avenue had become the largest civil rights story shop in history.

The physical process of editing 16mm film was a half-industrial, half-artisanal, half-magical, half-cerebral process, more than the sum of its parts. Every 11-minute roll of 16mm negative film we shot and shipped from the field was developed at Precision Labs in New York but was unwatchable until they made a positive workprint copy. We shipped the corresponding audiotape to our in-house sound facility, where Meredith Woods transferred it to a separate reel of 16mm full coat magnetic film, then synchronized it by hand to the corresponding roll of silent 16mm workprint, frame for frame. Then an identical pair of sequential inked edge code numbers was stamped onto picture and sound reels once every foot, so that the editor could manually keep them synchronized. Meanwhile, an audiocassette of the sound had been sent to a typist, who banged out a paper transcript on a typewriter. Finally, sometimes weeks after we shot, the workprint, sound, and transcript arrived at Blackside's editing rooms, where teams logged them before the editors set to work putting together a first cut. The virgin original film negative stayed in a New York vault. Months or sometimes years later, before the finished show could be released, a second technical team hot spliced the original negative to precisely match the cut workprint, following a second set of latent edge codes optically exposed in the original manufacturing process. From the hot-spliced "A/B rolls" negative a watchable 16mm answer print was finally created. How did we ever make movies?

Each editor worked on a $30,000 400-pound 6-plate Steenbeck flatbed editing table, the size of a baby grand piano. The editor would loop the picture film and two tracks of sound film over, under, and around twenty-eight different rollers on the console, lock all the retainers, swing the master control lever to "forward," and it was off to the races. Synchronized picture and sound played in parallel on a little speaker and a little frosted-glass screen, so that when a person spoke, the words came out of his mouth at the right time.

After screening rushes (so called because they are rushed from the lab and give you such a rush), taking copious notes, and huddling with the director, the editor would mark the start and finish of a shot on the picture and sound film with grease pencil, then with a splicer (one brand appropriately called a "guillotine") physically cut both the workprint picture and the corresponding magnetic sound film to the exact length, connect it to the next shot with special adhesive tape, and finally splice placeholder leader back into the original rolls back at the gap. To shorten or lengthen the shot, the editor peeled the tape off (Walter Murch writes, "They made a little screech as they came apart, almost as if they were crying out in pain"), recut picture and sound to the new length, and then respliced the remaining tiny trim back into the roll of original rushes. A poorly executed splice would derail film speeding through the machine's toothed rollers and shred several feet of workprint and full coat before the editor could hit the brake.

Even describing the process is exhausting, but editors and their assistants repeated this miniature stitching operation tens of thousands of times on *Eyes*. Was the filmmaking any better because it was arduous? Possibly. Was something lost in years to come when we could edit with lightning digital speed? Possibly. Every tape-spliced edit had a fleeting permanence about it that demanded clear forethought based on experience, patience, and what Dan Eisenberg called "measured experimentation" about how the scene and story would unfold. We may never know, but all that deliberate physical motion—assistants passing in the hall with stacks of film cans, editors swiveling in their chairs to reach hither and yon for trims, the muscle power it took to rewind a set of thousand-foot reels, the dexterity and concentration to execute perfect tape splices— gave Henry's editing rooms the purposeful air of a high-end kitchen with its chefs and sous-chefs. Those toilsome mechanics, even the seconds spent splicing, forced directors and editors to really think before they cut, to contemplate where the film had come from over the previous minute of screen time and where it was headed in the next couple of minutes. Like ceramics or surgery, it required the artisan to commit to a plan before firing the kiln or slicing the tissue.

Today the mechanics have all but vanished into firmware and software, devoid of any physical effort whatever beyond the tiny motions of mousing, right click, and left click.

The mechanical work is secondary to the editor's real job, which is to see the order of things differently from the rest of us, sifting, sorting, and arranging thousands of sounds and images into a powerful, transparent, and seamless film narrative. The good film editors were ones who could previsualize a sequence in all its cinematic power or frailty, before anyone had the benefit of test-flying a few different versions on a computer screen.

Henry mostly allowed the producers and editors to find their own way through the forest of civil rights, knowing that his "salt-and-pepper" teams and well-experienced editors would hash it out in the cutting room, keeping a check on each other, each coming up with ways and means the other might not think of. Except for Judith, none of the producer/directors had ever before successfully wrestled with the structural problems of a one-hour narrative documentary, let alone a six-part series.

In a wise and risky early move, Henry had decided to construct the six programs not around the themes or ideas, like equal protection under law or nonviolence, but around specific battles on specific fronts—Selma, Ole Miss, Birmingham, Emmett Till, Montgomery, Mississippi Freedom Summer— which would carry the themes and ideas as stowaways. With minimal guidance from narration, Henry trusted the audience to unpack the embedded meanings on their own.

Blackside teams were engineering a "people's history" that had to work as truth telling but also as high-profile prime-time television, up against *Cheers* or *60 Minutes*. Editors began to shape the battle stories. Because we were telling a *few* strong tales from the history, not the whole history, most of their work involved stripping away what was not useful, and rearranging the 1 percent that remained in exactly the right order for maximum power, "condensing a gallon of Dunkin' Donuts coffee into one cup of espresso." Editors had the infernal job of squeezing all the force, nuance, simplicity, and complexity into a compact "PBS hour" (54 minutes and 20 seconds exactly) that would satisfy the competing demands of PBS executives; historians; critics; veterans of SNCC, CORE, SCLC, the NAACP, and Citizens' Council; former Panthers; white suburbanites in Iowa; teenagers in Harlem; ten million prime-time viewers of all ages, genders, classes, and races; and Henry Hampton.

So what did the editors actually do all day? What, for example, is the best order in which to arrange the telling of Emmett Till's murder and the trial of his killers, the tale locked away in Henry's mind for thirty years, and likely unknown to the vast majority of Americans in 1985? In a sense, all of *Eyes* was bound up in how much the Emmett Till story meant to Hampton. It was the pearl in the oyster.

The ordeal of Emmett Till can signify very different things depending on the *order* of telling. Like any piece of historical narrative construction—the Watts Riot, the race between John Henry and the steam drill, the Tet Offensive—this would be a puzzle in time, temporal not spatial. Starting with Orlando's edit back on *America, We Loved You Madly* in 1979, there probably remains not a single reasonable ordering of the Emmett Till story that was not tried at some point over many years during the creation of *Eyes on the Prize*. Literally dozens were constructed on paper or in the editing room.

The historical chronology was simple: In 1955, a fourteen-year-old middle-class Negro boy, naive about southern racial codes, travels from Chicago's South Side to his great-uncle's sharecropper cabin in rural Mississippi. He buys candy from a white store owner's wife, and says, "Bye, baby," as he departs. Four nights later the store owner, J. W. Milam, and his half brother, Roy Bryant, abduct young Till at gunpoint from his great-uncle's house in the middle of the night, beat him, and shot him in the head. Fishermen find his bloated, naked body in the Tallahatchie River with a 75-pound cotton gin fan tied around his neck with barbed wire. The boy's mother insists on publicly displaying her son's ravaged corpse in Chicago, the bones in his face and skull smashed. The murder trial in Mississippi plays out in suffocating August heat before a hundred reporters and photographers from around the world. Every white attorney in the county joins the defense team. As tension rises in the courtroom, the boy's sixty-four-year-old great-uncle, Moses Wright, finds the courage to stand up before the all-white, all-male jury, point his finger, and identify the murderer, which no black man had ever before done in Mississippi and lived to tell about it. "Thar he," says Wright. Twelve white jurors, told by the prosecutor, "Every Anglo-Saxon one of you has the courage to find these men innocent," acquit the murderers of Emmett Till. Mose Wright flees for his life, leaving his cotton ready to pick in the field, and never returns to Mississippi.

After acquittal Milam and Bryant then unapologetically told the whole story of how they killed Till to *Look* magazine reporter William Bradford Huie in exchange for four thousand dollars cash. That published story and the *Jet* magazine photo of Till's smashed face gave tangible horror to the abstract notion of southern racial violence run amok with full support of the white community. The story was out, creating a national sensation and galvanizing Henry's generation with both fear and resolve. Jesse Jackson called it "the Big Bang" of the civil rights movement. Only a few months after Mose Wright's lone black gesture in that white court-room, fifty thousand black citizens of Montgomery, Alabama, rose up to-gether to boycott segregated buses in the first successful mass protest of the modern civil rights movement.

As the opening scene in the opening program of *Eyes on the Prize,* the story would be our carnival barker, our noir tease, and our declaration of theme, purpose, and style, a chance to strut our narrative stuff. It had all the moral power of a Tolstoy parable with the trappings of feudal Southern Gothic: a creepy poison stew of erotic fear and hatred in the Mississippi night, a weighted corpse sinking into the moonlit muddy river, a black sharecropper-preacher standing up in court to accuse a redneck thug. There were cigars, toddlers, and gooey French kisses in the courtroom, em-battled poor whites, black witnesses disappearing into the steamy night.

Should events on screen unfold as events in life unfolded, or should they be torn apart and reassembled in nonlinear order? Should we open with the foreordained absurd verdict, or end with it? Begin with the B-movie kidnapping of "the boy that done all that talk," as Christopher Metress does in his book *The Lynching of Emmett Till?* With the river it-self, as in Stanley Nelson and Lewis Erskine's film, *The Murder of Emmett Till,* or with a text about the theory of civil order, as William Faulkner did in his lament about the Till case? Or Till's baby pictures, as in Keith Beau-champ's *Untold Story of Emmett Till.* What about opening with Mose Wright picking cotton as the narrator says, "His story begins . . ."?

Or perhaps Ralph Abernathy ruminating, "That could have been me," or Ella Baker decrying the death of black mothers' sons. Should Mose Wright's act of solitary resistance, looking in the courtroom photo for all the world like a sharecropper Adam reaching out to touch the finger of God as he points at the murderers, be the very first image in *Eyes on the Prize,* proudly planting the flag of resistance, or should it be the very last image? Or should we veer far outside the box and begin with the line poet Ezra Pound wrote at the end of World War II, announcing the death of Emmett Till's father in Italy: "Till was hung yesterday for murder and rape with trimmings." What about opening with Bill Huie interviewing the murderers Bryant and Milam, all three parts read by black actors, as in Mike Wiley's play *Dar He?*

Should *Eyes on the Prize* start with ghosts, building the Till story around the evocative footage of Bryant's dilapidated store that Henry, Or-lando, and Jean-Philippe Boucicaut had shot back in 1979? Or should we go down there ourselves with a dolly, generators, lights, and a big crew to shoot our own spectral noir images of the now abandoned store in the moonlight, a haunted landscape overgrown like Auschwitz in Alain Resnais's classic documentary of ethnic horror, *Night and Fog.*

Where, for maximum emotional punch and understanding of cause and effect, should Judith and Dan deploy the photo of Till's pulverized face? End with it? Place it at the point in the story when Henry and millions of young African Americans saw it in *Jet*? Certainly not open with it—that we could agree on. Should they deploy it at all (Henry never did in *America, We Loved You Madly*), at risk of a few million viewers scrambling to cover their eyes and switch channels to *The Jeffersons*? Should the narrative be retold from start to finish several times, each with new revelations, *Rashomon*-style: first Bill Huie's version, then the same events spun differently by the defense, then events as they filter out to black teenagers across the country in 1955?

It could make your head explode. Depending on how the interviews and archive footage were edited and the narration written, this was either a police procedural leading up to solving a murder mystery, or it was a Kafkaesque court drama leading up to Mose Wright's act of courage, an impressionist deep dive into the Dark South, a remarkable first step that finally sparked a mass movement, a eulogy for all martyrs of American apartheid, or all of the above.

And over the years Henry's own sense of the story's meaning had changed. For teenage Henry Hampton in 1955, the crux had been the murder itself and what it said about his own vulnerability as a black teenager. But later in life, when he came to understand the agency and hope in Mose Wright's testimony and its role in kindling the movement, "The story of the uncle was equally if not more powerful, that act of courage of people saying 'No more.'" The nephew Emmett as leading actor gave way to his uncle Mose as leading actor, and what begins as a television story of black *victims* (the murder) could shift 180 degrees to a launching pad for black *victors* (the Montgomery bus boycott). Hampton and Fayer battled over what it could and should mean on television: Henry the chronic optimist had over the decades come to view the blurred photo of Wright courting death as the most heroic of American gestures. Steve saw in it all the irrational hatred of the killers, the worst in American society.

What was the core practical *reason* for spending all that time and money on this story? Certainly not simply to recount the casual barbarity, grieving once again for the thousands of murdered black men whose killers walk free. Fayer remembered Henry reacting to an early draft that ended with the horror of the boy's death. "I'll be damned if I am going to end the story on that note, white guy versus black guy. It's got to end on the old man, Mose Wright, standing up and pointing his finger at the killers and saying 'Thar he' . . . bravery in the face of almost certain death."

No, Henry knew all along that everything hinged on the nationwide media attention, especially from the tenacious black press. That coverage allowed his generation to discover its mission, just as social media coverage would rouse a future generation to discover its mission with the death of Michael Brown in Ferguson, Missouri.

Associate producer Llew Smith and researcher Lewanne Jones were scrambling to gather material, but for the moment editor Dan Eisenberg and producer/director Judith Vecchione had little to work with for the scene: a few newsreels from Mississippi and Chicago, faded photos, headlines, our interview with cousin Curtis Jones, and a fine interview with influential black *New York Amsterdam News* reporter James Hicks that Henry had done back in 1979. Dan said, "It all amounted to little more than a few shards, and we stretched the shards."

But among the shards were eyewitness accounts from Jones, who described the scene at the store and was sleeping next to his cousin Emmett when Bryant and Milam burst in. Hicks explained on camera his efforts to get Mamie Till's black Chicago congressman, Charles Diggs, into the courtroom after white deputies had turned Rep. Diggs away. Hicks managed to approach the bench with Diggs's United States House of Representatives business card when the judge said, "'Just a minute, just a minute.' He called a deputy over . . . and the deputy said . . . 'This nigger here said there's a nigger outside who says that he's a congressman . . . but the sheriff won't let him in, so he's sending his card up there with this guy.' And the judge said, 'A *nigger* congressman?!?' And the deputy said, 'That's what this nigger said.' I said to myself, my God, I have never seen anything like this in my life. And so . . . the sheriff says, 'I'll bring him in here, but I'm going to sit him at you niggers' table.'"

But what of the material the Blackside archivists couldn't get: newsreel film of Money, Mississippi, tied up in a rights dispute, including a 1955 interview with Till's other cousin, who wouldn't talk to Orlando and Henry six years before. Some of the Cap Cities footage was apparently lost forever. Johnson

Publishing would not license the *Jet* photo of Till's face until Llew called John H. Johnson personally and made the case that "it was a matter of history."

And what of the dark eddies that we couldn't even consider in the brief screen time allotted, like Medgar Evers smuggling a witness out of the county in a casket, rumors that as many as a dozen locals had joined in torturing Till, or Mississippi senator James Eastland's masterstroke of leaking the U.S. Army's charge that Till's father had raped two women and killed a third in Italy during the war.

Talk is cheap; but fortunately for us, professional editors have neither the interest, time, nor patience for floundering around with all the options. They set to work with a plan, building the tale from material they have rather than moping about material they wish they had. "If it's not in the room, it's not in the film."

Judith's editor, Dan, already an established and well-respected avant-garde film director in his own right, was whip smart and no stranger to the mysteries of story order. Dan said it was his job "to deliver something that was legible, accurate, and honest."

They decided early on to position the photo of Till right after the open-casket funeral, and to withhold Huie's recitation of guilt until the very end. Cousin Curtis Jones and reporter James Hicks, the only ones claiming direct experience, would anchor the scene, but Dan would shape the narrative around the emotional flow of events, not around character development. They mapped it by cutting and pasting ideas into notebooks and pinning 3x5 cards on a big bulletin board.

In their first cut they chose to open with the night abduction, then flashed back to the incident at the store, then flashed forward to Mrs. Till's insistence on displaying her son's corpse in Chicago, then back to the actual discovery of the body, then the trial, Wright pointing at the murders and saying "Thar he," the verdict, and finally, the just-the-facts story from beginning to end as told by William Bradford Huie.

Judith, Llew, and Dan all loved it, felt they had succeeded in setting forth a coherent rhythm of emotion and thought. But Henry was fuming, convinced that by unfolding the story in this order, and giving it no context, Judith had sapped it of all its power, leaving just another jumbled story of victimization. It was a whimper, not the Big Bang. He did manage to affirm that most of the elements of the story were there, but asked, "Have you gotten to the significance of all this? Why should people give a shit?"

Was the problem simply that he had been playing the same chronological, linear Till mind-movie over and over in his head for decades? Dan felt that Henry "had accumulated meaning and significance to things outside the event itself . . . but the material did not communicate those things. . . . His reactions were often enigmatic and unclear."

Judith remembered, "We had cut it so that we first said, 'This is a story about a kid who gets killed,' so that you know right up front that he's dead. But Henry said, 'You've taken all the wind out of it by doing that. You have to put it in chronological order.' And we said, 'No, Henry, that's not what this story is about. This is not the story about he's dead, it's the story about *why* he's dead, and how people reacted and closed ranks.' . . . To me that drove much more powerfully to the photograph in the casket. I thought Dan had done a beautiful job of cutting it. And Henry came upstairs and we went around, and he said, 'No, I really want to see it the other way'. . . . the way he had it in his head.

"He's the executive producer; I have to do what he wants. Dan was fuming but very professional and recut it to be chronological . . . took every one of those damn splices apart and cut it beautifully chronologically to hold back the death, until we discover the body in the river. And Henry thumped up the stairs and looked at it and said, 'Put it back.' Dan had steam coming out of his ears he was so mad. But Henry had had, I'm sure, for years, an image of this story, maybe the experience that *he* had, of the shock of discovering the body, and that's where he thought the power was." Hampton said the program didn't get to the heart of "what it means for Mose to testify. . . ."

Judith, coming at it fresh, as "a relatively ordinary American white woman" new to the Till story, had done what she considered the most clear and effective factual story for the mass diverse audience we wanted to reach.

Henry could easily have said to his white director and white editor, "Not only am I the executive producer who is paying your salary, *I* was a young black man in 1955, and I understand this in ways you never can and never will," but he didn't. Not once, in all our years making racially charged films with Henry Hampton, did I hear him play the race card.

So early in the process, Till became a battered scene at the heart of a long and expensive creative battle. No matter what the storytelling order, the Till story line was always broken for someone somewhere inside Blackside. (For some it's still broken.) And from the start the team was hamstrung by having to do the whole saga in fourteen minutes, so like many others in *Eyes,* this story shrank over the coming months as most of the Faulknerian texture was necessarily stripped away.

And there was the nagging suspicion that Bill Huie's account of the murderers' version was not entirely trustworthy. Did Till really flaunt the picture of the white girl in his class to the murderers? Llew said, "We had discussions about it. His account of Milam as a rational, calm man making the decision to shoot Till is at odds with the accounts of witnesses hearing screaming—Till being beaten and tortured from the start—not a deliberate tipping point." Had Milam and Bryant lied to Huie? Did implicit bias sway Bill's account? Historian Terry Wagner argued in 2010 that Curtis Jones's account of events at the store is also unreliable and perhaps even fabricated, that he had not arrived in Money until after the events at the store. Had Jones lied to us?

Then we had the problem of judging how our ordinary mainstream American prime-time audience might enter this first-ever television construction of the Till/Wright story *before* we guided them through a descent into the racist netherworld of American apartheid. Henry felt that without establishing the underlying terror against which he stood. We could not ask viewers to experience the Till story and Wright's courage in a vacuum. Henry often said, "I've never met an audience that wasn't collectively smarter than I am," but he could have added that we have never met an audience that was better informed about the *context* of the story, that is our job. They had planned all along to construct a tease and introduction to segregation leading up to Till, but had not had the materials or time to do it.

It goes to the heart of every documentary's opening dilemma: How much scene setting and background does the audience need for the drama to make sense? Constructing the opening of a film is like launching the space shuttle; nearly all the heavy lifting happens in the first five minutes, the long, million-mile flight is the easy part, until you have to land safely. (Judith added that if you weigh the opening down with too much baggage the thing will crash before you reach orbit.)

In Fayer's original 1978 treatment he told of the incident at the store, the abduction, and the murder in exact chronological order, and then put the Till story on "pause" for a few minutes of flashback while he laid out an ingenious overture. He traced young Emmett's trip from Chicago on a mystery train thundering through the night toward the Mississippi Delta, evoking an American *Heart of Darkness,* with evocative footage that carried the boy deeper and deeper into a dystopian South, marking out the history of slavery, Reconstruction, Jim Crow, the Klan, and lynching, until the young innocent finally stepped off the train, alone and about to die in Money, Mississippi. Fayer then snapped the audience back into the middle of the trial, with all of the white spectators "who lived in a sea of black people" carrying sidearms in court and the judge questioning "a nigger congressman?!?"

The battle royal over Till was well under way when I flew in from California on January 20, 1986, the first Martin Luther King national holiday. I stayed up late over Scotch with Orlando at his apartment on the top floor of the U-boat talking about the reelection of Ronald Reagan, who had opposed the King holiday and then grudgingly signed it into law when faced with overwhelming veto-proof support in the House and Senate. Henry had noted that we were trying to get a grant from the NEH, directed by Reagan appointee Lynne Cheney, whose husband, Congressman Dick Cheney, had voted against honoring King with a holiday when the bill first came up. Both of us were down in the dumps at being away from our families, and both worried that Henry was so distracted by fund-raising that we might never have him again as a creative force.

The next morning I wrote a ten-page memo praising the good work Judith and her team had done, agreeing that no one could judge work-in-progress versions of the Till story until it was set up by a prologue describing the moral moonscape in which it unfolded. They set to work and emerged a few days later with a riveting exposition of segregation that at last articulated what black people in Mississippi were up against in 1955, and what white people were afraid of, a journey through the decades, emphasizing the psychology of both blacks and whites trapped within a brutal system. Judith's remarkable narration laced it all together beautifully. Now the magnitude of young Till's blunder, his killers' audacity, and the courage of his great-uncle's testimony carried new weight.

The final version opened on Mose Wright picking cotton, with the narrator identifying him and saying, "His story begins . . . ," then immediately revealed the discovery of the body and snaked its way forward and backward to the final "Thar he," Huie's coda, as Judith's swing narration throws us to the Montgomery movement.

I know that we never got the Till story exactly right for Henry. I doubt he would have liked the way later filmmakers handled it. So it is with so many stories. Yet as finally broadcast, that opening sequence of *Eyes on the Prize* celebrates Mose Wright, the dirt-poor sharecropper-preacher whose grandparents had been born as property, utterly powerless in slavery, becoming a courageous political actor on the national stage through his own force of will. *That* gave Henry satisfaction. It went on to introduce the Montgomery bus boycott as an action sparked by the Till case, succeeding when people banded together . . . making a clear connection between remarkable acts of personal courage and a remarkable mass movement.

And Till was only *one* of the sixty scenes Henry's teams had to wrestle into compliance for *Eyes I*. Rough cut screenings were scheduled only a month away. In order to regain momentum and hit some benchmark of forward motion, I argued we should stick to the original dates and with a wink and nod call them "in-house first assemblies" instead of rough cuts. Henry and Judith agreed.

At the end of October, sensing I couldn't really contribute much with the films scattered in scenes as the editors cobbled together the assemblies, I headed back to California to have Christmas with my family and shoot a commercial for Froot Loops to supplement my meager Blackside pay.

Blackside was one of the last predigital documentary companies, shooting on 16mm film negative well into the 1990s. (Ken Burns kept shooting documentaries on 16mm film up through 2010, and I actually shot Super 16mm doing second-unit work on *Fruitvale Station* in 2012.) We took our temporary music off vinyl records, did real "cut and paste" on scripts with scissors and glue, drew up schedule charts by hand, and made long-distance calls on phones with cords and logged them on notepads. We used the U.S. Postal Service, gathered around the new "facsimile machine" the day it arrived, and marveled at the new FedEx overnight delivery service that fall. Until Orlando brought a 20-pound Kaypro word processor from California, with its little green CRT screen and 5¼-inch floppy disks, we had no computers of any sort beyond Kenn's primitive DEC. Our researchers worked in the massive card catalog and stacks at Harvard's Widener Library and the Boston Public Library. Today, sitting among venture capitalists in a Silicon Valley café as I write, pulling up street views of Money, Mississippi, with a few keystrokes, I look back on those quaint times not with warm nostalgia but with consternation at how quickly we could have accomplished so much more without all that molasses in the infrastructure.

The office at 486 Shawmut endured a blizzard of memoranda, any one of which could be a dozen single-spaced pages, crammed with detail to encourage forward motion, sustain morale, and most of all, make the cuts shorter and clearer. We cooked up a hodgepodge of homilies, fables, and homemade rules designed to help producers structure their stories.

Returning from California, I devised the "Parable of the Peach Pits," a long shaggy-dog fable in which the wise king offers his kingdom to whoever among his subjects could fit the most peaches into a box of a given size. One by one the supplicants put peaches into the box, squeezing in a dozen, then thirteen, then fourteen, beginning to squish them, then shaving off skin and slicing away little bits of peach flesh to fit in fifteen, then twenty, chopping off more and more from each peach until all that remains is a box of peach pits. In making films we so often try to cram in so many different incidents, characters, backstory, names, numbers, policy points, eddies, textures, detail, exposition, and lessons that we wreck them all.

At the end of the peach pits parable, the winner gathers eight perfect peaches and twenty perfect interstitial grapes that together fit exactly into the box without violating any individual peach.

Judith, who somehow managed brilliant analyses of everyone else's cuts while producing two fine shows of her own, patiently explained the difference between a chronology and a chronicle: "Chronology is not story." A chronology gives equal narrative screen time and emphasis to everything that happened, say week to week in England in 1390, or day to day in Selma in 1965, whereas a *chronicle* devotes time and attention to a handful of pivotal dramatic incidents arranged for maximum impact, as in *The Canterbury Tales* or the *Eyes* documentaries we were constructing that winter in Boston. Our twelve iconic tales constituted stories *from* the history, not the whole history; a chronicle, not a chronology.

Then there was "pendulum management," for guarding against overcompensation in editing. And "slinky-izing," in which historical time expands and contracts, Slinky-like. We devote different screen duration to different events, seldom corresponding to their real-time duration: it takes about five minutes to walk across the Edmund Pettus Bridge in Selma, two if you run, but in a film it can take thirty seconds, or thirty minutes, depending on the gravity, goal, function, and positioning of the crossing.

And what about "pieces of the True Cross," i.e., the real thing. We were a company drowning in metaphors.

To illustrate our handy paint-by-number structure lessons—peach pits, chronologies, chronicles, Slinkys, space shuttles, and Fayer's reliable man-up-a-tree story arc—Judith walked us through a case study of *Vietnam: A Television History,* and I did a chalkboard schematic of my own *Day After Trinity.* I convened a little seminar on Rob Epstein's *The Times of Harvey Milk,* one of the most brilliantly structured documentaries ever made. In that film, the story of Milk, the first openly gay public official ever elected in America, appears to march relentlessly forward from birth to meteoric success to his death at the hands of the assassin Dan White. In fact, filmmakers Rob Epstein and Deborah Hoffmann scrambled the real-world chronology to produce more powerful intellectual and emotional forward motion, so skillfully that we mistake it for a natural chronological flow of events. Milk's first forty-two years of life consume three minutes of screen time and his last few seconds consume ten minutes. Coming from San Francisco, where few people thought twice in 1985 about having gay friends, relatives, and coworkers, I had introduced it as "a film about another people rising up," but the parallel between gay people in California in the eighties and black people in the South in the sixties did not really resonate at Blackside.

What emerged from 486 Shawmut that winter was not only a television series, but a new way of making documentaries. Henry gave us a creative space that was both wide open and fiercely disciplined, "with form but formless," in Orlando's words. This remarkable documentary incubator reflected in its very processes parts of the remarkable movement it chronicled. Within his force field on Shawmut Avenue, Henry created a welcoming place where time moved quickly and flares of dysfunction erupted, but where you could try anything as long as it was serious. Orlando remembers, "Walking through the doors of Blackside . . . you walk in, and you start walking up those steps, and you know you're in another space and you just transform into that space." Later, Orlando and many others would learn that escaping that space could be hard.

The nasty contradiction built into letting the producers spread their wings, solve their own problems, and seek cinematic solutions amid "the abrasion of good minds" was that we had a finite budget, a deadline, cash-flow troubles, and a boss. Each of the Blackside teams was producing two one-hour films in fourteen months, twice the pace of standard PBS projects. As work progressed, so did the accumulation of stress, tension, overruns, and anger, but so did passion for what we were accomplishing.

Henry gathered everyone together just before Christmas and said, "I don't know if I'll have the cash to continue. I can't afford to pay anyone but the editors. Can you stick with me for a couple of weeks?" Callie Crossley remembers "freaking out. This is what my parents warned me about; I'm going to have to go home and live with them." In an astonishing testament to Henry and his vision, everyone held on, no one quit or even slowed down. Laurie Kahn said, "I thought he should have sold the damned Jaguar," but stayed by him. Cash from another grant came in.

After a rough week struggling to get people unstuck from obsessing over detail and back to the job of churning out crude first versions of shows, I wrote E. B. White's advice to farmers on the chalkboard: "Once you've given your pig an enema, there's no turning back," and next to it Francis Ford Coppola's homily: "No film is ever as good as the rushes or as bad as the first rough cut." I skedaddled for the airport, headed back to shoot a cereal commercial with Colossal Pictures in San Francisco. It was a different world; arriving on the set at seven in the morning the next day, I found two food stylists sorting through thousands of Cheerios with tweezers to cull the perfect from the imperfect for the hero shot.

Then I worked with the special effects unit on *Top Gun*, blowing up big scale-model jet fighters on a desolate mountaintop east of San Francisco. They paid me well to shoot handheld 35mm for a faux "documentary feel." Go figure. Director Tony Scott was a wisecracking, cigar-smoking mensch with silver-tipped cowboy boots and an apparently endless supply of cash, not burdened with the financial clouds that hovered around Henry Hampton. It was fun helping the pyro guys set igniters in their little explosive cocktails—black powder and homemade napalm (naphthalene, Tide detergent, and gasoline) inside condoms stuffed into Dixie cups. Henry would have loved it. The crew patiently delayed blowing up a 9-foot F-1 fighter jet because a dove landed on the nose and refused to leave. Twenty-five of us spent most of one twelve-hour day on the clock waiting for pyro to prep dozens of mortar pipes, only to scramble for cover when the pipes all misfired prematurely, unleashing a shower of burning phosphorus projectiles. The dove returned. Most of the days produced one or two seconds of screen time and cost at least as much as a month of running Blackside.

CHAPTER FOURTEEN

Messy History

1986

The painter Wayne Thiebaud's metaphorical advice to artists is always useful to filmmakers. He says of rough gesture drawing, "Don't work your way around the golf course with a putter; use a driver." You don't want Michelangelo fretting over the rosy details on some cherub's butt when he should have seen that it was one cherub too many. You don't want a film editor polishing the opening scene when perhaps it should really be the closing scene, or not even be in the movie.

The editor's crude "first assembly," an expansive sketch, is the first time anyone sees the elements working together, the different textures and flavors first coalescing—or not. A vivid anecdote that took your breath away on location now falls flat in context, another draws strength from the footage around it, a voice-over suddenly breathes life into a humdrum still photo. A documentary assembly is a curious, overlong mashup of raw material, without narration, music, or anything we would really call "editing." It must simply give a big blunt feeling of the forward motion, with characters banging against one another, foreshadowing how the pieces may eventually play together in the same movie—a gesture drawing.

The fun part is the tremendous rush from seeing for the first time that a coherent *movie* might lie somewhere in that two-hour sprawl of shards. The not fun part is seeing how that first assembly reveals the whole differential equation laid out before you, with too many variables, too many multiple solutions, too little time. But not so fast. So much of what makes cinema *cinema* boils up with the editor's gift for layering, braiding, matching action, sound/picture interplay, visual rhyming, and rhythms that cannot possibly be achieved in a hasty assembly.

Henry had been on the road much of that fall raising funds, but now he returned to convene work-in-progress assembly screenings in January 1986 at the head of the Big Table. With his black beard, barrel chest, and red power suspenders, he looked for all the world like a man who had taken the afternoon off from his job as a jolly lumberjack to guide us through Socratic dialogue on "the arc of the moral universe." In these meetings he was as far as I could tell the smartest guy in the room, though he seldom showed it: warm and exuberant but modest in the extreme. He listened closely and gave few comments, letting others state the obvious, then weighing in only when he saw that no one else was going to bring up an important point. Mostly he asked his pointed questions: "What's at stake?" "What will make a seventy-year-old white lady in Peoria give a damn about this film?" "How could that guy remember that meeting when we know he was five hundred miles away?"

Despite years watching my own assemblies go down in flames, I hoped creative lightning would strike, that those *Eyes* assemblies would arrive as inspired works of raw genius. But that was not to be. Jim and Callie's Birmingham/Albany cut was workmanlike and historically clear, which pleasantly surprised me, since on the road I had doubted Jim had the chops, but it was surprisingly colorless except for Ralph Abernathy's singing. Where was the verve of ordinary foot soldiers, and what about those long confusing eddies chronicling the inner workings of Birmingham city government?

Orlando and Prue's Freedom Rides assembly had the opposite problem: magnetic characters floundering in storytelling confusion. But years later, Jim DeVinney told me, "I remember a turning point for me. It was in Orlando's show, the black woman talking about her son being locked up in jail, and she is laughing and crying at the same time. I realized *then* that this series was about the *courage* of black people. It was *not* about outrage at denial of rights, *not* about white people freeing black people." Jim had grown up in Indiana, with a fair amount of interaction with black people, but he had come to Blackside with little interest or understanding of the movement. Here in the assembly screening was the transformation of an ordinary white person, Blackside's own Jim DeVinney, embracing a ground truth long understood by the rest of the staff—certainly all the black staff. It was exactly the transformation that Henry hoped to achieve when millions of Americans watched *Eyes on the Prize*.

Though the assembly screening was the first time Henry had really seen much of what his directors and editors were up to, he said little. So the rest of us took up the slack with rowdy discussion of the works in progress and some much-needed praise shouting for all the hard work. Here I first saw Henry struggle with a problem that would bedevil

Blackside's moviemaking for years: he could ask dazzling questions, but could very seldom clearly articulate what he didn't like in a cut, and seldom offered a practical solution. We searched for telltale cues from the boss—hand on chin means he likes it, hand on brow means he doesn't, putting hand over mouth means he doesn't like that particular moment, or (the worst) sphinxlike gaze out window means he doesn't like *any* of it but can't say why. His reluctance to give clear editorial marching orders cost him and the rest of us untold sleepless nights, and cost the company a fortune over the years.

The next day Judith and Llew's Montgomery boycott assembly did, in fact, succeed in dispelling the "tired seamstress" trope by bringing Rosa Parks's lifelong activism to the foreground. Abernathy's hushed singing of "Leaning on the Everlasting Arms" came alive in the context of an unfolding struggle and radiated emotional power to everything around it in the cut.

Talking shop that evening over dinner at Chef Chandler's, Henry was glum. I did not yet understand that he was almost always glum after screenings, so I tried to buck him up, slapping a smiley face on the progress his teams had made. He was at best guarded, unable to bust out with any sense of relief or satisfaction that we actually had decent first assemblies on the *Eyes on the Prize* shows, an important benchmark, even if they were messy. I typed out my notes for the producers every night that week, sometimes trying to decipher, articulate, and usually temper the extreme frustration Henry often unloaded over dinner.

Whenever I came in from the coast, I got a mass download of pent-up troubles from everyone—producers, assistants, the accountant, the editors. I was happy to serve the talk therapy with the staff, who suspected I had a back channel to the boss. But I could seldom muster a solution to the unending organizational problems swirling around Henry's aversion to budgets, deadlines, discipline, and timely feedback. Maybe it was just me, because I am descended from German Lutherans, who never saw a deadline they didn't love. Jeanne Jordan (who kept a photo of Virginia Woolf over her Steenbeck) and the other editors lived by order, and Henry was comfortable with disorder. Dan Eisenberg made clear that the editors' job was to deliver comprehensible cuts on time and on budget, but Henry neither practiced nor truly appreciated the professional discipline of an editor. His comfort zone was visionary informality; less charitable staff said his comfort zone was turmoil.

• • • • • •

Now in the dead of winter, Boston could seem Dickensian, and we took to calling Blackside "Bleakside." On bitter-cold bad days I could almost hate that city. How could people live like this? Compared to our California paradise, Boston could seem permanently wounded, narcotized by sports, ashen, frigid, and everlastingly racist. Henry's black staff didn't feel comfortable sitting in the bleachers at Red Sox games because they risked heckling by whites. Henry mistrusted every cop in our neighborhood. I could even hate the innocent streets themselves, tangled little eighteenth-century cow paths redesigned by bitter civil engineers, now choked with cars, trucks, buses, and dirty snow.

But that winter our financial picture had brightened; we had $1,400,000 (and rising) committed of the $1,750,000 (and rising) production total. The money chase was mostly Henry's chase, and he was cultivating Silicon Valley entrepreneurs in hopes of a fat donation. (He respected big money almost as much as he respected big ideas.) I was at that time doing a fair amount of shooting with young Steve Jobs on various documentaries, and Hampton was awestruck when I told him about filming a meeting with a couple dozen Apple staffers in their twenties who were all millionaires. When Jobs cashed out of Apple in 1985 for $100,000,000, Henry noted that it was enough to run Blackside for about fifty years. Our *Eyes* shortfall was $350,000, what Jobs made in a week. Around the time of Apple's Rosa Parks "Think Different" ad, Mike Chin and I were setting up for an interview in Steve's Cupertino office while he chatted on the phone with Kurt Vonnegut, and it crossed my mind that I should ask Steve Jobs to give Henry Hampton a million dollars. I chickened out.

Inside our Blackside bubble we suspected maybe the money hassles were all our imagination, that the fund-raising frustration just went with documentary filmmaking, but then one day the *New York Times* ran a big article about the trouble Henry Hampton was having funding his series about civil rights, naming corporations and foundations that had turned us down: Carnegie, Rockefeller, Xerox, IBM, GE, Hallmark, and dozens of others. It wasn't our imagination.

Blackside's struggle for support unfolded in what most of us considered the darkest days of the Reagan retrenchment. Henry, always the champion of all-diversity-of-all-sorts-all-the-time, had somehow managed to hire a young Republican intern away from the Reagan White House; the guy did a great job. To the consternation of his generally anti-Reagan, anti-Republican, anti-imperialist, antijingoistic, antinativist, antinationalist (though never anti-American) crew, Henry again insisted on seeing lots of American flags on screen, particularly in the hands of black boys and girls. He said it was mostly to position our series firmly in the mainstream, and as he often reminded us, "It's our flag too. Don't let them take it away."

As soon as we made it through screening six assemblies, with their high wide view of the decade-long movement story, the gaps were obvious. We could see clearly now what final parts of the *Eyes* puzzle still needed to be filmed in the field, mostly pickups for the Mississippi and Selma stories. We were months behind schedule, and rough-cut editing had just gotten under way.

Meredith Woods, Judy Richardson, and Callie Crossley had finally gotten a fine interview with Dr. Bernice Johnson Reagon, who delivered a stirring discourse on the power of freedom songs. As a minister's daughter in segregated Albany, Georgia, she had learned singing in the congregational style, with song leaders but no soloists: "So I grew up in a church with the sound of people singing, and the first instruments are hands and feet, and to this day, that's the only way I can deal comfortably with creating music."

In her teens she joined Albany's NAACP and then SNCC, sitting in at lunch counters by day and organizing community meetings at night. "There was more singing than there was talking. So most of the work . . . had to do with nurturing the people who had come. The singing is the kind of singing where you disappear. What we did in the mass meeting was extend ourselves beyond our bodies." Reagon swiftly became recognized as the southern movement's greatest song leader.

Movement leaders knew that in the end the forces of segregation had a monopoly on violence, but could not overcome nonviolence, and Bernice knew that one thing the Albany police could not overcome was singing. "Singing is different than talking, because no matter what they do, they would have to kill me to stop me from singing. Sometimes the police would plead and say, 'Please stop singing!'" (Bull Connor had dumped a load of Freedom Riders back across the Georgia state line because "I couldn't stand their singing.")

The *Eyes* crew had a terrible time with Dr. Reagon, who was by turns reluctant, grumpy, brilliant, "sharp tongued about white folks," and outright hostile during the setup, reminding them that it's pronounced "Al-BEN-ey." She could be famously prickly, but as we so often found with *Eyes* interviews, the moment the camera rolled, the movement itself took over, and she slid back into her warm, wise, and spellbinding self, her movement self, time traveling back to Albany, Georgia, in 1962.

And there was no singing like Albany singing. "If you have a gold mine, then there is a point in the gold mine where you have the richest part, and that's called the mother lode; that's what Albany is to black people, just the concentrated essence of the spirit of the people.

"You know the verse in 'Steal Away' that says 'God is on our side'? There was a theological discussion that said: maybe we should say, 'We are on God's side.' But you know, God was lucky to have us in Albany doing what we were doing. What I think about is just being very alive and very clear, the clearest I've ever been in my life, . . . I was doing what I was supposed to do."

She sang:

Oh, come and go with me to that land
Come and go with me to that land
Why don't you come and go with me to that land, where I'm bound.

I had heard young Bernice Johnson Reagon and the Freedom Singers sing the same song on that night years before in college in 1963, and soon after decided, indeed, that I would follow them to Mississippi.

When shooting slopped over from 1985 into 1986, we updated ourselves from the Fourteenth Amendment tour to "the Fifteenth Amendment 1986 World Tour," a nod to the constitutional provision that "The right of citizens of the United States to vote shall not be denied or abridged by the United States or by any state on account of race, color, or previous condition of servitude" (as long as they were male).

We returned to New York, where it had all started with Andy Young only three months before; it seemed like years. Mike and I met Bobby Shepard for a huge sushi dinner at a place on Amsterdam Avenue. Chin, who had mysterious friends in high places from his previous careers, disappeared for twenty minutes and returned to present me with a freshly autographed copy of Richard Avedon's *In the American West*. For those of us from the American West, visiting New York in the 1980s was like doing time: the Bronx permanently on fire, crackheads in every alley, and God only knew what went on down there in the subway; so it was nice to have Bobby as our guide and guardian.

Next morning we set up in a bare conference room at WNET on Forty-ninth Street to interview former SNCC executive secretary James Forman, whom I had not seen since the day I left the Atlanta office twenty years before. He seemed well and fit, had aged more than most of the SNCC crowd, but was sharp as a tack. I remembered Jim as a thoroughgoing intellectual, more skilled at blistering midnight analysis than anyone except maybe Stokely Carmichael or Al Lowenstein.

He had given Callie a lively preinterview over the phone, clear-eyed about deep divisions between SNCC and SCLC. But those same analytical chops that had served Jim so well in movement debates in the 1960s now made it tough for Callie to guide him past dialectical critique to simple storytelling. Jim wound around and around, modulating tactical differences, parsing meeting after meeting about traditional Negro leadership's objection to the draft of John Lewis's speech at the March on Washington, without ever saying what, exactly, it was that they objected to (talk of "revolution," "the masses," and John's metaphorical reference to a "scorched-earth policy").

In frustration, Callie abruptly stopped the interview, sent me and the rest of the crew out of the room, turned to Forman, and told him he was wasting her time and wasting her film. Jim said, "Miss Callie, I can see you are upset." Callie replied, "I am more than upset. Now, I am going to call the crew back in here and you are going to do better telling me the whole story." When we resumed the interview, Jim did a little better, but in Callie's words, "He simply wanted to revise his hotheaded youthful reactions to the now revered MLK."

In the end he simply declined to articulate those fierce differences between SNCC and SCLC that had been to us so obvious and toxic back then when the two organizations could go at it like Cain and Abel. It is our job as filmmakers to help people make the leap from dense exegesis to simple narrative, and with Jim Forman we did not do well. Perhaps the intervening twenty years had given him too much time to interpret it, write about it, circle around it, deconstruct and reconstruct it, analyze it into paralysis. Television, intolerant of dialectic, thrives on blunt fact bluntly told. Perhaps we were just too late.

After we wrapped our gear out of the PBS offices, I drove up to Precision Film Labs to drop off the exposed film for processing and pick up a batch of new workprint. But the lab manager wouldn't release anything to me until Blackside paid $50,000 in overdue film-processing charges. After a very unpleasant phone call to Henry, a long, empty-handed drive back to Boston, and a long nap by the side of the expressway while the sushi food poisoning wore off, I stayed up late talking with Orlando about Forman and the news of the day from Cape Town.

The film that I couldn't get from the lab was an interview Orlando had done weeks before with Myrlie Evers, Medgar's widow, the same Myrlie who had so moved Judy Richardson ten years before. He filmed it in Los Angeles while he had been home over our Christmas break. Orlando was extremely devoted to his family, who were not happy about his doing yet more work for Henry Hampton during his few days of winter vacation in California. "It wasn't going over real well with my family. . . . But there was a sense of mission that I was on . . . Cira and Jaffar and I would talk about that." We all knew that Orlando's wife and kids were getting tired of his mission, just as a lot of Blackside families were growing tired of competing with Henry Hampton. To us he was our warm, fearless, and enigmatic leader; to them he was a faraway phantom.

Medgar Evers had been the NAACP's first field secretary in Mississippi. As children on their way to school, Medgar and his brother, Charles, had to walk for days past the bullet-riddled hanging body of a family friend who had been lynched and then used for target practice by local whites. Evers had served as a sergeant in the segregated army in the Normandy invasion, only to be addressed as "boy" when he returned home. He had worked undercover with Amzie Moore, disguised as a sharecropper, investigating the murder of Emmett Till. Evers was the first black person to apply to the University of Mississippi law school, and had received death threats ever since the school turned him away.

Early in the evening of June 12, 1963, President John F. Kennedy had addressed us, the American nation, on prime-time television, saying,

"The heart of the question is whether all Americans are to be afforded equal rights and equal opportunities, whether we are going to treat our fellow Americans as we want to be treated." The president finally found his sure footing on the civil rights high ground that night, made a resolute and politically risky public statement supporting the movement's goals, and announced he would be sending new civil rights legislation to Congress. "The time has come for the nation to fulfill its promise."

After the broadcast Byron De La Beckwith, a member of the KKK and Citizens' Council, hid behind a stand of flowering honeysuckle with a high-powered rifle, took aim, and shot Medgar Evers in the back as he walked from his station wagon to the house where Myrlie and the kids had stayed up late waiting for him.

Orlando told me that that night in 1963, when news of Evers's killing reached New Hampshire, was the first time he ever saw his parents cry.

Only Myrlie Evers herself, not a historian or journalist, could tell us about Medgar's assassination; but she had never before agreed to an interview with anyone. Orlando persuaded her, but when they arrived at Mrs. Evers's home in Los Angeles, it was clear to Mike Chin that she was ready to back out. Orlando managed to talk her into at least letting them set up camera and lights.

Then the crew patiently waited as the sun began to sink, just as we had waited while Orlando talked with Diane Nash in Chicago and Freddie Leonard in Nashville, and as the crew would patiently wait for hours while Orlando talked with Malcolm X's brother in Detroit a few years later. Film crews are always keen to take care of business before the light changes, often forgetting a director's particular rhythm, but Orlando was never in a hurry. He was always blessedly able to insulate himself from the mandates of fading light or a crew on the clock, focused instead on what the audience would actually hear and see on screen a year in the future.

"I sat down with Myrlie and started talking . . . suddenly we have all these photos spread all over the floor. And I could tell that sitting down with her there, and she was going back, and she was finding comfort in being able to talk about her husband. . . . Mike had seen this happen before, so he knew what was going on."

On camera Orlando coaxed from Myrlie stories of her first meeting with Medgar during the first hour of her first day at all-black Alcorn College, their falling in love, wedding, starting a family, and the frequent painful separations when he traveled for NAACP work around the state, a man on a mission. . . . "He represented a type of savior for me with all of the anger and the frustrations that I had had myself growing up in that segregated society, and not knowing anyone who talked about them and who talked about doing something about them." They were in the thick of the bloody integration of the University of Mississippi by Medgar's friend James Meredith, and the wave of Freedom Riders rolling through the South in 1961. A firebomb landed in their carport.

"Medgar was my husband, my friend, the father of my children, my love." She recounted their last day together. Orlando gently asked her to tell about their relationship again, no less than seven times, until both she and he were satisfied with the telling.

"And we came to realize, in those . . . last few months, that our time was short; it was simply in the air. You knew that something was going to happen, and the logical person for it to happen to was Medgar. It certainly brought us closer during that time. We didn't talk; we didn't have to. . . . It was a touch, it was a look, it was holding each other, it was music playing; and I used to try to reassure him and tell him, 'Nothing's going to happen to you. Everybody knows you. You're in the press. They wouldn't dare do anything to you.'

"He said, 'Honey, you've got to be strong' . . . when he left that morning and went out of the door, told the children how much he loved them, turned to me and said, 'I'm so tired, I don't know if I can go on, but I have to.' And I remember rushing to him and holding him and he kissed me and he said, 'I love you, I love you. I'll see you tonight.'"

Then, whether out of compassion or a realization that the story could never be told better, Orlando filmed her account of Medgar's death in one take:

"Late that night . . . the children were still up; I was asleep across the bed, and we heard the motor of the car coming in and pulling into the driveway. We heard him get out of the car and the car door slam, and in that same instant, we heard the loud gunfire. The children fell to the floor, as he had taught them to do. I made a run for the front door, turned on the light, and there he was. The force of the bullet had pushed him forward, . . . and the strong man that he was, he had his keys in his hand and had pulled his body around the rest of the way to the door. There he lay, and I screamed, and people came out. Our next-door neighbor fired a gun . . . to try to frighten anyone away, and I knew then that was it, that the man that I loved, had shared my life with, he had shared his life with me, where I had been a reluctant . . . supporter of his in the beginning and wanted him for myself and for my children, but understood when he said, 'I belong to my people, and to my state, and I want to help them. . . . I'm doing it for you, I'm doing it for the children, for other wives and other children.'

"I rushed out and saw him lying there, and people from the neighborhood began to gather; there were also some whose color happened to have been white. I don't think I have ever hated as much in my life as I did at that particular moment, with anyone who had white skin. I screamed at the neighbors. . . . And I can recall wanting so much to have a machine gun . . . in my hands, and just stand there and mow them all down. I can't explain the depth of my hatred at that point."

All-white juries twice declined to convict Byron De La Beckwith. While Myrlie Evers was testifying during the second trial, former Mississippi governor Ross Barnett interrupted the proceedings to shake hands with Beckwith. Evers was laid to rest with full military honors at Arlington National Cemetery.

In 1994, based on new evidence, a jury of eight blacks and four whites found Beckwith guilty of murder in the first degree.

When we got the film after the lab bills were finally paid, Jeanne Jordan walked into Henry's office and asked, "Have you *seen* the Myrlie interview?" and forced him to come down to her edit room to watch. As I remember, Henry called me that afternoon and allowed himself some satisfaction and rare Hampton praise for what Orlando had accomplished.

I, too, was a man on a mission, and in February 1986, for the first time, I was ready for the mission to be over. Mike Chin and I flew to Montgomery and met Llew Smith for an interview with Alabama's former director of public safety, Floyd Mann. In the absence of city police at the Montgomery bus station in May 1961, Mann had probably saved the Freedom Riders' lives when "I just put my pistol to the head of one or two of those folks who were using baseball bats and told them unless they stopped immediately, they were going to get hurt." He looked back with sadness on the failure of Alabama's governor John Patterson and city officials to intervene when the Freedom Riders entered their state.

Prue interviewed former governor Patterson himself, as courtly and rugged as the day in 1958 when, with the unapologetically racist backing of the Ku Klux Klan, he defeated the young racial moderate George Wallace for governor in a landslide. He spoke of the Freedom Rides:

"Robert Kennedy started calling me on the telephone. Robert started calling the president of the Greyhound bus company, making demands on them. They had trouble getting drivers to drive the buses because they were concerned about their buses and themselves, I guess.

"Well, my personal feeling was that I thought that they should stay home and mind their own business and let us try to work out our problems down here in some legal way. I even asked the attorney general and the president to just simply ask these people to mind their own business and obey the law."

Llew Smith and I spent a day going through musty stacks of old film at WFSA, the NBC affiliate in Montgomery, sat there for hours watching Alabama house fires, Alabama beauty pageants, Alabama political picnics, speeches, for a few scraps of Rev. King and George Wallace. At the hotel the TV news buzzed with grenade attacks on police in South Africa, some fracas in Damascus, and Governor Wallace tearfully announcing his retirement plans after four terms: "I have climbed my last mountain."

Back in California, at my son Lincoln's soccer game in Woodside, it seemed I had never seen so many white people in one place. The bicoastal experience on *Eyes* was odd. We lived happily at the end of a gravel road in the Santa Cruz Mountains high above Silicon Valley, which was well on its way to becoming the greatest legal accumulation of wealth in human history. Nothing had a rough edge. We soon observed the newly established Martin Luther King holiday more as an excellent long Sierra ski weekend than a time to contemplate a great leader's moral lessons.

On May 11, 1986, I took a red-eye from the coast, happy to be back in Boston with spring at last in the air, a breeze that could somehow be both warm and chilly at the same time. In coastal California our benign seasons have little meaning except for the sudden spectacle of natural disaster, floods, drought, and flamboyant wildfires, but New England had the brutal foil of winter. The South End's little neighborhood garden plots were bursting out with baby greens, and for a change everyone at

Blackside seemed rosy and full of energy. Affordable housing condos were now under construction across the street. That Friday evening I could hear two guys singing a beautiful call to prayer back and forth across Blackstone Park.

Blackside had shed its cloak of melancholy. Judith was great fun, in good spirits, and announced she was getting married. Henry, just back from a well-earned vacation in Barbados, was relaxed over dinner, bubbling with enticement to get me more involved in the future he was conjuring up: Did I want to produce the Black Panther show in *Eyes II*? ("How close to Oakland is Woodside?" . . . About a million miles.) I told him I was exactly the wrong guy—what was he thinking? Ah, Henry . . . it was so nice to see him really happy at last. Around this time, in an expansive mood, he said he wanted to give everyone on the team a piece of the action. Like so much at Blackside, these generous impulses were never committed to paper, and as far as I know none of us ever saw any of whatever mysterious profit *Eyes* may have earned in years to come.

He wanted to expand into platforms beyond film, so had recruited the seasoned literary editor and agent Bob Lavelle to set up a publishing arm in the basement at Blackside, which would soon set the standard for documentary engagement and outreach. The immediate task was producing an *Eyes on the Prize* companion book.

To get the book written efficiently in the short time remaining, Henry hired a sharp and friendly young *Washington Post* reporter, Juan Williams, who quickly became known for his willingness to take contrary positions, to push against the Blackside consensus. Fayer remembered him "leaning against the crowd, toward the right, pointing out that we were often self-censoring." But soon Williams managed to alienate most of the staff, who vehemently objected to much of his writing. They felt it was often out of tune with the tone of the series, sometimes inaccurate, even unsympathetic toward the characters on screen.

Now, as it would with regularity over the next ten years, 486 Shawmut took on a siege mentality in the ramp-up to rough cut screenings. Virtually every person I know who ever worked at Blackside says being there was a high point—if not *the* high point—of their careers, our miniature version of the Bauhaus in 1925, the Left Bank in 1930, Motown in '65,

American Zoetrope in '75, Apple in the '80s. And within that Blackside experience, nothing rises in memory to match our love/hate for Hampton's rough cut screenings, unlike any others in the industry, the mother lode in Henry's gold mine.

Coming on the heels of a barely watchable assembly, the rough cut feels more or less like a movie, a little too long, about the right tone, about the right rhythm, still tenuous, ragged, and malleable, but recognizable as a film and ready for useful comments from both civilians and advisors. At WGBH, or ABC News where I had worked, the producer/director typically kept their cuts shrouded in proprietary secrecy, except for tense little salon sessions, with a few suits huddled around the Steenbeck and maybe an assistant taking notes in the corner. When the lights came on, the exec would give detailed comments and then hash it out with the producer/director. In the presence of a very strong executive, younger staff were often reluctant to contradict his or her critique of what worked and what didn't.

We screened in a big theater at the Boston Film/Video Foundation. It took a lot of nerve on Henry's part to make his producers/directors trot out awkward, incomplete, and easily misunderstood works in progress. He could bring in fifty people or more to view a rough cut—advisors, funders, PBS executives, friends, college kids, high school students, production assistants, researchers, the bookkeeper, the night janitor Ditch, and then invite them all to give their reactions. I certainly had never seen anything like it before, and DeVinney remembered, "Those meetings rambled on forever, for hours, on into the evening. There was a luxuriousness about them. You could really talk everything through. . . . They were wonderful for their honesty." Of all the many lessons I learned at Blackside, the importance of early unrestrained criticism in open screenings was the most lasting and important. Compared to the Silicon Valley meetings I have filmed over the past quarter century, so exquisitely engineered for maximum decision-making metrics per meeting minute, the Blackside sessions sprawled and roamed with inclusionary verve and genuine searching. I remember SNCC meetings careening on into the night the same way twenty years before.

It was in these large public screenings that Henry seemed his most democratic, presiding from the side of the room, though seldom offering an opinion himself. When the lights came on, it was usually a more senior professor who spoke up first. Henry gave the profs the reins for a while, but if discussion between our alpha producers and alpha scholars became too contentious, defensive, or lost in the academic weeds, he might call on an intern sitting in back or a visiting high school kid to get the real scoop on how the film was playing. The blessedly naive strangers saw things we could never see, surprised us with what moved them and what didn't. The civilians gave us a hard reality check on what we could expect ordinary viewers to know beforehand about the history. Some of their comments opened big philosophical doors: "Why didn't they shoot back?" Others set us right on basic clarity: "Who was that fellow Allard Lowenstein?"

From the start, the discussion of Judith and Llew's Till-Montgomery rough cut was fiery, passionate, and contentious, with strong opinions, a real sense of something at stake. That was a good sign.

Hard as it is to believe now, very few of the stories in *Eyes on the Prize* had ever before been told on television, and none ever in a connected series. In years to come Emmett Till would be the subject of plays, feature documentaries, nonfiction books, articles, novels, radio programs, rap songs, poems, ballads, a musical, *Emmett Till, The Opera,* and at least four feature films have been in development for years. But Blackside's rough cut screening in 1986 was the first time anyone had ever seen it on screen. After months of reordering the triggering incident at the store, kidnapping, murder, trial, and verdict in different ways, just when we thought the Till story was finally well structured, the whole affair blew up again.

Judith, Llew, and their editor, Dan, now sat there gracefully and took notes. Juan Williams said, "The organization is peculiar." Clay Carson said Till didn't give the sense of a struggle starting, and asked them to move more clearly from the idea that oppression created fear and the inability to act to a willingness to overcome fear and begin the struggle in Montgomery. But Ruth Batson felt Till worked wonderfully and the story lost its way *after* Till. Aldon Morris said we hadn't connected Till to the history of lynching; Vincent Harding and I wanted to connect Till to Medgar Evers. Harding added that the show "must have a healing function," and wanted to put the American struggle into the context of global liberation, reminding us that the French colonial army and Foreign Legion were at that moment in 1955 fighting their last stand against Vietnamese revolutionaries at Dien Bien Phu. Wow.

Then a non-Blackside woman whom none of us had ever seen before stood up and said, "Till blew me away." Henry's secretary Sara Chazen, who had not seen anything in all the time she had worked in the office, raised her hand and, near tears, said the story was wonderful and dramatic.

After enduring an hour-long blizzard of contradictory suggestions, praise, and sharp criticism, Judith finally stood and wisely summed it all up: "The emotional shape and the intellectual shape are not working together." It was missing that transformative surge from blacks as victims to blacks as fighters that was the core function of the Till story in *Eyes*. Henry was again quietly infuriated by the lack of drama.

I thought Orlando, Prue, and Jeanne's Freedom Rides rough cut was one of the most powerful films I had ever seen, with such searing moral simplicity that I had to go for a walk during lunch just to regain my composure. But Jeanne and Orlando thought it was the worst screening ever, "not a story, just a bunch of things living next to each other . . . I knew we had to fail in order for us to come together." And it turned out that some of the people in the audience thought that fair-skinned, hazel-eyed Diane Nash was *white*; who would have guessed?

Then their Mississippi show rough cut was an emotional triumph but a structural wreck.

After the Till/Montgomery debacle, we all feared the worst for the rough cut of Vecchione's other film, school desegregation in Little Rock and the University of Mississippi. But the tables turned and it was a knockout, full of powerful drama as the Central High story unfolded entirely from the point of view of the young students, and Meredith's bloody entrance into Ole Miss almost entirely from the point of view of warring state and federal officials. Telephone recordings of President Kennedy forcing Governor Barnett into submission electrified the film. Like so many of the *Eyes* battles, these were stories of presidents (Eisenhower and Kennedy) deploying federal power to protect the rights of black citizens made powerless by local ordinance, state law, or the failure of local law enforcement. Henry was at last pleased and relieved, and after the screening he and I, Judith, and her team actually made it through a whole review of the film without a shouting match.

Among Henry's many gifts to us was the steel nerve we developed over those years in his brutal rough cut screenings, the understanding that as a filmmaker you *must* invite the most severe criticism early in the game, embrace it as a blessing that is sure to make your film better. He abhorred praise for praise's sake; the point is not to be liked, the point is to find out what works and—most important—doesn't work.

On the final morning, just as we were about to screen the Selma rough cut, the giant Siemens double-system film projector jammed and everything ground to a halt. Sensing a vacuum, Judy Richardson jumped up to lead the big crowd—interns, professors, PBS executives, Henry, observers, everyone— in freedom songs. Callie soon joined her, and Julian Bond led us:

> I read it in the paper just the other day,
> The freedom fighters are on their way!

I remember that week of rough cut screenings as a time of daily creative combat. Vincent Harding, wisest of the wise elders, set a pastorly tone; at times he seemed to be channeling Howard Thurman. The word-centric advising crew, academics all, placed inordinate value on text, so narration came in for particular scrutiny. Every edit and every line of narration had to be defended. Henry would ask, "How am I going to explain that to Lynne Cheney?"

We had particularly sticky times when the memories of people in our films were inexact, revisionist, incomplete, or simply wrong. Callie and Dave Garrow got into it over a question of how much Coretta King would have known about a detail of her husband's tactics. "But it actually ended up being better, of course, as these things do. Because I ended up with Ralph Abernathy at the end."

Then Professor Carson and Professor Garrow questioned whether after the March on Washington, Ralph Abernathy could have been at the deserted National Mall watching the wind blow discarded programs. (That exact beautiful image appears in James Blue's USIA film *The March*.) Apparently all historical records indicate he was on the other side of town with members of the Kennedy administration. This was the only instance I know of in *Eyes* when Henry gave executive approval to use a suspect memory.

Clay and others remember that through it all there was an underlying tension about Henry Hampton wanting to be celebratory. Carson and Harding would have left more questions at the end of each program, more nuance and ambiguity, rather than the resolved affirmation of the American system, even triumphalism, favored by Henry. When Henry raised a concern that too much nuance might affect ratings, Vincent shot back,

"My grandchildren are more important than ratings. . . . Democracy works when people work for democracy, and we must see this as a critical experiment in democracy which must happen *every* generation."

And after enduring months of rant from me about shortening, thinning, dumping, squeezing their shows for maximum cinematic power, the producers now endured a fresh blizzard of complaints from scholars about what was missing.

What was gained by this costly to-ing and fro-ing? Only a fool would ever argue that *Eyes on the Prize* or any other documentary puts forward absolute truth, fairness, or unmediated history. But we all could argue that the expansive, grueling, and expensive rough cut review process made these shows the most true, the most fair, inclusive, and historically accurate we could create in 1985. Andrea Taylor of the Ford Foundation told me years later, "Ford gave a *lot* of money to Blackside because of the integrity of the approach. The integrity was obvious in the meetings, people challenging each other."

The next evening at Legal Sea Foods over a relaxed supper, Steve Fayer, Juan Williams, Orlando, and I made one last attempt at getting Henry to change the title of the series. Someone at the network suggested "Revolution in Black." Anything was better than that, or the long-forgotten *America, We Loved You Madly,* but *Eyes on the Prize* might have little meaning to ordinary Americans outside the movement, and it sounded to me like a quiz show, something petty. Fayer thought people would make fun of it: "I'ze on de prize." While I was getting beers at the bar, Henry scribbled alternate titles on a napkin: *We Shall Overcome, We Shall Not Be Moved, Freedom Now, Freedom Road, We'll Never Turn Back,* but it was absolutely clear he was committed. He argued that the title he had selected years before from Judy Richardson's list of freedom songs would immediately click with audiences, and history has shown that he was absolutely right. He said finally, "The title of the series is *Eyes on the Prize,*" and we drank a toast to it.

Once again Henry drove me to Logan in his Jag, and once again he asked me to finish *Eyes* if anything happened to him; I know he asked others the same question, and I always wondered if he knew something we didn't. Back in California again, I dove into a series of Clorox commercials. These were dreary affairs with washing machines and kitchen sinks on the sound stage and a big bored crew, including a guy everyone called "the Dirt Fairy," a functionary from the Federal Trade Commission who brought different kinds of grime certified by the FTC for cleaning product commercials. But it paid well and it was grand to be home with Nina and the kids.

On break during a shoot I called Henry from a pay phone and he told me brass at CPB had watched the rough cuts and declared them "boring and unwatchable." I remember telling him, "Fuck them." Time to circle the wagons around Henry.

PBS weighed in with a generally positive response. But still Henry got pleas from network executives to tamp down the factual side and punch up the emotional side: "Use nonperiod music to build grandeur and punctuate emotions. . . . I want you to tear at my emotional strings. . . . Do something really provocative . . . not something loaded with facts . . . dry . . . give us plenty of tears along with the facts. . . ."

It was at Blackside where I learned that the test audience is always right when they tell you something is wrong, and they are almost always wrong about how to fix it. Audiences never lie; if they tell you they are confused, bored, or unmoved, you can't tell them they are not. And the problem they cite seldom lies where they point to it: if a line from John Lewis falls flat in the third act, it's because maybe you needed a setup in the second act, or because it repeats something from the first, or because we haven't heard from Lewis for thirty minutes. The editor Walter Murch calls this "referred pain," as when the pain in your leg is caused by a pinched nerve in your back. "The audience can tell you where the pain is, but not the source of the pain." We had plenty of referred pain.

We had been at it for less than a year.

Advisor Paul Gaston informed us that bootleg copies of our rough cuts had been screened in South African townships; our stories of civil rights organizing were being used to help anti-apartheid organizing.

Henry, Orlando, and I talked often about South Africa, which was in the late 1980s tearing itself apart in the last desperate spasms of apartheid, worse than anything Alabama or Mississippi could have imagined in the 1960s. It was from Henry I first learned that black South Africans were not citizens of South Africa, not endowed with any governmental power or protection. However bad things were in Alabama, the civil rights movement succeeded because even if local authorities kept them from voting, African Americans were still legally citizens of the United States of America. In the end, when persuasion failed, appeals from blacks in Selma to the government of the United States succeeded in a way that appeals from blacks in Soweto to the government of South Africa never could. Henry got to the core of it: "At least we were citizens. . . . We did it right. The difference is that we have a constitution that gives rights to everyone, and they don't."

Simmering with resentment, I flew back to Boston on Father's Day 1986 for fine cuts. I was a "Hampton hostage"; it had about it some of the same intensity as working for SNCC except that I was now a grown man with a family and a home mortgage. The company still owed me expenses from the fall of 1985.

Over those years in the air, Orlando and I missed many milestones in our children's lives—soccer games, first dance, half a dozen birthdays. Orlando had expected to be done and home by now, but was making plans to bring eight-year-old Jaffar from Los Angeles to spend the summer in Boston. Nina had called from California to say that our nine-year-old Lincoln had asked at Little League if I would be there by the last inning.

Henry convened nearly two hundred people to view our fact-checked fine cuts in a big theater at MIT. Among the advisors that day were Peter Edelman, Ben Chavis, Sam Allen, Jack Mendelsohn, Darlene Hine, Paul Gaston, Dave Garrow, Clay Carson, Wiley Brandon, and, of course, Vince Harding. Looking down on it all from the balcony with his bemused smile was the great American documentary maker Richard Leacock, one of the cameramen who had filmed George Wallace in the schoolhouse door, now a professor in MIT's film department. Chuck Scott's old car had broken down in Central Square and he ran a mile to MIT with the film cans under his arm.

In their introductory remarks for the day, Callie and Henry reminded us that in our own small way we were part of an unending liberation struggle, she in celebration of "Juneteenth," the day in 1865 when news of emancipation reached slaves in Texas, the westernmost slave state, and Henry by marking the tenth anniversary of the 1976 Soweto uprising.

The Till/Montgomery program fine cut, with its riveting new introduction to segregation, now had style and verve. The school desegregation show marched right along, with the courage of James Meredith and the Little Rock Nine at the forefront, and prompted Guy Carawan to ask, "How did they get so strong?"

Orlando's Mississippi fine cut was more powerful than ever. He remembers, "We came into the second screening much more bold, and I can remember the Mississippi screening specifically, where people were weeping. People had moved into another space where they weren't giving notes, they wanted to *testify*. . . . And we didn't know what we had until we started showing it to people, and even then it wasn't until the fine-cut screening that we realized that something was happening."

We could see Henry at ease in the screenings, allowing himself to really feel good about what we had accomplished so far. It all had heft, it had power, it was coherent, and it was almost done. Even Steve Fayer, the company curmudgeon, said, "It made my spirits soar."

But now it was time to finish the mop-up shooting and cut these things down to bare bones, all muscle, not an ounce of fat—drain the swamp, slash the underbrush, strip out the metaphors. Excise everything but the most dramatic truth.

Blackside buzzed with trading, trimming, and trying, sometimes micro detail: Should that be one second of silence or two seconds after the church bombing? And sometimes wholesale: Do we really need to see Lyndon Johnson on camera? Where, exactly, should we first meet Bull Connor, as a threatening colossus before the Birmingham demonstrations begin, or should he suddenly appear in the middle of the mayhem to ratchet things up?

My job as series producer was to parachute in from the coast as the relentlessly upbeat senior helper, urging people forward, on call as an editorial Mr. Fix-it and referee. The dynamics of compromise and horse trading were usually collegial, but sometimes exploded with anger and frustration, slammed doors, caustic memos, tears, and on at least one occasion, all of us on all the floors could hear tires screeching away up the block on Shawmut Avenue. If we were lucky, these great battles were over serious content issues, or why the hell we were always short on money (only Henry knew for sure). If we were not lucky, they were simply months of pent-up petty frustration exploding over perceived favoritism or over who failed to buy the doughnuts that week.

And Blackside, like most American institutions, had its own simmering internal issues around race and gender. Orlando, Judy, and other staff knew that Hampton was likely to favor men over women in meetings, and sometimes white men, myself included, over everyone else. I tried to take a backseat in the big screening discussions, convinced that the feedback had to go unfiltered directly to Henry and his producers. In meetings when I was the most senior white man in the room, I sensed that it bent the flow of conversation in my direction. I noticed more than once that advisors would treat me as senior to Judith, Orlando, or Callie, which I was not.

Noland Walker said Henry was flat-out harder on black employees, whether out of his own implicit bias or because he wanted to force them to excellence, we were never sure. With women, Jeanne Jordan noted the conundrum that he was "very old-school, fairly sexist, but gallant. Every Valentine's Day he would give all the women Blackside-logo lotion or bubble bath. He took people to lunch and would pull out the chair, gentlemanly, sweet," but he was progressive in seeing that women excelled and advanced in the documentary profession.

Among the hints of division along racial lines was the matter of CPT, "Colored People's Time," the stereotype of African American meetings always starting late. I had first heard the term from Jim Forman in the SNCC office in 1964. We will never know whether it actually had to do with who was white and who was black, who was northern or southern, but I remember white staff fuming when visiting funders and PBS brass were kept waiting for a meeting that started late.

Judith Vecchione remembered, "Henry began a practice of having little flowering plants brought to each of our desks. Each week, without comment or explanation, the old one would be whisked away and a new tiny pot would appear. If it was a particularly hard week with producers desperate and furious at the largest target—Henry, of course—we would look at those flowers and curse: Do you think it makes me feel any better? . . . and, of course, it did."

He had thirty frayed tempers crammed together at Shawmut Avenue, with no air-conditioning (the primitive DEC computer shut down in the heat). The long hours, working weekends, constantly shifting deadlines, and daily diet of film violence strained our band of brothers and sisters nearly to breaking. Kenn Rabin said, "I felt responsible for everything; I never took a vacation, and then when I finally did I felt guilty about it."

Laurie Kahn said, "We all worked seventy or eighty hours a week . . . because we cared so much about it." Judy Richardson said Henry had "a maddening penchant for pushing his producers to greater artistic achievement . . . to make them go far beyond what they thought was their best work . . . and then ask for more." Many Blackside alumni later said that working for him drove them nearly crazy, even if it was the greatest time in their lives. It had the ferocity of working for Jobs at Apple in the eighties, but without the million-dollar stock options. (I remember thinking, "Henry's just like Steve. They're both geniuses but neither of them can manage their way out of a paper bag." But Henry was a warm, welcoming, and generous person, great fun to be with, blessed with a clear sense of civic responsibility. Steve, in my limited experience, had few such blessings.) And we endured the relentless unspoken suspicion that Henry (and even we ourselves) expected us to make *the greatest television series ever about the greatest movement in American history.*

In contrast to his gracious listening to all comers at the big screenings, absorbing it all and saying little, he could be merciless, adamant, and undemocratic in the edit room. It was odd for such a warm person. There a different sort of executive producer emerged, clearly stating his dislike for things in a cut. Dan Eisenberg saw an autocratic contradiction between his micromanaging style in the edit room and the content—expansion of democracy—of the shows.

After one particularly baffling intellectual flight about symbolism and meaning in the Mississippi rough cut, Jeanne Jordan told him, "Henry, speak English." Jim DeVinney remembered, "He never critiqued a show about its filmmaking, it was always *all* about the content, which had sometimes been locked in his head for years." He could give clear notes around the politics, philosophy, and social science, but could be tongue-tied when it came to the actual filmmaking.

Through it all, from those first days of *Eyes* to the final Blackside series in the late 1990s, Hampton never pretended his company was a democracy; he was the boss, with final control and final cut. He had assumed all the risk; the rest of us were quick to forget that Henry lived with the prospect that he would be the public face of *Eyes,* the big visible target of whatever scorn was certain to come if we got this wrong. I'm sure few of his producers ever knew or understood what it meant to have his neck stuck out so far, what it meant to wake up every morning knowing he might have to mortgage his home yet again to meet payroll (as he did more than once) for *Eyes on the Prize.*

Meredith Woods remembered, "There were moments when the *entire* Blackside staff was in revolt against Henry." On May 27, 1986, six producers and associate producers walked into Henry's office and presented a petition threatening "nonviolent direct action" unless he acted on budget transparency, rational deadlines, paid-up lab bills, and an upstairs bathroom by Friday. (This reminded Judy Richardson that in 1965 five women staged a sit-in in Jim Forman's office at SNCC headquarters to force men as well as women to take minutes at staff meetings.) They asked for an explanation of the mysterious "FU" extra social security deduction that appeared on their pay stubs, the "Fuck You deduction." Most people had come from large, well-managed institutions like WGBH or ABC with a big firewall between them and the legal department, development department, and finance department. Few understood that Henry could not pass the buck on up to any higher authority. Although Henry took on substantial risk again and again with apparent outward calm, he was in fact extremely uncomfortable with it.

That evening, after "The Great Blackside Sit-In," Henry and I went over to Roberto Mighty's studio to record temporary "Keep Your Eyes on the Prize" vocals for the series logo. The petition had really gotten to him, and I had never seen him in such a funk. But the session was fantastic, with a great a cappella group from the Berklee School of Music, and Henry's friend, a tenor sax man named Gates, who could eat your heart out riffing on that old freedom song. But even that magical music couldn't lift Henry's spirits, and he retreated deeper into silence as the night wore on, until he finally asked me to direct Gates, which both Gates and I knew was a bad idea. When I told him that the Georgia Humanities Council had given us $20,000, he responded, "I'll be doing paperwork for the Georgia Council for the rest of my life."

For him, "the abrasion of good minds" had turned ugly, and he told his sister Judi that his producers, with their mix of race, gender, temperament, and opinion, were "raw, nasty, uncontrollable." Inside Blackside the mood could swing from melancholy to giddy to wrathful. One by one, producers taped up newspapers over the glass doors. Judith and Dan Eisenberg took to locking their edit room door every morning out of self-preservation. Meredith Woods remembers the tension, mostly between

Callie and Jim. "At some point when Jim and Callie were at loggerheads over whatever, Judith walked right into the editing room where Chuck was working with them, closed the door, and I heard Judith screaming through the door. Really screaming." Many Blackside alumni remember Henry and Judith in screaming fights, slamming doors. They were both geniuses, and as Dan remembers it, Judith was "tuned to a very high frequency."

Exhausted by combat with his warring producers, Henry more than once had to simply decamp and decompress at his little cottage a couple hours north in rural New Hampshire, sometimes with his friend Leslie Harris, sometimes alone. I understood the comfort he described in "going up there and just sweating a solder joint on some broken copper pipe." Unlike anything at Blackside, it was direct, simple, and physical; the plumbing either leaked or it didn't, and if it leaked you could fix it. Madison Davis Lacy remembers going up there with Henry and seeing that it was "an emotional retreat of the first magnitude. We hauled water, split wood, behaved like a couple of idiots and had a great time."

We all got angry at Henry at some point—some people are still angry—but we never got angry at the civil rights movement. When Martin Luther King talked about "the long and bitter and beautiful struggle," he could have been talking about the making of *Eyes on the Prize.*

We were headed toward broadcast on PBS, which boasted a hundred million viewers a week in 1986. But our zeal to make great public television was matched by the Reagan administration's zeal to put public television out of business. Republican presidents, senators, and congressmen had scorned PBS from the moment of its birth in 1967, and the network had tried to stem the attack by becoming softer, more risk averse, and more boring every year. In a flight of cultural blindness, Reagan's FCC chairman Mark Fowler, an aggressive deregulator who had led the repeal of the fairness doctrine, defined television as simply "an appliance, a toaster with pictures," not a public trust vital to democracy, but a blunt instrument of commerce like any other. Reagan, like Nixon before him, called for total elimination of public funding for all broadcasting, including NPR and PBS, arguing they should sink or swim in the marketplace. CPB board member Richard Brookhiser, said, "The Bolshoi is fine. . . . Nature programs, little things grazing in the tundra. Fine." Despite the efforts of a few courageous insiders, the original bold and noble mission of public television was slipping away.

Lynne Cheney, now head of the NEH in 1986, wrote that PBS had become highly politicized, particularly by Republicans, that journalists in public broadcasting tended to be liberal, and that corporate America for the first time had significant influence over PBS because its corporate funding now surpassed public funding. "Programming for minorities and other special groups, which seldom holds much interest for corporate underwriters, is kept alive with public funding and foundation money." Henry was well aware.

As congressional support faded in the 1980s, PBS became more dependent on thinly disguised commercials, heading toward the moment when *The Civil War* would be very visibly sponsored by General Motors. S. L. Harrison, in a well-reported 1986 *Washington Monthly* article, wrote, "PBS officials say they are now having trouble finding sponsors for several documentaries, including one on unrest in the Philippines, one on the civil rights movement in the U.S., and one on black heroes."

Together Henry and I did an "Oreo cookie pitch" over a fancy dinner at a rich lady's townhouse up on Beacon Hill. He was a champ at squeezing funds from reluctant supporters, and with the coming of the new year 1986 some significant money at last started coming in: $600,000 from CPB, $200,000 from WGBH. The budget crept upward.

Henry was unsure about the issue of black armed self-defense. For him, guns were the third rail, not so much for skittish funders as for that great moderate middle of the American class/race/gender demographic he so dearly wanted to reach. As Charles Cobb described in his book, *This Non-violent Stuff'll Get You Killed,* nonviolence was clearly a *tactical* weapon, the only one that worked in the end. But except for Quakers and men like James Lawson and Bayard Rustin from the Fellowship of Reconciliation, very few in the movement were pacifists. Many, including SNCC leader James Forman and King's brilliant tactician of nonviolence, James Bevel, had served in the military and knew their way around guns. Ralph Abernathy, Medgar Evers, and Henry Hampton himself owned guns and knew how to use them, but they understood that guns would not win the struggle. King sometimes traveled with armed guards, and the very presence of weapons could sometimes deter white violence. For most southerners, nonviolence was by its very nature an abstract and impractical idea, so it is not surprising that few embraced it as a life philosophy. Cobb quotes his friend SNCC organizer Ivanhoe Donaldson, "The civil rights movement was about civil rights, not about nonviolence. Nonviolence was a tool . . . I didn't go to Mississippi to celebrate nonviolence; I went down there to fight for the right to vote."

Henry had done an extraordinary interview back in 1979 with North Carolina NAACP leader Robert Williams, who had organized black Marine Corps veterans into a chapter of the National Rifle Association and fought back against the Klan. "We had dug foxholes, we had sandbags, steel helmets, heavy rifles, and we also had introduced the Molotov cocktail to the civil rights movement." Blackside interviewed him when he returned to the United States after twenty years in exile in Cuba, North Vietnam, and China. But Williams was so wrapped up with guns and Communism—the other third rail—that Henry, fearing Red-baiting, just didn't want to go near him for *Eyes on the Prize.*

Would young men and women in 1986 care about Vincent Harding and Howard Thurman's insistence that violence was a "tragic last resort"? It would not be until *Eyes II* that Henry fully explored the questions of weapons with the programs about the Black Panthers, Malcolm X, and the urban rebellions of the late 1960s.

In July, just off the plane, I was winding down in the yard at home when a producer called me in tears, asking what Henry had meant in the meeting they had just finished. I had no idea. I was three thousand miles away. Minutes later the phone rang again; it was Henry, spitting mad, asking what in hell the producer had meant in the meeting.

We spoke almost every day. He might call any time, anywhere, with an idea or a problem, or just because we enjoyed talking. I got phone calls from Hampton on the set of a Nike commercial in Rome, a Cocoa Puffs commercial in San Francisco, and in the high country of Yosemite. *Eyes on the Prize* invaded my sleep: I once dreamed that I was dreaming in a tent in the High Sierras when a phone rang; it was Henry, distraught over conflict between two of his producers, asking me to come to Boston right away. In my dream within the dream I got up, packed up my tent and sleeping bag in the moonlight, and followed a telephone cord miles and miles down the mountain, all the way to the airport, and set out for Boston. Ah, Henry.

Now we finally had to force the whole juggernaut to completion. By spring the only thing between us and great television was more work and more money. We couldn't get an interview with any member of the King family, and George Wallace wouldn't talk to us.

CHAPTER FIFTEEN

The Selma Show

1986

In the name of the greatest people that have ever trod this earth, I draw a line in the dust and toss the gauntlet before the feet of tyranny, and I say: segregation now, segregation tomorrow, segregation forever.

—Alabama governor George Wallace, Inaugural Address, 1963

Henry Hampton knew from the start there could be only one climactic event in a documentary history of the civil rights movement, and that was the battle royal at Selma.

On March 7, 1965, in that ordinary town on the fall line of the Alabama River, a few extraordinary men and women churned up the final battle of the classic civil rights movement. The world watched as Alabama state troopers clubbed, bullwhipped, and tear gassed their way through six hundred unarmed black men, women, and children who had set out to deliver a voting rights petition to Governor Wallace. That nationally televised attack, today a crystalline moral icon of the era, would force the White House and Congress to enact the greatest in a series of laws overturning a hundred years of legal and quasi-legal segregation. Henry would position Selma to mark the swift culmination of a century-long fight against American apartheid, one of the great sea changes in our history.

He himself had marched there with Martin Luther King twenty years before, and knew that nothing mattered more than that voting rights campaign, waged in blood and pictures. Nothing would make stronger television.

Henry understood that the white citizens of Selma harbored a particularly bitter sense of insult from northerners. A major slave-trading and munitions center before the Civil War, their town came under siege in April 1865 by Union regulars and the Chicago Board of Trade Artillery.

The Confederate defenders, an ill-trained muster of volunteer militiamen, kids, and old men, were no match for the northern troops, who ran them out of their hometown, then spent the night looting and burning. It was the last major battle of the Civil War, and it is still reenacted annually on a field outside of town, with the Confederates conquered again, year after year.

In 1963, the presiding state judge, James Hare, told a reporter, "Slave traders of two centuries ago had scraped the bottom of the barrel by the time they got around to bringing in slaves for Selma." The high bridge leading out of town to the South was named for Confederate general Edmund Pettus, grand dragon of the Alabama Realm of the Ku Klux Klan. Local black leader Amelia Boynton's mother had taken her around in a horse and buggy in the 1920s, fruitlessly encouraging black people to vote. She and her husband had managed to become registered back in 1934, but when Henry Hampton arrived in 1965, registrars had allowed only 2 percent of Selma's fourteen thousand black citizens to register— fewer than three hundred people—compared to 90 percent of Selma's whites. In neighboring Lowndes County 80 percent of the citizens were black, but not a single one was registered to vote.

Among the devices routinely deployed to disqualify black applicants was the arbitrary requirement to interpret any section of the Alabama or U.S. Constitution, chosen at random, to the satisfaction of the white registrar. By the mid-1960s, nearly a century after passage of the Fifteenth Amendment, which unambiguously declares, "The right of citizens of the United States to vote shall not be denied or abridged . . . on account of race, color, or previous condition of servitude," the percentage of registered black voters in Alabama was actually falling.

The display of savagery, moral heroism, and political triumph in Selma stood at the crossroads between what Judy Richardson reluctantly called the "good" classical civil rights movement of 1955 through 1965 and the bittersweet "bad" movement of the late 1960s. It was the climax of both the movement and of our TV series, the hinge between all that came before and all that came after in the sixties. And like Waterloo or Hiroshima, Selma was once simply a place, and then it became a moment in time, and then a watershed of history, and finally, in the twenty-first century, an idea. Lyndon Johnson had been exactly correct when he said it was "a single place to shape a turning point in man's unending search for freedom."

In the freedom struggle up to that time and in the first five episodes of

Eyes on the Prize in 1985, campaigns across the South had decisively won laws and regulations guaranteed to protect the rights of black Americans, but many of the southern states simply failed or refused to enforce them. Back home in California after a week in Selma in the fall of 1985, I had a hard time explaining to my eleven-year-old daughter why Alabama blacks couldn't vote in 1965. "I thought that's why Lincoln freed the slaves," she said. And in Selma, blacks still sat in the colored section of the lunch counter and went to segregated schools; streets in black neighborhoods remained unpaved; and the threat of violence against anyone who objected hung in the air. Riding in the front of a bus in Montgomery or eating a hamburger in Birmingham had a social meaning, but no meaning whatever in deciding who would govern. The decade of desegregation campaigns had earned no political power to black citizens.

Andy Young had said when we interviewed him earlier that fall, "When the four little girls were killed in the church in Birmingham in '63, we felt that that was directly a result of the kind of inflammatory political rhetoric coming from George Wallace. . . . That incident convinced us that unless you changed the *politics* of Alabama, that you couldn't really change the society. You really didn't want to have to go out and demonstrate every time there was a grievance, and the only way to avoid that was to *elect* the public officials yourself."

Diane Nash talked about the murder of the four little girls in 1963: "We said that we had two options. The first one was, we felt confident that if we tried, we could find out who had done it, and we could make sure they got killed. And we considered that as a real option. And the second option was that we felt that if blacks in Alabama had the right to vote, that they could protect black children. And we deliberately made a choice . . . and promised ourselves and each other, that if it took twenty years, or as long as it took, we weren't going to stop working on it and trying, until Alabama blacks had the right to vote."

Seeing that black registration in rural counties had enormous political potential, SNCC opened a base in Selma. Jim Forman told us, "We were laying a trap." Only a new direct assault on voting, which had only been marginally successful in Mississippi, would guarantee full participation in electoral politics and power in Alabama.

In his 1983 treatment Davis Lacy wrote, "White savagery against unresisting civil rights protesters could provoke the national response necessary to move the administration and Congress. . . . The strategy hinged on provoking a particular individual, James G. Clark, Selma's volatile sheriff." Arrayed against Clark and George Wallace would be the combined moral energy of SNCC, SCLC, Malcolm X, John Lewis, Martin Luther King, the black citizens of Selma, and thousands of northern supporters descending on the town. Yapping around the edges would be the American Nazi Party, and caught in the middle were Selma's fumble bunny young mayor, Joe Smitherman, and its very professional world-weary police chief, Wilson Baker. It had all been recorded on news film, and as television drama it would be unbeatable.

Henry and Fayer decided the Selma show would be the only one of the six *Eyes* episodes that told one complete and unitary story, set in one place, with a single cast of characters, a clear arcing Aristotelian drama, with its own full hour of screen time.

In Boston in 1985 Callie Crossley and Jim DeVinney wrote yet another treatment—the fourth—based on Davis Lacy's original work, exploring the thematic question: Who's in charge here? The Selma city government? The county sheriff? The police chief? The state of Alabama or the United States? As Joe Smitherman explained it: "Wallace . . . had gotten involved in states' rights; that was a big issue. We still believed that the state had the right to govern itself and set its standards. If we wanted a poll tax, if we wanted to set standards for qualified people to vote, we felt we had that state's right." George Wallace himself later told us, "The government was taking us over and swallowing us up and becoming our master instead of our servant. The segregation issue was one of those things that was latched upon as the usurpation of authority; we were going to do it ourselves, but they wanted to do it *them*selves."

Our rollicking national drama has been sustained over two and a half centuries by many things, but to this day it is driven by the ferocious and often healthy competition for sovereignty between the local, state, and federal governments. Who can decide to dam the Grand Canyon, or ban assault rifles or soda pop, or end slavery? Without ever actually telling viewers, *Eyes on the Prize* would serve up this Federalist versus anti-Federalist debate by stealth, smuggled inside a compelling collision between white cops and black petitioners, the governors and the presidents.

That fall the Blackside team had fleshed out the program's second big idea: the messy history of internal conflicts, between both black movement leaders and different white authorities in Selma—late-night arguments, backroom deals, bitter fights over tactics on both sides, horse trading in Washington.

What would eventually become the Selma campaign in 1965 had emerged quietly two years before in February 1963, when Bernard and Colia Lafayette of SNCC began organizing with Amelia Boynton, a few ministers, and Dallas County's only black lawyer, J. L. Chestnut. Andy Young described Mrs. Boynton and the others as "local people who had PhD minds who never had an opportunity to get the formal training that enabled them to have the impact on the society that they ought to have had." Joining them was the equally smart and genial Rev. Frederick Reese, "one of those people who lived in small towns who had no intention of living anywhere else, and was just determined to make his town a good place to live." Father Maurice Ouellet, a white priest at the local Catholic mission, quietly provided mimeograph machines, telephones, and a place for visiting SNCC workers to sleep.

SNCC organizers saw themselves as radicalizing shock troops, parachuting in behind the lines to work for months and years with local insurgents in rural Mississippi, Georgia, and Alabama, without the newsworthy magnetism of leaders like King. And to be a local leader on the streets of Selma in 1963, risking everything in hopes of full citizenship in your own country, was not unlike being a local leader in Soweto twenty years later, almost as frustrating, and just as dangerous. On the same night that Klansman Byron De La Beckwith assassinated Medgar Evers in Mississippi, a band of whites beat Bernard Lafayette nearly to death in front of his home, stopping only when his neighbor fired a rifle in the air.

At first they worked at desegregating all the restaurants in town, except for the Silver Moon Cafe, an all-white watering hole too dangerous for a sit-in. Before long, SCLC's fiery young Birmingham veteran, Rev. James Bevel, and his new wife, Diane Nash Bevel, joined the Lafayettes. The newly formed Selma voter registration project quickly moved beyond the lunch counter forays and with guidance from SNCC's Prathia Hall went right to the real source of power: voting. Rosa Parks had organized Alabama voting drives back in the 1950s, and SNCC, SCLC, and the local Catholic mission had been training local people in voting workshops for some time, but still could not get them actually registered.

Meanwhile, the new president, Lyndon Johnson, edged cautiously toward action, and Special Assistant Bill Moyers and Attorney General Nicholas Katzenbach quietly began planning to present either new voting rights legislation or a constitutional amendment. Johnson, a New Deal white southerner, had broken the longest filibuster in history to pass the Civil Rights Act of 1964, and was now ready for action on voting. The president chafed under the imperatives of Cold War world opinion: How could the nation that liberated Europe from Fascist thugs continue to let racist thugs run amok in southern streets? The political pump was primed; many of us at the time believed that Johnson was at last convinced in his heart, but needed external pressure to force his executive hand. When we began *Eyes,* Henry pushed hard for running a behind-the-scenes simultaneous Washington, D.C., plotline while the violent theatrics played out on center stage in Selma.

SNCC's campaign in Selma was clearly aimed at registering blacks in one southern town, but we all knew its greater purpose was to provoke white resistance so vicious and flamboyant that Washington would have no choice but to enact sweeping voter reforms across the entire South. Opening the floodgates to black voting would—one hoped—defeat racial injustice at its constitutional core, once and for all.

Selma's whites would have none of it. The movement saw voter registration in town as something far greater than itself, and whites, like their ethnic brethren in Mississippi, *also* saw it as the leading edge of a much larger revolution. Mayor Joe Smitherman put it well. "You grew up with this: 'If you give into those black people they'll end up marrying your sister. . . . You want 'em marrying your sister, and your son marrying a black?' The Citizens' Council would say, 'Stand your ground, you're fighting for the white man's rights.'" Mrs. Boynton, Rev. Reese, SNCC, the White Citizens' Council, Sheriff Clark, SCLC, the Klan, and Governor Wallace *all* understood that black voter registration in large numbers would upend the system; on that they all could agree. "We were coming to destroy their world," said Andrew Young.

In a series of "Freedom Days" in 1963 increasing numbers of African American citizens patiently lined up in front of the courthouse to register, even on the twenty-eight days a month that the registrar's office was closed, in a ritual of political shadowboxing. Clark and his men began arresting demonstrators, then began beating them, then shocking them with electric cattle prods, happy to lock up mothers and fathers, children, and grandparents together, first by the dozens and then by the hundreds. SNCC brought James Baldwin and Dick Gregory to town. On one blistering hot Freedom Day, four FBI agents and two Justice Department attorneys watched as Clark's posse stopped SNCC workers from bringing water to 300 applicants lined up at the courthouse. Clark arrested 165 teenage and elementary school marchers and then, out of view of news cameras, sent them on a forced cross-country run for miles in blazing summer heat, pushing them along faster and faster with cattle prods until they vomited, before locking them in jail. On the Fourth of July, his posse attacked newsmen, and then went after the crowd with nightsticks and tear gas. The federal government did not interfere.

Often the same demonstrators would go back on the line as soon as they were released on bail. An early *Eyes on the Prize* script noted that at one point Dallas County had twenty times more black citizens in jail than on the voting rolls.

In the summer of 1964, while the mass-media spotlight was focused across the border on Mississippi Freedom Summer, Judge Hare issued a patently unconstitutional injunction barring any gathering of three people or more, and naming Nash, Bevel, Boynton, and thirty-nine other individuals, specifically enjoining them from meeting with any others. Rev. James Bevel and Mrs. Diane Nash Bevel could not legally meet with each other. The judge's action effectively stopped voter registration work in Selma, affirming that Clark's men could now beat and jail protesters with official sanction under state law, while ignoring federal law. Clark told us in 1985, "I was doing my doggonest to enforce the law of Alabama in Selma in 1965." After quoting the Alabama constitution at length to us, he said, "It doesn't say anything about the U.S. Constitution, only Alabama. It is not written anywhere that a county sheriff must enforce the U.S. Constitution." SNCC had "bet the farm on Selma," but with no federal protection, the voter registration effort was for the moment defeated.

The movement's strategies against the harebrained notion of local police authority trumping the U.S. Constitution were not always unified, and that messiness appealed to Henry Hampton. The Blackside writers understood that SCLC, the NAACP, CORE, and SNCC, like the Founding Fathers or the sparring anti-Fascist Spanish factions Orwell described in *Homage to Catalonia,* or even the Klan and Citizens' Council, had contradictory but complementary plans. Telling this story on television would demand striking a delicate balance between the charismatic leadership of Dr. King, at that moment a moral supernova in the American sky, and SNCC's dogged, patient groundwork with local people. Attracting national publicity to get national legislation passed was what King did well; local organizing was what SNCC did well.

But Ella Baker, SNCC's elder mentor, had proclaimed, "Strong people don't need strong leaders." Jim Forman explained for us SNCC's reliance on leaders from the local community. "We felt that there should be a projection and an organization of indigenous leadership . . . from the community. . . . We kept explaining to King the . . . real danger in trying to project a charismatic leader because of a possible assassination. If you didn't have a broad-based movement, the assassination of a leader could lead to a decapitation. We wanted a movement that would survive the loss of our lives."

Most of Dallas County's black population in 1965 were sharecroppers, with little access to television, but the few black professionals—teachers, clergy, the two doctors—had seen dogs and fire hoses on TV and were encouraged by the success of the movements they saw in Montgomery and Birmingham. Some TV stations in the South, particularly in Mississippi, blocked the appearance of any blacks and put up a "Technical Difficulties" card when civil rights stories came in on the network news feed.

Now it seemed the only way to really get Selma on TV and on Congress's radar was to deploy Dr. King. Mrs. Boynton and the Dallas County Voters League decided to leapfrog over SNCC, and appeal directly to SCLC in Atlanta. The thirty-six-year-old Rev. King had just returned from Nobel Prize ceremonies in Stockholm as a moral celebrity, *Time* magazine's "Man of the Year." He could generate massive media attention that SNCC by itself could only dream of. The major news networks and wire services, based in New York and L.A., depended on local white stringers in small towns where the movement did its most intimate work, but national correspondents and crack camera crews looking for a good story after Mississippi Freedom Summer might now shine a very bright spotlight on the trouble in Selma.

Mayor Joe Smitherman was a thirty-four-year-old appliance salesman and civic booster with his heart set on bringing new business and industry to Selma. Andy Young told us Smitherman was a lukewarm good old boy, "not particularly courageous, but neither was he particularly evil or bad . . . he was just a man caught in a trap and didn't have the personal strength or courage or wisdom to make any changes. He was sort of swept along with the tide."

Smitherman tried to cool the situation behind the scenes. He told us in 1985, "We offered concessions; we would start hiring more black people, paving streets . . . but the blacks had solidified their leadership through Martin Luther King. Wilson Baker had an idea that we ought to go ahead and register some, but we couldn't convince the appointed registrars to do that. I even called three prominent black leaders, tried to make a deal with them. I said . . . 'I've got some state money if you three will come out publicly and demand I pave a road . . . you'll get credit for this and I'll respond. And we don't need this Martin Luther King in here.' Then there was this black con man going around to the various counties where you had a large black population and he . . . claimed that for $10,000 he could keep Dr. King out of here."

On January 2, 1965, Martin Luther King arrived in Selma and violated Judge Hare's injunction by speaking at a mass meeting in Brown Chapel A.M.E. Church before a thousand parishioners, with a half dozen camera crews, the FBI, and the state police recording it all. King was in high form with his "Give us the ballot" oration that night, announcing that the movement was here to stay until blacks had the right to vote in Selma, "symbol of bitter-end resistance to the civil rights movement in the Deep South."

As *Eyes on the Prize* would point out, SNCC leadership was smarting at the fact that "De Lord" had come in to hijack the credit and purpose of a local movement they had worked for years to build. They decided to deploy more SNCC personnel to Selma, which was ramping up to be the biggest show in the movement that winter. So to get more bodies into the field and outplay SCLC by sheer numbers, most of us on the Atlanta office staff shipped out to Alabama.

I was then a twenty-year-old forty-dollar-a-week staff worker at SNCC's bustling national headquarters in Atlanta, enduring my first frigid southern winter. After Freedom Registration work as the lowest-level foot soldier in Mississippi, I had joined SNCC as the lowest-level bureaucrat, northern campus coordinator, handling all the organization's fund-raising on a hundred northern college campuses. SNCC was struggling after the collapse of the MFDP at Atlantic City. I was a clueless fund-raiser, in over my head, only able to coax a few thousand dollars a month from all those students at all those colleges, with suggestions like "Try putting on an Anti-Jemima pancake breakfast on your campus!!!!!" In that midwinter time of low morale, we were glad to get out of the office and back into the field.

SNCC's photo coordinator Tom Wakayama sent me off with the first real camera I'd ever held, a Pentax single lens reflex with a 100mm Angenieux lens. I set out westward with Julian Bond, *Washington Post* reporter Paul Good, and half a dozen others, arriving in Selma late on January 10, 1965. We went straight into a meeting with James Bevel and John Lewis about how to get three hundred people safety from the church to the courthouse the next morning. I did not learn until I went to work for Henry Hampton twenty years later that that same day the Johnson administration had secretly finished the first draft of its Voting Rights Act, and another draft of a constitutional amendment. Contrary to later fictionalized accounts, Johnson by then strongly supported civil rights, and now all the administration needed was a trigger.

We spent the night at an empty house on the edge of town with no indoor plumbing and no insulation, with a bitter wind whipping through the cracks. What I remember from that first night was trying to sleep on the floorboards with no blanket, bone cold in my army jacket, worried not that night riders would kill me, but that I would die of asphyxiation from the propane oven we left burning all night for warmth. Unable to sleep, we rolled out at dawn and made it over to movement headquarters at Brown Chapel Church. I spent the morning shooting stills of preparations for the day's march, the morning mass meeting, and portraits of Bob Mants and other civil rights workers. SNCC's Ivanhoe Donaldson asked me not to take his picture. "No photos, you never know where that picture's going to end up . . . FBI, sheriff's office, who knows." Oh, those innocent days.

Around noon a few hundred of us fell in line behind King and set off toward the courthouse, along the unpaved streets of the black section, past the little houses raised up on cement piers. I took some shots of King at the head of the line, in winter light coming through the bare trees, marching next to SNCC's John Love, the first man I ever saw wearing an earring.

Somewhere along the way I again shook King's hand—the man himself—and was again surprised at how big it was, even beefier than I remembered from Meridian, more like the hand of a boxer than a preacher; it was like greeting Joe Louis, though King was only about five and a half feet tall. I remember thinking that by walking so close to Martin Luther King, I might get shot. Following behind King and his aides, we rounded the corner of Lauderdale Street and Alabama Avenue, and there in front of the courthouse was the other man himself: Sheriff Jim Clark, big guy in his forties with a .38 revolver on his right hip, cattle prod on the left, khaki uniform. Milling around the building were twenty or thirty of his uniformed deputies and volunteer possemen in World War II helmets and construction hard hats, pistols and long clubs on their belts, looking oddly middle class and middle aged, like a baleful militia of armed accountants.

The whole scene radiated menace. By then several dozen African Americans, dressed in their Sunday best with overcoats against the damp cold, led by Mrs. Amelia Boynton, had lined up on the sidewalk, waiting quietly for the registrar's office to open, knowing it never would. Bevel had trained them all in the techniques of nonviolence. Dr. King had peeled off from our group, and watched from a car with his aides across the street, parked in front of the FBI office. Bevel and a white SNCC field secretary, Frank Sorraco, unintimidated by Clark, posted themselves on the sidewalk. Boynton, a striking, statuesque black woman in her fifties, walked up and down the line giving encouragement. When Clark ordered the three organizers off the sidewalk and into a side alley, they looked him in the eye, refused, and continued encouraging the demonstrators.

Suddenly Clark seized Mrs. Boynton by the back of the neck and began manhandling her with all his might down the sidewalk past the others. How she stayed upright on her high heels as he gave her the brutal bum's rush, I'll never know. He did it in front of half a dozen network news cameras, accelerating her all the way up the block—not a perp walk, but a perp run—around the corner, into a patrol car, and off to jail.

Clark had delivered the goods, the gaudy media goods, exactly as movement strategists hoped, exactly as Selma's few moderate whites feared. Within minutes, sealed cans of news film were in the hands of couriers headed for the developing lab in New York. The scene would flash around the country on TV that night, and appear on the front page of the *New York Times* the next morning—and in Henry's documentary decades later. It was an explosive image, a 220-pound, six foot two, balding white sheriff, infuriated that anyone would question his authority, unafraid of brutalizing a dignified black woman in front of helpless black men, in front of her neighbors as they petitioned peacefully for the right to vote, on national television.

Three of us from SNCC went across the street past King's car and burst into the FBI field office, demanding that "the federal government

take immediate action to protect the right to vote in Alabama!" The bewildered woman behind the counter didn't know what to make of us. The
agent behind her, who looked exactly like an FBI agent, calmly explained
that whatever was happening across the street was a county matter, and
the FBI would not intervene.

When we came out, Clark's men were arresting marchers, and we
watched them herd dozens of people into a prison bus. As the bus pulled
out we could see it rocking from side to side in rhythm and we could hear
the people inside belting out "Ain't going to let Jim Clark turn me around,
turn me around, turn me around . . . !"

At least no one was hurt that day. Who could know that Clark rousting Mrs. Boynton was only an appetizer for the carnage yet to come when
a trooper would beat her unconscious on "Bloody Sunday"? Sitting with
Henry in a Boston editing room twenty years later, looking at that news
film of those two tribes facing off at the courthouse, it seemed so obvious
that Jim Crow's days were numbered, that Clark and his posse represented nothing more than a last desperate stand for American apartheid.
But on that day in 1965 no one knew whether the center would hold. Who
could predict that Mrs. Boynton might soon win a seat on the Selma City
Council, John Lewis a seat in Congress, that Jim Clark would wind up in
jail, or that we would live to see a black president of the United States
clasp Mrs. Boynton's hand as they lead eighty thousand marchers across
the Pettus Bridge on the fiftieth anniversary of Bloody Sunday.

As police brutality went in those days, what we had just seen was kid
stuff, but Clark's manhandling of Mrs. Boynton reenergized the community, as Rosa Parks's arrest had electrified Montgomery. That night hundreds of people jammed into Brown Chapel Church. The courageous
minister, Rev. Lewis, knew perfectly well that the 16th Street Baptist
Church in Birmingham and dozens of others across the South had been
bombed and burned to the ground for opening their doors to mass
meetings. As the congregation thundered out freedom songs—"Oh-o
Freedom! Oh-o Freedom!"—I could feel the floor shake. It was suffocating, the steam heat turned up all the way.

Ralph Abernathy cranked up the crowd with his patented "rousements" before throwing it to King. Just as Martin took the podium there
was a small muffled explosion on the left side of the sanctuary, and the
crowd surged away to the right, until we quickly saw that it was a burst
pipe on a radiator, not a bomb. What struck me was that the news crews

all immediately had lights on, cameras rolling, rushing *toward* the danger while everyone else rushed away. King calmed the crowd, as he had before in churches under siege at night, and let loose with a powerhouse oration calling for a "veritable *symphony* of *justice* in Selma."

Though popular history pegged white resistance in Selma as monolithic in its nasty resolve, the white community was, in fact, divided over how to stop the rising tide of demonstrations. A precious few Selmans, mostly Jews and Catholics, quietly supported their black neighbors. At the upscale Albert Hotel, white businessmen met secretly with local black leaders, who had to enter through the back door. Father Ouellet was evidently the only white man among Selma's fifteen thousand whites to speak out openly and forcefully against Clark's brutality.

Clark, like a man possessed, could not stop himself from behaving badly in front of the cameras. A few weeks later, in freezing rain, Rev. C. T. Vivian confronted him on the courthouse steps, called Clark a Hitler, scolded him for stopping people from voting, with the cameras rolling and the sheriff seething in silent rage. Both the sheriff and the reverend knew that the black citizens who watched had never seen a black man so fearlessly get in a white cop's face. Clark suddenly lunged forward and punched Vivian square in the face with a lightning jab so hard that it broke a finger in Clark's left fist. Clark told us later, "I just don't even remember hitting him, to this day I don't, even though I saw it on television that night, I didn't remember it." We could only imagine what Clark did in the woods and back alleys, out of the cameras' view. The bloodied Rev. Vivian refused to retreat: "We're willing to be *beaten* for democracy!" In 1985, he told us, "It was an engagement like none other. You don't walk away from that. That's what movement is all about."

John Lewis saw Clark as a fearful victim of the system. Unlike many other Black Belt law officers those days, Clark actually had a thought-out position on race. John Fleming of the *Anniston Star* did a series of interviews with the former sheriff late in life. "Jim Clark was no ignorant racist who simply went along with the crowd, beating blacks and their white allies just because it was the thing to do. . . . He was prone to talk about race science, the duty he was bound to carry out under the Constitution of the state of Alabama in 1965, the orders of his superiors, including George Wallace. Martin Luther King was a communist, and the communists were funneling him money. King had a girlfriend in Selma, he was a failed preacher."

Both the movement and Henry Hampton's team chose their sheriffs carefully, judging their battlegrounds in part by the quality of available villains: bad actors like Bull Connor, the proud bigot of Birmingham, who unleashed the dogs on cue with operatic fury, or the restrained and courtly Laurie Pritchett in Albany, Georgia, who by studying Gandhi and lecturing his officers on nonviolence, had managed to get King out of town without giving the movement any real gains. And, of course, they chose Selma's increasingly unhinged buffoon, Jim Clark. It was a particularly disgusting blood sport: heavily armed, helmeted officers, under the cloak and sanction of state law, bludgeoning, fire hosing, arresting, pushing, shoving, punching, cattle prodding, whipping, and tear gassing defenseless, nonresisting ordinary people who had declared their commitment to nonviolence. It happened month after month throughout the 1960s.

I can't remember exactly how long I stayed in Selma, fifty years ago as I write. It seems like months, but was probably only a few weeks: pitching in at the church, making sandwiches for marchers, sending info and photos back to the Atlanta office, doing the routine of daily marches. I became fascinated with the clean-cut white guys with skinny ties and reporter's notebooks who followed us, and then sprinted for the telephone booths whenever anything big happened; this was obviously the real deal: genuine journalists filing genuine news stories on deadline (stories that Blackside researchers would dig out twenty years later). What mattered in Selma was the media coverage.

Henry said, "The civil rights movement was the first big television event in this country over a sustained period. . . . Television was very much like a good policeman for people in the fifties and sixties; if you attract television cameras they would literally keep you alive. The civil rights movement would have happened with or without television . . . but it was gasoline that could be tossed on the fire of this southern rural movement. . . . The industry learned that this was not only something that would, in fact, draw ratings, but that people would immediately understand and react to. The movement learned from this that they could stay alive and at the same time reach people in Seattle and Minneapolis and

Boston and draw a constituency into what at that point had been a local movement."

Today anyone with a cell phone would capture Clark manhandling Boynton and post it around the planet within seconds, but back then it took real skill and the resources of a major news organization to record those pictures and get them on television. I had never before seen news cameramen at work, mysterious guys who appeared like moths out of nowhere with their heavy hardware, anointing the scene with gravity, absorbed with their technical rigmarole. The networks would not get caught flat-footed again, as they had in Dallas, when the assassination of President Kennedy in public, in broad daylight, in front of hundreds of people, was captured by Russian immigrant Abraham Zapruder, an 8mm home-movie hobbyist, but not by a single news camera.

White crowds, convinced the northern television networks were against them, often went for the cameras. In making *Eyes on the Prize* we did a sequence about the horrific night after James Meredith tried to enter the University of Mississippi. It was a hell of a scene, but Henry's researchers could find little film, because the mob attacked the press, smashing cameras, killing a reporter from Agence France-Presse execution-style, before shooting thirty-five federal marshals. Mobs understood the postmodern power of images long before the postmodernists did.

Yet fortunately for Blackside and generations of documentary makers to come, those twentieth-century news cameramen, correspondents, field producers, and soundmen stuck with it month after month, like combat photographers. Without them we never could have made *Eyes on the Prize*. On the streets of Selma, and later in the anti-Vietnam mayhem in Berkeley, I saw them throw themselves into the scene, utterly fixed on whatever was flaring up in front of them, often putting the shot above their own safety, with the adrenaline of a hunter on the kill. It took steel nerves, skill, and physical strength to navigate the bedlam between marchers, police, and hostile mobs, shouldering a 20-pound camera, reloading film every ten minutes. When the fracas was all over, they would vanish as quickly as they had appeared. Watch the unflinching footage that Robert Roy shot for ABC in Selma, or Stephen Lighthill shot for CBS in Berkeley, month after month; not only did they muster the same intensity that the police and demonstrators fired up, they had to stay miraculously calm, oddly detached, and focused, both literally and figuratively, sometimes shooting from inside a gas mask.

Haskell Wexler says, "When you shoot, you're there, but you're not there." Any cameraperson who has ever slipped through the looking-glass viewfinder into the fever dream of real violence will know what I'm talking about. In the beginning they probably felt it was not their fight. They were constrained by their network's and newspaper's standards of journalism from partisanship in newsgathering. These crews eventually could not escape their own growing sympathy with the movement. Recording the routine brutality against peaceful demonstrators, many of them flipped over to the side of the protesters, and could barely conceal their desire to join in reforming America with their pictures.

In Selma they made their sympathies known by their courage and craft. When *Eyes* began editing in Boston in 1985, we could see it in the hundreds of hours shot during that dreary, violent winter, in their understanding that they were not simply filing nightly spot news, but were seizing history on the fly. Henry pointed out that camerawork that in simpler times might have been merely a couple of shots for the evening news now became worthy of patient observation and visual storytelling, long sustained shots of courageous local people, with clearly recorded narrative dialogue. By the time Clark attacked C. T. Vivian in the rain, the newsmen had endured Selma for weeks, and refused to back down when deputies shoved them and ordered them to stop filming, covered the lenses with their hands, or when Clark yelled at them to turn their lights off.

When Rev. Reese led Selma's black teachers, thirty-one of whom had been fired by the all-white school board for trying to register, in a dignified march to the courthouse, a nameless CBS cameraman patiently let his camera roll. The teachers, dressed in their middle-class business attire, quietly approached the door again and again and the helmeted Clark again and again swaggered down the steps to drive them back with his nightstick. That grainy old footage had all the narrative power and subtle terror of a feature film. In *Eyes on the Prize* it plays virtually uncut, without commentary, only the sound of shoes on the pavement and Clark's squawking. Chuck Scott explained, "The editors used the footage to actually *tell* a story, not simply to illustrate a story. That was something new. We had such good material and it had not been seen before *this* way." Archive footage *drove* the story rather than simply illustrating it.

Video of Clark manhandling Mrs. Boynton or the attack on the Pettus Bridge today goes for about two thousand dollars a minute. But it was work for hire, and today not one of the cameramen who filmed it ever got a credit or a penny of the archives' license fees. ABC, CBS, NBC, and Getty Images profited handsomely in 1986 when Henry paid tens of thousands of dollars for news film, and again in 2005 when the Ford Foundation paid half a million to renew the licenses.

Henry and I both thought that the imagery was a triumph of war won or lost on pictures. The objective ground truth—whether a few people got registered that day—paled against the subjective picture power of massed marchers and police. Joe Smitherman looked back years later: "They picked Selma just like a movie producer would pick a set. You had the right ingredients, I mean you would have to have seen Clark in his day, he had a helmet like General Patton, the Eisenhower jacket and swagger stick; and then Wilson Baker was very impressive, and I guess I was the least of all, I was 145 pounds and a crew cut and big ears."

Selma's days of isolation were over, and that winter, movement strategists consciously used the television crews to get the brutal pageantry in front of 30 million ordinary American viewers, 435 congressmen, 100 senators, and one president, at a time when the nation was not yet numb to television violence.

The ritual played on . . . black veterans marched, black cosmetologists, black morticians, black clergy. King and Abernathy went to jail (police chief Wilson Baker made it a point to arrest them before they got to the courthouse, so that Sheriff Clark could not get his hands on them). A congressional delegation came to town, and on February 4, 1965, SNCC brought Malcolm X, whose fierce-eyed northern urban rhetoric about burning down the master's house in the context of global liberation drew polite applause, but was a hard sell for southern blacks accustomed to the warmer style of southern preachers. Malcolm said, "I don't believe in any kind of nonviolence. . . . I think the people in this part of the world should give Doctor Martin Luther King what he's asking for and give it to him fast before some other factions come along and do it another way." A member of the American Nazi Party got close enough to King to punch him. Mrs. Annie Lee Cooper attacked Sheriff Clark, sunk her teeth into his arm, and hung on until he beat her off with his nightstick.

Up in Boston in 1965, young Unitarian staffer Henry Hampton was watching it all on television.

CHAPTER SIXTEEN

It's Our Flag Too

1986

O ur Blackside film crew pulled into Selma on December 4, 1985. The last time I had crossed the Edmund Pettus Bridge it was just another ugly bridge, not a national historic site. Mike Chin, Sekou Shepard, and I stocked up on George Wallace Community College sweatshirts, and when the clerk volunteered, "You're not from around here, are you?" we said we were from San Francisco, and he added, "the land of fruits." We met with the affable Mr. Corneil of the Selma Chamber of Commerce, who handed out "Selma: The Butterfly Capital of Alabama" and "The Queen of the Black Belt" stickers and took us to The Sisters soul food restaurant for black-eyed peas and fried chicken. The food was excellent, but the conversation was all thumbs, Callie, Laurie, and I not quite sure how to chitchat with this white civic booster about his town's top ranking in the annals of racist bad behavior. Surely he suspected we harbored animosity for his town and everything it stood for.

Selma's lovely historic district, frozen in time somewhere between 1850 and 1950, had a southern charm I had not noticed back in 1965. Seen from the opposite bank, the town, with its luxuriant trees and nineteenth-century buildings perched on the bluff above the easygoing Alabama River, the air alive with swallows, looked for all the world like a quiet town in southern France.

But gone forever by 1985 was that deep provincialism and flavor we northerners had sensed so keenly back when states had their own customs, speech, brands of food and drink: Rebel and Nehi pop, Jax Beer, Dixie Crystals sugar. I remember some states even had different markings down the center of the road. But now from the Holiday Inn at the strip mall next to Interstate 80 I could count the national franchises: FedEx, Exxon, McDonald's, Wendy's, Quincy's, Shell, Walmart, Taco Bell, Chevron, KFC. The local white and black news anchors all sounded as though they had gone to Columbia Journalism School, and the topic for the day on the local talk show was a Birmingham, Alabama, demonstration against South African apartheid. The South in 1985 seemed to me finally wrestled into submission by national brands and national consciousness, tamed, domesticated, its old spirit both broken and liberated. Gone was segregation by law, but vanished with it in those early days of homogenized global culture was much of the precious regional culture; it seemed an odd price to pay for full democracy.

By 1985 the town was smaller (down from 28,000 to 20,000), blacker (68 percent), and poorer (31 percent below the poverty line) than the last time I had been there, though all the streets were finally paved, and all the houses hooked up to the city sewer system.

Joe Smitherman was still mayor in 1985 after eight consecutive terms, now navigating the late twentieth century's political and social shoals with exuberant smarts and good humor. His old nemesis Andrew Young was mayor of Atlanta, and they would bump into each other at the United States Conference of Mayors and reminisce about the good/bad old days. When he was elected as a moderate in 1964, a member of the White Citizens' Council, "Segregation was not an issue, because *everyone* was a segregationist," until he was swept up in a civic hurricane. By 1965 he was trying to control thousands of invading northern liberals, the arrayed freedom armies of the movement, thousands of local black citizens, his own sheriff, and the full power of the international media that had descended on Selma. Then came the National Guard, and before it was over regular troops of the U.S. Army entered Selma once again, as they had a century before.

Blackside's Selma story was evolving as a television show of Shakespearean complexity and menace, with the long-suffering and ever-civil segregationist director of public safety Wilson Baker doing everything to restrain hypersegregationist Clark, while SNCC and SCLC did everything to unleash Clark for the world to witness.

Henry was uncomfortable heaping scorn on white southerners as a monolithic group, and loved stories of decent people caught in bad dilemmas, so he was fascinated by Baker. Andy Young had described Baker to us as "one of the most intelligent and sensitive law enforcement officers I ever met. He was a remarkably knowledgeable and reasonable man, skilled at managing conflict, exactly what you want in a police chief." Baker taught criminology at the University of Alabama, saw that integration was inevitable, and made it his business to actually talk with movement leaders and even debate on the street with Henry Hampton's Unitarian boss, Dana Greeley (Greeley's Yankee blue blood mojo was no match for Baker's Alabama mojo).

Baker, who knew all along that if he couldn't control the violence Lyndon Johnson would send in the army to control it for him as Kennedy and Eisenhower had done before, often interposed himself and his men between Clark's posse and demonstrators. As *Eyes* researchers later discovered, Baker also secretly initiated dialogue with the Department of Justice in Washington.

Henry and Davis Lacy had built these puzzles into their original Selma script, knowing that Smitherman grew up on welfare with his widowed mother in the farm economy where every poor white knew that "If you wouldn't do the job for that price, there was a nigger who would." Smitherman understood he had something in common with poor blacks and may even have harbored sympathy for their plight. In January 1965 Clark's and Smitherman's locker-room talk spilled over when Smitherman made the mistake of referring to Martin Luther King as "Martin Luther Coon" on national prime-time television, to the delight of Blackside's editors twenty years later.

But Joe was nothing if not flexible, and after universal suffrage became the enforced law of Alabama in 1965, he bent his style and personal beliefs to align with the times, and apparently became a real leader, appointing blacks to key positions in city government, courting the black vote. When we interviewed him in 1985, Joe was Selma's longest-serving politician. He greeted us with little ice-cold eight-ounce bottles of Coca-Cola you seldom see outside the South, which he fetched from a refrigerator in his office, and made sure to remind us that "My fourth and fifth term I got eighty percent of the black vote."

He was a funny, chain-smoking, fully matured Alabama hipster, one of those winning southern politicians unencumbered by too many circuit breakers. Smitherman's candor served him well in his *Eyes on the Prize* interview, as he forthrightly conjured up the plight of a naive boy mayor seeing his world change forever: "I know that's very demeaning to say that, but you thought that . . . they were just satisfied with living in these shacks, and they were happy people. Hell, I mean you just grew up with that sort of thing, 'cause you grew up among a lot of poverty yourself."

He was still resentful at how his city had been used back in 1965. "Kids would come in, students to get their spurs in Selma. I remember I had a phone call from the University of Minnesota and some young girl said, 'We're coming to your city tomorrow.' . . . They chartered an airplane . . . came over here, marched two hours, got in the bus, went back, caught the plane back. I find today in dealing with federal agents, many of them with prominent jobs marched here in Selma, that's part of their portfolio."

By the end of the interview, with his warm Alabama voice, easy laugh, and outstanding sense of irony, the new Joe trumped the old Joe. As we were packing up he gave us each a jar of pickled quail eggs, a central Alabama delicacy, including one for Henry. "Here's one for your boss."

The next day Callie, Jim, Mike, Sekou, and I went over to Brown Chapel A.M.E. Church, now protected as a National Historic Landmark, and shot an interview with Mrs. Amelia Boynton. She had aged into a stately grand dame of the movement, with an unfortunate rhetorical style honed from having told the same story a thousand times over until the words felt scripted, disconnected from real experience. But Mrs. Boynton did fill in key parts of the Selma narrative for us. With a flourish she autographed the photo I had taken of Sheriff Clark rousting her down the street twenty years before. She lived to be 104 years old.

Back at the Holiday Inn that evening Sekou and I took a six-pack over to Mike Chin's room to watch our umpteenth football game on TV. I don't remember the game, but I vividly remember the commercials. It was the golden age of Budweiser and Miller Lite beer commercials. (My friend Patrick Crowley had that same year done a 30-second Miller beer commercial with Haskell Wexler that cost $1,500,000, almost the entire original budget of all six *Eyes on the Prize* documentaries combined.) Those luscious beer ads offered up a perfect dream of pluralist America, set in cheery taverns packed with laughing African Americans, Euro-Americans, Latino Americans, and Asian Americans having the time of their lives bonding over beer. It was a bizarre stage on which to witness the integration in which Henry so deeply believed, but had yet to be achieved in reality in 1985.

Amelia Boynton, Jim Clark, Rosa Parks, and young Joe Smitherman could never in their wildest 1965 dreams have imagined seeing these hyperintegrated beer worlds on television in Alabama, but they filled me with crazy hope that if Madison Avenue could do it, maybe the rest of the nation could follow. Advertising would carry on its unlikely mission as evangelist of all-multicultural-all-the-time for decades, a leading exemplar of American diversity. Go figure. My dad joked that there were more black women in the L. L. Bean catalog than in the whole state of Maine. The most perfectly integrated multicultural crowd I ever saw were the extras on a Sprint commercial I shot for Barbara Kopple in 2005; that same week, at an evening performance at the Berkeley Repertory Theatre, my wife, Nina, surveyed the all-white crowd and said, "The only way to integrate this place is for us to come in blackface."

In 1985, Mike and I subsidized and supplemented our low wage on *Eyes* by shooting television commercials with multiethnic casts, mostly for breakfast cereal, tennis shoes, and snack food. Like many progressive filmmakers of the time, or like Henry's original crew at Blackside in the early seventies, we did not really face up to the contradiction between our documentary work and our commercial work. We did our best work with big crews, big equipment, and big budgets, selling sugared cereal to children, while at the same time doing our other best work with a tiny crew and tiny budget to record the freedom struggle of African Americans in Selma, Alabama.

Those former segregationists who seem to have changed with the times, like Joe Smitherman, Sheriff Mel Bailey, Chief of Police Laurie Pritchett, and some architects of South African apartheid, describe what history now judges to be past sins—their own and their society's—with dark, droll irony, regret, and a bit of revisionism. They, and maybe even George Wallace, had gone through the crucible of civil rights and seem to have emerged as different men. Some had learned to chuckle, often with pain, at their old selves, even if their victims did not. Perhaps they would talk with Blackside because they knew this history was important, regardless of which side they had been on, or how self-serving they could become.

Then there are the Jim Clarks, who would unapologetically tell us how he wouldn't change a thing, because they believe that we, not they, landed on the wrong side of history. Reason, Christian persuasion, and overwhelming public opinion may have converted a lot of white southerners, but made no dent in Jim Clark's enduring pathology. He had begun his political career as a liberal on racial matters, but as sheriff had abruptly and completely flipped his views. Ralph Abernathy had described Jim

Clark to us as "an awful, mean, cruel, fat man, white man," Henry called him "Sheriff Mindfuck," and around the Boston office he was "the Pinch Hitler," for interns too young to remember the real one. Clark grew up hardscrabble, and had served his country as a gunner on bombers during World War II. On his uniform he wore a lapel pin emblazoned with "NEVER," and controlled what amounted to a personal army of two hundred armed men: the "walking posse" and the "mounted posse." He was a cartoon, but a dangerous one.

Prudence Arndt, Orlando's white associate producer, and I drove over to meet him in Anniston, Alabama, picking up a local all-white crew out of Birmingham, just to be careful. (Selma producer Jim DeVinney had wisely chosen to attend his own wedding that same day back in Boston; dedication to Blackside had its limits.) Clark met us at his mobile-home dealership, on a gravel road in the woods outside of town, graciously ushering us into his office in a double-wide. Neither life nor history had been kind to him: after losing his bid for reelection to Wilson Baker in 1966—the citizens of Selma had had enough—he decamped to Anniston, the boneyard of segregation, where Klansmen had burned the Freedom Riders' bus back in 1962. He slid through a series of odd jobs and finally, in 1978, was arrested by agents of the federal government he so despised and convicted of smuggling three tons of marijuana from Colombia, and served nine months in prison.

Greeting us in 1985, Jim was bald, losing his hearing, thinner, a welcoming white supremacist on his way to becoming a broken-down old man. He was surprisingly meek compared to the big thug in uniform we had feared in Selma back in the day. He showed us with pride his lineage in a book of Confederate descendants.

I had a hell of a time lighting him, making that stark trailer interior look like anything interesting. I did not have the nerve to ask Jim if I could see the teeth-mark scar on his wrist where Annie Lee Cooper bit him.

Prue forged ahead with the interview. Most of what Clark had to say in his elderly genteel way was patently delusional, but he clearly believed every word of it. "Martin Luther King was there with three white prostitutes and it was all a matter of record . . . and I felt like that he was coming in with a crew there to agitate things along with the American Nazi Party.

"Amelia Boynton led the group to the courthouse and directed them to come inside and to take over the offices and to urinate on top of the desks and throw the books on the floor, and she was the one that was telling them what to do and how to do and I went out and tried to persuade her to leave the premises."

On the mayhem at the foot of the bridge, when Clark's mounted posse attacked with bullwhips: "Just as the troopers were advancing . . . I saw the demonstrators come up with ice picks and straight razors . . . and they just voluntarily lay down on the ground as the troopers came up, then that's when they started on the troopers with the weapons. . . . We were trying to keep a low profile as law enforcement, and to keep everything quiet as possible."

When we finished, Clark said, "Y'all were fair." Unique among everyone we interviewed for *Eyes on the Prize,* Clark alone was lost in time. A few months before he died in 2007, he told the *Montgomery Advertiser* that he "would do it all over again the same way."

Seventy white Alabamans, led by Lutheran pastor Joseph Ellwanger of Birmingham, marched to the Selma courthouse in support of voting and sang "America." They were largely drowned out by a hundred whites revving their car engines and singing "Dixie," while a hundred blacks across the street belted out "We Shall Overcome." The local whites then attempted to beat Ellwanger and the marchers before Wilson Baker broke it up and hustled the group out of town.

By February 1965 Selma had settled into a rain-soaked stalemate. The press now maintained a permanent presence, covering more or less daily confrontations between massed marchers and white authorities at "the Selma Wall," a rope barrier behind which Chief Baker penned demonstrators into the George Washington Carver housing projects so that Sheriff Clark could not get at them. King shuttled in and out from northern fund-raising and from his pastoral duties in Atlanta.

I wrote home to my parents in California: "Selma will probably get worse before it gets better . . . there have been 3000 arrests in the last two weeks . . . we're exasperated at what the press does with Dr. King, talking about his 'two week old voter drive,' when SNCC has been working there since '63. . . ."

SCLC in turn could be contemptuous of SNCC's impetuous confrontational style, and Wyatt Tee Walker insisted to us that "SNCC was in over its head." With few exceptions, most notably SNCC chairman John Lewis, a young minister, King acolyte, and staunch believer in lived theology, SNCC people were generally secular, focused on political and economic power. Nearly all the leadership and staff of SCLC were pastors, driven by a belief in the power of moral suasion, faith, and bonds of "the beloved community"; King had not yet articulated his more radical political and economic positions. Despite their fierce differences, leaders of the two organizations warmly admired each other.

SCLC had credible influence in the White House, while in SNCC we held a palpable distrust of President Johnson and the liberal Democrats who had in our eyes derailed our effort in Mississippi the summer before. But together SNCC, CORE, SCLC, and the NAACP maintained a barely united popular front that winter in Selma. Unlike factions in many other social movements in the twentieth century, they kept their collective eyes on the prize, in solidarity with the people of Selma for the sole purpose of winning a strong federal voting rights law and the enforcement to go with it.

My own feeling in those desperate months—and while we were making *Eyes* years later—was that if it took King's unequaled rhetorical power and attentive press corps to force the issue of massive voting reform, so be it. If he (or *Eyes on the Prize* years later) made a few moderate southern congressmen or my segregationist relatives in Florida finally flip and see state racism for what it was, then fine. If mainstream American was not quite ready for SNCC, we could wait.

I was back at work in Atlanta when the fuse for the final confrontation was lit during a night march on February 18, 1965, in the quiet little farming town of Marion, Alabama, twenty-five miles from Selma in Perry County.

Perry County had not a single black voter in 1965. Local police had jailed SCLC's James Orange on charges of contributing to the delinquency of a minor after he organized young people's marches in support of voter registration. Fearing he might be lynched, five hundred people assembled at Zion Chapel United Methodist Church just after dark, and Albert Turner led them on a peaceful one-block march along the town square to sing hymns in front of the jail. They were met at the post office by lines of deputy sheriffs, city policemen, state troopers, and Selma's Sheriff Clark. Suddenly the streetlights went off. Police and local white civilians attacked together, thrashing the protesters and news photographers, smashing cameras, spraying lenses with black paint, and severely beating NBC correspondent Richard Valeriani. Not a single photo or frame of news film of that night's melee ever got out, so in 1985 we relied on Valeriani's and Turner's vivid firsthand account.

State troopers chased Jimmie Lee Jackson, a twenty-six-year-old army veteran and youngest deacon of the St. James Baptist Church, his eighty-two-year-old grandfather (the son of a slave), and his mother into Mack's Cafe, where they beat the old man to the floor. When Jackson's mother tried to stop them, they beat her. When the unarmed Jackson threw himself over her to protect her from the blows, trooper James Bonard Fowler slammed him up against a cigarette machine and shot him twice in the stomach. As troopers beat him on the head with their nightsticks, Jackson staggered out and collapsed bleeding in the street. He died in the hospital, but not before Al Lingo, commander of the state police, arrested him in his hospital bed for attempting to murder a police officer. Jackson had attempted five times to register to vote. State trooper Fowler claimed self-defense, was neither questioned nor charged, and killed another black man in Birmingham the following year.

Decades later Orlando and I flew into Birmingham's Shuttlesworth International Airport and drove to Marion to work on a film for the Southern Poverty Law Center. The little town square was charming, the sort you might discover on a back-road holiday in England; it must have been paradise for a moderately well-off white person in 1950. By 2014 uncontrollable kudzu was closing in on the peaceful little burying ground where Jackson's body lay buried amid wooden crosses, next to the two-lane road from Selma, his granite tombstone pockmarked with bullet holes.

Andy Young told us, "You expected death, you knew it was going to come, but you couldn't let it slow you down, you couldn't." With Jackson's death the political heat in Alabama and Washington rose. On February 23, 1965, thirty-one Republican senators, governors, and congressmen condemned not only the situation in Alabama, but the administration's refusal to announce just when it was going to propose new federal voting legislation. Republican senator Everett Dirksen said, "The time is now." The *New York Times* reported, "Television broadcasts and news accounts of Sheriff James G. Clark's treatment of Negroes seeking to register in Selma has been an element" in decision making.

Back in 1979 Albert Turner had told Orlando and Henry, "We were infuriated to the point where we wanted to carry Jimmie's body to George Wallace and dump it on the steps of the capitol. We had got about like the white folk are." SCLC leaders saw they could finally break the logjam of frustration in Selma. James Bevel proposed marching all the way to the state capitol in Montgomery, fifty-five miles away, to confront Governor George Wallace with a petition. Wallace's racist pandering had, in King's words, "caused these people to feel these acts were aided and abetted by the highest office in the state." It would mirror Gandhi's 1930 march to the sea, which sparked worldwide press coverage and led to the eventual collapse of British colonial control of India.

James Bevel told us, "In a nonviolent movement, if you went back to some of the classical strategies of Gandhi, when you have a great violation of the people and there's a great sense of injury, you have to give people an honorable means and context in which to express and eliminate that grief and speak decisively and succinctly back to the issue. Otherwise your movement will break down in violence and chaos. So agreeing to go to Montgomery was that kind of tool that would absorb a tremendous amount of energy and effort and it would keep the issue of disenfranchisement before the whole nation."

The FBI had uncovered a plot to shoot King at the head of the march, and on Sunday morning, when no one knew his whereabouts, SCLC's Hosea Williams and SNCC's John Lewis prepared to lead, flanked by Bob Mants and Albert Turner. King then called from Atlanta and asked them to call it off, but Hosea protested that six hundred marchers, some children, many carrying bedrolls, were formed up and ready to go. The disciplined column of twos left Brown Chapel Church with a handful of cameramen tagging along, wound through the eerily quiet downtown and up Broad Street onto the Edmund Pettus Bridge.

Cresting the bridge, they descended a hundred yards down to where the highway leveled out. There a line of two hundred helmeted Alabama state troopers, James Bonard Fowler among them, blocked their way. John and Hosea came to a stop at the head of the column, standing quietly as Major John Cloud announced through a bullhorn that the march was illegal, and ordered the marchers to return to their church. "May we have a word with you?" asked Hosea Williams. "There's no word to be had," Cloud replied.

Sheyann Webb, who was eight years old at the time, told us, "As we got closer and closer to the bridge, my eyes began to water, that's just how afraid I was. And I wanted to turn back and I didn't want to turn back. And I said to myself, if they can go, I can go too . . . and I began to just cry. And I remember the ministers who were at the front of the line saying, 'Kneel down to pray.' And I knelt down and I said to myself, Lord, help me."

What happened next is now the stuff of civil rights legend. Bill Cook, one of the *Newsweek* reporters I had seen at work, wrote, "The charge was swift and horrible. Impersonal behind their gas masks, the troopers clubbed their way through the screaming demonstrators. Blue-gray clouds of eye-stinging tear gas were released. When the clouds lifted, I could see the full enormity of the brutality. Hurt and unconscious Negroes lay on the highway shoulder. A trooper walked by and dropped a tear-gas grenade by each fallen Negro. Across the highway, hundreds of white spectators cheered."

Sitting in the church twenty years later, Mrs. Boynton described it to Callie. "And the men came from the right side, from the left side, from in front of us, they came upon us and started beating us with their nightsticks, they started cattle prodding us, they started gassing us. . . . One of the officers came to me, state trooper, and he hit me across the back of my neck . . . he hit me again, and I remember having fallen to the ground. . . . They tried to run the horses over some of them, and the horses would not step on them . . . somebody said, 'She's dead.'"

The image of bestial racism, a tableau of Christian martyrs worthy of Dante or Michelangelo, would flash on televisions throughout the country that night, and again when *Eyes* aired in 1987 and 2016, and would be dramatized in *Selma* in 2014. Here was the massacre of the innocents: Southern sheriffs in their pig-face gas masks gone berserk against African Americans who stood there and took it. It would be a staple in history texts and documentaries, and in 1965 it was a public relations catastrophe for George Wallace's Alabama.

Astonishingly, no one fought back. Henry Hampton had said of nonviolence, "There is no reason why a people oppressed, treated the way African Americans were in this country, should have chosen these extraordinary and unusual weapons to make this change in a country that glorifies violence. It was a miracle: not once over the ten early tumultuous years can you find a documented case of a black killing a white in civil rights demonstrations. It was the perfect working example of a democracy attempting to cleanse itself. . . . I never lost a bet during those years with my production team: 'Find me one case where black Americans in anger killed whites around the issues of civil rights.' It is absolutely astounding."

State troopers chased hundreds of screaming and weeping marchers—those who could still move—back up over the bridge toward town, where Clark and his possemen went after them with bullwhips. The dazed and injured demonstrators sought refuge inside Brown Chapel Church. Wilson Baker, furious, forced Clark's posse and the troopers to withdraw a block back from the church. In the parsonage next door, Medical Committee for Human Rights doctors and nurses from New York set up a triage center.

As the cameras rolled, troopers and possemen spread out into the adjacent George Washington Carver housing project, where enraged citizens finally began throwing rocks and bottles, and the officers began beating everyone they could lay their hands on, marcher or not. On an open phone line to headquarters in Atlanta, SNCC's Willie Emma Scott reported, "We have a problem—the guys are not nonviolent any more. They're ready to fight. About two or three busloads of possemen are in front of the church beating people, throwing tear gas . . . the church is full of tear gas. Broken arms, legs." Like many southerners, black men in the projects owned pistols and hunting rifles. Yet SNCC and SCLC had by then deeply rooted the practicalities of nonviolence in Selma's black community. Months of workshops on nonviolence had done their job.

When we talked to him in 1985, Andy Young explained, "Here were people who were well armed; but we always trained people that the one thing that the police could not deal with was nonviolence. They could deal with violence and all you had to do was for one person to fire a shot, and that gave them an excuse to mow down hundreds of people. And we were very pragmatic and practical about it, and we explained violence . . . as suicidal. And that it required, I think the term that Bevel used to use was, 'a kind of revolutionary patience.'

"You had to talk them down by simply asking questions, 'What kind of gun you got, thirty-two, thirty-eight? You know, how's that going to hold up against the automatic rifles and the twelve-gauge . . . you know how many ten-gauge shotguns that they've got? There are at least two hundred shotguns out there with buckshot in them. You ever see what buckshot does to a deer?' And most of them had. . . . It's one thing to be brutalized by yourself on a dark night when nothing can be done about it, but when you're brutalized together on national television, something in the society is going to change."

I had left Alabama in February 1965, not with a noble bullet wound the way George Orwell had left Spain, but with a bad leg in need of medical care back home, and was at my parents' house in Sacramento drinking a glass of milk when I saw the images on the news that night with the helpless terror of a dream. I recognized John Lewis, whom I had just seen at his desk a couple of weeks before, standing with such quiet dignity, iron willed, his overcoat blowing in the cold wind as the troopers advanced. John had been beaten many times before and he knew exactly what was coming, knew what it was like to be clubbed on the head, but he stood silently with his chin up. I saw him hit the ground, and picked out Mrs. Boynton in the retreating crowd as she went down, disappearing into the gas. When the reporter said that troopers had fractured John's skull, I threw the glass of milk at the television.

George Wallace later told us, "The media has always been unfair to the people of our region of the country. Frankly the media did play it up more than it ought to have been played up because it wasn't all that important, but they always have done that." But Wallace's troopers had bestowed ferocious media leverage that movement leaders themselves could hardly have imagined. Henry Hampton said, "People in Oregon, in California, people in Idaho watched those people on the bridge at Selma, and became *part* of it because they felt the moral force of what people were trying to do."

Joe Smitherman said, "I didn't understand how big it was until I saw it on television . . . that looked like a war. And then . . . the wrath of the nation came down on us." The display of unprovoked savagery had gone so far over the edge that even southern congressmen couldn't take it. In Washington, Texas Democrat senator Ralph Yarborough rose to declare, "Shame on you, George Wallace, for the wet ropes that bruised the muscles, for the bullwhips which cut the flesh, for the clubs that broke the bones, for the tear gas that blinded, burned, and choked into insensibility," and then he began to cry.

CHAPTER SEVENTEEN

A Great Story

1965

In times of great challenge movement leaders would put out a "call to the community of goodwill." So the night of the Bloody Sunday attack, King called on religious leaders to come and "join me in Selma for a ministers' march to Montgomery." SNCC, CORE, and SCLC had learned by then that escalating violence could only be staunched by huge media attention, community solidarity, and immediately saturating the zone with more demonstrators, including northern whites. Hundreds of outraged clergy mobilized.

Henry Hampton was sitting with the Unitarian national board of directors in their annual meeting at headquarters on Beacon Hill when King's telegram arrived. The board promptly adjourned, and with Henry as their spokesman, headed for the airport, ready to bear witness in Alabama.

Henry, Orloff Miller, Bob Hohler, Jack Mendelsohn, Royal Cloyd, James Reeb, and the Unitarian's charismatic eminence grise, six foot three Dana Greeley, "the Liberal Lion," took a night flight and caught a nap in the rental car lounge in Atlanta. They hopped a small plane to Montgomery, where SNCC workers drove them "behind a flatbed truck full of ministers" to Selma for a few hours' sleep. Henry was twenty-four, trim and fit, in his second year as director of information for the Unitarian Universalist Association. By Monday, the Unitarians had forty-five ministers in Selma, joining up with a thousand locals and a thousand other northern ministers, priests, rabbis, nuns, and a few southern whites, ready to put their bodies on the line for racial justice.

Andrew Young called it the "second coming of the Union Army," Judge Hare called them "self-appointed saints," and Mayor Smitherman told us, "Here they came . . . I'm going to be frank with you, some of them were very scummy people . . . and now we had some scummy people trying to stop 'em. We became the march capital of the world. They converge on your city and you see things that you've never seen before . . . you would have a black woman carrying a white baby with a white man, or you'd have a blond-headed white woman with a black man and a black baby. . . . We were trying to handle it peacefully and hope we would wear 'em out and they'd get out of town."

Then liberal federal judge Frank Johnson issued an injunction against marching. King and SCLC had been willing to break state laws and orders across the South—and pay the consequences by going to jail—but not federal laws or injunctions.

As Henry and the others arrived at their quarters in the housing project late that night, an intense all-night meeting was under way across town: SNCC leaders Jim Forman, Stokely Carmichael, and John Lewis argued that the march should go all the way, violating Judge Johnson's order, while SCLC's King and Young argued that it was madness to fly in the face of a federal order.

Jim Forman told us, "We explained to Dr. King that . . . those injunctions should be fought. So consequently we did not feel that there should be any types of deals worked out with Justice. . . . Find out what's the principle and fight for the principle. . . . So we had a meeting from about eleven o'clock to five o'clock that morning where we were trying to lay out to him the necessity to keep his word to the people that the march would *not* be called off. And so about five o'clock he called Robert Kennedy and said that they were gonna go forward with the march. . . ." A hundred and fifty carloads of extra state troopers came in during the night.

So on Tuesday morning, after hours of waiting, Henry, Rev. Reeb, and the other Unitarians joined two thousand marchers forming up for a second attempt to cross the Pettus Bridge. Smartly dressed in suits, ties, and clerical collars, they headed toward the same waiting phalanx of troopers who had savaged the fleeing demonstrators only forty-eight hours before. Walking with effort, his leg in the brace, Henry knew he would not be able to run. If and when they confronted officers at the county line on the other side of the bridge at the site of Sunday's debacle, they would be in violation of Judge Frank Johnson's court order, and the troopers could repeat the Bloody Sunday carnage with complete legality.

"We knew there was going to be a confrontation," remembered Rev. Orloff Miller. They crested the bridge and saw two hundred helmeted troopers arrayed across the highway, daring them to come forward.

When they reached the far side of the bridge, near the spot where Lewis and Hosea Williams had paused the march on Sunday, King stopped and knelt in prayer. Somewhere in the throng stretched out behind them on the bridge was Henry Hampton, but we could never find him in the newsreel footage.

What Henry and those two thousand marchers, hearts pounding, did not know as they moved toward their destiny was that King had sealed a deal just after sunrise in a phone call with Johnson's aide LeRoy Collins. So according to the plan, on cue, they stopped just shy of the county line, knelt to pray, and then sang "We Shall Overcome." Then King and Abernathy turned around and began leading the bewildered marchers, who had come to Selma to see this thing through all the way to George Wallace's doorstep in Montgomery, back toward Brown Chapel Church, still singing the now bitterly ironic song.

Orloff Miller remembers thinking, "Are we not going to go through with this confrontation? What's happening? All of a sudden I realized that the people in front were turning around and coming back and I was aghast. . . . But we were well disciplined, so we turned around too and marched back over that bridge with a terrible sinking feeling. I felt just awful, it wasn't what I had come for."

Slouching back into Selma instead of on to Montgomery, now surrounded by seething SNCC workers and local teenagers, Henry didn't know what to think, but suspected that the moral relativism of national politics had caught up with the raw, principled clarity of the Selma movement. It was then and there that Henry had his epiphany: Someday someone is going to make a great story out of this." And so *Eyes on the Prize* was conceived even before its own story was complete.

That afternoon, March 9, 1965, Henry helped the Unitarians regroup, make some sense of the tactical retreat, and decide what to do next. Rev. Orloff Miller told us, "We never fully understood what had gone on in the negotiations behind the scenes. . . . But we did understand King saying, 'As many of you as can, could you stay a few more days?' Henry tried to convince Rev. Reeb, who had come to Selma over his wife's strong objections, that he had done his job in Alabama and should go home to his family and his pressing work in Roxbury. Reeb changed his mind several times, and then called his wife to say he would stay one more day. He, Miller, and Berkeley, California, minister Clark Olsen walked to Walker's

Cafe in the black section of town, and over dinner discussed their frustration with King for having summoned them all this way for a fizzle and then asking them to stay on. As well, they went over plans for a goodwill college student exchange program with America's Cold War enemy, the Soviet Union.

After supper, Reeb, Miller, and Olsen took a wrong turn into a white neighborhood, and as they passed the Silver Moon Cafe (the only restaurant SNCC had avoided in its sit-ins) a man yelled, "Hey you niggers!" Four whites attacked them with clubs. Olsen looked over just in time to see one land a roundhouse swing with a club on Reeb's head, heard his skull crack, and watched as he fell to the pavement. As the attackers punched Olsen and kicked Miller in the face, one of them yelled, "Now you know what it's like to be a real nigger!" Miller and Olsen managed to get Reeb to the SCLC headquarters at Boynton's Insurance, and finally, in a commandeered hearse, to the black clinic in Birmingham.

The next morning, after a sleepless night, Henry joined a march led by Ralph Abernathy from the church to the courthouse, but Smitherman and Baker blocked them before they got past Sylvan Street. In Washington, D.C., a dozen demonstrators who had snuck into the regular White House tour began a sit-in in the first-floor hallway. Lyndon Johnson was meeting with legislators and National Council of Churches clergy trying to sort out the Selma crisis, when word came that Jim Reeb had died.

King preached his eulogy that night at Brown Chapel Church, with Henry Hampton and virtually every Unitarian minister in America in the pews. "The beast had to strike back. . . . Now our brethren know what it's like to be a Negro in Alabama." President Johnson sent yellow roses, and offered Air Force One to bring Reeb's widow and her husband's body home to Boston. Mississippi senator John Bell Williams rose on the floor of the Senate to declare that Reeb had "found the trouble he was looking for." Sheriff Clark claimed that someone from the civil rights movement had killed Reeb.

Fifteen thousand people attended an ecumenical service in Washington, D.C., and twenty thousand in Boston, and hundreds of demonstrators lay down to block traffic on Pennsylvania Avenue in front of the White House. The Roman Catholic Diocese of Worcester, Massachusetts, proposed sainthood for James Reeb. I joined a picket line with people from our church at the federal courthouse in Sacramento; young

Clayborne Carson did the same in Los Angeles. The death of a northern white clergyman had accomplished what the death of Jimmie Lee Jackson, the young black Alabama deacon, could not.

Stokely Carmichael called it: "What you want is the nation to be upset when anybody is killed . . . but it almost seems that for this to be recognized, a white person must be killed."

With the attack on Reeb, Wilson Baker had had enough, and later that night the feud between Sheriff Clark and Baker escalated to a physical confrontation that "ended only when Mayor Smitherman stepped between the two men's raised fists."

Clark Olsen, fearing that his life was now in danger because he was the only witness who had seen the murderers' faces, got out of state as fast as he could. He returned to testify, but the attackers were acquitted by an all-white jury.

Most everyone in the movement understood the notion of the Social Gospel, but for many the Sermon on the Mount was wearing thin. SNCC leaders were by then disgusted with what they saw as King's capitulation and moved their operations to Montgomery, for a new round of bloody confrontations just blocks from the state capitol. Wallace held firm and unyielding. Eloquent as always, SCLC's King preached, "Selma, Alabama, became a shining moment in the conscience of man. If the worst in American life lurked in its dark streets, the best of American instincts arose passionately from across the nation to overcome it." In stark contrast, across town SNCC's Jim Forman, with a different eloquence and fire in his eyes, snarled to the crowd after being attacked by mounted possemen, "If we can't sit at the table, we'll *knock the fucking legs off*!" When *Eyes on the Prize* was telecast in 1987, this would mark the first time the network ever sent out a program with the word *fucking* to its local stations. In his former self in 1965, Jim had with those fierce words summoned all the raw expression that eluded him in our tortured and deconstructed *Eyes* interview in New York twenty years later.

Then, on March 15, 1964, Lyndon Johnson spoke to a joint session of Congress, invoking the "long-suffering men and women peacefully protested the denial of their rights as Americans. Many of them were brutally assaulted. One good man—a man of God—was killed." In what was certainly the most powerful speech of his presidency, Johnson compared Selma to Lexington and Concord, "a single place to shape a turning point in man's unending search for freedom," and called loud and clear for legislation to outlaw any denial of "the right of any citizen of the United States to vote on account of race or color. . . . Their cause must be our cause too. Because it's not just Negroes, but really it's *all* of us, who must overcome the crippling legacy of bigotry and injustice. And we *shall* overcome!" That white cracker president Lyndon Baines Johnson, son of the segregated South, had come to Jesus in ways that few could have imagined just the year before. It was exactly what SNCC and SCLC and the people of Selma had worked so hard to achieve.

James Bevel told us in 1985, "I think it's classical, in terms of a man rising above being a southerner, being white, and being anything, and just in that moment was *possessed* by the spirit of being a man looking at America, looking at the Constitution, looking at the struggling people." In Boston we had shot an interview with C. T. Vivian upstairs in Orlando's tiny living room, with the smell of Laotian food in the air. C. T. recalled—as he would in countless documentary interviews—the tear rolling down Martin Luther King's check when Lyndon Johnson said, "We shall overcome," on national television in 1965.

But Smitherman said, "Lyndon Johnson came on . . . and said, 'We shall overcome.' And that just like you'd stuck a *dagger* in your heart . . . *what's* this guy *doing*?!?! . . . the South's very patriotic—but it just destroyed everything you'd been fighting for."

Judge Johnson, too, saw footage of the attack on the bridge, and on March 17 reversed his order, allowing the march to Montgomery to go forward, and the movement once again called out the liberal armies. On March 21, King, Young, Forman, Lewis, and a host of labor leaders, celebrities, and clergy (including Catholic nuns from Henry's old diocese in Kansas City) led eight thousand marchers in a third attempt to cross over the bridge, carrying their petition to Wallace. This time—by federal order—there were no Alabama state troopers stopping them, but rather fifteen hundred federalized National Guardsmen and two thousand regular army troops protecting them. A sullen Sheriff Clark stood at the county line and said, "I'm happy to see they go. I wish they would come back and get the rest." A small plane overhead dropped Klan leaflets.

After a week on the road, the column of black and white marchers, swelling to twenty-five thousand, surged, ran, and danced up that final mile to the doorstep of George Wallace's State House in Montgomery. As the governor peered though the blinds at the mass jubilation below, King delivered one of the great speeches of his career: "How long? *Not* long . . .

because truth crushed to earth will *rise* again . . . How long? *Not long . . . because the arc of the moral universe is long, but it bends toward justice!* Glory, hallelujah! Glory, hallelujah! Glory, hallelujah!"

Johnson sent the voting rights bill to Congress the same day.

With the Smitherman interview, our Alabama filming was complete, except the big empty hole where George Wallace should be. We drove back to Montgomery along the route of the final march, through Lowndes County, past the desolate spot where Klansmen killed Unitarian activist Viola Liuzzo, a white mother of five who had been inspired by the death of James Reeb to join the struggle in Selma. On that same road a state trooper had stopped the car containing Henry Hampton and Dana Greeley on their way back to Montgomery and taken them to the police station before sending them on their way. In a stroke of genius after King and the marchers passed through in 1965, Stokely Carmichael had stayed behind here in Lowndes to recruit local people for the original Black Panther Party.

While we were on the road Henry, Llew, and Bobby Shepard had done a fine interview with Coretta Scott King, and editing on the Selma show was already at rough cut.

In October, Tom Layton hosted a fund-raising dinner at his home in San Francisco with sixty foundation people, and there was Henry Hampton showing clips, dazzling them with his stirring pitch. He was clearly tired, and seemed aged from the man I had met only a year before. He came down to our place in the Santa Cruz Mountains for the weekend, enjoying hanging out with the kids, chattering nonstop about his vision for the sequel, *Eyes on the Prize II.* On Sunday he drove down to Pebble Beach and managed to get in eighteen holes of golf with three guys he met on the course, construction executives from Texas, arriving back at our place late that night, aglow.

If you're going to make a documentary about Christ, you'd better interview the Antichrist. George Wallace lacked the pure public malice of a Jim Clark, Bull Connor, or the hooded Klansmen, but his vast enduring popularity and political power made him a far more effective driver of legitimized racial violence.

Henry had been after the Alabama governor ever since the days of *America, We Loved You Madly* back in 1978. Callie and Jim had turned the world upside down for a year trying to get an interview with Wallace, and "All the formal people that you go through to request an interview said, 'No, no, no, no, no, no, no, no, no, and *no!*' Forget it, forget it, forget it, no, no, and *no,*" said Callie.

"But . . . one of the great things about working at Blackside is that so many people had little leads for you, because they wanted us to succeed. . . . It could have been one of the scholars . . . or I may have gotten a lead from the mayor of one of those small towns in Alabama . . . said to me, 'You know, you really should talk to Betty from the symphony. . . . Well, she can get you in . . . she's a big deal with the symphony in Atlanta.'"

Callie called Betty and "I pulled up all of my Tennessee roots and threw them on the phone . . . all of my accent from Memphis . . . said, 'I'm just having the most *horrible* time trying to get to George Wallace. . . . And, you know, of course I *must* talk to Governor Wallace.' She said, 'Well, of *course* you *must.*' She said, 'Well, *certainly,* I can look into that.' The next thing I knew, I got the call from the guy who'd been blocking me, saying, 'It's OK.'"

Back in 1963 Wallace had famously planted himself "in the school-house door" at the University of Alabama, backed by beefy white state troopers. There, mocking national and international opinion, confronting what he saw as federal usurpation of Alabama's rights, he personally stopped the assistant attorney general of the United States from escorting a young black woman and black man on their way to enroll. He was every inch the defiant champion of states' rights, on national prime-time television, chest puffed out, standing up against integration, agitators, Negroes, the federal government, and everything northern.

Rev. Shuttlesworth told us, "George Wallace was like a bantam rooster in a courtyard trying to show how brave he was. At that time you could get publicity by challenging the federal government. . . . The effect of it was like a feisty dog barking at the sun trying to keep it from shining." In fact, few people that day noticed that Bobby Kennedy's assistant Nick Katzenbach quietly escorted the students in the back door a few hours later, as planned all along, after indulging Wallace in his show of rebellion.

By the time we got to Governor Wallace he was slouching toward the finale of one of the most bizarre arcs in American politics. He began civic life as a staunch populist, in the mold of Huey Long, a liberal defending the little guys against the big guys, the first judge in Barbour County,

Alabama, to insist that white attorneys address black attorneys as "Mister." The NAACP endorsed Wallace in his first run for governor in 1958, prompting his landslide defeat at the hands of the fiercely unapologetic white supremacist John Patterson. The vanquished Wallace then made his deal with the devil of race, declaring, "I will never be out-niggered again." And so began his two-decade rampage of incendiary pandering racism, sometimes as a master politician, often as an insolent demagogue, the personification of southern resistance, and for most northerners the emblem of concentrated evil posturing as politics.

Henry felt we could in a way position Jim Clark and Bull Connor as fringe crazies, but by 1968 Wallace's snarling rhetoric won him ten million votes in the presidential primaries, and he carried five southern states in his fourth run for president. As American politics became ever more unglued in the late 1960s, Wallace dared to tell his political base of working-class whites directly and clearly that they were under attack by beatniks, "little pinkos," and elitist race mixers.

We interviewed him on March 10, 1986, in the last lap of his final term as governor, eighteen years after a would-be assassin shot him five times. But he was gunned down for no particular political reason by the young unhinged Arthur Bremer, who wanted to impress his sixteen-year-old girlfriend with "a statement of my manhood." The assassination attempt left Wallace a paraplegic, wheelchair-bound, in constant pain, and in John Fleming's words, "oozing remorse."

Waiting in a State House anteroom for him to appear, his bodyguards chatted with us about how much they loved public television. (In my experience, all bodyguards love public television: Andy Young's in New York, Hamid Karzai's in Kabul, Jerry Brown's in California.) For an instant, when two plainclothes state troopers wheeled him into the room, I though it was a mannequin; the real George Wallace was detained elsewhere on important business, but we could set up our lights on the dummy before the busy man himself rolled in front of the camera. Could this sickly old creature possibly be governing Alabama? Could this possibly be the fire-breathing bully who unleashed so much pain and terror back in the day?

His beefy, black press aide bent over him in his wheelchair, shouting into the governor's less deaf ear, introducing Mike Chin, Callie Crossley, and me. Facing Wallace on that day in 1986 were a Chinese American activist camera assistant, a clear-thinking young black woman producer, and a former civil rights worker. We had come, in essence, to ask why he had unleashed all that racist rhetoric that got so many people killed, injured, and jailed twenty years before.

We will never know what George Wallace thought—slumped there waxy and shrunken, trapped in his useless, bullet-ridden old body, struggling to form words, with the great seal of the State of Alabama looming behind him, at the mercy of all these hectoring elitist race mixers from Boston. He may have thought he had died and gone to hell.

He had declared himself a born-again Christian ten years after Selma, had come to Jesus after "five bullets gave me a thorn in the flesh, according to the Apostle Paul," and apologized to civil rights leaders. By most accounts his reversal on race was genuine, but Callie wasn't buying it. John Lewis said his old enemy Wallace had picked up the phone and, "like confessing to a priest, poured out his heart and soul . . . he said, 'I was wrong . . . I don't hate anybody.'" And so unfolded a surreal final chapter, in which George Wallace chummed up and apologized to the very people he had scorned and brutalized. He built schools for blacks, appointed more blacks to state government than any leader in the history of Alabama. Andy Young had told us, "George Wallace, I think, was an opportunist and a charlatan who I think, frankly, did undergo some level of repentance after his own suffering." But today, there would be no baring of the soul, no deathbed contrition.

Callie recalled it: "We get settled, and we sit down, but nobody really explained to me how hard of hearing he was. So I asked the first question . . . background on *Plessy v. Ferguson,* blah-blah-blah, all the richness of it, and he goes: 'HUH?'

"And now, as I think back on it, maybe the guy that kept blocking the interview was not blocking it so much for content, as he understood that he wasn't going to be able to hear me well, and there was going to be like a big tragicomedy."

Conscious now of how loud she would have to talk, Callie dove into her interview questions, thundering, "GOVERNOR WALLACE!!! AS A BACKDROP TO OUR UNDERSTANDING OF THE SOUTHERN SYSTEM OF SEGREGATION, I WONDER IF YOU COULD GIVE US A LAYMAN'S EXPLANATION OF *PLESSY V. FERGUSON,* WHICH WAS THE LEGAL BASIS FOR THAT SYSTEM?!?!?" My chair vibrated. Hard of hearing myself, I let loose a cruel chuckle.

Wallace responded, "It was just that the great mass of people, of white people, felt it was the best interest of both races, it was not an antagonism toward black people, and that's what some people can't understand."

It was our policy at Blackside to really let people themselves explain their own positions, whatever they were. Callie asked Wallace about states' rights. He responded, "All you gotta do is read the constitution of the nation . . . the Tenth Amendment says that 'all power not especially delegated to the federal government is left to the states, or the people respectively of the states'; that's the substance what it says. Well, they had a right to . . . determine the qualifications of attendance of school, and that had been so in a prior Supreme Court decision. But in the long run, that decision was wrong because integration must come . . . segregation could not last and it shouldn't have lasted. . . . it wasn't a segregation issue, it was a usurpation issue."

But he was charming and gracious, and gave us a decent interview, hemming and hawing on many questions, reminding us many times that it was black voters who got him reelected for a fourth term in 1982, attributing his long-ago positions on segregation to states' rights, not racism. It sounded high-minded, but it had been racist code. The logo of the Alabama Democratic Party up until 1966 was a banner emblazoned with "White Supremacy" above a white rooster (Stokely called it "a white cock"). Like some other reformed segregationists we spoke to, he led with anecdotes about how much black people now loved him, about how much he has done for black people, about his old black friends and his new black friends. He showed us the red leather-bound honorary degree from Tuskegee, a black college, gruffly acknowledging the irony of it all.

Speaking about his own rhetoric: "I never made any statement that offended black people, unless I said in those days I was for segregation. I never made any statement about inferiority or that sort. . . . I was born and raised among black people and they're my friends . . . if I had said anything that the Eastern press said I did, and did, no self-respecting black would ever have voted me, for a hundred years; yet I won ninety-five percent of the black vote in the last election in Alabama. I love black people, I love white people, I love yellow people . . ."

As Callie navigated him through an hour of discussion about states' rights, segregation, and the attack on the Pettus Bridge, George Wallace— ever the on-message politician—found opportunities to bring up his Tuskegee degree four more times, at one point asking Callie, "Do *you* have an honorary degree from Tuskegee Institute?" To which he himself responded, "*I* have an honorary doctorate degree from Tuskegee Institute."

On voting in Alabama in the 1960s: "Yes, black people were allowed to vote except they had to be able to read and write your name and some of the other things before that really kept blacks from voting. . . . But yes, there were some discriminatory measures passed by other folks regarding voting, not by myself."

Our advisors and nearly all historians believed that he had deliberately failed to block the violence on Bloody Sunday, regretting it only later. Wallace remembered his orders to Colonel Al Lingo, commander of the state police on Bloody Sunday: "I do know that I gave orders not to let what happened at the bridge there . . . do nothing that would stir up any trouble there, just don't let anybody attempt to hurt anyone. . . . It enraged me because I didn't intend for it to happen that way. I said, 'For goodness' sakes don't let anybody do anything to cause any disturbance or violence.' Now this thing when it happened at the bridge in my judgment was just something that happened. There was no violence, beating people down and putting them in the hospital, not a single person was injured in that march . . . they were trying to keep them getting through because they were afraid something might happen." He claimed at least a dozen times that back then "relationships were very fine between black and white." Really?

We took snapshots and George Wallace graciously autographed an 8x10 glossy photo of himself, "Best Wishes to Henry Hampton." Callie was morose in the car afterward. "He was as revisionist as he could be. . . . But it was the best we could do. I think we all had that peculiar feeling you have the day after a big final exam, when you expect to be exploding with elation at having finished, but it's just another day."

I thought for sure Wallace had given us his last interview, if not his last breath, that he would die before we left the building, but he fought on for another ten years. In his last decade, the governor agreed to many more interviews about his actions in the movement days. Even after he had lost the power of speech, he made a reptilian, silent appearance in Paul Stekler, Steve Fayer, and Dan McCabe's sweeping masterpiece, *George Wallace: Settin' the Woods on Fire,* and silently smoked a cigar for Spike Lee's riveting *4 Little Girls.* By then he had declined badly, and his presence on Spike's screen is simply ghoulish—by design, I suspect.

With Wallace in the can, there was nothing left for us to shoot.

......

Everyone knew that Henry had a "peculiar drawn-out way of closure." Sometimes Hampton would spend a day preaching quick wrap-up with a team and then he'd say "No."

Ricky Leacock gave Chuck Scott a big hug after the Selma fine cut, but the final week was a nightmare. Vecchione wrote me in California, "Morale is for shit around here." Nina and I canceled our twentieth-anniversary vacation; I flew to Boston and directly into a crisis meeting with Judith. We managed to lock the narration words on her school desegregation film on schedule—elated—and were all walking on air when Henry blew a "big fucking hole in the hug fest" by announcing that, actually, he wasn't satisfied with how Judith had handled the national context of the story. That triggered the first of many sour fights that week between Hampton and Vecchione, culminating in her flying into a rage over—you guessed it—Henry's suggestions for yet another adjustment in the Till chronology. She accused him of turning her film into "a dog's breakfast" and stormed out of the building shaking and crying, finally after all these months fully defeated by his dogged refusal to let go of the story, and her suspicion that we were all conspiring to take control of her film. Orlando and I ran out of the building and tried to calm and comfort her, but she drove off. You could cut the air with a knife.

I went to the ground floor and spent six hours fine-tuning the Freedom Rides show with Orlando, Prue, and Jeanne in their editing room under the watchful eye of Virginia Woolf. By then Judith had returned, and a few hours later Henry and I trudged up four flights of stairs to face the hasty recut that she and Dan had done on Till. Henry, still not pleased, made a few comments until Judith once again savaged him and he—you guessed it—walked out of the room. It was probably the right thing to do, because if he hadn't they would have been throwing chairs at each other. A bit later I met him in the Selma editing room and we set to work mopping up the final lock on those two deferred lines of narration.

Series writer Steve Fayer's professional calm helped, and his narration memos are a testament to the writer's craft: "Use solid nouns, simple declarative sentences. Pg 32 opening sentence—too involved, and it is all prepositions. Sort out characters . . . drop dependent clauses . . . tell me why whites don't want blacks to vote in Selma . . . do you have to say 'night' when Valeriani says it for you . . . the seven lines are not working for you, target for half the length, mention John Lewis's name only once. . . . Is this line necessary . . . is this line necessary? 'In a meeting with President Johnson, Gov Wallace used the issue of protection to illustrate federal intervention in a state issue.' I have the feeling many viewers would have a tough time figuring that one out on the printed page."

My job now as series producer was to enforce the latest cease-fire. Judith said, "Henry and I were ready to kill each other by the end." But wonder of wonders, Judith had completed finishing touches on the spectacular 6-minute opening for the whole series, an eloquent, tightly constructed prologue you could not take your eyes off . . . flags, kids, tears, marches, songs, songs, songs. It was sheer genius, at once a tease for what was to come over the next six hours and a complete intense telling of the whole civil rights story in miniature. And through it all Judith churned out clear-thinking memos packed with schedule and postproduction details. When did this woman sleep?

We had long argued over who would narrate the series. I sent memos advocating for a woman. Henry from the start wanted Julian Bond, who had done the on-camera commentary in the original 1979 project. Julian and I had become friends in 1965, both of us flourishing in the camaraderie of SNCC's Atlanta office, and had corresponded and visited over the years after I left Georgia. He was prep school educated, urbane, funny as hell, and like Hampton came from a life of privilege in the segregated South. They were about the same age, and he, too, had been rattled as a teenager by the news of Emmett Till's murder, saying, "I felt vulnerable for the first time in my life. This could easily have been me."

Julian told me that when *Eyes* reinvented itself in 1985, Henry told him, "You can be in it or you can narrate it, but not both, you choose. I told him I'd rather be in every show as a narrator."

Bond was a fine poet blessed with a fine voice, a natural for the job, but I thought he was far too loaded down with progressive political baggage for the middle-American audience Henry was after, and he might be a lightning rod for right-wing criticism. Julian had been a full-time paid SNCC leader, and the Georgia state legislature had refused to seat him after he was elected in 1966 because he publicly opposed the Vietnam War and had refused to ban Communists from SNCC. He was at that moment in 1986 just beginning a bitter high-profile election campaign for the House of Representatives against his former SNCC colleague John Lewis. I worried that *Eyes* would sacrifice its hard-won journalistic evenhandedness by putting a partisan in the pulpit, and asked Hampton if it would be appropriate for Lyndon Johnson's press secretary to narrate a film about Vietnam.

Henry insisted on Julian, and once again, I was wrong and he was right. As history would show, Bond did a magnificent reading of the *Eyes* narration in his industrial-strength velvet voice. In his unhurried way he nailed it because he knew *exactly* what each word meant. And as far as I know not an eyebrow was raised or a single criticism made because *Eyes on the Prize* was narrated by a civil rights activist.

Overages had pushed the budget up and up, and by the end it would top 2.5 million, nearly twice the original estimate.

The deadline was upon us. Orlando's safe-house apartment on the fifth floor was full, so I brought a sleeping bag and slept on the floor of Henry's office. Everyone was running on empty. In the car on the way to pick up his dry cleaning late one evening, I joked he needed a servant. He said, "I need a wife."

With editorial threads still loose in each of the six films, I proposed we end it like a labor negotiation, sweat-lodge style. Each team would go into an edit room with Henry, Fayer, me, and Judith, have pizza sent in, force the final nipping and tucking, and not quit until every single image and sound was locked. The longest session—"The Selma Death March"—went twenty-one hours, stalled by debate over how to position news film of Sheriff Clark decking Rev. Vivian. Henry locked the Till/Montgomery film, which must have been hard. Finally, knowing perhaps that he himself was actually incapable of declaring the final film actually finished, Henry ordered *me* to order *him* to declare Orlando's Mississippi show locked. As we walked out of that final picture-locking session on July 25, 1986, someone exclaimed, "Free at last! Free at last! Thank God Almighty, we are free at last!"

Henry took me to Logan Airport, driving fast with skill and confidence. I got home at 3 A.M. and told Nina, "I think it's over."

Weighed against great sea changes in modern history, the classic American civil rights movement achieved tremendous goals in an extremely short time with very low casualties compared to wars: about a hundred deaths directly caused by civil rights activism compared to tens of millions in World War I, World War II, and the American and Spanish civil wars. Compare the 4 young men arrested in America's first sit-in in

Greensboro, North Carolina, in 1960 with the 70 blacks killed and 180 wounded in South Africa's Sharpeville Massacre only a month later. Compare a thousand synagogues burned down on Kristallnacht in Nazi Germany in a single night in 1938 with about four hundred churches bombed or burned during the entire ten years of the civil rights movement.

Our *Eyes* capstone was Lyndon Johnson's signing of the Voting Rights Act on August 6, 1965, five months after Bloody Sunday, with Amelia Boynton at his side. It prohibited literacy tests, placed federal referees and monitors in places with clear practices of disenfranchisement like Dallas County, Alabama, and Neshoba County, Mississippi, and gave the Department of Justice the responsibility for enrolling black voters. The question "Who's in charge?" was answered. The significance of Selma to Henry's television series and to the history of the nation rested on this notion: the legal affirmation of full citizenship for all Americans, enforced by the federal government. It was as simple as that.

The Voting Rights Act was a triumph of the classic civil rights movement. It was a response, the Supreme Court said, to "an insidious and pervasive evil which had been perpetuated in certain parts of our country through unremitting and ingenious defiance of the Constitution." And in the decades to come, it gave African Americans political power that simple desegregation never could. Black voter registration in Mississippi jumped sevenfold the next three years. And never again could blacks be excluded from a southern jury because of their race, as they had in the Till trial. Henry said, "The civil rights movement was a miracle. One of the great models for the world."

But as it turned out, the battle of Selma would not end the struggle for racial equity, and passage of the Voting Rights Act of 1965 would not stop voting discrimination in America. We had little reason to suspect or notice in '65 when shortly after the VRA's passage, determined conservative organizers began a methodical forty-year campaign to gut it, culminating, for the moment, in 2012 when the Supreme Court struck down one key provision of the law in *Shelby County v. Holder.* The ceaseless contention continues to this day, as increasing numbers of black citizens find their right to vote diminished by newly enacted voter I.D. laws, purges of voting rolls, and polling place irregularities.

Longstanding inequity and de facto segregation in education, housing, and employment and police violence against blacks exploded in the Watts section of Los Angeles only two weeks after Johnson signed the

Voting Rights Act. That posed an immense problem for *Eyes on the Prize*. On public television in 1985, the rush to redemptive endings at all costs was in full swing, and Henry certainly did not want to squander his one shot at making tens of millions of Americans feel good and proud about race, if only for one evening.

He knew it would be dishonest to put a happy face on the harsh realities and messy history of 1965. As we had stood in front of the Dallas County Courthouse back then, he and I could both sense the ominous winds blowing far from Selma: a fatal fracturing of the civil rights movement; droning segregation and exploding violence in northern cities; drugs anesthetizing alienated young people, black and white; deep systemic racism that could not be rooted out with pictures of whites and blacks holding hands in Selma. And some of those same young black men who marched for freedom from Selma to Montgomery, some of those young white soldiers who protected them and draft-age thugs who taunted them would soon ship out together to Vietnam, along with Alabama state trooper James Bonard Fowler. Henry wrote, "We regrouped and went on to fight and win a monumental battle to end a bad war, but our chance to transform this society into one based on true equity was lost for the moment and for us. We entered a different time." The last line of narration in *Eyes on the Prize* is this: "In the euphoria of the moment no one could know that the civil rights movement would never again be the same. The fragile coalition that had shaped the movement for so long was coming to an end."

So television viewers in 1987 would have to take the triumph at Selma with a lump in the throat. With the unanimous agreement of Henry and the staff, Jim and Callie pinned two one-sentence epilogues to the end of the Selma show, one noting the murder of Viola Liuzzo after the glorious rally in Montgomery, and a second showing newsreels of Watts in flames.

A year after we wrapped it all up, the Selma *Eyes on the Prize* episode would go on to win an Oscar nomination for Callie and Jim, whom Henry had trusted with the story even though she had never made a documentary and he had known nothing about the movement. (Callie would be forever grateful, especially when they walked down the red carpet at the Academy Awards two years later, that her producing partner Jim had been wise in the ways of awards rules, and insisted to Henry that they both have a "producer" credit rather than "coproducer.")

On April 12, 1988, in the luxury-equipped stretch limo driving us all down Hollywood Boulevard on the way to the Academy Awards, someone slipped a tape into the VHS player, and up popped George Wallace proclaiming: "Segregation now! Segregation tomorrow! Segregation forever!" I had never seen Henry Hampton laugh so hard.

CHAPTER EIGHTEEN

A Great Healing Machine

1987

What Henry Hampton had achieved was heroic, lasting, and beautiful.

When Louis Massiah, who would later become a key producer at Blackside, saw a work-in-progress preview of *Eyes* at the Flaherty Film Seminar in 1986, he wrote that he had seen "a great healing medicine that was being created in Boston. . . . The film had woven testimony and images of another time to affirm an experience that had shaped so many of us directly and indirectly, an experience that was being neglected, twisted, or denied." For years I misread the lines, and thought Massiah had written, "a great healing *machine*," which for me conjured up a different but equally appealing achievement.

Eyes on the Prize: America's Civil Rights Years finally premiered theatrically on the big screen at New York's Public Theater on November 8, 1986, and then, with support from Sandy Heberer, Barry Chase, and a few other resolute PBS executives, on nationwide prime-time broadcast in February 1987. Critic Walter Goodman wrote in the *New York Times,* "The nobility of America's civil-rights struggle comes through with the directness and strength of a spiritual. . . . The battle shown here is between oppressors and oppressed, between brute force and steadfast endurance, until the legal, physical and moral weight of the Federal Government brings victory."

By year's end, the series would reach twenty million Americans, and was headed for a hundred million more viewers worldwide. It won six Emmys, including one long overdue to Fayer for writing, and the Oscar nomination for Callie and Jim. (Many Blacksiders scratched their heads about Academy Award rules under which Henry himself was not nominated.) It won the prestigious duPont-Columbia, Polk, and Peabody awards, was named *TV Guide*'s "Best Documentary of the Year" and the Television

Critics Association's "Program of the Year," earned a spot on *Time* magazine's "Ten Best of the Decade," and was quickly adopted by the New York
City Board of Education and many school districts across the country for
wide curriculum use. Used in nearly half of America's colleges, it would
before long become the country's main source of education about the
civil rights movement. Soon a telecourse, VHS and laser disc sales to the
home video market actually began bringing in some money.

The reviews were stunning. Writing in the *Hollywood Reporter,* Arthur Barron called it "glorious . . . a vivid penetrating examination of the
civil rights movement in this country . . . in a cool but compassionate way,
this series chronicles how the civil rights movement grew in stature and
purpose, a social cause not just for the dignity of one people but for the
decency of all." The painstaking effort to reflect more than one viewpoint
was not lost on critics, who praised the "refusal to sentimentalize the civil
rights movement, refusal to focus exclusively on the achievements of
iconic black leaders, and refusal to overlook dissension within the movement." In the *Washington Post,* Tom Shales wrote, "'Eyes on the Prize' is
not only bound for glory, it gets there in a hurry."

The southern press weighed in. The *Dallas Times Herald* wrote, "everything a TV documentary should be . . . balanced, powerful. . . . I cannot
remember learning more from any television program." The *Atlanta Constitution* said, "An excellent piece of historical journalism . . . evenhanded. . . . The series' true strength is in its sense of history . . . a history
lesson well worth learning."

Geoffrey C. Ward, in his *American Heritage* review, wrote, "Defeated
white opponents are heard from along with civil rights workers who over-
came and outwitted them. Nor does the series ignore the genuine contribution made by white participants. . . . It does not flinch, either, from the
conflicts over tactics and clashes of generation and personality that inevitably made the Movement's tasks more difficult."

Louis Massiah wrote, "I have this image of Henry Hampton, Moses-
like, carrying the sacred tablets containing the lessons of the civil rights
movement to a nation that had been seduced by the golden calf of the
Reagan era." And Louis joined others in seeing that Henry's achievement
was not simply in rescuing long-neglected content: "Sometimes I think
that our hunger for the history contained in *Eyes* has made us slow to appreciate that one of the greatest gifts of Blackside is the style engineered
by Henry and others who've been instrumental in shaping the Blackside

sensibility." In their attention to the very subject matter of *Eyes on the Prize,* most critics and probably most viewers understandably missed one of its greatest accomplishments: a subtle change in the form of prime-time documentary television, pushing ordinary people to the forefront of their own story.

Though complaints may have come to local PBS stations, I could find no record of anyone ever being able to nail *Eyes on the Prize* for factual inaccuracy. The only negative comment I could locate in the archive was from Bishop James Dees of the Anglican Orthodox Church in North Carolina, complaining about Orlando's Mississippi program. "I do not consider this program to be in any way indicative of the feelings of the South generally towards our colored brethren, and I resent it vehemently." PBS vice president Barry Chase wrote back immediately, challenging the bishop to "support your charges with at least one reference to a misstatement, overstatement, or misrepresentation of fact in the program you attack. . . . It will withstand the most searching scrutiny."

Henry was dismayed that some reviews mistakenly said his documentaries were based on the book by Juan Williams, rather than the other way around.

We were all proud and a little surprised at the accolades, and the past year's blood on the floor began to fade away in a haze of relief that it may have been worth all that trouble. Henry could now, at last, bask in affirmation of his brash impractical conviction: a mass audience would sit still for a well-told television history, even if it was messy, and even if it was mostly about unknown black people, and then ask for more. He had made a series in which the ordinary people of the movement carried the day, and in which none of the emotional power was not earned.

In triumph, the offices at 486 Shawmut Avenue at last grew calm. Henry headed off to vacation in Nepal.

He had by 1988 become a bit of a national celebrity, and everyone wanted a piece of him—Oprah, the *New Yorker,* the NAACP, Oliver Stone, the newly installed Bush White House, Hollywood. When Henry got his well-earned session with Terry Gross on *Fresh Air,* he led by talking eloquently about Emmett Till. Lynne Cheney and the long-suffering Romas Slezas sent congratulations, and Henry got a big hug from Rosa Parks.

He was at last a happy warrior. I was overjoyed for him. In a culture that often could not help itself from rewarding the wrong people for the wrong reasons, I felt that justice had finally kicked in for this warm, stubborn, and most brilliant of men.

It was also a triumph for public broadcasting. The brass at WGBH were apparently caught by surprise and astounded at the success of *Eyes,* a program for which Henry felt they had shown only tepid interest at the start when he really needed support.

And in December 1987, *Flying* magazine published a glowing profile, with a striking photo of Hampton next to his airplane, looking for all the world like a steely action hero.

Bill Cosby, perhaps the most popular black man in America in 1989, sought out Henry and thanked him for reclaiming stolen and forgotten history. Cosby told me that Henry had set right the problem, that "*Eyes on the Prize* was more than a documentary. The fictionalizers of history will have us forgotten. . . . The story had been in the hands of the racists . . . the need for the slaver to extricate the truth from the slave . . . to erase the truth. Not all of this was beatings and hanging, but what white people have eradicated from history." Henry soon became friends with Bill, who called him often after-hours at the office, just to talk, and invited him to the set of *The Cosby Show* in New York.

Henry had just turned forty-eight, president of his now twenty-year-old company, and president of the Museum of African American History in Boston, which could have been a full-time job in itself. Soon he was developing a dramatic miniseries about Selma with Cosby. The building on Shawmut Avenue may have grown quiet for a moment, but Henry jammed his enterprise into high gear, chasing that first hit, not wanting to waste an ounce of social capital.

And so began a ten-year explosion of projects: *Eyes on the Prize II: America at the Racial Crossroads;* films about Africa, minority scientists, the African American Church; Orlando Bagwell's stunning portrait of Malcolm X. And to show the world Blackside was not just black, a strong multipart series about the Great Depression and another about the War on Poverty.

He hired a personal organizational specialist to help impose rational forward motion on it all, but in all those years I worked with Henry, he could never get ahead of his own enterprise. At Blackside we were constantly racing to catch up with everything, including Henry. He began keeping a diary, but after a few weeks apparently couldn't find the time to continue it.

Now a national go-to guy on race, he was quickly swept up in the controversy surrounding *Mississippi Burning,* a 1988 popular Hollywood feature film that reduced the 1964 Freedom Summer to a crime thriller in which white FBI agents liberated black Mississippians, who were themselves reduced to little more than sad-song-singing victims. In a letter to me he said, "I grow angry about the manipulation of history and the culture it reflects. I should do something, shouldn't I?" The film shrinks Dave Dennis's explosive cry for power to a polite mumble quickly drowned out by a swelling Hollywood score. Whites have 95 percent of the dialogue, and the only individualized black character in the film is an FBI agent. (The FBI had not a single black field agent in 1964.) It perpetuated *exactly* the media whitewashing we had worked so hard to counter in *Eyes.* Henry and many others, including Bernice Reagon, who refused to do music for the film, expressed anger that *Mississippi Burning* gave not an ounce of credit to the courage, smarts, resolve, and agency of black Mississippians.

Henry felt a duty to fill space and time with good work. His older sister, Veva, psychiatrist and mother of two, had just become dean at New York University's medical school, the first woman and first African American ever to hold the post. "And my younger sister is an executive with Mobil Oil in New York. Both of them feel some responsibility, but I'm a bachelor and I don't have a family demanding my time." So he devoted sixteen hours a day to the African America film enterprise.

Back during the frantic days of *Eyes I* fund-raising in 1984, Henry's proposal and sample reel had come across the desk of PBS executive Suzanne Weil, who thought it was "the most brilliant thing I've ever seen before or since," and told her colleagues, "I don't know who this guy is, but give him everything he wants."

In 1988, at a public television conference after the release, Sue, recently widowed, again bumped into Henry. They struck up a conversation, and before the day was out were headed for their first date. "He said, 'We could go to this new Thai place, or we could take my plane and fly out to the Cape for lobster.'" Off to Cape Cod they flew, Henry at the controls of the Cessna, each of them telling their life story.

And so began a very close relationship that would last nearly ten years. They were exceedingly discreet; few around Blackside knew they were a couple, and I don't ever remember seeing Sue at the office. She was coordinator of performing arts at the Walker Art Center in Minneapolis, where she took Henry backstage at *Prairie Home Companion* to meet her friend Garrison Keillor. She was at the same time directing the Arts and Culture program at PBS, so they saw each other on weekends and she occasionally stayed at 88 Lambert. But mostly they flew or drove out of Boston in his Jeep, picked up a Big Mac, and cruised up to his little house in Lyman, New Hampshire, driving a snowmobile up the final hill, to escape their turbo-drive lives and constant deadlines. Sue remembers the neighbors: "Fred and Rose lived at the bottom of the hill, and were a little puzzled at the situation—a black man and a white woman. Henry was the only black person for miles around. . . . We spent weeks there—he was in heaven. We cooked. He *really* relaxed. Most of all, he took a lot of naps."

We all knew he got out of Dodge on the weekend, but that was about it. Looking back now at Sue's snapshots of their time in New Hampshire, I see a completely relaxed, unplugged, and unwound Henry whom hardly anyone ever knew, lounging in his pajamas, reading a novel—off the clock in a way that was unimaginable for those who worked with him. He and Sue looked for all the world like a couple of carefree newlyweds, relaxing in the warm, sunlit kitchen, a vase of flowers on the table. Judi and Veva liked Sue, and they all spent family holidays together, with "lots of pies." They exchanged heartfelt love notes when they were apart. And over those years Sue and Henry traveled together on long trips to India, Nepal, Portugal, and Costa Rica.

I spent hugely enjoyable evenings with them over long dinners, but never really understood until years later how happy they were together, or how important they were to each other. For all the warmth, they felt they had to keep their relationship cloaked in shadow, certainly from coworkers. "The black women didn't like me. Black/white was bad enough, and then there was the whole business of blacks and Jews. . . . We kept it discreet . . . there was also the business of a conflict of interest because I was a mogul at PBS and we were funding him."

During his life, Henry had many serious girlfriends, both black and white, most of them strong, confident executives, but he never married.

He and Sue never talked about marriage, never considered it, though Sue says, "He should have had kids." Blackside was his life.

He said that *Eyes I* had taken him "to the porch of the old folks' home." But now all eyes were on Henry Hampton, the documentary tycoon of the moment, expecting the next big thing.

Even before the premiere of *Eyes,* Henry had begun development work on *Eyes on the Prize II.* He expressed at times that he didn't want to tackle the post-1965 "bad movement"; it wasn't really his period and he didn't really like it. But in the wake of *Eyes I*'s success, who other than Henry Hampton could have picked up the essential thread of history?

He said, "Now a wise man would have stopped, gone home, and decided not to take the history beyond '65 because everybody warns, 'Oh boy, you're getting into rough stuff now.' . . . But you cannot stop, because in one sense all that history before was an anomaly." He said that the original *Eyes on the Prize* "covered a period for which historians have had a chance to apply all the filters, and there is very little doubt about what was going on. *Eyes on the Prize II: America at the Racial Crossroads,* on the other hand, deals with matters that are less straightforward."

By 1965 black liberation was not complete, Martin Luther King had more than one speech in him, and history did not stop in that glowing moment when voting rights and equal treatment under the law seemed to have been won. Years later, in his commencement address at Washington University in 1989, Henry, ever-optimistic guardian of the dark view, said, "The events at the bridge at Selma marked our first victory—and the beginning of the end. We had dismantled in . . . an eyeblink in historic time a system of apartheid that had prospered for centuries. And in a sense one could make the argument, as outrageous as it would be for a people who had been here from the beginning and whose labor had been used to create the great American fortunes, that we were immigrants in our own land, free for the first time to compete without the shackles of legalized segregation. It was a moment of exuberance and promise—not unlike today—and it was lost."

The *New York Times* reported the possibility of a sequel to *Eyes.* "The stalling of the civil-rights movement in the 1980's was 'one of the great crimes of our century,' Mr. Hampton said. . . . 'Many of the issues, such as poverty and homelessness, that preoccupy America today . . . were problems that the movement tried to eradicate but failed.'" Strong words for such a sanguine fellow.

Times had changed in the years since Johnson signed the voting rights bill, fearing he had "delivered the South to the Republican Party for a long time to come," which, of course, he had. In 1968, Richard Nixon shrewdly welcomed the former slave states into the party of Lincoln. Ronald Reagan had in 1980 vowed "to restore to the states and local communities those functions which properly belong there." (Like racial segregation?) George H. W. Bush deployed his infamous Willie Horton commercial featuring a black rapist during his successful 1988 campaign.

When we were making *Eyes I,* the rights and wrongs had seemed so beautifully simple, especially for white viewers. "Mosaic and conciliatory," Henry said. Now the steely gaze of Malcolm X edged out doe-eyed Rosa Parks, the Black Panthers' guns trumped prayer vigils, power displaced persuasion. With *Eyes on the Prize II,* Hampton would introduce a more rich and unruly cast of characters, some threatening both to whites and to many blacks in a way that Martin Luther King never could be. Henry himself was often uncomfortable with militancy, but now explored black nationalism, affirmative action, black incarceration, wage and wealth inequality, northern segregation, the underclass, urban rebellions, the rampaging war in Southeast Asia, and the nationwide rage of 1968.

He was about to tackle "Vanguard movements . . . like the Black Panther Party . . . things that shot across this landscape like shooting stars. For many blacks, there are moments of personal recognition in the sequel," he continued. "They will remember when people stopped saying 'Negro' and went to 'black.' Whites will remember the riots and fear at hearing 'black power.' The experience can't allow them to look beyond that and see some of the marvelous things that happened." Sometime around this historical moment in the early 1990s when we were beginning *Eyes II,* the American national conversation adopted the term "African American." (Henry asked, "Why now?") I sensed another page had turned when white people talking with other white people began saying "African American" instead of "black."

Churches, community organizations, and even Henry's relatives gave what they could for the new series, but a hundred corporations and corporate foundations turned him down. Even though, as Judy Richardson said, "He was one of the few black people in public broadcasting that people would listen to," his celebrity was not enough. He said, "I got suckered by my own enthusiasm." The proposed total budget swelled to $6.2 million and would rise further. Tom Shales wrote in the *Washington Post*, "The first 'Eyes on the Prize' was considered a major miracle, and producer Henry Hampton the major miracle worker. . . . Considering that the first series was a triumph in every conceivable way, it's strange that Hampton couldn't have just been given a big fat grant by PBS to produce the sequel."

Hampton could be conservative in predicting viewers' tastes and tolerance, but he never sanitized his proposals for the sake of funding. Corporate funders who had shunned the original series were even less interested in putting their company logos on urban rebellions, assassinations, prison riots, and busing. Barry Chase at PBS told me, "Henry was not an angry black man," but surely potential sponsors saw in the "angrier" *Eyes II* a grim ride without the resolution and redemption that audiences and critics had found so appealing in the original *Eyes I*. Henry said, "No one ever says, 'Malcolm X? No way!' The reality is, you never know why. There were some companies that said they'd like to sponsor us—but after the series was finished, so they could see it first. It's a little like saying, 'I'd love to be pregnant. Can I see the baby first?'" He hated begging for money, and the tension ate him up, even if he gave the appearance of a strong front.

PBS, CPB, Ford, and Lotus Software, which under then chairman Mitch Kapor had granted $200,000 for the first series, now stepped up under Janet Axelrod and new president Jim Manzi with $300,000 for the sequel. Manzi said, "The first one was so great that it was easy to fund the second. . . . As for the content of *Eyes on the Prize II*, . . . we didn't think twice about it, but we understood that other people would."

With his meager seed money, Henry convened a planning session with his scholars and senior staff.

In August 1988, with the new series still short of money, *PBS NewsHour* correspondent Charlayne Hunter-Gault arranged for Camille and Bill Cosby to host a fund-raising cocktail party at their baronial town house on the Upper East Side of Manhattan. The gathering was specifically designed to help sever dependence on white funders. Hunter-Gault said, "I wanted to invite people who were the direct beneficiaries of the movement—heirs to the legacy of Dr. Martin Luther King and all those people who put their bodies on the line for them to be investment bankers, lawyers, journalists, doctors, and other participants in America's economic mainstream."

The *New York Times* reported, "Mr. Cosby, puffing on his signature cigar, told the group that blacks were now in a position to take responsibility for a broader range of problems within their community, and must do so to insure that issues that are of importance to them are addressed. The national goal set by the party's organizers was to raise $500,000 from blacks." Surveying the room crammed with fifty black professionals, under a giant regal portrait of Mr. and Mrs. Cosby, he mused, "'There's a lot of money in this room.'"

It was by some accounts an odd evening because Cosby referred to Henry as "the gimp," and after delivering his come-to-Jesus money-raising pitch told the crowd, "Come on, give the guy money; he's a cripple." Judy Richardson remembers, "There is a titter, because people assume this is a joke between the two of them. . . . And then he does it again, and there is less laughter." Andrea Taylor recalls that people cringed; "Cosby was cruel, just cruel." Judy asked Henry, "What was *that*?" and he replied, "I don't know, it made me uncomfortable, but I'm in the man's house, he's giving a fund-raiser for us."

Cosby ponied up with $42,000 of his own, and by the night's end Henry had commitments for another $80,000. PBS joined the Ford Foundation in eventually granting a million dollars.

Transition to every new series meant a mass exodus and mass influx of people at 486 Shawmut Avenue. To Henry's surprise and sorrow, all but one of his producers, exhausted and alienated by their service on *Eyes I,* declined generous offers to return for *Eyes II.* They had overpaid their dues, wanted to rebuild their frayed personal relationships, get to know their kids again, work five or six days a week instead of seven. I know he pleaded with Callie, Orlando, and me half a dozen times to reunite for another round. Callie was out of work; I was doing Gummy Rabbits and MTV commercials. Judith, wishing that "there could have been some less bloody way to do *Eyes I,*" had returned to the relative calm of WGBH. Callie finally went back to WABC-TV in New York, feeling she could "never replicate the specialness" of *Eyes I.* Judith's ever-patient editor, Dan Eisenberg, went directly from Blackside to a documentary about Sigmund Freud; perfect. Orlando, by then directing his own films in Los Angeles, said Henry "called and said he wouldn't do it without me, offered me senior producer position and $15,000 to move the family to

Boston. . . . I said, 'I'm not sure I want to be on it, because I bring all the good and the bad of *Eyes I*. I don't want to poison the water . . . so it's best that I don't."

But all documentary roads now led to Boston, and Hampton had no shortage of eager, skilled replacements ready to drop everything for the promise of Shawmut Avenue. Massiah wrote, "Blackside was one of the great twentieth-century destinations for independent filmmakers. I remember when Jennifer Lawson, the senior vice president at PBS, came to visit Blackside, reminding us that like WNET in the late 1960s and the fabled UCLA film program of the 1970s, the nexus created by Blackside would have an important impact on the American filmmaking and television community for years to come."

Again, Judy Richardson made an impassioned plea that with all of Blackside's hard-earned credibility, expertise, and determination, the new series about the new era could and should be made by all-black teams: *Black*side. "For me it would have made a difference if we had done this with an all-black production team." But he was "against all-black anything," adamant that he would not segregate the company. He stuck to his guns on "the Blackside Method" of multiple perspectives orbiting around a vital center.

He said, "We have secrets from one another, generation to generation, race to race. When you say 'police,' I see one thing and you see another. When you say 'law,' you see one thing and I see another. . . . We are talking across a great abyss." Fayer remembers, "He wanted black people to have to explain, he wanted white people to have to explain to black people."

Speaking widely in the media about the makeup of his production teams, Henry said, "We are . . . integrated simply because integration provided us with much better program product for the national audience . . . each program team will be headed by two coequal producers, one black, one white, and integrated by gender as well. . . . I know it is inefficient to have two chiefs for each hourlong program, two visions that must be shared and compromised. I also know that many of the conflicts and frustrations of the larger society are played out within those teams . . . I know that such a system costs me money and time. It also creates oceans of stomach acid for those who have to work together. . . . Still I insist on it. . . ."

He assembled four teams to make eight films. Jackie Shearer, black Blackside veteran from the early days, teamed with white political documentary director Paul Stekler, Blackside's first PhD, who was at the time playing in a band in New Orleans after being denied tenure at Tulane "because I didn't want to spend time writing scholarly academic papers, I wanted to make films." WGBH veteran Terry Rockefeller, trained as a historian, teamed with Louis Massiah. Veteran documentary maker Carroll Blue joined up. Jim DeVinney, the only returning alum, worked with Cap Cities survivor Madison Davis Lacy, and Spike Lee's editor Sam Pollard teamed with white writer Sheila Bernard, just off Michael Ambrosino's latest series *The Ring of Truth*. They were joined by a couple dozen new assistants, associate producers, and researchers, including Janet Lawrence from the BBC and a young radio producer, Joe Richman.

Many of the new arrivals had lived through the '70s events in question. Some had on their own initiative closely studied *Eyes I*. Paul Stekler said, "*Eyes on the Prize I* was my film school. I outlined all the episodes when it was first released, what was archive, what was music, interviews." Val Linson, a production assistant on *The Cosby Show,* was blown away by *Eyes I,* thought, "This is what I want to do," and when Henry visited the Cosby set she asked him for a job.

As he had done before and would do again, Henry carved out room in the budget when he spotted a novice with potential, in this case young Noland Walker. At a party at Howard, Noland had said he wanted to be a documentary filmmaker, and a friend asked if that was a realistic goal for a black man. "After seeing *Eyes* in my senior year it was clear that was it. . . . I used to go by his office once a month, ring the doorbell, and say 'Noland Walker for Henry Hampton.'"

Meredith Woods now returned after two years working for Ken Burns. She enjoyed her time assisting the legendary film editor Paul Barnes on *The Civil War,* but said, "Blackside was my model. It was *completely* different in every way. . . . I was the only black person who ever worked on *The Civil War* . . . the final scholars' meeting for the locked picture was all white men except for me. There was no critical content discussion. It was really a celebratory sign-off; nothing in the series got changed."

The ever-steady Steve Fayer worked as full-time freelance series writer on *Eyes II*. Orlando, Callie, Judith, and I served only as advisors. And as we had before, Henry and everyone else looked to Judy Richardson as "Blackside's moral compass."

At 486 Shawmut creative chaos on *Eyes II* picked up where *Eyes I* left off. None of his production teams had ever met or worked together before. Fayer said, "Some woman bailed out and another guy left after a day." Meredith Woods added, "There was this guy Tony, who was supposed to produce with Judy Richardson on *EOP II*, and one day he went out and never came back. Henry hired Sam Pollard to replace him. Stanley Nelson was at *EOP II* school and I never saw him again." Carroll Blue and Henry clashed.

In an attempt to keep the new series on even financial ground, he brought in crack supervising producer Alison Bassett, who had earned her stripes under the New York disciplines of MTV, ABC, and broadcasting legend Fred Friendly. Bassett quickly learned that even before starting, *Eyes II* was $27,000 over budget and still paying off bills from *Eyes I*. The company now had to pay cash up front or put down deposits with vendors who had had a bad experience collecting on the first series.

Back on *Eyes I*, Henry had hired Harvard senior Bennett Singer to help in the publishing operation. Like so many new staffers, Bennett's office was a door on top of two file cabinets between the coffeemaker and the Mississippi editing room. (He had no choice but to memorize all the Mississippi dialogue.) "I worked like a fiend, and felt embarrassed when I had to ask if I could have the day off for my graduation." Bennett thought, "What's with the Jag?"

Now working on *Eyes II* as Terry and Louie's associate producer, Bennett was one of the company's first out gay employees. He sensed that within this fiercely multicultural institution the notion that gays deserved equal inclusion in the expansion of democracy had not yet gained full traction.

Henry had several gay employees, but "they kept their heads down." Bennett said, "If you were gay inside Blackside it was chilly day to day . . . there was a wall of silence." He felt that if Henry resisted making connections between black liberation and gay liberation, it likely stemmed not from animus, but from his proper midwestern upbringing, "because he had nothing to go on in his experience with gay people." Speaking of the 1950s and '60s, Henry's childhood friend Ellen Sweets said, "*Gay* in St. Louis?? Not on your life!"

Bennett had come to Blackside partly because of his interest in the interaction between civil rights history and LGBT history, "trying to understand it because I was living it." He joined a million others in D.C. in 1987 for the March on Washington for Lesbian and Gay Rights. Afterward he spoke eloquently about the experience on NPR. But when several Blackside staffers invited Henry to listen to Bennett on the radio, Hampton was clearly uncomfortable.

Singer decided he would have to make a film of his own about the point where gay rights and civil rights intersected, and went on to produce *Brother Outsider,* a fine feature documentary about Bayard Rustin, gay chief organizer of the 1963 March on Washington. Bennett told me, "I hope the Rustin film extends Henry's vision in a way that he would appreciate."

On *Eyes I: America's Civil Rights Years,* Hampton had an organic starting point (Emmett Till) and, more important, a clear landing point (the 1965 Voting Rights Act). *Eyes II: America at the Racial Crossroads* had neither. Nor was the post-1965 period blessed with a clear plot arc of battles, building one success or setback upon another. The new series would look at an obvious constellation of themes and topics—black nationalism, self-defense, affirmative action, urban rebellion, control of schools, the transition from protests to politics—but at the outset lacked a settled road map of stories. The end point was especially hard to identify, and few on the teams were completely sure what "America at the Racial Crossroads" actually meant. And undergirding it all was the late-1960s existential panic that this time the center really might *not* hold.

Planning meetings now explored dozens of story options. As before, Hampton asserted, "As television producers who specialize in social history, we are as much interested in the lives of washerwomen and day laborers as in generals and presidents." Newcomer Noland Walker remembered, "When the producers were trying to figure out the slate for *Eyes II* . . . Henry had Will Conroy and me move a huge Ping-Pong table, so that when things got tense people could play Ping-Pong . . . and it felt like twelve angry men in there, going round and round and round . . . about what the series was going to be."

Advisors and staff finally settled on eighteen stories less known than the iconic tales of the early 1960s' *Eyes I.* The first program in the new series focused on Malcolm X and the emergence of Black Power during the 1966 King-Carmichael "Meredith March," the last great march of the civil rights movement; the second on King's frustrating efforts to move the movement north to Chicago and on the Detroit riots in 1967. Show three looked at the election of Cleveland's first black mayor, Carl Stokes, the Oakland Black Panthers, and the racially charged school conflict in New York's Ocean Hill–Brownsville district. Number four was devoted entirely to the last year of King's life; five to Muhammad Ali, the student takeover of Howard University, and black nationalism; and six focused on the Attica prison rebellion in 1971 and the Chicago Panthers. Program seven covered the 1975 Boston school busing crisis, the election of Atlanta mayor Maynard Jackson, and the *Bakke* affirmative action case in California. The final show explored the destruction of Miami's Overtown neighborhood to make way for an interstate highway and the election of Chicago's first black mayor, Harold Washington, in 1983. While *Eyes I* had looked mainly at relations between white Americans and black Americans, *Eyes II* delved equally into relations between black people themselves.

And the role of whites in the movement would be tested. Stokely Carmichael wrote in 1966, "One of the most disturbing things about almost all white supporters of the movement has been that they are afraid to go into their own communities—where the racism exists, and to get rid of it. They want to run from Berkeley to tell us what to do in Mississippi. Let them instead look at Berkeley."

Depending on how you looked at it, *Eyes II* was either a collection of loosely connected stories that lacked *Eyes I*'s biblical trajectory toward redemption, or it was a powerful anthology of Black Power's lurching vital energy, as the movement transitioned from mass protest to rebellion and electoral politics. Either way, Dave Garrow put it well in a 1987 memo to Steve Fayer, Paul Stekler, and Henry: "The story of the last 19 years for black America has NOT been a good one . . . the record is far more one of failure and deterioration than stories of success and progress. EOP II must not take on any self-congratulatory air."

Davis Lacy and other producers wanted to loosen up the rigid *Eyes* style, give it more snap, make it attractive to a younger audience. Paul Stekler said, "Henry was very progressive in his politics, but very conservative in his viewership. His idea of audience was in line with his own upper-middle-class upbringing, always asking, 'How will this play in Peoria?' Everyone on *Eyes II* made a different film for Henry than they would have made for themselves. He wanted to speak for *all* Americans."

Neither Henry nor the producers intended to simply repeat *Eyes I*, but he wanted to keep *Eyes II* within the artistic wellsprings of *Eyes I*. Chuck Scott said, "After *Eyes* we knew it could be done: proof of concept. The challenge was how to make *Eyes II* more aggressive, but still be *Eyes*. Henry's guidance made this happen. Most of the producers wanted something more edgy, more militant."

Right out of the gate there was resentment at Henry for not embracing the role of black women in the post-1965 liberation movement. Terry said she, Louis, and others "pushed hard for an Angela Davis story, but Henry wouldn't touch it. . . . The role of women post-'65 was pushed off the table. . . . Henry was not a feminist." And it did not help that Davis had been a leader of the American Communist Party, which the right (and center) had succeeded in branding permanently toxic. Henry did not want to engage that discussion on prime-time television.

On the other hand, Henry was now ready to explore black nationalism and armed self-defense. He tied himself in Jesuitical knots over how to address the growing "blackness" of the movement. He tangled with Richardson so badly that he once kicked her out of an advisors' meeting after arguing about the use of a Marvin Gaye song. "And it had become clear that Henry and I really are on different pages in terms of the way we see this second period. I go totally into black movement . . . the 'bad movement.'

"There were times Henry and I were barely talking to each other. . . . We were driving home and he had that little convertible and we're coming down the expressway. . . . I was so mad that I thought I've got to have a red aura around me. I actually thought if I ask him to leave me off here on the side of the road, can I figure out how to get back to town. So he knew at the beginning of *EOP II* that we are really of two different minds but still kept me on. As angry as he and I get with each other over political things, he left room for people like me, who had totally opposing views, to be heard."

The choice of music was a good cultural and political barometer of the new series and its filmmakers. Nearly all the producers wanted more modern music, including hip-hop and rap, which Henry detested, to connect with a young audience. Davis Lacy said, "*Eyes I* music felt reverential; it felt like the preachers were telling the story. I wanted a different soundscape, hot fucking music, urban, modern." The Panthers and Malcolm X had no use for freedom songs. Malcolm X said, "It's the twentieth century, and if you're walking around singing 'We Shall Overcome,' the government has failed you. Singing is not going to help you. You've got to stop singing and start swinging." The producers in the end deployed disco, salsa, James Brown, Jimi Hendrix, Aretha Franklin, Sweet Honey in the Rock, Curtis Mayfield, Bob Dylan, Dinah Washington, Marvin Gaye, freedom songs, and the funk band War.

Hampton would sometimes send Vincent Harding on missions to accomplish what Henry himself felt he could not, as when he assigned Vince to talk Jim DeVinney and Davis Lacy out of a secular Wilson Pickett song at the end of the Meredith March in *Eyes II* and replace it with a spiritual. Jim and Davis Lacy prevailed, arguing that the whole point of using the nonchurch song was to underscore that the liberation struggle was moving away from the church.

Some moments in *Eyes II* are as good or better than anything in *Eyes I.* The second series was built more overtly around themes and ideas than *Eyes I,* sometimes less elegantly camouflaged in narrative, and was consequently less cinematic. But the stories could soar.

One story is worth looking at closely. Louis Massiah and Terry Rockefeller produced a powerful *Eyes II* sequence about the killing of Panther leaders Fred Hampton and Mark Clark by Chicago police in 1969. Twenty-one-year-old Fred Hampton may well have been the only Panther who might have created a real alliance with working-class whites and Latinos, leapfrogging over the swagger of Huey Newton, Bobby Seale, and Eldridge Cleaver to fulfill J. Edgar Hoover's own nightmare of an effective "black messiah."

The Blackside filmmakers were initially hamstrung because the Chicago police, the FBI agents on the case, and the state's attorney wouldn't talk, but by dogged research Bennett Singer located William O'Neal, who had been one of the FBI's informants inside the Chicago Panthers. O'Neal lived under various pseudonyms and had never publicly revealed his role in the killing. He agreed to an interview, but only on the condition that the team be ready to meet in one of three cities, and he would reveal his location only when the time came for the interview. On the appointed day, Henry Hampton, Terry Rockefeller, Louis Massiah, Bobby Shepard, and Sekou Shepard met O'Neal in Manhattan.

O'Neal arrived wearing sunglasses and wanted to keep them on during filming, but Bobby convinced him to take them off. He said he was traveling with a bodyguard and asked Henry Hampton if he was related to Fred Hampton. As a young petty criminal on the streets he had gotten arrested for joyriding in a stolen car across state lines and was facing serious prison time when FBI agent Roy Mitchell proposed that O'Neal could either rot in jail or join the Chicago Panther chapter as an informant, though he never used the word. (The taciturn Mitchell had played a key role in solving the Philadelphia, Mississippi, civil rights murder case in 1964.)

Young O'Neal had always wanted the power and even respect accorded policemen in his neighborhood. "So all of a sudden I was working for the FBI. . . . So I felt good about it. I felt like I was working undercover, doing something good for the finest police organization in America."

Before joining he had thought of the Panthers as little more than just another street gang, but "the first set of reference books I saw inside the Black Panther Party was *The Selected Works of Mao Tse-tung*. . . . And it wasn't too long after that that I started seeing books like the *The Communist Manifesto*. . . . The Panthers would sit down and . . . study these books. We would go through political orientation. Fred Hampton and Bobby Rush would explain to us, the new membership, basically what it meant . . . and they drew parallels to what was going on in the past revolutions in the various countries . . . like China or Russia. . . . I expected . . . we would be out there doing turf battles with the local gangs, but they weren't about that at all. They were into the political scene: the war in Vietnam, Richard Nixon, and specifically freeing Huey. That was their thing."

O'Neal quickly rose to security captain for the Chicago office under Bobby Rush's command, and for seven months was Fred Hampton's personal bodyguard. In his sometimes contradictory soliloquy, he said, "We were buying weapons at that point. I carried two guns every day for seven or eight months. . . . Once in a while I'd pick up a locker of C-4 explosive. . . . We had five hundred members and everybody was aggressive." Then he pivots to "It was a game we were playing—the leather jackets, the berets, the military format, the guns—it was all to impress the people, really. We never intended to take on the police department to overthrow the government. It was rhetoric; it was shock treatment for white America.

"We tried to develop negative information to try to discredit Fred Hampton. . . . I tried to come up with signs of him doing drugs or something and never could. He was clean." O'Neal clearly began to admire Fred Hampton, but his stay-out-of-jail ticket required that he report to FBI agent Mitchell, with whom he developed an unlikely friendship. "He always said, 'You're working for me,' . . . I was treated well, I had been to Mitchell's home, I have held his child in my arms . . . he was a role model for me when I needed one. I mean, we had very few role models back then; we had Malcolm X, we had Martin Luther King, we had Muhammad Ali, and I had an FBI agent."

Tensions rose when Panthers killed two officers in a shoot-out on Chicago's South Side in December 1968. Now Agent Mitchell described going to their funeral and "wanted to know the locations of weapons caches, he wanted to know if we had explosives. He needed to know who was staying at what locations, who spent the night where. . . . We knew that the police would react in some way."

O'Neal drew a floor plan of Fred Hampton's apartment for his FBI contact. "I knew it would be a raid, but I didn't feel like anyone would get killed, especially not Fred. . . . I understood what was going on. He didn't have to tell me. I knew . . . what he could do to help the police department do something about it."

After work at the Panther office on December 3, 1969, O'Neal walked over to Fred's house on Monroe Street, where "The women were cooking a big dinner . . . chili and a big pot of spaghetti, and most of us who had labored that day at the office and were just looking forward to . . . eating dinner and reading and just being together." At 11 P.M. he walked home and went to bed. At 4 A.M. twelve Chicago policemen smashed their way into the apartment, fired fifty-one rounds, and, guided by O'Neal's diagram, killed first Mark Clark and then Fred Hampton as he lay sleeping next to his pregnant fiancée.

O'Neal got the news the following morning and went with Bobby Rush to the Monroe Street house. "It hit me after I walked into that house. It was cold and it was blood everywhere, and it was holes in the wall and then . . . I just began to realize that the information that I had supplied leading up to that moment had facilitated that raid. I knew that indirectly I had contributed . . . and I felt bad about it. And then I got mad. . . . And then I had to conceal those feelings, which made it worse. I just had to continue to play the role. And I think it was at that point that . . . I lost something. . . ."

O'Neal himself could easily have been killed if he'd stayed later. "So I felt betrayed . . . I felt like I was expendable. I felt like perhaps I was on the wrong side. . . . I'm not going to sit here now and take the responsibility for the raid, you know. I didn't pull the trigger. I didn't issue the warrant. I didn't put the guns in the apartment . . . but I do feel like I was betrayed."

The FBI gave O'Neal a three-hundred-dollar bonus for the diagram and information that led to the raid. "There was quite a few informants back then. . . . I mean, what am I supposed to do? Feel guilty right now about it? I didn't feel guilty then; I was hurt because Fred Hampton died."

Terry Rockefeller and Henry shared the questioning. Bobby Shepard remembered O'Neal furiously twitching his leg off camera throughout the session. As professional documentary makers often do, Henry and Louis asked O'Neal to tell the story one more time for the camera. The transcript of that interview says it all:

> *Interviewer:* Once again I want to ask you about your feelings when you learned about the raid, Fred Hampton's death, or walking through the apartment with Bobby Rush.
> *William O'Neal:* I can't do it again. I, I just can't.

Afterward, he asked Henry, "Did I do a good job?" When Bobby Shepard asked O'Neal why he had decided to talk with them, he said, "Because I want my daughter to know." He told the whole story—the only filmed interview he ever gave—and then vanished. A week later all three of his phone numbers ceased to function. Because Henry, the team, and O'Neal's lawyer, Flint Taylor, had lingering doubts that perhaps they had filmed an impostor while the real William O'Neal was elsewhere, Taylor flew to Boston, watched the rushes, and confirmed that it was, indeed, Mr. O'Neal.

Then, on January 15, 1990, Martin Luther King Day, the week of the nationwide broadcast premiere of *Eyes on the Prize II*, William O'Neal threw himself into oncoming traffic on Chicago's Eisenhower Expressway. The medical examiner ruled his death a suicide. When news reached Blackside, there was a stunned silence. Louis Massiah remembered talking with coworkers. "Was it a suicide? A murder? Was the death faked so he could go back into hiding? I don't remember if we blamed ourselves, but we couldn't help but wonder if there was a causal relationship between what would be the imminent revelation of O'Neal's role in Hampton's death and the suicide." The U.S. government eventually settled a civil suit, paying $1,800,000 to the family of Fred Hampton and others killed and wounded in the raid.

In a dreadful precursor to our present disputes over mass incarceration, New York's Attica Correctional Facility exploded in a massive rebellion in 1971, when one thousand inmates seized the cell blocks and took forty-two guards hostage. They were protesting appalling conditions. Blackside's researchers had secured footage shot inside the yard, images that overturned the public perception of inmates as "horrible faceless guys running amok." After state troopers stormed the prison, killing thirty-two inmates and eleven guards, officers tortured "Big Black" Frank Smith, one of the leaders.

Producer Sam Pollard described his conversation on camera with Smith.

We had shot the interview with him, asked him the question about what had happened after the National Guard retook the prison, and he gave me a very perfunctory answer. . . . We cut the camera off. I turned to Bobby and I turned to Judy Richardson. "I don't think he really gave it to us." I said, "Do you think I should go back and ask him again?" Bobby said "yup," Judy said "yes." So I went over to him and I leaned over and I said, "Black, your telling of the story was fine, but you didn't really go back and really dig deep and remember how painful that story was. Now if you tell me you can't do it I won't shoot anything. But if you think you can really go back and really remember the pain and the brutality of what they did to you, we'll roll." He thought about it for a few seconds, and he said "OK." So we started rolling, and he went back, and right before we were getting ready to say "cut," Judy, Bobby, and myself, we were all crying.

"They ripped our clothes off, they made us crawl on the ground like we were animals . . . they lay me on a table, and they beat me in my testicles. And they burned me with cigarettes and they dropped hot shells on me and then put a football up under my throat and they kept telling me that if it dropped it they was going to kill me. And I really felt, after seeing so many people shot for no apparent reason, that they really were going to do this. They set up a gauntlet in the hallway and they broke glass up in the middle of the hallway and they made people run through the gauntlet and they had . . . forty police on each side, with clubs they called nigger-sticks, and they was beating people. And it just hurt . . . another human being treating a human being this way, you know, and it really hurt me, even sitting here now. . . . They broke my wrists, opened my head up, took me to the hospital, and dumped me on the floor. . . . You know I went through this all that afternoon and then they took me up to the cell and played Russian roulette with me, left me in the cell nude, nothing to wrap up in, and I'm trying to get up on the pillow to keep myself warm." He was crying.

Sam said, "I felt terrible after that, you know, being so manipulative." It seemed to me that what Sam saw as manipulation could also be seen as liberation of a dark memory.

Huey Newton was to *Eyes II* what Stokely Carmichael was to *Eyes I,* a still-living critical player and lightning rod of the times.

Like Wallace, Newton had nearly died from gunshot wounds in 1967, shot by Oakland police during a traffic stop gone bad. His wife, Frederica Newton, read about Henry's *Eyes II,* called Blackside, and ended up facilitating an interview. Newton had by then earned a PhD from the University of California, Santa Cruz, entered a drug abuse program in 1984, and had recently been released from jail on a parole violation. Terry arranged for me to shoot the interview since Chin was unavailable. When he walked into the Oakland Holiday Inn room exactly on time, healthy and fit at forty-six, shorter than I expected, and agitated, but not in a bad way, I looked him over, as cameramen do, and said, "You don't have a gray hair on your head," to which he replied, "It's not that I didn't try."

He spoke of the early Panthers role in Oakland. "The police were the government; all the police were southerners. As a matter of fact in the sixties they were still recruiting from Georgia. And they said that white southerners knew how to handle these Negroes. So the police were impolite, and they were very fast to kill a black for minor offenses . . . such as black youth stealing automobiles. They would shoot them in the back. It was widespread dislike for the police because of their inhumane treatment of blacks."

He described the Panthers' ten-point program, their bold tactic of following the police around on Oakland's streets with guns and law books, and he linked the connection between black nationalist groups in the United States with African liberation movements. "That connected us to the international movement of the workers' movement, the international proletarian movement, such as was happening in Cuba . . . we were very impressed by the Cuban revolution. And, at the time of the creation of the Black Panther Party, I was introduced to Marxism and I think I had read a book called *Imperial Materialism and Empirical Criticism,* by I. V. Lenin."

His smarts and charisma were undiminished. It was during this session with Newton that I first heard the aphorism "No one gets out of this life alive." A couple weeks later I picked up a paper in Paris and read that he had been found dead on the sidewalk in the Oakland neighborhood where he had spent years organizing, shot to death in a dispute with a drug dealer.

The government's COINTELPRO program and the Panthers' own fratricidal battles had slowly brought their heyday to an end. Some, like Bobby Rush, began successful careers in electoral politics, but I know Henry was unsure how much their work had improved life for minorities in America.

During *Eyes on the Prize II,* Henry was still ensconced at his beloved compound up in Roxbury, driving to the office in his old Jag. Still enmeshed, as he would be for the rest of his life, in the rat's nest of BSI finances, he could now count his personal assets at around a million dollars, apparently not counting his equity in *Eyes on the Prize I.*

He made short-lived plans to "really get organized," "to lay out a life plan for a) living spare, b) retirement, c) investing, d) learning how to get organized, and e) life." With the help of a life coach he set out to adopt a rational work calendar, reining in the many large projects now in his queue by freezing the research and preproduction time. And in a move we all would have cheered had we known about it, he resolved to conquer his chronic procrastination by adopting a rigid schedule. None of these resolutions lasted long. In his equally short-lived "daybook," he drew from memory diagrams of golf courses.

Noland Walker still unloaded antiques from the Jeep when Henry returned from his rambles. Walker said the house up on Fort Hill "looked more and more like 'The Fall of the House of Usher,' an antiques store where no customers came."

He was physically strong, but post-polio syndrome was now advancing. The condition affects some patients decades after their initial bout with the disease, with the bitter irony that the more active a polio survivor has been, the more likely and acute the post-polio malaise. Henry was now plagued with renewed muscle weakness, atrophy, pain, and fatigue, cruel burdens for a man so full of life, energy, desires, and bursting with goals. He could no longer manage to swing a golf club, and he had trouble climbing up into his airplane.

He mostly kept the pain and discomfort to himself and mustered such verve that we who worked with him could sometimes forget that he was disabled. Years before, when she first met him at a party, Ruth Batson said, "Henry was executing some fancy moves on the dance floor."

Parking his car with Vincent Harding one evening, Henry produced a handicapped parking placard, and Vince asked, "Where the hell did you get that?" But the times I shepherded him through those quarter-mile concourses in the Atlanta airport—he declined a wheelchair—were agony. During one of his visits to California we had a little time to kill, and since he had never seen Stanford University, I thought it would be fun to walk around the Quad, but realized after the first fifty yards that he was having no fun, so we headed back to the car. Shortly after that, he started using a cane. As he aged, his friends and staff would find a reason to dawdle in a crosswalk to give him more time to cross.

He now had fifty people working for him. As before, discussions and screenings unfolded around the Big Table, Henry presiding. Val Linson remembered, "That table leveled the playing field. Around that table women would not let Henry stop them. It was great for me as a young woman of color." Jackie Shearer with her genuine Boston accent and Boston grit pushed back against the boss as Judith Vecchione had on *Eyes I,* becoming a model and mentor for younger women.

Signing off on completed *Eyes II* programs was no easier than signing off on *Eyes I* programs. Now the series ran half a million dollars over budget, "so we would send him out on the trail to make speeches," said Alison Bassett.

Richardson said, "At Blackside it's *never* just a movie." Alison said, "Working at BSI was frustrating because we all wanted to do a good job. It was so important to get these people's story right. Henry created a feeling that we were doing something special, part of the exclusive *Eyes on the Prize* Club. We all have wounds to show for it." Bassett quit over the sign-off issues, and again over budget, but then returned to finish the series.

Though it may leave a trail of personal and financial wreckage behind, and even destroy institutions, there is no contradiction between bad management and great art. Our great documentary pioneer Robert Flaherty ran every single one of his films far over budget, and Vincent van Gogh nearly bankrupted his generous brother, Theo. Thinking about Henry, Ellen Sweets said, "Name me a single great artist who was a great manager."

After the locked picture screening of a show about the first use of the term "Black Power" on the Meredith March in 1966, everyone turned to Henry, who didn't say anything for a long time, and then simply walked out of the room. Jim DeVinney stalked him to the coffeemaker and said, "You got to give me something." Henry replied, "I keep thinking about the white people in the march, with white people on the sidelines screaming at them, how did they feel." Simple. Jim and the team went back in and found a white kid who says he left the Meredith March and put his energy into stopping the Vietnam War. Henry saw it, and said, "OK, lock it," though he was never satisfied that the series adequately articulated white fear of black power.

Andrea Taylor said that when she visited 486 Shawmut as *Eyes II* was nearing completion, "You could hear a lot of cursing and screaming. Tension was everywhere: around the process, around Henry, and there was tension in the room between the two producers on each show." Sam Pollard looked back and said, "The *reason* he hired us all is that we're going to fight." Racial tensions simmered, and unbeknownst to Henry, the black staff had a black Fourth of July party because, in Judy Richardson's words, "There comes a point where you get tired of always explaining your position to white people. They needed a break. It was great."

But underlying it all was a profound and moving sweep of American history, which could have been forged nowhere but Blackside. Henry Hampton said that the overwhelming image he carried away from his experience on *Eyes II* was the sight of editor Lillian Benson crying at the Steenbeck as she worked on the back-to-back assassinations of Martin Luther King and Robert Kennedy.

Finally, with 80 different archive sources, 175 interviews, 157 different songs, a dozen rowdy open screenings, rewrite upon rewrite, they locked all eight films.

I was only an advisor on *Eyes II* but supervised creation of the animated *Eyes* series logo at Colossal Pictures in San Francisco. In some symbolic sense, all the tensions of this new messier history distilled themselves into arguments over logo design. Battling abstractions—affirmative action, armed self-defense, black nationalism, Black Power—now took on new life as battling images that had to coalesce into a 20-second animated cameo of *Eyes II*. I asked the whole staff for theme and image suggestions and got back a bewildering laundry list: political guy, kids, woman,

Malcolm X, white woman, black nationalist flag, flames, ballot box, Africa, Afros, Muhammad Ali, fists, American flag, feet marching, Black Panther logo, white fear, Black logo, line of marchers from *EOP-I,* MLK, lots of Malcolm X, *no* MX, *no* MLK, Statue of Liberty with head bowed. For this series in which guns were so important, Hampton told me "guns are off-limits," and I had heated phone calls with him in which he asked me to remove the "angry people," black nationalist flag, and flames from an early version. And, perhaps now scared by the "bad movement" narrative he had unleashed, he asked that we use the same *Eyes on the Prize* song from the first series, and said "raised fists dominate too much." I found myself arguing for the black nationalist and Black Power images to my black executive producer. Ah, Blackside!

The job involved hundreds of hand-cut, hand-inked animation cells. After accommodating change after change, Colossal's CEO chose to absorb several hundred hours of their own staff time and a thousand dollars of expenses, saying, "I guess we can't give it all to the rain forests this year." Colossal's long-suffering director Drew Takahashi decided to absorb the overage costs himself, and I paid their final invoice out of my own pocket.

Eyes on the Prize II: America at the Racial Crossroads premiered on Martin Luther King's birthday in February 1990 to good reviews, all noting how much more complicated it was than *Eyes I.* Walter Goodman, the curmudgeon of the *Times,* said it left "a jumble of feelings . . . admiration for those who put their bodies on the line mixed with distaste for some of their messages and tactics." Tom Shales of the *Washington Post* said, " 'Eyes on the Prize II' brings back a time of great communicators who had something great to communicate. . . . If the eight-part sequel . . . seems less stirring than the original, it is partly because the movement itself seemed to become stalled, a victim of establishment intransigence and of factionalism and competition within the ranks of those protesting."

At what turned out to be his last birthday party in January 1968, Martin Luther King's staff sang "Happy Birthday to You," the most recognized song in the English language. Like many filmmakers before and after, Henry paid Warner/Chappell Music an ample license fee to use that nineteenth-century tune with 1930s lyrics in *Eyes on the Prize II.* For decades, until a court finally ruled the copyright effectively invalid in a 2015 legal action brought by filmmakers, some producers paid as much as $20,000 for one verse.

We may be tempted to think of "Happy Birthday" or the "I have a dream" speech as community property for all Americans, part of our common cultural inheritance in the public square, like the Gettysburg Address or a recipe for apple pie. Do we not all contain some of the "I have a dream" in our American hearts and minds, as part of what makes us a nation, a culture, and a civil society. The nasty fact is that most public speeches are private property, often controlled by Fox, General Electric, the King estate, ABC, or Bill Gates's Corbis Motion, now itself controlled by a Chinese company. Given the realities of copyright and intellectual-property law, they are no more your birthright or mine than your Apple computer's operating system or a lumber company's old-growth redwood forest. King's speeches in *Eyes on the Prize* are assets to be monetized.

His masterful 1963 "I have a dream" oration, some of which he improvised on the spot, riffing on Psalms, Shakespeare, and lines from a long succession of activists and pastors who came before, rose from the power and passion of preaching. *On the Media*'s Jamie York says, "the rules of preaching are in profound conflict with the rules governing intellectual property."

As archive material came into Blackside back in 1986 on *Eyes I*, we got little hints of "some weirdness" about the rights to all the King speeches we used. It rattled me, but I was too busy with other things, and Henry must have solved whatever the problem was, because it apparently went away. *Eyes I* and *Eyes II* were completed and broadcast in 1987 and 1990, respectively, with short-term but squeaky-clean licenses paid to networks for all the news clips of Martin Luther King.

Coretta King herself had given a long, heartfelt interview for *Eyes I,* and had sent a warm letter of congratulation to Llew Smith saying how much she appreciated what Henry and the team had done. She then went on to do a second interview for *Eyes II.* Dr. King was, of course, all over Jackie and Paul's stunning elegiac tale of King's last year, exploring his courageous opposition to "the giant triplets of racism, extreme materialism, and militarism." Blackside had certainly done its part to stem what Cornel West aptly called "the Santa Clausification" of Martin Luther King.

Flash forward to July 1991. Henry called me in an angry panic, saying he had just received a letter from the estate of Martin Luther King, not to congratulate him for ten years of struggle to make the finest, most nuanced television shows yet about their father and the movement he led, but to claim that all Blackside's use of the slain leader's speeches in all of *Eyes on the Prize I* and *II* was illegal. They argued that the license fees we had paid to networks covered only the actual film they shot, not King's words or image *in* the films. A confidential internal Blackside memo stated that the heirs asked for language stipulating that "Blackside agrees that it will not make any use of the name, image, voice, writings, and speeches of Dr. King that will reflect negatively on him or his reputation."

The memo reaffirmed that the portrayal of King in *Eyes* was overwhelmingly positive, and that Blackside could agree that any new version of *Eyes* could be consistent with that, "but we cannot agree to have our journalistic integrity compromised beyond that, especially as it relates to other projects. If all individuals that *Eyes on the Prize* dealt with asked for the same stipulation, a balanced and accurate history would not be possible." The memo also makes clear that the company was fighting not only for their own documentary ethics and freedom, but for filmmakers in the future.

Kenn Rabin remembered, "The issue was just not on our radar. No clip owner ever said, 'Contact the King estate first.' The King estate came to Blackside and said they owned all the material, image, likeness, text, audio, everything, and wanted money and veto power over use. 'You've got to pay, and we will have control over future use.' As far as anyone knew, it was the first time ever that King's children had approached any media organization with these demands."

Here was a sudden existential threat to the series, serious business that Henry could not ignore. His able attorney, Ike Williams, told him, "As long as that threat's out there, we've got to disclose it to people who want to license *Eyes on the Prize* for distribution, and it's going to intimidate a lot of licensees."

Back in 1963, a month after the March on Washington, Martin Luther King's attorney, Clarence B. Jones, had filed for copyright registration on the 17-minute "I have a dream" address in King's name (King committed all the profits to the civil rights movement). Jones shortly brought suit against Twentieth Century Fox Record Company and Mister Maestro to stop unauthorized vinyl record sales. Since King's death in 1968 his estate had not really sorted out how to apply the law to newsreels of King.

But now with the success of *Eyes I* and *Eyes II,* they wanted a piece of the action. Williams said, "It was about the kids . . . it's not about Henry, it's about them. 'Dad's legacy belongs to us, and we have the right of publicity.' You can't make a beach towel with his picture on it, you can't sell a framed picture, you can't sell a recording of 'I have a dream.'" The state of Georgia recognizes the "right of publicity" by common law, which gave the family the right to go after everybody.

"The rights of publicity say that if you exploited your likeness, voice, stance, costume, like Dracula with a cape . . . during your lifetime for profit, then your heirs have the right to license it for a very long time; most states do fifty years after the death of the person. Humphrey Bogart's heirs: you can't wear a raincoat and a slouch hat and sort of talk like him with a cigarette to advertise a bank without hearing from them and their representatives." Orson Welles's daughter retained a lawyer whose business card read "Artists Rights Enforcer."

The legal doctrine of "fair use," which makes a copyright exception for brief clips in news programs, was just coming into use in documentary. Lawyers for King's son Dexter rejected Blackside's "fair use" claim and threatened to sue not only over the right of publicity issue with Martin Luther King's words and image, but over the sticky problem that Coretta King had crossed out "in perpetuity" on her *Eyes II* release, replacing it with a handwritten "3–5 years." They claimed the right to King's "image" even when he did not speak; Blackside's attorney argued that this was completely without legal precedent.

It was every filmmaker's bad dream: an unexpected aggressive legal challenge just at the moment of triumph. Henry abhorred combat (except within his teams), but now he was thrown into a fight not of his own choosing, to quite literally protect his life's work. To make the problem go away and avoid a nasty public dispute, he offered King's heirs a substantial sum.

The estate countered that it wasn't nearly enough because *Eyes* and Blackside were profit-making enterprises, with *Eyes* videotapes on sale at Blockbuster. *Eyes on the Prize* was, in fact, at that moment bringing in only modest returns. Henry said, "They seemed to have the notion that millions of dollars were available." They also demanded control over all the archive shots and recordings of King throughout the entire fourteen-part series, which meant de facto control over *Eyes on the Prize*. That control was unacceptable to Henry and a red flag to scholars, and would mean the actual end of distribution.

Henry bore the brunt of the struggle, with help from Ike Williams, and from the skilled Bob Lavelle, who ran Blackside's publishing and outreach arm, and had a lot of experience with literary rights. Blackside made plans to comply by creating a special version when the estate requested specific cuts in the *Eyes II* King show. An upcoming giveaway of *Eyes* videotapes to public schools was put on hold. PBS heard about the rumble, became wary, and decided not to rebroadcast *Eyes on the Prize* during Black History Month in 1993, a move that Michael Eric Dyson called "a sure travesty for the interests of the civil rights community and African American history, not to mention King's legacy."

Attorney Williams now told Henry he had little choice but to fight back in court, or risk losing *Eyes on the Prize*. "Given their claim that he couldn't show *Eyes* without a tithe, that would have made it impossible for Blackside to exist. . . .He very reluctantly finally came to say, 'Well, OK, I'm doing it.' I had a lot of respect for the difficulty he had in making the decision."

And so Henry Hampton, the premier media chronicler of civil rights, went to the United States District Court for the District of Massachusetts and filed a declaratory judgment proceeding against the estate of Martin Luther King. As he explained to Dyson, Henry alleged that the family's threats and demands for exorbitant payments "had a chilling effect on Blackside's right of free speech." Henry was distraught but now calm. Williams remembered him saying, "Much as I'm stunned that the kids are taking this position about a film that honors their dad, you know for me as an African American, to be a litigant adverse to the King family is something I never thought I'd do in my life."

Dexter King shot back that Henry's suit was an attack on his family. Henry and Ike met with Dexter and his advisors at their counsel's office in Boston, "seeing if we could agree on what the legal issues were and whether it was possible to find common ground for a settlement. Henry wanted to settle. He wasn't interested in a judgment against King's estate. He just didn't want the films to be killed. Dexter was sticking to his demand for a piece of the action every time *Eyes* was shown."

Meanwhile, the King estate was also in a protracted legal tussle with his alma mater, Boston University, over the disposition of a portion of Martin's papers. "And the law didn't look good for them . . . on that one I think they began to realize that there wasn't big money to be gotten," said Ike. BU's lawyers were friends of Ike's, so they joined common cause.

Blackside eventually struck an out-of-court settlement "for whatever we ended up with. It was a really nominal amount."

Though Henry was rattled and exhausted by the melee, *Eyes I* and *Eyes II* were free at last from the King estate's control, but the general question of rights to the speech had not really been settled. In 1999, judges in *Estate of Martin Luther King, Jr. v. CBS* upheld the estate's ownership of "I have a dream." Lewis Hyde says that ever since, "Martin Luther King's heirs have treated his created work as a commercial property. They have used King's work, sold it to advertisers . . . a reformulation of King's image and message, moving it from the political and spiritual sphere in which it began into a completely commercial sphere."

Since *Eyes,* the King family has indeed succeeded in significantly monetizing their father's image and speeches, licensing them to Apple, Alcatel, Cingular Wireless, Bell South, Chevy, Target, Coca-Cola, Walmart, McDonald's, Kellogg's, Delta Airlines, and a cell phone ad featuring Dr. King with Kermit the Frog and Homer Simpson. Mercedes-Benz licensed his image in an ad for a $175,000 car.

In a 2001 Alcatel TV commercial, the martyred King is put into service as a representative for a telecommunications corporation, delivering his "I have a dream . . ." to a masterfully computer-generated empty Washington, D.C., National Mall in support of the company's message: "Before you can inspire, you must first connect." One wonders if the ad agency understood King's late-life skepticism about the forces of capitalism.

And according to Kenn Rabin, for a time in the late 1990s, networks would not release any King archive footage to documentary makers without clearance from the estate. Jamie York reports, "The estate has sued or demanded steep fees from academics, journalists, and news organizations, charging intellectual property violations. And, almost without exception, they've won." The screenwriter on Ava DuVernay's feature film *Selma* was given the thankless task of paraphrasing Dr. King's speeches because the estate had already licensed the actual original words to Steven Spielberg.

The "I have a dream" speech is recognized by more Americans than any other. But for years because of the King family's aggressive action, despite Henry's legal action, video of this oration so central to our American experience often could not be found in its unabridged entirety anywhere on the Internet. You could see licensed bits of it in books, in *Eyes on the Prize,* in Orlando Bagwell and Noland Walker's *Citizen King,* and other documentaries, but elsewhere it was ephemeral. "I have a dream" came and went in bits and pieces, an oratorical Whac-A-Mole, some days up on YouTube, but most days replaced by a takedown screen: "Removed at request of copyright holder." One afternoon in the winter of 2012 I could find it only on a Swedish middle school teacher's Web site.

But in 2013, in celebration of Internet Freedom Day, the advocacy group Fight for the Future posted "I have a dream" in its entirety, in open defiance of the estate's copyright. Several of these videos remain easily accessible online, and it appears the King estate has stopped fighting the tide.

CHAPTER NINETEEN

Will the Circle Be Unbroken

1998

A ll fourteen parts of the full *Eyes on the Prize I* and *II* were now safely launched and well on their way to a place in the canons of both American history and television history. Henry's aim was to leverage Blackside's popularity, street cred, academic reputation, and broadcast ratings record beyond civil rights and black liberation. Twenty-two years after launching his company, Henry Hampton could at last really explore the expansion of democracy, messy history, and "the responsibilities of the government to its citizens and vice versa."

Like many rising documentary stars, Henry for years had his eye on Hollywood, partly starstruck simply because it was Hollywood, and partly because he felt constrained by nonfiction.

"I have this compulsion to get big ideas on film and out to audiences. I think I've got to try." So he set out to "conquer Hollywood." At a cordial one-on-one dinner with Tony Bill, who had just won an Oscar for producing *The Sting,* they discussed a film about the Tuskegee Airmen, and another on African American chemist Percy Julian. Henry pitched *Selma, Lord, Selma* to television director Peter Werner. His portfolio included dramas about the civil rights movement, a neighborhood activist in Boston, a Black Panther project to be directed by Charles Burnett. He got development money for a feature about the last day in Martin Luther King's life, and scheduled meetings with Ossie Davis, Danny Glover, Harvey Weinstein, Norman Lear, and a half dozen progressive movers and shakers.

Many of us suspected that Hollywood fiction filmmaking would be a poor fit for him; he was too dedicated to the independent telling of true stories. Didn't the world already have enough brilliant people making feature films? Did he have any *idea* how they would smother his autonomy and then grind him to dust? Nothing substantive came of all the huffing and puffing in Hollywood, and like so many fine documentary makers, Hampton fortunately returned to doing what he did best.

Walking across campus on a sunny afternoon in January 1991, one of the very first calls I received on my first cell phone was from Henry; he told me he had just gone to the doctor with an innocent cough and came out with a diagnosis of lung cancer. Startled, I remember almost losing my balance. He may have called me in particular because I had dealt with cancer several years before, and I was completely cured, healthy, and fit. I said, "Henry, I wanted to share many things with you, but never this." I did a lightning-quick mental inventory of the decades of punishing pressure he had absorbed, the smoking, fast food, the lack of exercise, the ceaseless tension. It was devastating; only in the abrupt, stark knowledge that he could die did I imagine the void that would remain where for all these years he had been my teacher, leader, and dear friend.

Doctors had found a rare oat cell carcinoma of the lung, but a newly developed course of autologous bone marrow transplant and chemotherapy could now in some patients put the disease into striking remission. His particular cancer had "sure and rapid progression to death" without treatment.

He was determined once again not to be defined by illness but knew the treatments would be so grueling that he could not run the company. He called Orlando, who was by then doing films for *Frontline* and *American Experience* through his own company, in New York. He told Orlando, "All these people think I'm going to make it, but I don't think I have the best chance, and I want to make sure the company is OK." Orlando went to the hospital, where "Henry made me sit in the room as they did procedures, to see how sick he was."

Bagwell could not say no, and reluctantly agreed to relocate his family to Boston and take over as executive vice president, new de facto head of Blackside. His return after a three-year absence was heartily welcomed by many, but churned up resentment among some longtime staff who felt that Henry should have chosen them to run the company.

Henry's treatments made him about as sick as a person can be without dying. To cheer him up, the staff sent a video with each one of them telling jokes. And then he began to recover, inch by inch, as his body began producing healthy red blood cells. After six months, as much to his own surprise as everyone else's, he returned to Blackside to oversee production on *The Great Depression* and development on *The War on Poverty*. He was weakened and had lost weight, but he was back.

We all tried to forget about his cancer, but now in the wings was the constant suspicion that Henry and even Blackside might not be immortal. From then on as projects worked their way through the pipeline, Henry regularly asked me, Orlando, Sam, and others, "Can you finish this if I can't?"

He and Sue Weil drifted apart and finally separated. Henry had begun seeing Marita Rivero, an old friend from *Say Brother* years before, and now a highly respected vice president at WGBH. "We went together to Julia Child's eightieth birthday, one of the first times he'd been out after his treatment. . . . He was a winner. . . . It wasn't a smooth relationship . . . it was a rocky road because we are both who we are. Henry was a flirt, a total flirt.

"Parts of our lives were similar. Our parents were black upper-middle-class families, which gave us a place to push off from. . . . Henry and I came along at a time when our parents were part of a small group; not that many black people had that. It was the kind of experience you can talk about."

Orlando said, "I was happy to know she loved him and he loved her, happy to know she made him happy."

Henry understood that many precursors of our beloved civil rights movement lay in the Great Depression of the 1930s and the government's response to it. Here was a time when people decided America was worth saving, and a chance for Henry Hampton to show the world that Blackside could branch out. It could look beyond race to class, economic democracy, and the core functioning of government itself in the 1930s—a prequel to *Eyes on the Prize*. Henry said, "*The Great Depression* series was not victims, not people standing in soup lines; once again, mostly it was people fighting like hell to surprise and move the economic and political system." This new series through history would range from the crash of '29 to the New Deal to the eve of World War II.

Fayer wrote a proposal to the NEH, wary of its chairwoman Lynne Cheney, who was reported to have said, "Steve Fayer has a distorted view of American history." But when NEH staff fact-checked the proposal, all was correct and squarely in line with prevailing scholarship; we got the NEH funding. Now the corporate underwriters and many foundations that had supported *Eyes I* but not *Eyes II* were even less eager to step up. Those sorry that they had missed an opportunity with *Eyes* now "did not want to put their brand on the Great Depression. Are you *kidding*?" said Martha Fowlkes, Henry's new director of development. We cut the series from eight shows to seven, even before we began.

Henry returned to work with us, and I was glad to see him. When his hair began to grow back, it came in straight. I had endured the sunburn and petty social barbs of baldness since my early twenties, and told him that straight hair was better than no hair.

He was exhausted by mother-henning his two-chief teams and decided it was time to put the original pure "Blackside Method" out of its misery, while keeping resolute "salt-and-pepper" biracial/bigender diversity across the board. He had plenty of young recruits. Suzanne Malveaux and her twin sister, Suzette, had just finished Harvard, and Suzanne said, "Everyone who graduated from Harvard and wanted to go into journalism went to Henry Hampton and learned how to put together a story." He assigned each film a single producer/director, with a supporting staff—"Blackside Method Lite"—the teams still black and white, but with one person in charge at the top. This was vastly cheaper, faster, and more efficient, but could it deliver the rich tapestry of perspective that fueled *Eyes I* and *Eyes II*?

Stephen Stept, Dante James, Terry Rockefeller, Rick Tejada-Flores, and Lyn Goldfarb signed on as directors, with Nell Irvin Painter, Alan Brinkley, Jim Green, Robin Kelley, and Arthur Schlesinger among its advisors.

I directed the flagship first episode in *The Great Depression* series and opened a "Blackside West" office in San Francisco with Leslie Farrell and Lillian Benson. It represented a radical departure from the successful *Eyes* historical film formula: a single producer/director in charge, a middle-aged white male—me—and an episode focused not on a person of color, but on a middle-aged white male industrialist—Henry Ford. With Ford as our American King Lear, we explored the onset of the Great Depression simultaneously through the eyes of this most powerful industrialist in the world and through the eyes of his workers.

As always, Henry was skittish about anything that smacked of doctrinaire left-wing critique. Searching for a comparison between Henry Ford's wealth and his workers' lack of wealth, I wrote the line "Ford gave his son, Edsel, a million dollars in gold bullion on his twenty-first birthday, about what one man could earn working in Ford's factory at five dollars a day for seven hundred years." He read it as overly clever lefty snark, lacking in Blackside's signature restraint, and asked, "Is that the facts speaking or is that the filmmaker speaking? You're making a workers' film. How are you going to explain that to Terry Gross?"

At the rough cut screening, Vincent Harding was the first to speak when the lights came on. "I'm not at all sure we should be making a film about Henry Ford." Henry said nothing. I was stunned and suddenly very scared that I had unknowingly created some monstrous celebration of bad white capitalists. Our intention to use Ford's employees as a lens through which to look at the collapse of a great economy was submerged just too far below the surface in the rough cut. Now for the first time I saw that with some spare narration and subtle editing changes we could flip the viewer experience so they would see a film about Ford's diverse force of workers rising up rather than a film about Ford himself.

Henry was nervous as ever exploring Communism, even in the 1930s, when the collapse of western capitalism was a possibility. I showed mourners at the funeral for slain Ford workers raising their fists under a huge portrait of Lenin and used their anthem, "The Internationale." But I had to negotiate with Hampton until we finally agreed to play *both* "The Internationale" and "The Star-Spangled Banner" back to back.

We got the seven shows done and broadcast, more or less on time and more or less on budget. They got good reviews, except I got slammed in my hometown paper, the *San Francisco Chronicle*.

We all thought Suzanne Malveaux made a big mistake when she left Blackside after *The Great Depression* for CNN, little suspecting she might one day be their anchor and White House correspondent.

Henry was by then in a friendly rivalry with Ken Burns. When *The Civil War* premiered in 1990 to forty million viewers, with the highest rating for any show ever on PBS, Henry sent Ken a congratulatory note saying, "Leave something for the rest of us." Henry greatly admired Ken but didn't really care for many of his films, and the two men certainly ran different operations. As it would turn out, the civil rights movement remains for the moment one of the few major chapters in the American Studies canon that Burns has not chronicled.

Nineteen ninety-three was an excellent year for Henry and Blackside, the company's twenty-fifth birthday and his fifty-third. His cancer was in remission. He was happy being with Marita. He taught his nephew how to fly a plane that year. He had just given the keynote address at the annual PBS convention, eloquent as always, noting that in the rapidly fracturing media landscape PBS was still the only home for *Eyes, Civil War, Vietnam,* and *Frontline.* He made a plea for more civility and more history on television, and said that public broadcasting was still too white and too male. That year Blackside released *The Great Depression* series in prime time to twenty-two million viewers and ratings 60 percent higher than normal, and PBS rebroadcast our original *Eyes I* and *Eyes II. The Great Depression* shows won another pack of Emmys for the company. Blackside was soon in production on a series about minority scientists with a young astrophysicist, Neil deGrasse Tyson.

With such a head of steam, and Orlando working as Henry's executive vice president, the options seemed unlimited: proposed specials series and dramatic features about the African diaspora, black music with Quincy Jones for HBO, Reconstruction, the underclass, Haiti, black conservatism, the story of SNCC, blacks and Jews, Malcolm X, Selma, jazz, Kwanzaa, African American scientists, the history of the American family, the Great Migration, black soldiers in World War II, the women's suffrage movement.

While Spike Lee was in production on his feature *Malcolm X,* he told Henry he liked *Eyes on the Prize,* but added, "Only fifteen minutes for Malcolm?" PBS's Judy Crichton, one of the few television executives whose vision rivaled Henry's, had long wanted to take on the Malcolm X story, but waited patiently for the right people to make it: executive producer Henry Hampton and director Orlando Bagwell. Funding for Blackside's two-and-a-half-hour *Malcolm X: Make It Plain* came from CPB, Ford, and Camille and Bill Cosby; no corporate sponsor would get anywhere near it. Bagwell's portrait of Malcolm depended for its power on people who knew him best, mainly his family, most of whom had never granted interviews.

In Detroit, O and I shared the interview crew (Mike Chin, Felipe Borrero, and Fred Nielsen) for our films about two men at extreme poles of the American experience, my white Presbyterian oligarch Henry Ford and Orlando's Black Muslim minister Malcolm X. When Malcolm's brother Wilfred Little failed to show up at the appointed time, Orlando called him and learned that Wilfred couldn't bring himself to get in the car and drive to the shoot. O talked him through it and Wilfred made it as far as the driveway, where he sat in the car for another hour. When he finally arrived at our makeshift studio in the Ramada Inn, Orlando talked with him again for a long time while the crew waited, as they had waited with Freddie Leonard, Diane Nash, and Myrlie Evers years before. O explained to Wilfred that he was not there to impose a Blackside script onto Malcolm's life, but to create the film in collaboration with those closest to Malcolm: "We need you to do this with us." Finally at ease, Wilfred spoke with moving and fluid precision for hours about the Nation of Islam, and his brother's life and death.

Malcolm X: Make It Plain is magnificent, the definitive documentary portrait of the man. It racked up another Emmy for Blackside. For me, the greatest revelation in it was to simply realize that over a lifetime of immersion in America politics and culture, I had never before seen Malcolm X smile, and a broad smile it was. On the contrary, a menacing frown had for decades elbowed aside the smile in mainstream media.

On one of his trips to California, Hampton and I played hooky, drove up to Stinson Beach, picked up a hitchhiker, Bernie, the Bolinas town poet, and enjoyed a lovely seafood dinner overlooking the Pacific. Orlando and I took our sons camping together in the Yosemite high country, and managed to talk hardly at all about documentary film.

Henry in his final years, like King in his, became increasingly concerned about education, jobs, and economic inequality. He spoke out about abandonment of the underclass, particularly young black men in the ghetto, who had been left behind when legal segregation ended and other African Americans moved upward. "As surely as I stand here I know that people without possibilities are dangerous people. As surely as I stand here I know we cannot build enough prisons, hold enough trials to save ourselves unless we reach to fight the third grand battle for equity."

With Leslie Farrell, Susan Bellows, and Noland Walker, now all Blackside veterans, he undertook a five-part series about the War on Poverty, a 1960s extension of the New Deal established in the wake of the civil rights movement, employing many of its people and tactics. I tried to convince him to host the programs himself, but he only laughed.

His cancer returned. Ox that he was, Henry came back from another round of treatments healthy enough to again run his company and to oversee *Hopes on the Horizon,* his two-hour film about democratic movements in Africa. It was the pilot for a planned ten-hour series about postcolonial Africa, meant to open Americans' eyes beyond famine and warfare. With its four-million-dollar budget (Alison Bassett called it "the most expensive pilot ever made"), *Hopes* also had the potential to stabilize long-term production prospects and cash flow for Blackside. Henry couldn't travel to Africa because his immune system was so compromised, so Judy Richardson, Sheila Bernard, and Terry Rockefeller wrote and produced the show, directed by Nigerian Onyekachi Wambu.

In all the years of chronicling American culture and history, no nonfiction television series had ever tackled the American Ur-issue, the constitutional original sin, mother of all American ills: slavery. Orlando now had developed a clear and eclectic style of his own, out from under Henry's strong shadow, and produced a massive series of his own at WGBH, *Africans in America,* with Marita Rivero as executive producer. He brought on young Blacksiders Susan Bellows, Llew Smith, Noland Walker, old-timer Jean-Philippe Boucicaut, and newcomer Jacquie Jones. Steve Fayer remembered, "Orlando extended the same freedom and trust that Henry had extended to him as a young man. It's very generous, and it costs a hell of a lot of time and money."

Those mid-1990s were a time of full employment for documentary makers in Boston, with *Nova* and *Frontline* at full tilt, and across town at 486 Shawmut Avenue, Henry was in production on *I'll Make Me a World,* three two-hour shows exploring a century of African American arts.

His company had finally become the full-blown documentary juggernaut he envisioned on that plane flight back from Saigon in 1968. Young new assistants now coming of age in the shop were amazed at how everyone anywhere, black or white, opened up the moment you said you were from Blackside. I sensed things had come full circle when a young rapper in *I'll Make Me a World* noted that his parents had made him watch *Eyes on the Prize.*

But with all the excitement, it was an open secret that every Blackside series was to some extent financed with funds from the next series. It was a constant struggle to keep the cash flowing.

A letter arrived at the office from the junior senator from Illinois, Barack Obama, who had been inspired by *Eyes on the Prize,* asking if Henry Hampton would have a look at his new book, *Dreams from My Father.*

But full enjoyment was snatched away. Henry's post-polio syndrome and the attendant fatigue worsened. New cancer treatments left him weak. Though he managed to put on a strong front, his health ever so slowly began to fade, and his focus began to diminish. He slowed down. The company tried to put an elevator into 486 Shawmut so that he could get up to the edit rooms, but the Boston historical commission said no.

None of this stopped him from launching what would be his final production, *This Far by Faith: African-American Spiritual Journeys*, a first-ever series chronicling the black religious experience.

Henry's own upbringing was not deeply religious, his Catholicism apparently perfunctory and clouded by skepticism. None of us knew him to be noticeably spiritual, but he certainly understood the power of the church and mosque in black lives. The idea had germinated for decades because so many of the civil rights movement's strategists had roots in communities of faith; a vast number of civil rights leaders were first and foremost preachers. Malcolm X was a Muslim minister. And he knew that in its upended form, the same Christianity that sustained black Americans also sustained slave owners and segregationists.

This new series would have a literally new twist for Blackside: each episode moved forward along two time lines, decades or even hundreds of years apart. For instance, the story of Thomas A. Dorsey, nineteenth-century composer of "Take My Hand, Precious Lord," was braided together with the story of San Francisco's activist preacher Cecil Williams. Slave rebel Denmark Vesey at Charleston's Mother Emanuel Church in 1820 was paired with the present-day Georgia Sea Island Singers. Noland Walker said of this time-dancing, uncharted territory for Blackside projects, "It was a hamstringer."

As he had on every series since *Eyes*, Henry had offered jobs to producers who had worked with him before; once again, many of them turned him down. Leslie Farrell came over from *The War on Poverty* project, and powerhouse senior producer June Cross from *Frontline*. Sharon La Cruise moved from a job at Coca-Cola in Atlanta. She said, "My God, I want to work at Blackside. They did *Eyes on the Prize*. . . . There was nothing else like it, a place that's run by somebody of color that's doing that kind of work." *Great Depression* veteran Dante James executive produced.

In the beginning *Faith* was guided in part by memos that Vecchione,

Fayer, and I had cooked up back on *Eyes* and *The Great Depression* covering style, method, fact-checking, and ethics. We had apparently cast a long unintentional shadow. Director Lulie Haddad, who had written her undergraduate thesis on white women and black women in *Eyes,* said, "You and Orlando living upstairs; that was the model, that kept us going, people moving to Boston. . . . Everyone, including me, would do anything, would lay down on the tracks. I felt we were being judged against the bar of *Eyes on the Prize.*"

Lulie continued, "I went to a different black church every Sunday, and a lot of them were tiny little ones in Boston, and I'd have to stand up and introduce myself, for eight months. I waited on line at Abyssinian because I was white. People were so accepting and so generous . . . so much heart . . . and because you're calling from Blackside, everybody talks to you, everybody within the black community." When Lulie, Mike Chin, and I filmed the chorus at Cecil Williams's Glide Memorial Church in San Francisco, who should pop up completely unexpected and unannounced but Bill Clinton. He knew every single verse to every single black hymn.

A 1995 profile in the *New Yorker* had observed, "Life has done its best to foster some resentment in Hampton, but apparently without success."

So far, the risky 1992 bone marrow treatment had given him six years of productive life, personal and professional. He racked up fourteen honorary degrees. He and Mike Ambrosino kept up their tradition of watching Patriots football games simultaneously at their respective homes and yakking on the phone after each great play. He traveled with Marita; they made plans to someday fly across the country in his plane. Whenever I went to Boston and visited with him, he was clearly weaker. *Hopes on the Horizon* and *I'll Make Me a World* were almost wrapped up, and *Faith* was just under way—all of them fraught with routine Blackside tension—when the final disaster struck in slow motion. In 1997, myelodysplasia, an aftereffect of the bone marrow transplant that had saved his life, now set in, and his rejuvenated marrow stopped producing new healthy blood cells.

Henry's cancer—"an ugly beast waiting, sitting somewhere in the quiet, waiting for my guard to drop"—had spread to his brain. The strong man who "thought when I had polio I had paid my dues," who refused to surrender to disease, was now savaged by new rounds of surgery, radiation therapy, and more chemotherapy. He sought every benefit of mainstream medicine, but also sent four hundred dollars to a quack in exchange for a letter claiming to describe "the latest cures and where they can be found."

He could no longer drive the Jag up to his home atop Fort Hill, let alone negotiate the building's stairs and passageways. Mike Ambrosino, Judi, Veva, and his nephews, Jacob and Toby, moved Henry into an up-scale conventional condo in Cambridge. On one of my trips from California we had dinner at a fine restaurant in Eliot Square, but Henry couldn't eat a bite. The waiter noticed the untouched rack of baby lamb and little swirly duchess potatoes, and asked, "Was it all right? Is there something wrong?" He replied, "I'm just not hungry." That evening as we talked about politics and films he was still Henry the smart-ass, Henry the charmer, Henry the intellect, Henry the sphinx, Henry the dark optimist, wondering about the future of his nation. But by the time we headed back across the street to his condo, he could barely make it, and was clearly in low spirits. I think he was scared.

Declining health had in fact over the past few years slowly made it diffi-cult for him to deal with important decisions about Blackside and its films. He had grown more out of touch and, in the words of Martha Fowlkes, "His brilliance became intermittent." To the outside world, his senior staff had circled the wagons and sometimes chose to project the appearance that he was still strong and in charge.

He was only fifty-eight, his face still gentle. I visited him in the hospi-tal, and he seemed spunky though pale and thin. We joked that he was on his way to looking like me, a skinny, bald white man. He was annoyed at having to piss in a bottle, at being kept from his films and from his long-abandoned golf game. He mustered some of his old shameless idealism as we talked about the transformation under way in South Africa now that Mandela was president and the nation's new constitution guaranteed the right to vote for all citizens.

He suffered a stroke. Sam Pollard remembers Henry from his hospital bed mediating a conflict between Sam and his coproducer. "Henry said, 'Sam, you got to pull back. . . . You've got to compromise.' I knew he didn't have long to live. Part of me felt I had to do it for him, so I did it. I cried, because I respected him so much."

He lived to fight a few more days and then slipped into unconscious-ness. His family assembled, joined by Mike Ambrosino, and the decision was made to remove his breathing tube. Mike remembers, "We waited, while his great heart beat on for hours. Henry's beloved nephews gently chided him for his well-known obstinacy as slowly he slipped away."

Mike Chin and I boarded a plane in San Francisco for our final "Hampton Air Force" flight, headed for Henry's memorial at the Arlington Street Unitarian Church, where Rev. Theodore Parker welcomed escaped slaves and wrote his "Arc of the Moral Universe" sermon with a loaded pistol on his desk. It was here, working for the Unitarians, that Hampton had forged his own sturdy philosophy of life and film. The guys from his old wheelchair basketball team sat down in front, flanked by kids from his neighborhood in Roxbury. Ken Burns, who was by then the face of historical documentary in America, sat up in the balcony. Looking around at the huge crowd in the church, Steve Fayer said, "If someone threw a bomb in here it would wipe out everyone who makes social justice documentaries in America . . . a good part of what's left of the civil rights movement, half the Harvard history department, and a few federal judges." To that he might have added: the president of the Ford Foundation, a quorum of grizzled Unitarian Mafia elders, every producer who had ever worked for Henry, and five hundred others whose lives he had touched.

We rose and sang a roaring "Keep Your Eyes on the Prize."

In life, Henry became uncharacteristically awkward when anyone gushed in public about his intelligence, courage, passion, persistence, his ten-year struggle to make *Eyes on the Prize,* or, God forbid, his vision. But today there was no stopping the flood as speaker after speaker sang his praises and foibles, and mourned his early death and the cruel thought of all those as yet unmade Hampton films and years of friendship now snatched away from us.

Henry's nephew Jacob ben-David Zimmerman recounted cleaning out the storied castle at 88 Lambert Avenue and finding seventeen cordless phones. His old friend the poet Sam Allen quoted the lament of suffering in Psalms 69:9, "The zeal of thy house hath eaten me up," and said God works in strange ways: "The America who wouldn't fund him is now stuck with him forever." Marian Wright Edelman called him "a great witness," and found in him "optimism in a dark hour, like Mose Wright."

Michael Ambrosino evoked Henry from the grave: "Tell everybody not to think that I'm gone. My heritage is very much alive. Ask all the folks who ever worked for Blackside to stand up. . . . Ask everybody to look at all those wonderful bright faces and realize that I am right here in every one of those hearts and minds."

Vincent Harding, most wise of the wise Blackside elders, shouted out:

"Who is left to change the world?

"We are left to change the world!

"We are left to tell the old story!

"We are left to keep our eyes on the prize!

"*We* are left, Henry. You can count on us, just as we could always count on you!

"Amen, Selah, Salaam Alaikum. *Right on!*"

His spirit filled the air, his huge heart still with each of us, his hand on our shoulders. Finally, dozens of Blackside alumni joined in singing "Amazing Grace," and it was over.

Henry Hampton was gone.

CHAPTER TWENTY

Freedom Is a Constant Struggle

1998–2017

Mike Ambrosino said, "Henry had a lousy sense of timing. This was his worst."

We hoped the Blackside film factory would somehow run forever on its own steam, powered by Henry's enduring spirit, the way Apple chugged along after Steve Jobs died or the Catholic Church after St. Peter. But the mojo had left the building. Henry spent his professional life exuberantly leapfrogging ahead to the next project, and the next and the next, ever alive with plans for next year and the year after. But now it dawned on us all that there was no next. And Henry left no plan for Blackside after the end he had long known was coming. This patient builder of institutions did nothing to ensure that Blackside itself, a creation as great as any single one of his films, would thrive, or even survive. For a man so famously averse to closure—was not a death foretold the ultimate closure problem?—it seemed maddeningly and pointedly authentic to who he was.

His nephew Toby Zimmerman said, "There were a lot of people who believed they were his best friend and that he would want them to run the company. He had that ability, to make you think you were important to him." Toby's brother Jacob speculates that his uncle didn't want to endure the fights over the company he knew would boil up if he put down on paper what the arrangement should be. Some believed he would not risk his beloved institution to a future he might not abide and could not control. One of his most loyal colleagues, Martha Fowlkes, noted the irony that this man so dedicated to pushing ordinary people to the forefront struggled with his own leadership at the end and perhaps "could not step out of the limelight and trust his team to carry on the legacy."

Jim Forman told us SNCC "wanted to build a movement that would survive the loss of our lives." But perhaps Henry really did want Blackside to die with him. Ike Williams said, "I think he had a very Egyptian notion. . . . He was going to be surrounded by everything he had worked on during his life . . . the good pharaoh. This was a personal journey he was on and he completed his journey, and the Ka slides down . . . into the pyramid and stays there, in the sarcophagus."

He left everything he owned, including now brittle Blackside, all its finished films, its unfinished *This Far by Faith*, its building, its tensions, its joys and sorrows, and its debts from previous productions, to his two sisters, Veva and Judi. This came as a complete surprise to everyone, including the sisters. Veva was a respected psychiatrist, Judi was a corporate public relations executive at ExxonMobil. Neither had any experience or interest in filmmaking, and neither lived in Boston.

It is no secret that the collapse of both *This Far by Faith* and Blackside itself was swift, unseemly, and bitter. One afternoon in 2000, senior producer Terry Rockefeller, just back from Africa and overseeing final work on *Hopes on the Horizon,* called *Faith* senior producer June Cross into her office. Terry informed June that the sisters were "paying our *Hope* staff salaries with your *Faith* money. You are going to run out of money."

Many knew that Hampton had often deployed funds from a new project to complete the previous project, long before his sisters took over management. This long-standing Blackside practice depended entirely on Henry's apparently endless ability to generate significant new money for significant new documentaries. It had allowed him to make one important film after another in times when documentaries by African Americans about African Americans were extremely hard to fund. Without the strategy, many of those films certainly never would have been made. It probably paid my salary.

His able and utterly professional director of business affairs, Lorraine Kiley, knew that while it may have been heroic, borrowing from one project to fund another was not exactly kosher. She told him, "I am not going to jail for you," and labored for fifteen years to keep the accounting clean. But there were few real controls, and Hampton was the final authority.

Now there was no charismatic leader who could walk into a room full of funders and gin up the next quarter million dollars. Deficit spending, Henry's longtime ally, had finally come home to roost. And because the rights to archive footage had expired, Veva, Judi, and Blackside, Inc., could not generate income by selling or licensing Henry's most valuable film legacy, *Eyes on the Prize.*

The other media assets that might have brought in cash, Blackside's considerable archive of original filmed material, had with Henry's blessing been transferred to ownership by the nonprofit Civil Rights Project, Inc. Storage fees were in default and Metro Storage was going to dump the archive material. So CRPI board member Bob Hohler arranged for Washington University in St. Louis to accept the material with $500,000 in support from the Andrew W. Mellon Foundation. He loaded up four tractor-trailer trucks with fifteen thousand videotapes, eight thousand cans of film, five thousand audiotapes, and one thousand boxes of paper files, and sent them on their way to Missouri. Relations between CRPI and Henry's sisters were seriously frayed. The archive's director, Nadia Ghasedi, said, "It is no secret . . . the sisters were concerned about us having the material. There was a lawsuit, and a settlement." Henry's nephew Toby, a lawyer, worked out a thirty-five-page agreement.

Under executive producer Dante James, the mostly young *Faith* producers soldiered on, their Blackside passion undiminished by Henry's illness and passing. Veva Zimmerman and Judi Hampton tried—some say foolishly, some say heroically—to oversee completion of their brother's final series without him, but the company's filmmakers quickly came into conflict with them. Many of the staff developed a fondness for Judi, but to a person they believed that the sisters had no understanding of Blackside's unique style of production or storytelling. Val Linson remembered, "It was surreal, a little dark. We were determined to get the films done the way he would have wanted, but there was a leadership void without Henry."

"The sisters came in guns blazing," said Lulie Haddad. One of their first actions, in April 1999, was to fire Judy Richardson, movement trailblazer and Henry's collaborator on every Blackside film for the past twenty years, revered by hundreds of staff and alumni as "the conscience of Blackside." And when the prospect was floated that Orlando, the visionary heir apparent (but not well known to Judi and Veva), might return to creatively guide Blackside, they asked him to submit a résumé and come in for an interview. When Veva asked me and Michael Ambrosino to join the Blackside board of directors, we both felt it was too late to make a difference and declined. Despite gallant efforts by remaining Blacksiders Michael Greene, Bob Lavelle, Martha Fowlkes, and Steve Fayer to keep the enterprise afloat, friction with the sisters and decades of Henry's high-wire management finally caught up with Blackside.

Veva and Judi hoped to sustain the company by producing training films for corporate clients, exactly what Henry had left behind a quarter century before. Faced with the financial and creative collapse of the institution they had inherited, Veva and Judi scrambled to stanch the bleeding, first by selling the storied Blackside building at 486 Shawmut Avenue (largely to pay overdue taxes and payroll). The whole *Faith* operation hauled itself to a remodeled industrial space in South Boston on a sketchy block just approaching gentrification, where prostitution still ruled the night. Lulie said, "The phones aren't working. Their fax don't work. Their e-mails don't work. The sisters insisted on cubicles in a large open room so there would be 'transparency'; they didn't understand why that wouldn't work, why you couldn't be interviewing somebody, crying over here and laughing over here." Health insurance coverage ended despite continued premium deductions from paychecks. One day a woman got off the elevator looking for Ms. Hampton because the rent had not been paid. It was just like the old days.

They shrank the *Faith* series from six episodes to five. "Then everything sort of came to a screeching halt. They stopped reimbursing credit cards and then they stopped paying salaries, and then they just sort of shut everything down," Sharon La Cruise said. Executive producer Dante James left after the locked picture out of frustration. The spot where Henry had always stood ready over the decades to inspire, cajole, bully, tease, and guide people in his own way was vacant. They had actually completed the creative editing, but none of the finishing, and none of the rights had been cleared when *This Far by Faith*, funded for $7 million, just simply ran out of money and came to a standstill.

The *Boston Globe* got wind of trouble at the city's most beloved film company, and reported that Blackside "was down to just one employee, an archivist . . . the old phone number no longer works, and doesn't provide a forwarding message to the new one." The press coverage tapped a wellspring of pent-up fury among the Blackside staff and alumni, unsparing in their anger and frustration at how Henry's sisters had apparently led the institution off a cliff. In print, none expressed nagging private suspicions that Henry himself had contributed to the debacle by not establishing a legacy plan.

A furious Judy Richardson spoke in the *Globe* of finishing *Faith*. "It is not going to happen unless it can be wrested from the hands of the sisters. . . . They destroyed something that exists nowhere else at this point," she said. "Blackside as an institution is gone."

In desperation, producer June Cross moved the *Faith* material to New

York. "Everything was in disarray. We'd gone through all the boxes and took the hard drives and as much as we could get for the *Faith* infrastructure, and then loaded it up in a van and drove it all away."

By 2002 Henry's company had regressed into a collection of desultory cardboard boxes in a hallway, much as Judith Vecchione found it the day she arrived to begin work on *Eyes on the Prize* seventeen years before. Andrea Taylor said, "Blackside was Camelot; for a short period of time, not to be duplicated."

It was a tragic loss. It did not have to end that way.

But against all these odds of extinction, the Blackside/Hampton force field lived on, though not at Blackside. The makings of resurrection bubbled up in New York, where Orlando Bagwell regrouped the best and brightest young Blacksiders in the Hampton style at his own Roja Productions for a six-year run, upstairs above a community nail salon in Harlem at 125th and Lexington, complete with a big table. (Henry had told him, "Never try to create what I've created here.") Bagwell was, like Hampton, a mysteriously charismatic man with his own fierce vision who could "go into a room and whip up enthusiasm and money" for a great film. He was by 2001 one of the preeminent chroniclers of American pluralism, executive producing his *Matters of Race* series, a bold exploration of post–black/white race issues at the dawn of the twenty-first century. After a skirmish with Ken Burns over who would make the definitive documentary about Martin Luther King, he and Noland Walker would soon launch work on *Citizen King,* the finest film ever to have its roots in Blackside.

Here in Harlem, Orlando gave June Cross free office space for *This Far by Faith.* June raised $650,000 in completion funding. "I communed with Henry every morning and every evening for two years to get it done." It was only through her heroic efforts—"like Moses," says Callie Crossley—that five *Faith* films finally made it to broadcast on public television in June 2003. *This Far by Faith* received decent reviews, many with a nod to the late Henry Hampton. The *New York Times* called it "splendid viewing." The *Los Angeles Times* said, "Like Ken Burns' 'The Civil War' or Henry Hampton's 'Eyes on the Prize,' it continually rewards faithful viewers with eye-opening lessons in an American history they may have thought they already knew."

· · · · · ·

Eyes on the Prize lived on for a while.

Though his fight with the King estate had nearly crushed him back in 1992, Henry had successfully retained control of *Eyes on the Prize*. But a new problem raised its head after he died: in the panicky final days of making *Eyes* we had in essence rented our archival clips, not purchased them. In 1987, we could only afford to license the hours of copyrighted material for ten years, not in perpetuity, and as the licenses expired one after another by 1997 all fourteen films had become technically out of print. A documentary with archive shots or music cannot be legally broadcast, reproduced, distributed, or publicly shown if the license on only one single shot has expired. Imagine the books lining the shelves in your public library vanishing one by one as the authors' rights to quotes in them expire.

Around the time Henry died, I began getting calls from librarians in rural towns and major universities, distraught because their threadbare decade-old VHS tapes had become unwatchable. Then, fearing legal action from corporations holding copyright on the archive material, even PBS itself had ceased its yearly broadcast of *Eyes* in 1994. Blockbuster and PBS Video withdrew all *Eyes* tapes a year later. Henry's long-ago dream of a television history that would "serve future generations" hit the wall. By 2004 the only legal way to get a playable copy of *Eyes* was to buy a VHS set on eBay for $1,400. Or you could buy crummy low-grade bootleg copies from a guy in Oakland. An entire generation of young Americans coming up through school was now shut off from "the principal film account of the most important American social justice movement of the twentieth century."

In the years since we began *Eyes,* the American copyright structure had transformed itself from a moderately rational legal framework to a dysfunctional vortex of greed. By 2003, when concerned people—Henry's sisters and nephews, foundations—began to explore relicensing and releasing the documentary legally, many of the original ninety-two independent collections and network archives from whom we had secured footage had been swallowed up by global media companies. *Eyes on the Prize* was held hostage to a half dozen corporate copyright owners. When Congress passed the Sonny Bono Copyright Term Extension Act in 1998, material that might have slipped into the public domain now required relicensing.

And finally, in addition to the original bad gene of short licenses, there emerged the inconvenient problem that Blackside had not really cleared every single original archive clip back in 1986. As copyright holders became more aggressive and litigious in going after violations, the broadcasters and distributors had to choose their battles, and they did not choose *Eyes on the Prize*.

Henry was seldom at a loss, and had he lived, he might have wrangled a solution, but now there was no one to manage renewing the licenses, and no money to renew them. The unintended consequences of insufficient funding, changes in archive ownership, and expansion of the copyright law had inadvertently achieved what white supremacists—Cosby's "slavers"—only dreamed of: they kept *Eyes* out of distribution. The commercial monster succeeded where deniers had failed. *Eyes on the Prize* for all practical purposes ceased to exist.

But the withdrawal of *Eyes* from public view coincided with the early days of Internet activism. Lawrence Guyot, fiery former Mississippi movement leader, teamed up with the online activist collective Downhill Battle, digitized the entire series from aging VHS tapes, and launched their "Eyes on the Screen" project. They distributed Henry's series over the Internet in open defiance of copyright restrictions. Guyot said, "This is analogous to stopping the circulation of all the books about Martin Luther King, stopping the circulation of all the books about Malcolm X, stopping the circulation of books about the founding of America. I would call upon everyone who has access to *Eyes on the Prize* to openly violate any and all laws regarding its showing." In a bold act taken directly from the movement strategy, they arranged for nationwide public community screenings in seventy cities of all fourteen *Eyes* episodes during Black History Month in 2005, as an act of civil disobedience. Some screenings were scheduled in the very same southern churches where the events in *Eyes* had been filmed by news crews almost half a century before, or where we had shot interviews in 1985.

Henry, no stranger to civil disobedience back in the day, might have loved it; we'll never know. He might have been intrigued that his iconic films about the civil rights movement were now used as an icon for the copyright reform movement. Or he might have fought like crazy to stop it; this was, after all, the man who sued Martin Luther King's estate to protect his signature work, *Eyes on the Prize*. Perhaps he would have mustered all his Jesuit savvy to spur a productive conversation between all the parties. But his surviving family members certainly opposed the Down-hill Battle action on all counts, partly out of fear that net streaming would undermine their effort to clear rights for legitimate rerelease. Henry's nephew Toby had gotten a judgment against the Oakland bootlegger, and his other nephew, Jacob, "made a hobby of getting takedown orders" whenever he caught DVDs being sold.

In the end, under legal pressure from Veva and Judi, Downhill Battle ceased streaming the series, and Guyot apologized. By then the tangled tech story had been picked up by *Wired* magazine and rippled through the growing community of media activists, historians, academics, and most important, the Blackside diaspora.

Andrea Taylor of the Ford Foundation, one of Henry's champions in the lean, early days, took notice and stepped up with Orlando Bagwell to arrange a large Ford grant to clear the rights for rerelease of all fourteen parts of *Eyes I* and *Eyes II* on DVD, and to broadcast it nationwide once again on PBS in prime time in 2007. It cost half a million dollars to reli-cense all the clips in perpetuity.

At last, one arc of the moral universe had finally bent toward justice, and Henry Hampton's *Eyes on the Prize* was safe, secure, and readily available for future generations.

Epilogue

The civil rights struggle is unfinished and ongoing. *Eyes on the Prize* plucked a few dozen events in the 1960s from thousands of battles in thousands of towns and packaged them in a narrative arc. In so presenting the movement we may have inadvertently planted in the public imagination a discrete black-and-white era that began and ended long ago, isolated from a continuum of constant struggle.

The "great healing medicine" may have been simply palliative. When PBS's WGBH World rebroadcast all of *Eyes on the Prize* nationwide in February 2016, with a special introduction tying the series to the Black Lives Matter movement, no one in the audience younger than sixty was born when the civil rights movement began. Just months before, a white supremacist gunman massacred black worshippers at the Mother Emanuel Church in Charleston, South Carolina, the setting for an episode of *This Far by Faith*. Not long after, barely coded racial and religious demagoguery unheard of since the days of George Wallace entered the presidential race. Ta-Nehisi Coates and other writers and activists began to explicitly reject the notion of an "arc of the moral universe bending toward justice."

The postracial American future we had imagined years ago has yet to rush in. In many quarters America remains nearly as divided by race as it was the day I was born: in housing, income, health, and wealth, while the mass incarceration of black males far exceeds previous levels. The political partisan divide in the Deep South is extreme: the Democratic Party almost entirely black and the Republican Party almost entirely white, unapologetically nativist. The classic phase of the civil rights movement met with sour revision when in 2013 the Roberts Supreme Court struck down a key provision of the Voting Rights Act of 1965, which had been enormously effective in guaranteeing African Americans the vote.

But who can deny the changes made since the era of legal segregation? Mississippi today has more black officials than any other state. Bobby

Rush and John Lewis serve in Congress, hundreds of movement leaders hold elective office, and all Americans together elected and then reelected the nation's first black president by a wide margin. No one can ever take that away from us. Andrea Taylor has gone so far as to say *Eyes on the Prize* helped lay the groundwork in 1987 for the election of Barack Obama in 2008.

The modern Black Lives Matter movement was fueled by the killing of an unarmed young black man in Ferguson, Missouri, only a stone's throw from the boyhood home where Henry Hampton's lifelong obsession with Emmett Till began. In 2015, Orlando Bagwell's film about the killing of young Jordan Davis played to a full house at Washington University, Henry's alma mater. John Lewis gave Washington University's commencement address in 2016. The Emmett Till Unsolved Civil Rights Crime Act passed in 2008, coordinating local and federal efforts to investigate racially motivated crimes committed prior to 1970.

Raymond Street in Atlanta, where Judy, Julian, and I worked at the old SNCC office, was renamed SNCC Way, under a city ordinance sponsored by Julian Bond's son Councilman Michael Julian Bond.

Dennis Sweeney and Allard Lowenstein had both inspired me to join SNCC's struggle in 1963. On March 14, 1980, Dennis, consumed by severe mental illness, walked into Al's New York office and killed him with five shots. Bill Cosby's career came to an abrupt end when more than fifty women came forward with accusations of sexual assault.

Henry might not recognize the public television of today, forced by the collapse of congressional funding to smother itself in commercials. Except for outliers within the system like *Independent Lens, POV, Frontline,* and the occasional *American Experience,* the bold programs that PBS set as its goal back in 1967 can now more often be found on cable and the Internet and in theaters. Few outfits can afford the expansive research and process behind so much of Blackside's work, and those rigid ethical standards that Judith Vecchione brought to Blackside documentaries now sometimes seem quaint.

In a double fit of irony, PBS, so utterly white male when Henry fought the good fight for diversity, abandoned much of its innovative thinking at the same time it institutionally embraced diversity. Cara Mertes, director of documentary at the Ford Foundation, told me she was recently at a big CPB meeting and "there were no white men in the room . . . half the people were from Blackside." The senior staff at WGBH and at documentary graduate schools around the country are well stocked with Blackside alumni carrying on Henry's work.

Henry's spare, plainspoken style might be a hard sell today. He never lived to see our present "fourth golden age of documentary," with its global popular reach and glorious anarchy of style. Funding headaches we will always have with us, but these are the best of times for documentary makers, with a wider landscape than ever. Had he lived, Henry would surely have spread his wings and exercised that big, bold mind and spirit of his to fill the space.

Among America's most important documentaries of the 1990s, Blackside alone sank beneath the waves. Other long-running shops—Kartemquin, Ric and Ken Burns, Barbara Kopple, Errol Morris, *Frontline,* Michael Moore, Telling Pictures—produced masterpieces at the same time as Henry and are still churning out major works.

Filmmakers who came after us have by now created many excellent full-length documentaries about virtually every one of the stories we attempted to do in abbreviated form in *Eyes:* Emmett Till, Little Rock, Ole Miss, Malcolm X, the Panthers, the March on Washington, Freedom Summer, and many others.

After *Eyes on the Prize,* Henry's most lasting legacy is the Blackside diaspora: hundreds of producers, writers, directors, and craftspeople who trained under his wing in Boston, and today carry on his work across this country and around the world. Andrea Taylor, who saw it all unfold from *Say Brother* all the way up through *This Far by Faith,* says, "We are all Henry's children." Scars and all, they are there because Henry had confidence in them and gave them a chance.

Orlando Bagwell, the talky kid just out of film school whom Henry hired in 1971, went on to make a dozen landmark documentaries, spanning the chronicle of race in America from slavery to Ferguson. In 2005, he was named director of media at the Ford Foundation, and took over running the world's largest nonprofit documentary production fund, which he oversaw from Andrea Taylor's old office, with a picture of Henry Hampton on the wall.

Acknowledgments

The world would be richer today if Henry Hampton had written this story himself, as he surely would have if he had not died so young. I heard rumors that he had begun sketches for an autobiography; if so, they remain hidden or lost. I began the work assuming after many decades in the film business that writing *any* book had to be easier than producing any documentary. How wrong I was.

I could never have done it alone. Judi Hampton made it all possible, extending patience, trust, and endless hours of conversation as I set off to explore her brother's life and legacy. And in the early stages it was the Ford Foundation that stepped up to support my research.

This story belongs to Blackside's band of brothers and sisters, all of "Henry's children" scattered around the country and the globe, who opened their memories and archives for me. In particular, Orlando Bagwell, Judith Vecchione, Callie Crossley, Steve Fayer, Romas Slezas, Dan Raybon, and Kenn Rabin endured repeated interviews and endless e-mail queries, as did Judy Richardson, whom I first met in Mississippi fifty years ago, little suspecting the future in store for us in Boston.

Among those who worked on and around Blackside projects over the years, many gave me time for long interviews: Michael Ambrosino, Prue Arndt, Alison Bassett, Susan Bellows, Hannah Benoit, Lillian Benson, Julian Bond, Jean-Philippe Boucicaut, Susan Brownmiller, Clayborne Carson, Michael Chin, June Cross, Howard Dammond, Jim DeVinney, Dan Eisenberg, Sandy Forman, Martha Fowlkes, Lulie Haddad, Vincent Harding, Leslie Harris, Mark Harris, Billy Jackson, Dante James, Henry Johnson, Jeanne Jordan, Laurie Kahn, Lorraine Kiley, Sharon LaCruise, Madison Davis Lacy, Carol Lawrence, Valerie Linson, Louis Massiah, Sam Pollard, Joe Richman, Marita Rivero, Terry Rockefeller, Chuck Scott, Bobby Shepard, Sekou Shepard, Bennett Singer, Llew Smith, Paul Stekler, Andrea Taylor, Noland Walker, Suzanne Weil, Ike Williams, Juan Williams, Meredith Woods, and David, Jacob, and Toby Zimmerman.

As well, many with special knowledge of Henry's early life, the 1960s, or documentary film production took the time to speak with me at length: Barry

Chase, Bill Cosby, Leslie Harris, Cara Mertes, Clark Olsen, Dan Raybon, Robert Patton-Spruill, Ellen Sweets, David Zimmerman, Toby Zimmerman, and Jacob Zimmerman. Melanie Ruiz helped me sort out the math metaphors.

Special thanks to Nadia Ghasedi, of Washington University's Film & Media Archives, Henry Hampton Collection, who guided my initial research and then read the manuscript start to finish, adding insights and catching errors. Thanks also to her predecessor David Rountree, her successor Brian Woodman, and especially to Chris Pepus at Wash U for his kind and thorough attention during my all too brief work at the archives. Many others provided detailed review of selected sections, both large and small: Clay Carson, Jim Rolin, Bill Couturiè, Andrew Gass, Hanna Miller, Kristine Samuelson, John Chater, Adam Hochschild, John Haptas, Dan Raybon, Judith Vecchione, Dan Eisenberg, Romas Slezas, Laurie Kahn, Chuck Scott, John Taylor Williams, Prue Arndt, Sekou Shepard, Dave Crittendon, Louis Massiah, Kenn Rabin, and Jim DeVinney.

I would have been sunk without the fact-checking skill and dogged attention of Mischa Benoit-Lavelle, son of Blackside's own Bob Lavelle, on *The Children's March* and King Estate dispute sections. Thanks to Samantha Clark for her photo research. Jackson Kelly as well did excellent research and fact checking.

Without realizing it, I probably appropriated a line or two from Steve Fayer, a far better writer than any of us. I apologize.

Dave Dennis, who oversaw work in Mississippi's Fourth Congressional District, where I labored in 1964, kindly gave me permission to quote from his 1964 eulogy for James Chaney. Thanks to Fred Wiseman for letting me sleep on his couch, and to the Portola Valley public library for its peace and quiet.

Long ago it was Loni Ding who introduced me to Mike Chin, who later put me in touch with Mark Zwonitzer, who said to call the extraordinary agent Flip Brophy, who deposited me at the doorstep of the excellent editor Wendy Wolf, who guided me through this new craft of book writing. Early on I was sustained by encouragement from Henry Hampton's original literary agent, Doe Coover, and by my colleagues at Berkeley's Graduate School of Journalism, Michael Pollan, Neil Henry, Mark Danner, Joan Bieder, Orville Schell, Adam Hochschild, and especially our national nonfiction treasure, Tom Engelhardt.

My greatest supporter, best reader, and most levelheaded critic throughout the long process has been my dear wife, Nina, who is particularly skilled at saving me from myself.

Note on Sources

Never intending to write a book, I took few notes other than production logs during my years working with Blackside, and few notes during my time in the southern civil rights movement. Henry Hampton left few private crumbs except for rare brief entries—usually with a weeks-long hiatus in between—in what he optimistically and unrealistically called his "daybook." I could locate very few of his letters. But fortunately he was a prolific generator of eloquent speeches, opinion pieces, and interviews spanning thirty years, and with those I have wherever possible allowed him to speak for himself. *Eyes on the Prize* was one of the last documentary projects produced without word-processing computers, so no digital records exist, but the thousands of paper and film records are well preserved at Washington University, thanks to the foresight of Bob Hohler.

Henry and I spoke on the phone many times each week for many years. I was present when many of the events described here unfolded, and in recounting them I began by sorting through the haystacks of memory. Wherever possible, I have gone to records, documents, press accounts, correspondence, and recordings of the same events and discovered that my recollections were often correct but occasionally fanciful or partisan.

Working on *Eyes on the Prize*, I stood in awe of the academic research scholars who surrounded us, and I can never claim their expertise or experience. But I have done my best to tell a true story. Transcripts of every one of the several hundred film interviews we conducted for the documentaries covered in this book are housed at Washington University, all easily accessible online, and I studied them all. As well, the collection's archivists were especially helpful in guiding me through the vast collection of Blackside papers dating back to the founding of the company in 1968.

Curator Frances O'Donnell helped me through the Unitarian-Universalist collection at the Harvard Divinity School, providing material on Henry Hampton's years working for the church. David Laughlin at St. Louis University High was helpful for the high school years, and Sonya Rooney at the

Washington University archives was able to locate material from his under-graduate years. I am indebted to Karen Cariani and Michael Muraszko at the WGBH archive in Boston, where I screened episodes of *Say Brother* as well as a particularly comprehensive on-camera interview conducted with Henry in 1995. Sadly, videotapes of *Say Brother*'s first year, in which Hampton often appeared, were lost in a fire.

To supplement my scant notes, letters, and photos from work in Alabama, Georgia, and Mississippi in the 1960s, I have relied on depositions, court documents, correspondence, as well as letters to my parents and my own SNCC correspondence and notes, and the Civil Rights Movement Veterans excellent online project. Along the way there were wonderful discoveries, like William Lawson's thesis about the funeral of James Chaney, Larry Spruill's dissertation about the SNCC photo department, Ralph Arlyck's marvelous essay about Steenbeck editing machines, and K. E. Hoerl's essay on *Mississippi Burning*.

I drew on extensive coverage of Henry Hampton, Blackside, *Eyes on the Prize*, and the civil rights movement from the *New York Times*, *Los Angeles Times*, *Boston Globe*, *Chicago Tribune*, *St. Louis American*, *San Jose Mercury*, *Meridian Star*, and *Jackson Clarion-Ledger*, and I must give a special shout-out to John Fleming of the *Anniston* (Ala.) *Star* for his fine in-depth reporting.

Bibliography

Books, Articles, and Transcripts

I stand on the shoulders of historians, reporters, and writers who were recording events while I was not. Among their works I found the following especially engaging and helpful.

Ambrosino, Michael. *A Well Seasoned Life: A Memoir.* N.p., 2010.

Association of Independent Video and Filmmakers et al. *Documentary Filmmakers' Statement of Best Practices in Fair Use.* Washington, DC: Center for Social Media (dir. Patricia Aufderheide), School of Communication, American University, 2005, archive.cmsimpact.org/sites/default/files/fair_use_final.pdf.

Barnouw, Erik. *Tube of Plenty: The Evolution of American Television.* New York: Oxford University Press, 1990.

Bernard, Sheila Curran. *Documentary Storytelling: Creative Nonfiction on Screen,* 3rd ed. Amsterdam: Focal Press, 2011.

Bernard, Sheila Curran, and Kenn Rabin. *Archival Storytelling: A Filmmaker's Guide to Finding, Using, and Licensing Third-party Visuals and Music.* Amsterdam: Focal Press, 2008.

Branch, Taylor. *Parting the Waters: America in the King Years 1954-63.* New York: Simon & Schuster, 1989.

Carson, Clayborne. *In Struggle: SNCC and the Black Awakening of the 1960s.* Cambridge, MA: Harvard University Press, 1981.

_____. *Martin's Dream: My Journey and the Legacy of Martin Luther King Jr.* New York: Palgrave Macmillan, 2013.

Carson, Clayborne, David J. Garrow, et al. *The Eyes on the Prize Civil Rights Reader: Documents, Speeches, and Firsthand Accounts from the Black Freedom Struggle, 1954–1990.* New York: Penguin, 1991.

Chafe, William H. *Never Stop Running: Allard Lowenstein and the Struggle to Save American Liberalism.* Princeton, NJ: Princeton University Press, 1998.

Cheney, Lynne. "Uncivil Wars." *Washingtonian,* February 1986.

Cobb, Charles E., Jr. *This Nonviolent Stuff'll Get You Killed.* Durham, NC: Duke University Press, 2015.

Cook, Bill. "Selma's Bloody Sunday." *Newsweek Memories,* 2012, newsweekmemories.org/cook.html.

Crosby, Emilye, ed. *Civil Rights from the Ground Up: Local Struggles, a National Movement.* Athens: University of Georgia Press, 2013.

Dittmer, John. *Local People: The Struggle for Civil Rights in Mississippi.* Urbana: University of Illinois Press, 1995.

Dyson, Michael Eric. *I May Not Get There with You: The True Martin Luther King, Jr.* New York: Free Press, 2000.

Epstein, Helen. "Meet Henry Hampton." *Boston Review,* December 1988, boston review.net/archives/BR13.6/epstein.html.

Everhart, Karen. "Blackside, Inc. Falters on Hampton's Last Series." *Current,* February 11, 2002, current.org/files/archive-site/hi/hi0220faith.html.

_____. "Henry Hampton: 'He Endured Because His Vision Was So Important.'" *Current,* December 7, 1998, current.org/files/archive-site/people/peop822h.html.

Fager, Charles E. *Selma, 1965.* New York: Scribner's, 1974.

Foster, Catherine. "A Legacy Lost?" *Boston Globe,* February 21, 2001.

Garrow, David J. *Protest at Selma: Martin Luther King, Jr., and the Voting Rights Act of 1965.* New Haven, CT: Yale University Press, 1978.

Green, Victor H. *The Negro Motorist Green Book.* New York: Green & Smith, 1937, New York Public Library Digital Collections, digitalcollections.nypl.org/items/88223f10 -8936-0132-0483-58d385a7b928.

Hampton, Henry. Commencement address, Washington University, St. Louis, MO, May 1, 1989.

_____. Keynote address, annual meeting of the Public Broadcasting Service, San Francisco, June 1992, current.org/1992/07/we-should-charge-ahead-with-thought- and-civility.

_____. "Television and Integration: Unfinished American Business." N.p., 1988.

Hampton, Henry, and Steve Fayer. *Voices of Freedom: An Oral History of the Civil Rights Movement from the 1950s Through the 1980s.* New York: Bantam, 1990.

Hansberry, Lorraine. *The Movement: Documentary of a Struggle for Equality.* New York: Simon & Schuster, 1964.

Harris, David. *Dreams Die Hard: Three Men's Journey Through the Sixties.* San Francisco: Mercury House, 1982.

Hochschild, Adam. *Finding the Trapdoor: Essays, Portraits, Travels.* Syracuse, NY: Syracuse University Press, 1997.

Holsaert, Faith, et al., eds. *Hands on the Freedom Plow: Personal Accounts by Women in SNCC.* Urbana, IL: University of Illinois Press, 2010.

Huie, William Bradford. *Three Lives for Mississippi.* New York: WCC Books, 1965.

Hyde, Lewis. *Common as Air: Revolution, Art, and Ownership.* New York: Farrar, Straus and Giroux, 2010.

Isaacson, Walter. *Steve Jobs.* New York: Simon & Schuster, 2011.

Judt, Tony. *The Memory Chalet.* New York: Penguin, 2010.

Klotman, Phyllis R., and Janet K. Cutler, eds. *Struggles for Representation: African American Documentary Film and Video.* Bloomington: Indiana University Press, 1999.

Kotz, Nick. *Judgment Days: Lyndon Baines Johnson, Martin Luther King, Jr., and the Laws That Changed America.* Boston: Houghton Mifflin, 2005.

Lawrence-Lightfoot, Sara. *I've Known Rivers: Lives of Loss and Liberation.* New York: Penguin, 1995.

Lawson, James. "A Righteous Anger in Mississippi." M.S. diss., Florida State University, 2005, diginole.lib.fsu.edu/islandora/object/fsu:181562/datastream/PDF/view.

Lewis, Andrew B. *The Shadows of Youth: The Remarkable Journey of the Civil Rights Generation.* New York: Hill and Wang, 2009.

Menand, Louis. "The Color of Law." *New Yorker,* July 7, 2013, newyorker.com/magazine/ 2013/07/08/the-color-of-law.

Metress, Christopher, ed. *The Lynching of Emmett Till: A Documentary Narrative.* Charlottesville: University of Virginia Press, 2002.

Minow, Newton. Address, National Association of Broadcasters, Washington, DC, May 9, 1961, americanrhetoric.com/speeches/newtonminow.htm.

Moon, Spencer. *Reel Black Talk: A Sourcebook of 50 American Filmmakers.* Westport, CT: Greenwood, 1997.

Morrison-Reed, Mark. "Selma's Challenge." *UUA World,* January 5, 2015, uuworld .org/articles/selmas-challenge.

Murch, Walter. *In the Blink of an Eye: A Perspective on Film Editing,* 2nd ed. Los Angeles: Silman James Press, 2001.

Naipaul, V. S. *A Turn in the South.* New York: Vintage, 1989.

Noam, Eli M., and Jens Waltermann, eds. *Public Television in America,* Bertelsmann Foundation, 1998.

Orwell, George. *Homage to Catalonia.* New York: Beacon Press, 1952.

Raines, Howell. *My Soul Is Rested: Movement Days in the Deep South Remembered.* New York: Penguin, 1977.

Smith, Valerie, ed. *Representing Blackness: Issues in Film and Video.* New Brunswick, NJ: Rutgers University Press, 1997.

Spruill, Larry Hawthorne. "Southern Exposure, Photography and the Civil Rights Movement, 1955–68." PhD diss. State University of New York, Stony Brook, 1983.

Taylor, Andrea. "Tribute to Henry Hampton." Address, 43rd Film & Video Festival, Council on Foundations, Denver, CO, April 25, 2010, fundfilm.org/resources/TributeHenry.htm.

Theoharis, Jeanne. *The Rebellious Life of Mrs. Rosa Parks.* Boston: Beacon Press, 2013.

Thurman, Howard. *Jesus and the Disinherited.* Boston: Beacon Press, 1949, 1976.

Tuchman, Barbara. *Practicing History: Selected Essays.* New York: Random House, 1982.

U.S. Congress. 106th Cong., 1st Sess. Clay, William. "Remembering Henry Hampton: 'Eminent Film-Maker.'" *Congressional Record* 145, no. 42 (March 17, 1999): E471–473, congress.gov/crec/1999/03/17/CREC-1999-03-17-pt1-PgE471.pdf.

Wade, Wyn Craig. *The Fiery Cross: The Ku Klux Klan in America.* Oxford: Oxford University Press, 1987.

Wagner, Terry. "America's Civil Rights Revolution: Three Documentaries About Emmett Till's Murder in Mississippi." *Historical Journal of Film, Radio and Television* 30(2) (June 2010): 187–201, tandfonline.com/doi/pdf/10.1080/01439681003779093.

Watson, Bruce. *Freedom Summer: The Savage Season That Made Mississippi Burn and Made America a Democracy.* New York: Viking, 2010.

Whitehead, Don. *Attack on Terror: The FBI Against the Ku Klux Klan in Mississippi.* New York: Funk & Wagnalls, 1970.

I was aided by myriad press releases, online newspaper and magazine archives, and online forums. Among the Web sites that I found especially helpful, smart, and even moving were the Unitarian-Universalist site at www.uuworld.org; the St. Louis city government site at www.stlouis-mo.gov; state historical sites for Mississippi at www.mississippihistory.org, Alabama at www.preserveala.org, and Georgia at georgiahistory.com; and the public broadcasting chronicle at current.org. And, of course, who today can undertake any major project without our longtime and usually reliable online friends Wikipedia and Google Maps.

Films

Before us and after us, many fine producers did work at least as strong and lasting as *Eyes on the Prize*. Productions I've consulted for this book include:

Always for Pleasure. Directed by Les Blank. Los Angeles: Flower Films, 1978.

At the River I Stand. Directed by David Appleby, Allison Graham, and Steven John Ross. San Francisco: California Newsreel, 1993.

Best of Enemies. Directed by Robert Gordon and Morgan Neville. Montreal: Media Ranch; Brooklyn: Motto Pictures; Los Angeles: Tremolo Productions, 2013.

The Black Panthers: Vanguard of the Revolution. Directed by Stanley Nelson. New York: Firelight Films; San Francisco: Independent Television Service, 2015.

Brother Outsider: The Life of Bayard Rustin. Directed by Nancy Kates and Bennet Singer. Brooklyn: American Documentary, 2003.

Color Adjustment. Directed by Marlon Riggs. San Francisco: California Newsreel, 1992.

The Devil Never Sleeps. Directed by Lourdes Portillo. San Francisco: Independent Television Service; Los Angeles: Xochitl Films, 1994.

Dirt & Deeds in Mississippi (aka *Ballots & Bullets in Mississippi*). Directed by David Shulman. San Francisco: California Newsreel, 2015.

Eyes on the Prize: America's Civil Rights Years. Various directors. Boston: Blackside, 1987.

Eyes on the Prize II: America at the Racial Crossroads 1965–1985. Various directors. Boston: Blackside, 1990.

Eyes on the Prize, 38-minute unreleased pilot. Boston: Blackside, 1980.

Eyes on the Prize, 8-minute fund-raising sample. Boston: Blackside, 1983.

Freedom on My Mind. Directed by Connie Field and Marilyn Mulford. Berkeley: Clarity Films, 1994.

Freedom Riders. Directed by Stanley Nelson. Boston: American Experience Films, 2010.

Freedom Summer. Directed by Stanley Nelson. New York: Firelight Films, 2014.

George Wallace: Settin' the Woods on Fire. Directed by Daniel McCabe and Paul Stekler. Boston: Public Broadcasting Service, 2000.

The Great Depression. Various directors. Boston: Blackside, 1993.

Harvest of Shame. Directed by Fred W. Friendly. New York: CBS News Productions, 1960.

How Jojo Beat the Hawk. Boston: Blackside, 1975.

King: A Filmed Record . . . Montgomery to Memphis. Beverly Hills: Commonwealth United Entertainment, 1970.

Malcolm X: Make It Plain. Directed by Orlando Bagwell. Boston: Blackside; Madrid: Fénix Cooperativa Cinematográfica; Boston: WGBH, 1994.

The March. Directed by James Blue. Washington, DC: United States Information Agency, 1964.

The March. Directed by John Akomfrah. New York: Cactus Three; London: Smoking Dogs Films; New York: Sundance Productions, 2013.

Matters of Race (series). Various directors. New York: Roja Productions, 2003.

Mighty Times: The Children's March. Directed by Robert Houston. New York: HBO Family; Montgomery, AL: Southern Poverty Law Center; Ojai, CA: Tell the Truth Pictures, 2004.

The Murder of Emmett Till. Directed by Stanley Nelson. New York: Firelight Films, 2003.

Nuclear Defense at Sea. Boston: Blackside, 1982.

Say Brother episodes. Directed by Billy Wilson, Stan Lathan, Russell Tillman, et al. Boston: WGBH, 1969–79.

Scarred Justice: The Orangeburg Massacre, 1968. Directed by Bestor Cram, Judy Richardson, and Samuel D. Pollard. San Francisco: California Newsreel, 2013.

Soundtrack for a Revolution. Directed by Bill Guttentag and Dan Sturman. Los Angeles: Freedom Song Productions; London: Goldcrest Films International; New York: Louverture Films; Berlin: Wild Bunch, 2009.

The Streets of Greenwood. Directed by Jack Willis. New York: New York Times Films, 1962.

This Far by Faith: African-American Spiritual Journeys. Various directors. Boston: Blackside; San Francisco: Independent Television Service; Boston: The Faith Project, 2003.

Vietnam: A Television History. Various directors. Boston: WGBH; Birmingham, UK: Central Independent Television, 1983.

Voices of a Divided City. Directed by Henry Hampton, Romas V. Slezas, and Alvin H. Goldstein. Boston: Blackside, 1982.

The World at War. Various directors. London: Imperial War Museum and Thames Television, 1973.

Index